M000305647

WICKED ERNEST

By the same author

Love and Drollery
Jest Upon Jest
The Demaundes Joyous
Kings, Lords and Wicked Libellers
The Caricatures of George Cruikshank
Juggernaut
Cruikshank 200
Lovers, Rakes and Rogues
The World of William Hone

Wicked Ernest

*The truth about the man who
was almost Britain's king*

An extraordinary royal life revealed
by
JOHN WARDROPER

Shelfmark Books

Copyright © John Wardroper 2002

British Library Cataloguing-in-Publication Data
A catalogue record for this book is
available from the British Library

ISBN 0 9526093 3 9

Shelfmark Books, 60 St Paul's Road, London N1 2QW

DISTRIBUTED BY CENTRAL BOOKS, 99 WALLIS ROAD, LONDON E9 5LN

Set in Palatino
And printed in Great Britain by Biddles Ltd, Guildford

CONTENTS

ILLUSTRATIONS

Those illustrations not credited are in the author's possession

By God, my lord, I am a damned infernal
sinner, and I know it, but I think it right
to go to church for the sake of example.
Prince Ernest to Archbishop of Canterbury

I wish I had no *feeling. That's not true;* I wish
not to lose a particle of what I possess but I
wish I could call that forth *whenever I liked,*
always in my own *Sanctum* ... My *foolish
foolish Eyes;* what *tell Tales!*
...Remember I *can love* & that not by halves.
Princess Sophia

I speak very little like a courtier tho' bred up
in the heart of Court (if Court has *any heart,*
which I much doubt). Poor Truth has a bad
life of it, yet it will sometimes out.
Princess Elizabeth

ACKNOWLEDGMENTS

I am grateful for the gracious permission of Her Majesty The Queen to quote from papers in the Royal Archives, Windsor; and for the efficient assistance of the archival staff.

My most extensive thanks go to the British Library (not forgetting its Newspaper Library) for their excellent service over many years. The Public Record Office, Kew, has been another valued and efficient source. Other public collections that have contributed are the British Museum department of prints and drawings, the National Portrait Gallery, Bodleian Library, National Library of Scotland, Leicestershire and Derbyshire Record Offices, Guildhall Library, London Metropolitan Archives, Family Records Centre, and the borough archives of Westminster and of Kensington & Chelsea.

Acknowledgments go to the controller of HM Stationery Office for references to Wellington Papers at University of Southampton Library; to His Grace the Duke of Wellington KG for a quotation in chapter 16 from a Wellington letter at Stratfield Saye House; and to the Hon Mrs Crispin Gascoigne for access to royal letters at Stanton Harcourt. The Niedersächsisches Hauptstaatsarchiv, Hannover, kindly provided the text of two letters.

For kind responses to my inquiries I am grateful to the Marquess of Anglesey, Lord Hastings, Lord Kensington, Sir James Graham, Bt, The Squire de Lisle of Quenby Hall, and many others.

Sources quoted are fully cited in the endnotes. I have strictly avoided putting any afterthoughts or supplementary facts in the endnotes (a practice tempting to authors but generally an annoyance for readers).

Readers who wish to explore further in the world of Ernest's life and times will find that many of the sources cited are a fruitful supplement to the bibliography.

Foreword

To be born a prince opens a man to temptations. In the closing decades of the Georgian era, when the British court enjoyed great wealth and much real power, most of George III's sons indulged in misbehaviour more dramatic than any we hear of nowadays. Wellington, though a high Tory, called them collectively 'the damnedest millstone' round the government's neck. The prince whose excesses are most familiar is the eldest, the one who became George IV. He often appears in this book; but its great subject is the fifth son, Ernest Duke of Cumberland.

He came within a breath of being our first King Ernest. It was a prospect that caused alarm. He was even suspected of plotting to thrust aside the heir-apparent, Princess Victoria. His turbulent nature, extreme Toryism and compulsive mischief-making made him disquieting enough, but accusations of grave scandal underlay all this. Two events that called for his most strenuous denials were a birth and a death: the birth of a son to his sister Sophia, and the violent death of a valet in St James's Palace.

A prince accused of crimes beyond the usual style of post-renaissance monarchies seemed to me worth inquiry. When I found that his assertions of innocence were unconvincing, yet were affirmed as royal truth by a long succession of biographers and historians, I was moved to search further. The pursuit was not easy, for Ernest had enjoyed the benefits of hush-money, perjured evidence, lawyers' tricks and the burning of secrets.

For Ernest, the most urgent burning was of documents stating the truth about Princess Sophia's son. That was achieved by a master hand at royal cover-ups, a well-rewarded official, not a Sir Humphrey but a Sir Herbert. Yet Sir Herbert could not abolish all clues, and Ernest himself proved helpful by creating some. When the son's origin became a public issue, for example, Ernest offered contradictory exculpations and published demonstrably false statements. A suspect's conflicting stories are gratefully noted by detectives. For confirmatory evidence I studied letters, diaries, newspapers of the day, and dust-laden court documents in the Public Record Office. What I have collated is now laid before my readers, the jury, so that they can decide if Ernest is guilty on both counts 'beyond reasonable doubt'.

This book goes far wider than a work of detection. The hyperactive Ernest takes it rewardingly into scenes both courtly and vulgar. The life of an age is revealed in the day-to-day words of contending performers. We encounter shady lawyers and journalists, royal doctors, politicians (Tory, Whig, radical and revolutionary in a time of turbulence), blackmailers, duellists at dawn and women of easy morals, high and low. Many of these appear thanks to my uncovering of the life of a character who until now has been little more than a cipher: the son of Ernest's sister. This man, with the unroyal name Thomas Garth, rides high with the fashionable Quorn Hunt, has a runaway affair with a baronet's wife, is outplayed by courtly Sir Herbert over his claim to 'a just title to rank and fortune', and spends five years as a uniquely royal inmate of a debtors' prison.

Far above such ungenteel things, Ernest's sisters languish at Windsor. While the princes range freely, six princesses suffer under an illustrious tyranny at the castle, which they call The Nunnery — a scene of cabals and hysterics. Their parents frustrate their longing for husbands. Here is the context of Sophia's misfortune. And she is not the only one who needs to conceal pregnancies. Her sister Elizabeth eases her mind with frank remarks about the heartlessness of courts: 'Poor Truth has a bad life of it, yet it will sometimes out.'

Elizabeth knew well that those who are Majestic or Illustrious by birth owe much to image-making and image-cleansing, arts often at odds with Truth. Writers about royal persons have been inclined to lack rigour (some examples, almost comical, yet virus-like in their effect, are given in an appendix). In Ernest's own time it was seen as a political necessity to protect him and others with the shield of untruth, but biographers and historians have no such justification, even though Ernest is a shaming presence in the British royal family. Those who find reasons to serve as royal palliators give Truth a bad life of it.

1
Birth of a royal baby

For the sake of George III's fifth daughter, Princess Sophia, the royal family's summer migration to the Weymouth seaside in 1800 was fixed for mid-July — 'earlier than they have ever gone there', a lady of the court reported.[1] But then came a delay. The king was not free to go until he had addressed his Lords and Commons at the closing of their session. Most inconveniently, William Pitt's legislative business dragged on through July. Sophia's need became so urgent that she was dispatched from Windsor in a small advance party, sharing a carriage with her young sister Amelia. Another advance arrival was their brother Ernest, Duke of Cumberland. This was curiously out of character, for hitherto he had hated the Weymouth routine of sea-bathing, excursions and family parties. More surprising still, he wrote to a friend that he planned to stay five or six weeks 'for the sake of quiet bathing'.

In the Speech from the Throne that George III finally read out on July 29, as drafted by Pitt, he thanked parliament for having created the United Kingdom of Great Britain and Ireland, the promised cure for Irish unrest. He also had to say that his people were suffering from 'scarcity', that they must make 'sacrifices', and that there had been 'disappointment on the continent' (bread and other daily essentials had never been so dear, new taxes were needed to fight Napoleon, an expedition to Flanders had been a disaster). The *Morning Post*, not yet bought over by the Tory government, commented subversively, '*His Majesty the People* yesterday took it into his head to be very angry with the Prime Minister of George III, and a numerous party of the *Swinish Multitude* followed Mr Pitt's carriage on his return from Parliament, hissing and groaning. It is a pity our Sovereign Lord the King is not of the same opinion with our Sovereign the People.'[2]

When the king and Queen Charlotte reached Weymouth on 31 July their thoughts were not on public clamour but on a family crisis. A royal physician, Francis Milman, was attending Sophia. She was not ill. Hints of the truth can be found in a summary of the court circular:

Saturday, 2 August: Princesses Augusta, Elizabeth and Sophia take 'an airing
   in their sociable [a carriage] on the sands'.
3 August: Sophia does not appear at church.
4 August: the king, queen and others, but not Sophia and not Ernest, take an
   'aquatic excursion' (in a warship).
7 August: 'Princess Sophia, being slightly indisposed, remained at the Lodge'.
8 August: 'All the Royal Family except the Duke of Cumberland and Princess
   Sophia went on board the Cambrian frigate', not returning from this
   excursion until 7.30 pm.

On that day Princess Amelia dispatched a letter to the prince of Wales
at Brighton: 'I am happy to be able to inform you that at last we have
the prospect of seeing our dear Sophia restored to health very
shortly... I feel most happy in being able to tell you this good News —
She is going on well — Pray pray sweet love, dont answer this & when
you come here pray take no notice to *high* or *low* of having heard from
me... I often think of my dear GP [George Prince] & lamented your
absence yes^y [her 17th birthday] — For fear of the Philistines I must
conclude... Your ever Aff^te Child   Amelia'

9 August, Saturday: all except Sophia have a merry time at the Weymouth
   theatre with *Love Makes a Man*, in which the noted actor John Quick plays
   Don Choleric Snap Shorto de Testy, opposite Don Dismallo Thickskullo
   de Half Witto; followed by a farce, *Barnaby Brittle*.
15 August: Sophia takes an airing on the sands.
18 August: Ernest at last joins an aquatic excursion.
2 Sept: Sophia 'is so far recovered as to take her daily excursions on the sands'.
11 Sept: Ernest rides out into the Dorset countryside with an equerry, General
   Thomas Garth (a name to note).
14 Sept: Sophia 'has derived great benefit' from the warm bath (heated
   seawater).
29 Sept: Ernest leaves, after an unprecedented two months at the seaside.[3]

And on 2 October the king dispatched a letter to the Duke of Portland,
his home secretary. Its content is made clear in Portland's reply. He
offers 'his most dutiful congratulations on the joyful event of Princess
Sophia's entire recovery', notes 'the satisfaction which your Majesty so
feelingly expresses upon it', and says he is acting at once on the king's
command to make Dr Milman a baronet.[4]

It is a reward for having brought the 22-year-old princess through a
pregnancy and the birth of a son on 8 August 1800.

In later years a story was put about that Sophia 'was dropsical, and
then suddenly recovered', and that the king was told 'she had been

cured by *roast beef* and used to tell this to people, 'all of whom knew the truth', as 'a very extraordinary thing'.[5] The king, noted as much for dissimulation as for eccentricity, may well have started this story himself. Amelia's letter and the baronetcy for Milman point to the truth, and much more is to come.

The boy was born into a troubled family. If George III and Queen Charlotte were strong in domestic virtues (as they are still often presented) they were unjustly rewarded with many ill-behaved and unfortunate children.

The princesses led unenviable lives. They called themselves the Sisterhood and Windsor Castle the Nunnery. Their brothers enjoyed separate establishments, drank and gambled, had a choice of mistresses, begot bastards and ran deep into debt (emulating and often outdoing great aristocrats). The princesses could dream of only one way to escape the Nunnery: by marriage. But with whom? The king ruled out British husbands, such as the noblemen who frequented court, so the princesses' best hope was that he would find them wooers from German principalities. But he even fended off those.

As he had seven sons who could sire heirs-presumptive, he might have felt able to allow his six daughters some latitude. His resistance to their marrying arose from selfishness. He called them his 'Cordelias'. (Though a play that touched on a king's madness did interest him, he absorbed no lesson from *King Lear* about royal folly and arbitrariness.) The princesses' role was to be devoted and console him, unlike his free-ranging sons, but it became more than they could bear.

A brief account of two of the Sisterhood will put Sophia's misfortune in context and will reveal some truths about court life.

Elizabeth, seven years Sophia's senior, born 1770, is an eloquent witness. Again and again she wishes she were not a princess. 'It certainly was a mistake *my* living at Court. It was certainly intended that I should have lived in the Country, been a younger brother's wife, for I do not understand *Court* quarrels.' She is 'poor Cinderella' who 'wishes sometimes to have the Wings of a Dove. Then would I fly away & be at ease, don't think me crazy that's all I beg.'[6]

This is from one of her hundreds of confidential letters to Lady Harcourt, a Lady of the Bedchamber to Queen Charlotte and wife of the 2nd Earl Harcourt, the queen's Master of the Horse. Although excessively stately in public, she was not a censorious confidante. She was a friend of Lady Jersey, the prince of Wales's notorious mistress of the 1790s. According to the well-informed journal-keeper Lord Glenbervie, George III 'amuses himself extremely' with his intimates 'about Lady Harcourt and her two bastard children by a Parson H, a handsome young clergyman who lived several years as chaplain in the house'.[7] Glenbervie says too that the king told his niece and daughter-in-law, Princess Caroline (in whom he was taking an amorous interest) that when the queen was lying in, Lady Harcourt 'humbly offered to supply Her Majesty's place till her recovery'. A Lady of the Bedchamber indeed.[8]

Lady Harcourt burned most of Elizabeth's letters. In a note in her collection she says that in one six-week period she received 123 from her. 'Most of these letters were immediately destroy'd, many others that it would have been imprudent to keep were so as soon as receiv'd, & I have now upon looking over the remainder torn 328.'[9] They will have told of things far more sensitive than the hateful ennui of Weymouth, such as this from Elizabeth, summer 1802:

'Shut your door & your window & I will honestly say in a whisper it is *Detestable* & I continue my prayers of *Oh how I long to be married, be married, before that my beauty decays*, etc etc. The weather abominable, the place itself *odious*... When I come home from a long drive (meeting no soul), from the excessive kindness of the Queen's new German Lady I amuse myself with an hour's German, then write & draw & dress for dinner, read to the Queen the whole evening till cards, when I play at whist till my eyes know not hearts from diamonds ... & when that is over, turn up cards to amuse the King till I literally get the rheumatism in every joint of my hand... News there is none but who bathes & who can't, & who won't & who will, whether warm bathing is better than cold, who likes wind & who don't, & all these very silly questions & answers which tire one to death.'

Like two of her sisters, Elizabeth adored an equerry. Hers was Lord St Helens, a distinguished ex-ambassador whom she called 'my Saint'. He is perfect and unattainable: 'It is always holiday with me when he is near, for I love him to *my heart*.' Some men are agreeable but 'not for one's own room'; but 'my Saint at all times, hours, minutes, days, nights, etc, etc, etc.' And again: 'I have just now been cheered by a visit from my valuable & delightful Saint... Every hour I feel more (if that were possible) attached to him. In short my dearest Lady Harcourt I have unfortunately strong feelings & my affection is of that kind that when I love I love unboundedly. This is a strange expression but it came to the tip of my pen.' Merely to gaze at him is a reward: 'I am happy enough with having my Saint here... This evening we have played at cards & I looked at him as he sat opposite to me.'[10]

'I love unboundedly.' Despite much burning of evidence, it is generally accepted that the warmblooded Elizabeth had two babies, and possibly three. In December 1785, when she was not yet sixteen, she was confined to her apartment in the Lower Lodge, Windsor. Accounts of her indisposition varied strangely — 'a scrofulous abscess on the left side', or shingles, or 'convulsive spasms'. In January one of her ladies, Caroline Howe, told Lady Spencer she was 'three days without any return of her convulsions'. These 'convulsions' perhaps served to account for cries in childbirth. Soon Elizabeth was 'surprisingly mended', and in February, the *Public Advertiser* reported, she reappeared 'very pale and much reduced'.[11]

Again 'indisposed' in 1788, Elizabeth retired to one of the royal houses at Kew. On 6 November *The Gazetteer* and other papers said, 'A favourable change seems of late to have taken place in the Princess Elizabeth's constitution.' Again weight-loss is noted: 'She is becoming less and less inclined to corpulency, which is attended with a proportionable increase both of appetite, spirits and strength. The princess is much addicted to reading, and particularly fond of poetry.'[12]

Caricatures could go further than newspapers. In 1792, when campaigners against the slave-trade were urging a boycott of West Indies sugar, Isaac Cruikshank created a palace tea-table scene in which Elizabeth holds out her cup and says, 'Indeed papa, I can't leave off a good thing so soon, I am sure of late I have been very moderate, but I must have a bit now & then.' Another princess says, 'For my Part I'd rather want altogether than have a small Piece.'[13]

The father of one of Elizabeth's children was registered as a royal page, according to a many-volume genealogical work, *Visitation of England and Wales*, whose chief compiler was the learned Maltravers Herald Extraordinary, Joseph Jackson Howard. Its account of the Battye family has a notable entry. The wife of George Wynyard Battye (1805–88) of the Bengal Civil Service is given as 'Marian Martha, dau of James Money by Eliza his wife, dau of George Ramus, Page to George III, by the Princess Elizabeth his wife, dau of George III'.[14] Marian Money was born in 1805, a date that accords with a mother born in 1786 or even 1788. The point to note about George Wynyard Battye is that his mother's brother, General William Wynyard, was an equerry to George III and her sister was a lady-in-waiting. Britain's establishment in India — army, East India Company and civil service — provided berths for many people with royal or other special claims. One whom George Battye will have known in Bengal was a son of the prince of Wales, George Crole, aide-de-camp to the governor-general.

Maltravers Herald Extraordinary's facts about Eliza and Marian, from the Kew church registers, must have been noted by a genealogist working before 1845, for in that year an odd thing happened. An iron chest holding all registers from 1783 onwards vanished from the church and is said to have been thrown into the Thames. George Ramus himself is something of a mystery. Royal archivists say that among various Ramuses in royal service no George can be found. It may be that he served as a cloak for a name more scandalous.

A letter from Princess Elizabeth at Weymouth to Lady Harcourt in 1794 suggests a third pregnancy: 'This town I shall ever look upon with thankfulness as it has been of the utmost service to *me*, but thank God a little *resolution* & a thorough reliance on the goodness of Providence has carried me through four weeks & as I feel I have acted *I hope* right, I trust it will not forsake me the two others.' Two more providential Weymouth weeks... (Might the phrase 'I feel I have acted *I hope* right' hint that abortion had been thought of?) Elizabeth continues, 'Make no remarks on all *this* but I feel happy in having said this to you, as I am certain nobody loves me more or feels more for me than you; did you know all, you *might* love me still better, for I have a hard part to act. I wish I could make all happy, but alas that is only a wish ... & it is not for us poor mortals to dispose of events or anything so I will not think of it —'[15]

The greatest afflictions were suffered by the youngest, Amelia, born 1783. She was smitten by the handsome Colonel Sir Charles Fitzroy, whose name shows his descent from one of Charles II's bastards. Fanny Burney, the author and sometime attendant on the queen, says that at 14 Amelia was so tall and well-formed that she looked 17, but with 'an innocence ... & a gentleness so caressingly inviting of voice & eye that I have seldom seen a more captivating young creature'. The story of her short life was first told in *The Romance of Princess Amelia* by William Childe-Pemberton, with access to her letters. She addresses Fitzroy as 'My own dear Angel'. It is a story of heartbreak.

That dear smile today gave me such pleasure... I dread your hating me.
I hope I shall be able to give you this, walking today at Frogmore. My own
dear love I am sure you love me as well as ever. If you can give me a kind
look or word tonight pray do, and look for me tomorrow morning riding...
I go to chapel tomorrow — now do sit where I may see you, not as you did
last Sunday morning... Did you tell P.W. [prince of Wales] how wretched
we both are?[16]

That she had babies is stated by strong witnesses, the sisters of
Matthew Baillie, a physician who attended Amelia. On a visit to the
sisters (Joanna, poet and dramatist, and Agnes) at Hampstead, the
author Maria Edgeworth discussed Amelia, then wrote to a friend,
'All about her children true.' One seems to have been born in 1799.
Princess Elizabeth to Lady Harcourt, December 1799: 'Amelia is
infinitely better. Tomorrow she sees the Archbishop & on Tuesday she
is to be confirmed — I trust she will not suffer what *I did* though my
dear Bishop was all kindness to me... The longer I live the more I am
sensible to kindness... I shall say no more on that head at present.'[17]

About 1807, Amelia writes to Fitzroy, 'Marry you my own dear
Angel I really must and will... O good God, why not be together?' She
is 'Your affectionate and devoted Wife and darling.' They did marry
secretly in defiance of the Royal Marriage Act. Amelia wanted to flee
Windsor to live with Fitzroy, but her friend Mrs George Villiers told
her how remorseful she would feel if the shock to the king 'produced
a return of insanity'. The king's fragile mind was often used as a
threat. Amelia yielded 'though she thought her life would be the sacrifice' — as indeed it was. And soon the king returned to his insanity.

Whatever her ailments were, heartbreak made them fatal. Mrs Villiers commented towards the end, 'And then one hears of the King
and Queen being patterns of conjugal fidelity and parental affection. I
am sure the Queen never had one grain of the latter quality in her
composition.' Amelia wrote to the prince of Wales a few months
before her death at 27, 'How much I wish the *rest* of the family had
hearts & feelings like yours... Anxiety & ill usage has preyed on my
mind & brought me to the state I now am.' The Baillie sisters said to
Maria Edgeworth, 'She died of atrophy [wasting away] ... anxiety of
mind accelerating or producing it.'[18]

Amelia bequeathed 'everything I have' to Fitzroy. When near death
she wrote, 'Leave Court as soon as you can... You are too good ever to
be happy here, and you know how little reason I had to love my

family, or esteem them... Beware of them.' She made the prince of Wales her executor ('him only do I trust'). She was too trusting. The prince told Fitzroy it would be awkward if the will became public, and persuaded him to give it up in return for a paper purporting to grant him Amelia's bequests (diamonds worth thousands, silver, books, pictures, furniture, etc). The prince gave him a fraternal hug. Mrs Villiers's husband, seeing the hug, was sure Fitzroy had been cheated. He was: he got very little.[19]

The princesses' subjection was publicized and deplored as early as 1794 by a radical publication, *The Female Jockey Club*. This was a sequel to *The Jockey Club*, which exposed the sins of princes and other 'jockeys' of the nation, and advocated a republic for Britain as well as France. The author was a journalist with knowledge of high society, Charles Pigott, a baronet's son, educated at Eton and Cambridge. *The Jockey Club* so wounded the prince of Wales with its slurs on himself, his cronies and his secret wife Maria Fitzherbert that he wrote to his mother denouncing it as 'the most infamous and shocking libellous production that ever disgraced the pen of man'. It must be prosecuted for propagating 'those *damnable doctrines* of the *hell-begotten Jacobines*'.[20] Pigott was to die in Newgate jail awaiting trial for sedition.

In *The Female Jockey Club* Pigott attacks 'the madness of entrusting one man with almost unlimited powers that are only to cease with his life', and declares, 'Wealth and power are without dispute the *grand* corrupters, the *petrifiers* of the human heart.' He is an English instance of what was then so potent in France: the condemnation, both rousseauist and rationalist, of society's corruption and injustices. *The Female Jockey Club* chiefly revels in the scandals of duchesses and others, but its chapter on 'The R–y–al B—t–sh P—c–ss–s' treats the princesses as victims.

'In the bloom of youth, in all the glowing exuberance of health, formed as it were by nature expressly for those ineffable delights from which this miserable etiquette of royal splendour has debarred them ... still are they less blessed than the poor peasant's daughter' who 'flies to her rustic lover's arms and there loses herself in a delirious trance of ecstatic joy'. Something stronger follows: 'To thwart *nature* must be ever fatal... What must be the character of courts, in eternal variance and contradiction to her immutable laws? But it is impossible to calculate the evils resulting from these *royal* exclusions. Have we not heard of the most desperate excesses, even of incest, being committed in consequence thereof? A sister raging with the fire of nature, checked in her course, flies to a brother's arms.'

What could Pigott have heard by 1794 to make him write this? Whom can he mean? It seems that Princess Elizabeth's first baby was born in January 1786. When one notes that Prince Ernest was soon afterwards sent away to school at Göttingen when just turned 15, one must suppress a temptation to speculate. Pigott says, two pages on, that he is not making 'the slightest imputation ... against the chastity of any of these sequestered virgins'. He takes an equivocally compassionate line: 'Let us then pass over the babbling tales of scandal... Nothing could be more barbarous than to plant thorns on the pillow of beauty, languishing for want of nature's best enjoyments.' He does not wish 'to abate the scanty means of any present indulgence, or to anticipate the approach of any future disaster'.[21]

When Princess Sophia's son came dramatically into the news years later, a similar thought about the thwarting of nature occurred to Charles Greville, the journal-keeping secretary to the Privy Council: 'There they were, secluded from the world, mixing with few people, their passions boiling over, and ready to fall into the hands of the first man whom circumstances enabled to get at them.'[22]

A sympathetic account of the princesses' miseries comes from a man who is no radical like Pigott but at the heart of affairs and on good terms with the king. James Bland Burges, under-secretary at the Foreign Office, reports to his wife in 1794 that the princesses 'are treated hardly better than children in a nursery ... never informed of what is going on, even by means of a newspaper (for these are contraband at Windsor)'. This was when the Duke of York was the inglorious commander of an army facing defeat by the French, and two other brothers, Ernest and Adolphus, were in the field.

'I do not believe there is a more unhappy family in the kingdom than that of our good king,' Burges writes, reporting what he has elicited from a court lady, Lady Elgin. 'They have lately passed whole hours together in tears... The king sometimes bursts into tears — rises up and walks about the room — then kisses his daughters and thanks God for having given them to him to comfort him — while the princesses are variously agitated, and sometimes so much so as to go into fits.' Sexual despair is part of this. The Princess Royal, aged 28, convinced that she will never be married, 'is fallen into a kind of quiet desperate state, without hope ... or in other words what is commonly called Broken Hearted', and a royal physician, Sir Lucas Pepys, thinks that only by marriage can 'her life or her understanding' be preserved.

The next, Princess Augusta, 'cries till she becomes composed and resigned'. Princess Elizabeth, the third, 'feels very strongly but soon recovers her spirits', and says 'she will try not to be such a fool as to make herself more unhappy than she is obliged to be'. She and others have however a further burden: large debts. Their parents do not provide the diamonds they must wear, and their allowances are insufficient. A royal jeweller, Duval, tells Burges that when he was asked to display samples at Windsor and the princesses admired them, he hoped the king and queen would make them presents — 'But Lord, my dear sir, no such thing! The poor princesses never got even a spark that they did not pay me for themselves.'[23] Yet the queen herself was a famous collector of diamonds.

In 1805, when only Princess Royal had escaped into marriage and Augusta was in her thirty-seventh year, the king said to the queen, 'I cannot deny that I have never wished to see any of them marry. I am happy in their company and do not in the least want a separation.' He had in fact spurned some proposals. One for Augusta from the Landgrave of Hesse-Homburg's heir he put in a drawer un-answered.[24] The younger princesses learned in girlhood to fear that they too would become old maids.

In her family Sophia was 'little Sophy', a fair, blue-eyed girl, possessing 'more sensitivity, energy and imagination than all the others together', according to her first governess. In her fifth and sixth years, 1782–3, her father underwent an ordeal that agitated the whole family. Defeated by his rebellious American subjects, blaming every-one but himself, forced to accept ministers he hated, he twice decided to abdicate and go to Hanover — twice drew back — and said in 1783, 'My sorrow may prove fatal to my health if I remain long in this thraldom.' By means of backstairs guile and election jobbery he escaped thraldom by making young William Pitt his prime minister.

His American defeat still haunted him. When he felt the great bout of madness of 1788–9 coming on, he said to Lord Chancellor Thurlow, 'I shall never lay my head on my last pillow in peace and quiet so long as I remember the loss of my American colonies.' Sophia's eleventh birthday (3 November) was marred by a painful scene. Mrs Papendiek writes in her court memoirs, 'On these occasions the princesses always had some amusement ... and were more than usual among the family. This day they were all to dine together for the King to see his children, but he took little notice of them or of anyone. At dessert he fell into a heavy doze.'[25] Five stressful months followed: the princesses' father raving, their mother distraught and weeping. And thereafter there was always the fear that the 'fever', the 'delirium' (the preferred terms) would recur.

Sensitivity is not a blessing at court. In 1793, in her sixteenth year, Sophia had a 'violent nervous disorder' with repeated faintings and trouble with her 'swallow'. Convalescing at Tunbridge Wells, she told her father she was fainting less, and her swallow 'came quite right before, and why should I despair?' (The king, when ill, was also troubled with his swallow.) Sophia entrusted a secret to the prince of Wales: 'Many more unpleasant things have passed since we met... I heard many a story that Princess Royal has repeated to the Queen... Things go on very *so so*... Nothing could have made me happier than your permitting me to open my heart to you; our conversation on Sunday was quite a cordial to my heart... One thing I must beg, & that is that you will not mention to any of my sisters what I said to you at the Lower Lodge, or I well know what a fuss it would make.'[26]

Her mother was one reason why things were *so so*. Prince Adolphus wrote to the prince of Wales: 'I am very sorry to hear that the ill humour of a *certain person* (you know whom I mean) continues so bad. Particularly her behaviour towards dear Mary & Sophia is so very singular... What can possess her to be so odd, & why make her life so wretched when she could have it just the reverse?'[27]

Sophia often had 'spasms'. One attack, 'a shocking cramp in her stomach', is described by Lady Susan Ryder, writing from Weymouth to her mother, the Marchioness of Stafford: 'She was so ill that she c^d not be taken home for some time & was taken to Mr Ryder's tent [at a military review], where I assisted in undressing her ... for the violence of the pain swelled her so much that she could not bear her cloaths on, & she was purple in the face. I was quite charmed with her patience.'[28]

Symptoms like hers are described in 1788 in a treatise on female diseases by Dr William Rowley. Before an attack, 'unaccountable lowness of spirits ... anxiety ... faintings'. 'During the paroxysm ... contractions like strangulation arise in the throat, with a sensation of a ball or globe ascending', and 'spasmodic contractions pervade all the alimentary canal'. Afterwards, 'debility, weariness'. Rowley sees 'extreme sensibility of the mind' as an underlying cause, and he speaks (a century before the word 'psychosomatic' became current) of 'surprising effects of the mind on the body'. A further thought is ventured by Dr James Wilson in a text on nervous disorders: 'Much of what is endured by women as "spasm of the stomach" is in truth the expression of disordered action in the uterus or its appendages.' The favoured medication was laudanum (tincture of opium).[29]

A milder affliction of Sophia's was short sight. Fanny Burney describes her on her twentieth birthday: 'She had a pair of spectacles on, which, with her uncommonly young face — its shape being as round as a baby's, & its colour as rosy — had a most comic & grotesque appearance.' (Spectacles were for *old* people.) 'She is so nearsighted as to be almost blind, and the queen now permits her always to wear spectacles.' Sophia is sensitive about them. She does not want to wear them on a visit to the theatre, for fear of 'some paragraph in the newspapers'. Her sister Augusta, the downright one, noted for not caring how she was dressed or coiffed, tries to persuade her: 'What, I ask her, can they say? *That the Princess Sophia wears spectacles.* Well, and what harm can that do her? Would it not be better they should say it than she should lose all sight of the performers?'[30]

Sophia, like Elizabeth, confided in Lady Harcourt. In August 1794 she wrote to her from Weymouth, 'Believe me My Dearest L^y Harcourt I shall ever remember with pleasure the last conversation we had together & shall do all I can to follow the good advice you gave me.' She speaks of 'ups & downs in this life', and goes on:

> I find that at present very much. My spirits are very weak, I am easily overset, however I struggle as much as possible... Dear Prince of Wales arrived yesterday... He is as charming as usual & a great comfort to us. Dear Ernest is as kind to me as it is possible, rather a little imprudent at times but when told of it never takes it ill.[31]

Here the 'easily overset' princess reveals an early fondness for Ernest. Imprudent is a word used for behaviour that caused people to talk. Six years later at Weymouth, Ernest was seen to behave publicly with imprudent affection, and people did talk.

But first some account is wanted of his formative years. This will take him to a point nine months before August 1800.

2

'Too wild for England'

Ernest began life in a hurry. Queen Charlotte attended a Drawing-room (one of the regular St James's Palace receptions) on 4 June 1771, George III's thirty-third birthday, and then a ball in the evening, 'and before morning His Royal Highness surprised everyone'. Ernest was the queen's eighth child in only nine years. Of the ones who really counted, the sons, he was the fifth. Like many younger sons, he would look to the army for glory.

His first year was a distressing one in the family. George III's mother, Augusta the Princess Dowager, who with her intimate friend Lord Bute had dominated the king's apprentice years, was dying of throat cancer. The king's youngest sister, Caroline Matilda, queen of Denmark, was imprisoned for adultery with her prime minister (he was beheaded). His rackety brother Henry married a woman of wanton repute and, what was worse, a commoner. This marriage so agitated the king that he insisted on the passing of an act that was meant to preserve royal dignity, but which caused little but grief. This was the Royal Marriage Act, which makes it a crime (still) for a British prince or princess to marry without the sovereign's consent. A rising MP, Charles James Fox, ventured to forecast in the Commons that the prince of Wales would 'marry a woman without the consent of his father, and live with her as his wife' — which indeed the prince did. Another MP called it an act for extending the royal prerogative 'and for the encouragement of adultery and fornication' — which also proved true. The king forced the act through by means of profuse honours and bribes, and sharp threats to 'deserters'.

The royal children's education began in a range of houses at Kew Green. They had teachers of English, French, drawing, writing and music. For the boys, discipline was strict. When the bishop of Chester was appointed the supervising tutor he asked George III, 'How would Your Majesty wish to have the princes treated?' 'Like the sons of any private English gentleman,' the king replied. 'If they deserve it, let them be flogged.' And flogged they sometimes were.[1]

Aged just 15, Ernest was sent away, accompanied by his younger brothers Augustus and Adolphus, to the university town of Göttingen in Hanover, the north German territory that had been under the British crown since 1714, when it supplied George I as a successor to Queen Anne. George III had sent his second son, Frederick, to Germany, but that was not until he was 18, and then chiefly to separate him from his loose-living brother, the prince of Wales. Frederick learned Prussian military manœuvres and also how to drink deep.

At Göttingen each prince had a governor, preceptor and gentleman attendant. In his first year Ernest reported to his father that he was reading Tacitus and being instructed in religion, morality, philosophy and geometry. (He was certainly a readier scholar than his backward father had been.) In music he was limited by extreme short sight: 'I now take lessons on the flute, it being the only Instrument that I could play, for I am able to be as near the Notes as I like.'[2]

His exile gave him mixed feelings. On receiving a letter from a Windsor page, Henry Compton, he wrote (aged 16):

> How much I wished at that moment to be in the Pages Room next the Concert Room, that I could see the King, Queen and Sisters without my being seen. This puts into my Mind the Recollection of many happy Hours passed in their Company, and which may happen I hope again. I must avow however that I would on no Account whatsoever return to Kew & live in the same subjection as formerly, for here I live very agreeably in company with so many young Men. It is very amusing as they are of so many different Countries.[3]

Despite his weak eyes he longed for military glory. At 19 he wrote to his father, 'All my Aim and my Desire is to command once an Army and have once the Character of being as good a General as the present Duke of Brunswick' — George III's brother-in-law.[4] (English seems to have become Ernest's second language.) He grew to six feet; was a good horseman; and entered the Hanoverian Hussars. By 1792 he was looking forward to action, for the revolutionary French were planning to liberate their neighbours from subservience to kings. Ernest's hero of Brunswick proclaimed a march on Paris, unwisely promising massacre and destruction for all who resisted him. The French responded fiercely, and Brunswick was unheroically hurled back.

Next year the British, Dutch, Austrians and various Germans tried again. George III insisted on having his favourite son, Frederick Duke of York, made the supreme command er, though he had neither experience nor talent for it. Ernest, a colonel at 22, fought in skirmishes and sent mettlesome reports. In August the royal family were 'in great spirits & happy to a degree with Prince Ernest's great doings', a court lady, Caroline Howe, reported. 'The King had a very excellent letter from him in which he lamented the necessity he had been in to destroy a man in order to save his own life, which he would certainly have lost had he not had the presence of mind to draw out a pistol.'[5] But York was soon retreating in disarray.

York's cavalry commander, General William Harcourt, had to watch over Ernest. His wife, sister-in-law of Lady Harcourt, the princesses' confidante, was with the general at headquarters that winter, and commented on Ernest in letters home. He 'would not do in England', she says. 'He talks too much, and I am sure he would not bear the life of Windsor three days. He is a true hussar [devil-may-care, swearing 'like a trooper'], but open, lively and very goodnatured. His manner, when he pleases, is good.' Ernest took her to see a convent near Tournai where he had been quartered. She reports, 'I had some difficulty in endeavouring to make him behave well. He would kiss the abbess and talk nonsense to all the poor nuns. I know a thousand traits of the goodness of his heart, but I fear he is too wild for England.' A few months later: 'In good hands he might be made a charming young man.'[6] One can read a good deal between the lines.

At headquarters he revealed traits harmful to his career: arrogant, quarrelsome and quick to feel ill-used. The Austrian commander, Walmoden, 'hellishly maltreated' him, he told the prince of Wales. 'I see clearly I am born to be the most unhappy of men. All my projects, all my desires, I see generally fail.' In May 1794 he was lucky to survive a passing cannonball. He suffered 'a strong contusion on my left arm occasion'd by the wind of a twelve-pound shot. My arm is quite dead except the elbow and fingers.' He had been under fire for three days and was nearly captured.[7]

He came to England to recuperate. After an eight-year absence he rediscovered sisters who had become strangers. Princess Sophia was now a girl of 16, a clever but vulnerable member of the Sisterhood. She saw a brother with the air of a hero: his rank now major-general (at 23), his arm in a sling, his tall, lean figure displayed in the gorgeous tunic and closefitting breeches of a hussar officer.

As Mrs Harcourt foresaw, Ernest could not 'bear the life at Windsor'. He wrote from there to the prince of Wales, 'Nothing is in my

Eyes so terrible as a Family party.' Faced next with doing his duty at Weymouth, he said, 'I must go on in the old humdrum manner, today, tomorrow and evermore.' He found diversions there, however. It was just a month later that Sophia wrote to Lady Harcourt that 'dear Ernest' was being so very kind that she had to warn him that he was 'rather a little imprudent'.

Ernest solicited the prince's help to have himself created a duke with his own household and funds. 'No one in the World is so much my friend,' he wrote. He was 'Ernst August, Major General' yet 'in every Sense Your poor brother'. From Weymouth he sent bits of news. 'The honoured Authors of our Days have had Yesterday a very long *Conversation tête-à-tête* which seemed to be very boisterous... The King was in remarkable good Spirits, but his Counterpart the very Reverse.' The subject was George. The 32-year-old prince had to marry before parliament would consent to pay his huge debts. A few years earlier he had had £160,000 paid off, promising never to offend again. Now MPs were very rightly rebelling at being asked to find, in the midst of a costly and disastrous war, a further £640,000 (say £35 million now). The king was in high spirits because he had just decided that his sister's daughter, Caroline of Brunswick, would be the spendthrift's bride. It was to be a famously strifetorn marriage.

Between brothers, the queen was a topic for jibes. Ernest reports a scene at the Weymouth theatre: 'There comes in a Milliner who says she had been bringing the Coiffures for her Majesty, which naturally set me a-laughing. This Laugh occasioned a horrid ghastly Grin more like that of Medusa than of Venus.'[8]

The Duke of York wrote to the prince of Wales: 'How do you like Ernest? He has I can assure you a great many good points about him. His greatest misfortune is his eyesight, which has got him already into two or three scrapes owing to his not choosing to acknowledge it.'[9]

Princes awarded ranks beyond all reason were an affliction for the army, and especially now against an ardent revolutionary force that promoted on merit. Returning to Flanders in November 1794, Ernest found he was reduced to commanding his Hanoverian regiment. 'How ill I am treated here,' he wrote to brother George. Previously he had commanded 3000 men (nominal command, but significant in his mind). 'And now as Major-General ... to be put back to the command of a Regt when three younger Major-Generals have Brigades & Corps is a thing by God I cannot bear.' More ill-used than ever, he had a violent scene with the Duke of York over the 'affront' of demotion and threatened to throw up his commission. A further affront was that Adolphus, aged 20, now had 'a Corps of four battalions & a Regt of Cavalry'. (How these royal pseudo-generals would have exhilarated the French!) 'My heart by God is ready to burst,' Ernest tells his 'dearest, dearest' brother George. 'The ill treatment I have met with will never be forgotten. How different can *brothers* be.'[10]

His furies were illtimed. York himself faced a far greater blow. Ministers relieved the incapable chief of his command, having at last overcome the resistance of the doting king, The army was again falling back in disarray — the men ill-provided, many sick and dying, as winter closed in. Doomed further efforts were made in 1795; and Ernest was still undervalued ('I am now a mere nothing, have no brigade'). The march on Paris was postponed for twenty years.

The king allowed Ernest to return to England in 1796. 'His left eye is shockingly sunk & has an amazing film grown over it,' the prince of Wales told the queen. Ernest had said this was caused by 'that unlucky shot', but doctors ascribed it to a 'humour' to which he 'had long been subject'. A few months later he was troubled by 'violent pains' in his head, he told the prince, and by a strange malaise: 'I find I need *Quiet* for I feel a Weight in my Head which should not be.' One must note here his lifelong flaring into rages. 'My heart by God is ready to burst' is echoed later by much more in that line.[11]

Now his great desire was a British command with the rank of lieutenant-general. Again the king ignored his pleas. In April 1798 Ernest issued a threat: if his wish were not granted, 'I will then Sir go into the Yeomanry as a Private.' The king made him a lieutenant-general … but merely in the Hanoverian army.[12]

A year later came a more solid advance: he was made Duke of Cumberland and Tiviotdale and Earl of Armagh, with an income of £12,000, later raised to £18,000. The dukedom made him a peer, a potential figure in politics. He acquired an entourage of gentlemen and servants. On better terms with his father, he joined his staghunts and harrier chases at Windsor, together with the king's equerries. More will be heard of one of these, General Thomas Garth.

Ernest had apartments in St James's Palace and also at Kew Green and Windsor. At St James's he and his servants occupied several floors along the palace's north side. The Lord Chamberlain's records show that in the last quarter of 1799 he began extensive improvements. New wallpaper cost £154 (the ballroom yellow with 'Etruscan' borders); new carpets £65. His bedroom especially benefited: a mahogany pembroke table with satinwood border; yellow chintz curtains and hangings for his fourposter bed; satincovered down pillows, a fine Marseilles quilt and counterpane; 'superfine blankets' at £5 10s the pair (four times the price of blankets for his servants); mahogany dressing-table with looking-glass, £15 10s; and in addition to existing mirrors, a large one over his bedroom fireplace, in a burnished gold frame, lit by a pair of gilt girandoles, £30.[13]

He valued mirrors. Joseph Farington of the Royal Academy writes in his diary in 1799, 'Prince of Wales very attentive to his person — dresses surrounded by 3 glasses in which he can see his person — the Duke of Cumberland follows his example.'[14] Six-foot Ernest could admire a handsome figure, free of the excess fat of his elder brothers. Clothed and wearing boots, in May 1799 he weighed 13 stone 7 lb (189 lb, 85.7 kg). This is known because, like other princes and many notables, he strolled to the wine merchants at the foot of St James's-street, now Berry Bros & Rudd, to have himself weighed (the records and the scales survive). The Duke of York was 15lb heavier, and before long the Duke of Kent passed 232 lb (105 kg). A short way up St James's-street lived the artist James Gillray, above Hannah Humphrey's printshop at No 27: ideally placed to observe passing politicians and princes. In July 1799 he gave the world Ernest (*plate 1*).

St James's Palace provided many comforts for an unappreciated general. Its wine-cellar supplied him and his entourage, as well as chaplains, maids of honour and Guards officers. The wine-cellar book of the Lord Steward's department makes pleasant reading, with its columns headed Claret, Madeira, Mountain (a Spanish wine), Sack, Port, Hock, Sherry. Ernest favoured port, madeira and claret.

A constant duty of the Lord Steward's office was the Pitcher List — a roll of chaplains, officers and others, down to mere footmen, served extra port, claret or ale on special occasions. Each royal birthday gave this boon, so a family of king, queen and thirteen surviving children, plus cousins, brought a merry sequence of pitchers. Wars were a boon too: pitchers all round if a town were captured, whether in India or Flanders. Pitcher-list people could not lose: there was no call for restitution if the British were routed, as they were once again in Flanders in September 1799.[15]

On Friday, 1 November 1799, a Lord Steward's ledger shows that beefsteaks, boiled chickens, cauliflower, potatoes and tarts were served at Ernest's St James's table. For the next eleven days he was at Windsor, in part perhaps to avoid paperhangers and carpetlayers, but a special occasion was Princess Sophia's twenty-second birthday on 3 November. The court circular records that after divine service at St George's Chapel there was, according to custom, a family party for her. Next day Ernest went with the king to view his farms, then 'took the diversion of hunting with the harriers'. That evening the Earl and Countess of Cardigan gave 'a grand supper to the Royal Family and a select party of Nobility at their apartments in the Round Tower'. On 5 November, Ernest joined the king on a staghunt. Next day the king, queen and two older princesses went to London (the king's weekly levee was on the 7th), leaving Princesses Sophia, Mary and Amelia at Windsor, where each had her own apartment in the Lower Lodge south of the castle. Ernest remained at Windsor. On the 9th, 11th and 12th he hunted again with the king.[16]

Long afterwards, he found it necessary to deny that he was anywhere near Windsor in early November 1799. The reason for the denial was the boy born nine months later at Weymouth.

3

A certain little boy

A princess troubled with a pregnancy had fewer options than other ladies. She could withdraw from view by becoming 'indisposed', but she could not travel to the continent, as Georgiana Duchess of Devonshire did when pregnant in 1791 by Charles Grey (the future Whig prime minister). Some ladies had recourse to accoucheurs who could be found in the classified advertisements, such as this in *The Times*:

> TO THE LADIES
>
> Any LADY whose Situation requires a temporary retirement may be accommodated agreeable to their wishes in the House of a Gentleman, eminent in his profession, whose honour and secrecy may be depended upon, and every vestige of pregnancy obliterated, so as to elude the scrutiny of the most sagacious.
>
> N.B. Children taken care of or adopted upon the most eligible terms.[1]

It is a question whether any worldly court ladies ever risked proposing the obliteration of every vestige of a princess's pregnancy.

Princess Sophia could be grateful at least that her time came in the Weymouth season. Away from the populous Windsor establishment she could be secluded with a few trusted ladies and servants. But how was this royal baby to be 'taken care of'? The first step was that he was baptized, aged six days, at St Mary's Church, Weymouth, as 'Thomas Ward, a Stranger [foundling], adopted by Samuel & Charlotte Sharland', and stated to have been born not on the 8th but the 5th of August.[2] The false date was perhaps meant to dissociate him from any flurry that might have been noted at the royal lodge. Sharland was a man of some standing, colonel of the Weymouth Volunteers, and had a house and tailoring concern on the Esplanade facing the sands. Also on the Esplanade were Gloucester Lodge and other houses where the king, queen, Sophia, Ernest and other royals were staying.

Weymouth, though convenient, had one drawback. In a small town, secrets are hard to keep. The Sharland arrangement soon unravelled. 'The good people of Weymouth were furnished with a delightful story

for scandalous gossip,' a Weymouth woman, Elizabeth Ham, who was
sixteen at the time, says in her memoirs. Charlotte Sharland had been
chosen for her role because she was having a baby about the same
time as Sophia. Elizabeth Ham says a 'medical gentleman' attending
Mrs Sharland (an apothecary/accoucheur, Abraham Beevor) 'sent the
monthly nurse away on some distant errand'. On her return, 'she
found two babies where she had left only one'. Mrs Sharland told her
the second was born after she left. 'But the nurse was not to be so
deceived. She insisted on knowing the truth, and the poor woman,
weak in mind as well as body, told her that a few minutes after she
had left the house, a carriage stopped at the door, and the doctor
brought a newborn infant and placed it by her side, with a purse of
money, and told her that she must say it was her own.' The nurse 'had
the pleasure of frustrating ... the well-laid plan for concealment'.

In the season, Elizabeth Ham's parents took in lodgers at three
guineas a week. 'There were aunts and other visitors staying at our
house,' she writes. They began talking about the princesses. 'I looked
up from my work and said, "I wonder what is the reason that the
Princess Sophia has never been seen out since the family came." Upon
this the whole party burst into a laugh, for it was evident that everybody had been thinking the same thing but had deemed it high
treason to give it utterance.'

Soon Ernest caused speculation: 'The reappearance of the Princess
Sophia was, of course, watched for with great interest. She was observed to be looking very delicate, and was always leaning on the arm
of the Duke of Cumberland. I watched them one day on their return
from a morning call... This pair were behind the rest of the royal
family and their attendants. As they passed the tailor's door, a woman
came to it with a child in her arms. They paused a few seconds, gazed
earnestly at the child and then passed on. Her brother must know of
her marriage, and is the friend of her husband, thought I. But I was
soon obliged to weave another framework for my romance.'

A royal party returned from a sea excursion and were rowed to the
pier in an eighteen-oar barge. The king and queen 'stepped over the
carpeted plank and ascended the steps'. Then Ernest, who had not
been on the excursion, 'darted into the boat, seized on the Princess
Sophia and kissed her, and then drew her arm though his and conducted her on shore'. The romantic explanation that Elizabeth Ham
now wove for herself was: 'The Duke of Cumberland was not really

the son of the King and Queen but of some foreign potentate, who for some political reasons they had brought up as their own son, but he knew all about it.'[3] To the royal party, Ernest's spontaneous brotherly devotion must have seemed 'imprudent', though it can be seen as doing him credit. This scene and the earlier one (the baby at the door) suggest a consensual affair — a point to be remembered.

The first account of Sophia's son to be published, long before Elizabeth Ham's memoir, was in the *Morning Chronicle* of 18 March 1829, when he was dramatically in the news. The article says that after the Sharlands' own baby was born the accoucheur returned 'about 3 o'clock the next morning ... with another fine boy in his arms'. That day 'it was announced to the Queen by Lady Cathcart and Lady Charlotte Bruce, who had been in attendance upon the Princess Sophia during the night, that a great change had taken place in the state of Her Royal Highness'. The baby was brought to the Sharlands wrapped in a silk skirt 'marked with a coronet' (this does seem careless). This was 'buzzed about the town, and the tailor acquired no small accession of trade'. The gentry came with orders 'for a new riding-habit or a new suit of clothes' as a pretext for seeing the baby. 'The tailor went about boasting everywhere of the great charge committed to his care, and at length went to General Garth', an equerry managing the affair, 'and required to know who were its real parents'. If he had hoped to increase his reward, he proved mistaken.

General Thomas Garth had been an equerry to George III since 1788. He and another of his vintage were 'fine gentlemen of the old school, in powder and pigtails'. The court circular records that on 11 September he and Ernest went for a ride together, an occasion for a discreet talk. The month-old baby was transferred to Garth's care. Being in command of all the troops on duty at Weymouth, he easily found a new wetnurse, the wife of a Scots Greys sergeant.

So it came about that the boy, his surname changed to Garth, was not brought up in a tailor's household but as the son of a bachelor equerry (born 1744) at Ilsington House, a fine mansion of the 1690s that Garth rented a dozen miles away at Piddletown. Many people came to think he was Garth's son, says Elizabeth Ham, 'but if a fair young princess was his mother ... is it likely that a little old man with a clarety countenance would be the object of her secret affections?' A sharper question is: if an equerry made a princess pregnant, would he soon after be given an elite regiment, the 1st (Royal) Dragoons (7 January 1801), be promoted lieutenant-general (1 January 1805) and to full general (4 June 1814), on the orders of the princess's brother, Frederick Duke of York, commander-in-chief; and also be made responsible for the household of the prince of Wales's daughter?

A day before the end of the century, 30 December 1800, more than four months after the birth, Sophia wrote a letter to Lady Harcourt that survives her burnings. She evidently could not bear to destroy it.

> I have long ere this intended troubling you with a letter, but you have received so many from hence that I think it cruel to trespass further on your time; but although silent I have often & often thought of you my dearest dear Lady Harcourt, & with that gratitude which will never end but with my life. You will easily believe that our private conversation has often recurred to my mind; how happy I am now that I had courage to begin it, for the excessive kindness of y^r manner has I assure you greatly soothed my distressed and unhappy days & hours.
>
> Be assured dearest L^Y H that I will do all in my power to prove I am not ungrateful for all y^r kind concern about me, by the prudence of my conduct, but you will allow I am sure that I require time to recover my spirits which have met with so severe a blow. — I have no doubt that I was originally to blame, therefore I must bear patiently the *reports* however unjust they are as I have partially myself to thank for them. But dearest L^Y H when I reflect of the difference of y^r behaviour & that of others it shows me how *insincere* the chief of this world are, & how we ought to *value* & revere a true friend, who is most justly stiled 'the most precious Jewel in life'.
>
> It is grievous to think what a little trifle can *slur a young woman's character* for *ever*. I do not complain; I submit patiently, & promise to strive to regain mine, which however imprudent I have been, has I assure you been injured unjustly... God bless you dearest L^Y H, continue y^r kindness towards [me], & love me a little...   Y^r affec^{te} friend   Sophy [4]

It is a touchingly confused, and artful, piece of semi-justification. 'A little trifle' may seem odd, but perhaps reflects a woman's sense of an unfair disproportion between the cause and the effect. She says nothing to suggest she has been the victim of an outrage.

Another woman in whom Sophia could confide at this time was her sister-in-law Princess Caroline, the spurned wife of the prince of Wales. He had banished her from his life in 1796, soon after the birth of their daughter Charlotte, George III's first legitimate grandchild (the next was not achieved until 1819). Caroline was given a separate establishment, down-river at Blackheath. Sophia wrote to one of Caroline's ladies, Frances Garth, a niece of the general, of her 'partiality for the amiable princess'. This annoyed the queen — no friend to Caroline. (When Caroline arrived in England to marry the prince, she found that her Lady of the Bedchamber, with the queen's approval, was his mistress, Lady Jersey; who intercepted her letters and betrayed their contents to the queen.) 'I grieve that it is not in my power to do any good,' Sophia told Miss Garth. 'You know I must be silent, and God knows in silence I feel most deeply attached to her.' And again: 'I cannot say what I don't think; therefore I hold my tongue, but it breaks my heart.'[5]

A good source for Caroline's court at Blackheath, as well as much else, is a journal kept, for his eyes only, by Lord Glenbervie, a junior minister with high connections. His wife, a daughter of Lord North, George III's unfortunate prime minister, was one of Caroline's ladies, and so were her sisters, Anne, Lady Sheffield, and Lady Charlotte Lindsay. In their gossipy letters they addressed Lady Glenbervie (no beauty but clever and amusing) as Dearest Quackler. Lady Charlotte to Lady Glenbervie: 'When we meet at Sheffield Place [Anne's house], I shall, I dare say, have quackle to tell you that won't do for a letter.'[6] Some news was best not put on paper. For one thing, postmasters and others opened letters for secret-service and other purposes. Whatever we may find in letters, there is much more that was never set down.

Princess Caroline enjoyed quackle and was artful at eliciting confidences. In March 1801, when Thomas 'Garth' was seven months old, Glenbervie told his journal that he had 'the most authentic information' about 'many of the circumstances of the Princess Sophia's extraordinary illness' at Weymouth, but 'of too delicate a nature' to commit 'even to this safe repository'.[7] The new-made baronet, Francis Milman, was then attending Princess Caroline... Three years later Glenbervie writes in his journal that the baby 'is now in a manner admitted by the people about the court to be the Princess Sophia's, and, as the story goes, by General Garth ... a very plain man, with an ugly claret mark on his face... But the Princess of Wales told Lady Sheffield the other day that there is great reason to suspect the father to be the Duke of Cumberland. How strange and how disgusting. But it is a very strange family, at least the children, sons and daughters.'

He notes an incident when the queen, Elizabeth and Sophia paid a morning visit. The queen went to another room with Caroline. The princesses talked to Lady Sheffield about a prudish sister of Lady Harcourt. Elizabeth asked, 'Do you really believe her to be a virgin?' 'Most certainly, Madam,' Lady Sheffield said. Glenbervie continues: 'Then says the Princess Elizabeth, turning to her sister, "You know, Sophy, I always say I do not believe there is such [a thing] as a woman being a virgin, unless she stuff herself with lead." The coarse, vulgar, stupid indecency of this speech shocked Lady Sheffield.' But 'stupid' is unjustified. Away from court, Elizabeth longed to speak freely.[8]

In 1810 Glenbervie learned more about Sophia from Mrs Walter Sneyd, 'a great favourite at court, and in the intimacy of the princesses'. 'Her Royal Highness complained for about nine months of a constant obstruction of the menses, and for the last four or five of them of strange motions and convulsions in the belly.' Mrs Sneyd put her hand on Sophia's belly and was sure there was a baby. 'But the princess neither on that nor on any other occasion ever spoke or looked as if she thought or suspected that others might believe she was pregnant.'[9] From childhood all the family had learned the art of dissimulation, with their parents as exemplars.

An account given by Sophia's brother Edward Duke of Kent of how she became pregnant is recorded by Glenbervie. Kent said Ernest visited her when she was in bed with a cold, 'took advantage of the family temperament in her, and, without her having any precise idea of what happened, got her with child'. Kent was friendly with Sophia — 'little Sosy, that clever little thing'. It seems likely therefore that he shaped this account to make her less blameworthy.

Of all 'the royal progeny', Glenbervie says, only Princess Mary, the sister between Elizabeth and Sophia, is not touched by 'the breath of scandal'. According to Caroline, 'it is now an established maxim with the princesses that as the king has told them he would never permit any of them to marry, they may indulge themselves in the gratifications of matrimony if they manage matters with prudence ... and form attachments as near to conjugal connection as the restriction imposed on them will admit of'. (Glenbervie was a lawyer, and it shows.) The 'restriction' was the Royal Marriage Act.[10]

The Duke of York's mistress, Mary Anne Clarke, writes in her suppressed memoirs, 'General Garth has always made himself very useful and accommodating to such of the Royal Family as have had little ones and are afraid or ashamed to own them. His residence, near

Dorchester, is called Piddle Town... I myself saw two very fine blue-eyed children there some few years since, and without any sort of prejudice but in their favour, I could not help remarking the likeness they bore to the Royal Family, and mentioned it to the Duke, who had given me the hint of what Garth had been liked for. "Every man has his fault," if not every woman too; and as to one family, whether it be royal or not royal, being held up to the public as paragons of virtue, why, it's all moonshine!' Mary Anne had the benefit of York's pillowtalk. She writes of the princesses 'supping in their own rooms': 'I do not mean that two or three of the princesses will sup together, but on the contrary, that each may have whoever she happens to invite or to like best — generally a male friend, perhaps one of the brothers or one of their friends.'[11]

Just three months after the birth of Sophia's baby there was a curious episode concerning a Page of the Backstairs named Ernst, with apartments in St James's Palace. He threatened somehow to cause great 'inconvenience' to the king yet could not simply be dismissed. To prevent the king's 'being further troubled', William Pitt, the prime minister, got Ernst 'out of the way' by making him comptroller of customs at Surinam at £800 a year, ten times his page's pay.[12]

Studies of brother-sister incest find several recurring factors. One is the separation and later reacquaintance of siblings. The parting of Ernest and Sophia came when he was 15 and lasted eight years. Notable instances of their time are William and Dorothy Wordsworth, who became passionately close after some years apart; and Lord Byron and his half-sister, who grew up apart and became lovers when she was 30. Other factors often noted are a lack of warmth in the mother, sadly true of the queen, and family instability and conflict.

Incest was then a frequent literary theme. At least one such work was read at Windsor: a gothic drama by Horace Walpole, *The Mysterious Mother*, in which a man marries a girl he had long ago unwittingly begotten on his evil mother (a girl thus both sister and daughter). Walpole gave copies, privately printed, to friends. One was Lord Harcourt, husband of Sophia's confidante. He lent his copy, astonishingly, to Queen Charlotte, and she lent it to Fanny Burney, who was a literary admirer of Walpole. Fanny arranged a reading with friends — tutors of the young princes. The reading was a shock ('truly dreadful!') and she begged the queen 'never to cast her eye upon it'.

The plot of one of Fanny's novels, *Evelina* (1778), twice touches on sibling incest — though only mistaken fears of it. Curiously, a real-life incest scandal much afflicted her in 1798: her brother James eloped with his half-sister. As Fanny was always friendly with the princesses, this affair is likely to have been an exciting topic at the Nunnery.[13]

When Glenbervie spoke of 'the family temperament' he was not thinking only of the royal children. The king himself, like his fore-bears, was a passionate man. At 21 he confessed to his mentor, Lord Bute, that he was distracted by 'the fair sex ... those divine creatures'. He so desperately wanted to marry the lovely Lady Sarah Lennox ('sleep has left me') that he begged Bute to 'consent to my raising her to a throne', or failing that, 'devise any method for my keeping my love'. No, he must not have her as queen or as mistress. Charlotte of Mecklenburg-Strelitz was speedily brought over as a bride.[14]

For the next fifty years George III's official image was of the exemplary husband. Other monarchs had mistresses, but not he. A few facts spoil the image. An unexpected entry in the records of Westminster School reads, 'Murray, Robert William Lathrop, natural son of George III; born December 22, 1780' — conceived, therefore, when Queen Charlotte was three months pregnant with her fourteenth child. During an erratic career this royal by-blow became a banker; then a lieutenant in the 1st Regiment of Foot; was convicted of bigamy and transported to Australia; married four times in all.[15]

The king, when deranged, avowed his passion for various ladies in gross and ribald words. When he was officially well, this behaviour would still erupt. After recovering from the madness of 1788–9, he persisted in pursuing Lady Pembroke, the beautiful wife of an errant earl. The Archbishop of Canterbury urged him to regard her as 'an affectionate sister'. Yet in 1804, when officially recovered from another derangement, he was still ardently wooing her (both aged 66). The prince of Wales's aide, Colonel John McMahon, reported that the king said he had 'humbugged' his doctors and ministers and would 'make them know who he was'. He would fit up the Great Lodge at Windsor for himself '& take Lady Pembroke into keeping, who shall live there with his two youngest daughters [Sophia, Amelia], but if Lady Pembroke declines his offer he will then make it to the D^{ss} of Rutland'. Meanwhile, he locked himself in a room with Sally, a housemaid, for three-quarters of an hour.

At Weymouth soon afterwards he was still wayward, rude, ribald. There was a shameful incident in the royal yacht in the presence of the princesses. One of the guests, a pretty Mrs Drax, had once amused him by exclaiming about a donkey, 'Dear pretty little ass, oh come here that I may stroke you.' Now he said to her for all to hear, 'Mrs Drax, you look very well, very well indeed, dear lovely Mrs Drax, how I should love to stroke you.' (Stroke = copulate with.) Officers and sailors 'could scarcely contain themselves' and some 'went below to have their laugh out'. He had exiled the queen from his bed. According to Mary Anne Clarke, the Duke of York and Ernest vied with each other 'in looking out for objects for the king's pleasure' and were 'ready in their supply' of young women.[16]

The blue-eyed boy with royal features had a childhood that must sometimes have been puzzling for him. His mother wrote to him, the *Morning Chronicle* says: 'Letters were brought from the princess by royal pages, with strict orders that they should be delivered to the general himself.' Another article tells of more dramatic contacts. It says the general placed the boy occasionally with a widow at the village of Clewer, just to the west of Windsor, and she was instructed to take 'the Young Gentleman (for so he was entitled)' for walks at stated hours. 'He was met by some person or persons who would caress him with all the warmth and tenderness of parents.' Once the widow was instructed to wait with the boy 'near a certain door' at the castle. A gentleman 'hurried from the castle ... caught up the boy with the eagerness of a parent who had long been deprived of the sight of a darling child, and suddenly disappeared with him'. After a time he returned, 'repeatedly kissed' the boy and handed him back.[17]

At Ilsington House the bachelor general became a doting surrogate father. Princess Charlotte, aged 18, visiting Ilsington in 1814 when he had been made head of her establishment, thought him indiscreet. To her redhaired Scottish friend Margaret Mercer Elphinstone ('dear dear Mercer') she wrote complaining of 'Garth's indelicate conduct about a *certain little boy*'. He had said to her, 'There is a young gentleman here who you may have heard of, & made some noise by some abominable stories of his (*sic*) being told, which were without a word of truth. Pray see & speak to him, as he would be dreadfully mortified if you took no notice of him.' The boy was Charlotte's first cousin, it is true, but she felt that the general was wrong to bring him forward.

She admired the boy, however. 'A more *lovely* boy was never beheld, I do think. I was so shockingly affected that I was ashamed of myself.' Her attendants were *'quite captivated'*. One of them, Lady Ilchester, was 'affected to tears'. This lady had difficulties over the general. First she told Charlotte she was astonished that he was 'continued at all in the family, and that he should be appointed about me', and was *'disgusted* at his *unfeeling & indelicate conduct'*, showing Tom 'with such unconcern'. She seems here to be trying for Charlotte's sake to keep to the line taken at court that Garth was the father; but ten days later she said that 'it *cannot* be & *is not* G's child, that he has the care of it, & is proud & vain that it *should be thought* his, & knowing he has it in his power probably to disclose whose it is if offended makes him so very bold & impudent about the whole thing'.[18]

Charlotte recalled that once at Windsor the queen asked Garth when he would be returning to Dorset, and he said he did not know, 'as *the boy he had adopted* was sick at Harrow School'.

As early as 1811 Charlotte had in fact a good idea 'whose it is'. She teasingly asked Frances Garth, the general's niece, what was to be done with the boy, and said, 'I suppose he will be in the army — in the 15th,' meaning the 15th Hussars, of which Ernest was colonel. Glenbervie, recording this, continues: 'Miss Garth looked grave. "Oh," says the Princess, "I know all that perfectly." It is shocking, very shocking... First the tailor and then General Garth were only cloaks.[19]

From Weymouth in 1814, Charlotte sent an account of the general indulging the boy. 'I never saw him in higher spirits... He tells me he *dootes on him* beyond anything & that he is afraid he spoils him, for that Thursday by rights he ought to go back to school at Harrow, but he is not to go yet, poor fellow. "When I named it to him," Garth said, "soon the tears came down his *fine blue eyes & dark eyelashes.*"'

For six weeks the boy has been 'hunting & shooting & fishing & riding all day long', Charlotte says. General Garth is 'of little or no use' in looking after her while the boy is there — 'he thinks of nothing else'. She is embarrassed when Tom, this boy with royal features, rides up and down the Weymouth sands (in front of the lodge where he was born) and 'a parcel of officers' as well as her servants 'look at him & then talk to one another'. The town is buzzing about him: '*All Weymouth* went to see the boy when he was at his hairdresser's.'[20]

A dozen years later the seductive charms of the overindulged blue-eyed fellow were to bring him into a court of law.

4

At the heart of the court

Ernest became a byword in his family, and beyond, for persiflage and mischievous, devious plots. It may be that he sometimes puzzled himself. To be born a Royal Highness, to be officially Illustrious, is a parlous gift, and all the more so if one is only fifth in line, is ambitious and assertive, yet has been frustrated in one's pursuit of glory.

He did have principles to cherish. One was the supreme virtue of royal blood. Another was the sacredness of the terms under which his family, the House of Brunswick, had come to the throne. The first rule, that neither the sovereign nor his heir nor their wives could be Roman Catholics, was of course not then challenged (George prince of Wales had secretly married a Catholic, Maria Fitzherbert; but he had to deny it). Next were the penal laws barring millions of George III's Roman Catholic subjects, some in Britain but overwhelmingly in Ireland, from serving as MPs or peers and from sharing in many other rights. To Ernest, these laws were rocklike, immutable.

A proposal to ease them came up soon after he took his seat in the Lords. Rebellion in Ireland in 1798 had been brutally repressed. In 1800 William Pitt's Tory government abolished Ireland's separate parliament by means of a great outlay of peerages and unlawful bribes (the start of the United Kingdom, still fraught two centuries later). In return, Pitt promised 'emancipation' — repeal of the proscriptive laws. After all, papacy no longer threatened Britain: the enemy now was Napoleon, no friend of the pope.

George III, having achieved his United Kingdom, rejected the quid pro quo. What? What? Have Catholics in his parliament? That would undermine the Church of England and his throne. Ernest and other anti-Catholics had worked him up to an illfounded belief that emancipation would violate his coronation oath. He vehemently declared to ministers and others at his levee in January 1801, 'I shall consider every man who supports that measure my personal enemy.' Pitt sent him a long letter 'humbly submitting' that emancipation was needed for the tranquillity of Ireland and would be 'no danger to the

Established Church'. He asked the king 'to deign maturely to weigh' the proposal. Otherwise Pitt must resign.[1]

The king would not weigh it at all. He passionately ruled out concessions 'forever'. Pitt resigned, after having served seventeen years. The king raged against him (as always, *he* was never to blame). A 'no popery' ministry had to be devised. According to Ernest, the king employed him 'to make the first overture to Addington' — Henry Addington, a feeble replacement for Pitt. Ernest bustled between Buckingham House and 10 Downing-street while Addington laboured to construct a cabinet. 'Faced by difficulties I only become stronger,' the king liked to say. But the stress overset him. He was 'feverish', the prince of Wales told the queen. She retorted, 'He is not! He has not been feverish' — for that was the palace euphemism for derangement. Every effort was made to hide the truth, but soon the doctors' bulletins went so far as 'a little fever', a phrase quickly decoded.[2]

In 1788 a Lincolnshire 'mad-doctor', the Rev Francis Willis, had been brought in. He imposed a coercive regime, often using the straitjacket to compel the king to obey his orders. On recovering, the king ordered that this monarch-dominator must never again be used. In 1801, however, two of Willis's doctor-sons, John and Robert, were summoned, and a third son, the Rev Thomas Willis, rector of St George's, Bloomsbury, played a delicate behind-the-scenes role.

Thomas Willis records in his journal a scene at Buckingham House early in the king's illness.

The king: 'I am now very well.' Willis says he is far from well.

The king: 'Sir, I cannot deceive you, you have found me out. I beg your pardon for having told you an untruth.' He devises an excuse, 'I was afraid to distress you,' and that is why he has also 'aimed to deceive the queen and my family'. Next, 'His Majesty wept bitterly and said, "Sir, I do indeed feel myself very ill ... and I have prayed to God all night that I might die or that he would spare my reason."'

If he takes the doctors' advice, Willis says, he can soon be well. Sobbing, hugging Willis, he begs, 'For God's sake keep from me your father, and a regency!'[3] His overriding thought is to avoid yielding power to the prince of Wales, a fate he had narrowly escaped in 1789.

The prince was indeed soon hopefully shaping a Whig cabinet. Addington and the court, to prevent a regency from being 'agitated' in parliament, had to conceal how ill the king was. It was a ticklish game. As soon as the king had a calmer spell, Addington wanted him to perform some royal functions. The doctors objected that to do so would hazard his recovery, but on 17 March, after a month of seclusion, the king was brought from his bedroom to preside at a Privy Council. As a result he became 'impatient of control'. Thomas Willis's journal spells out how much power meant to the king:

> He did not understand (and in the feebleness of a mind lately bewildered by a very severe delirium, just now opening to itself and yet in a doubt about everything, how should he understand) that he should sit at the head of his Council in the plenitude of his kingly power at one moment and be under the control of one of his subjects at the very next.[4]

Unknown to the nation, Willis became the channel of executive action. Addington drafted a proposal for peace talks with Napoleon, but it was Willis who put this in front of the king and obtained his assent. What might Napoleon have said about that?

In early April the king showed his gratitude for Ernest's support by granting him a precious honour, the colonelcy of the elite 15th Light Dragoons. The same day the king played backgammon for two and a half hours with his feet in a tub of hot water (to draw the 'humours' from the brain). He talked of his 'second recovery from a severe delirium'. Next day he was allowed to have dinner with the queen, three princesses and Ernest. 'He talked a deal about going to Hanover,' Willis notes; and there was worse, for the queen and princesses kept him afterwards to hear 'their lamentation and even despair'.[5]

Official bulletins were being worded so deceptively that Addington ('in great spirits' too over Nelson's bombardment of Copenhagen) proposed a thanksgiving service for the king. Willis astutely advised against it, 'as it would only tend the more to make known his complaint, which was hitherto, by having been completely managed, little understood.' *Managing* awkward truths is no recent upstart art.[6]

In any case, the king's state did not quite justify thanksgiving. He developed a disturbing fondness for Caroline, princess of Wales, his niece and daughter-in-law. On 18 April, after a feverish night, he slipped away from Buckingham House and galloped down to Blackheath, escorted or pursued by Ernest and two equerries. He told the princess he had thought constantly about her and had resolved that his first visit 'on his recovery' would be to her, to assure her of 'the greatest kindness from all his family', except one (her husband). That night he had a relapse — delirious and full of wild notions.[7]

Thomas Willis's chief contact at Buckingham House was Princess

Elizabeth. Almost daily she wrote him notes signed 'Y^r friend Eliza' or variations on that. His journal and her letters tell the truth behind the lies. She was agitated by the Caroline affair: 'My brother Ernest has brought a message from the Pss to the King which has set him off again about her. Mama thinks the C. [lord chancellor] should speak to E. about it as he really does mischief.' Ernest seems indeed to be promoting his father's passion. It was bad enough that the king fixed a day to settle a scheme with Caroline to share control of five-year-old Princess Charlotte, which would outrage the prince of Wales. The queen was 'frightened to death', Elizabeth wrote, because the king was 'most extraordinary about the Pss [Caroline] — you do not know how he torments & plagues Mama about it'. Extraordinary indeed: he was 'very full of taking the Pss of W over to Hanover'. He would 'take her away by stealth'. Caroline told Elizabeth that 'she never would reveal what had passed' when he came down to Blackheath.

Soon the king was declared, falsely, to be well. Elizabeth was tormented with fears of the truth emerging. To Willis, 25 May: 'I find he has that power over himself to conceal his real state from everybody but his own family.' He was demanding to go to Weymouth. 'Oh consider the precipice we stand upon... Here [in Buckingham House] we can keep all secret ... but at a public water-drinking place the thing's impossible & was he to expose himself there I firmly believe we should die of it, for what we go through now is almost more than we can stand.'[8]

News-management continued. *The Times*, then subsidized by the government, gave this loyal picture: 'His Majesty gains strength daily and recovers his former spirits. The only apprehension for his health arises from his extreme activity of disposition, which will not permit him to take the necessary repose.' On 4 June, his sixty-third birthday, he appeared for only an hour instead of the usual long ceremonial. Next day's *Times* said this was because 'the natural cheerfulness and good nature of the king's disposition leads him to exert himself beyond his strength'. Elizabeth wrote to Willis of a sharper concern. She had been 'frightened to death he would talk about the *princess*'. Details which she 'cannot write' she will tell orally.[9]

It was during these painful months of deception that Elizabeth was moved to write to Thomas Willis, 'I speak very little like a Courtier tho bred up in the heart of Court (if Court has *any heart* which I much doubt). Poor Truth has a bad life of it yet it will sometimes out.' And also, '*I can assure you* I have not a *hint* of a Courtier in me.' The court is 'the *Hot bed* of *Flattery Insincerity Jealousy* & a thousand other petty stings of uncomfortable littleness belonging to human nature'.[10]

By year's end the king was better; but in 1804, deranged again, he revived his scheme to win control of Princess Charlotte. He also pursued her mother more ardently than ever. He repeatedly rode down to Blackheath to dine with her, and took freedoms 'of the grossest nature'. She could not refuse to receive him alone, she told Lady Glenbervie, 'without declaring that he was still mad'. It came to this: 'He threw her down on one of the sofas and would certainly have ravished her', but she 'contrived to get over it on the other side'.[11]

She had many lovers ... the artist Thomas Lawrence, the politician George Canning, the naval hero Sir Sidney Smith ... but she drew the line at a man of 67 who was her uncle, father-in-law and king.

Ernest's first speech in the House of Lords was not about papist peril but about women's rights. Bishops and others, in response to disasters abroad and unrest at home, were as usual denouncing vice. They were concerned that divorce actions, a privilege of the rich, were revealing the unedifying lives of aristocrats to the middle and lower orders. A peer, Lord Auckland, introduced in May 1800 an Adultery Bill to prevent a guilty wife, when divorced, from marrying her lover.

Ernest's brother William, then living procreatively with the actress Dorothy Jordan, made a long speech quoting Jewish, Greek and Roman arguments against enforcing such rigour. Ernest was briefer. 'When I consider the arts and blandishments of the seducer, and the situation into which the sex may be betrayed by his designs, I think her condition a case rather of commiseration than severity.' He did not think the proposed law would prevent adultery. 'So few men are inclined to marry the women they have seduced that it would be cruel to deprive the females of this last hope.' Lord Auckland, though backed by dozens of bishops, got a majority of only 77–69, and the bill was defeated in the Commons.[12]

One must wonder whether Princess Sophia, in the seventh month of her pregnancy, read reports of Ernest's words about seduction and commiseration.

Ernest had begun practising seductive arts in Hanover. His biographer G M Willis, who consulted German records, says he showed 'his fondness for the fair sex' from 1791 and 'had many adventures'. In 1794 Ernest called Tournai 'one of the pleasantest garrisons, as I know almost all the pretty girls in the town'. A few months later he was a little love-distracted, for his brother Adolphus had to tell him he had received a letter 'meant for your mistress'. On returning to England, Ernest brought a son with him, George FitzErnest, but passed him on to Prince William's convenient nursery of illegitimates.[13]

A caricature by Isaac Cruikshank, 'The Illustrious Lover or the Duke of Cumberland Done Over,' suggests in 1801 that Ernest is besotted with a girl in the slummy St Giles district. A watering-can placed phallically between his legs besprinkles a flowering plant, next to which is displayed a cheap print, 'Twopenny uprights' (women available for twopence in alleyways). On the floor are papers saying 'My Dear Dear Dear Lovee' and a chest of 'Keepsakes' — hats, shoes, a cracked chamberpot ' *often used by M. Anne*'. Some of Ernest's enormous speech-bubble must be quoted:

> Not meet at St Giles's? D—n——n [damnation], worse than a Dog you treat me — not to be allowed to attend as Midwife, Nurse or Chamber-maid, D—n——n must I belong to nobody? — but I must not complain — I am always blubbering... I act the part of a Fool — O the dear Plant ... my adored, my Celestial... I cannot conquer this heaven-born passion... Let the Doctor feel your pulse... Only write me word you hate me, & by G— I shall adore the Paper, the Ink, the very grease of your hand... O that lovely loose dress — always be loose — then I call G-d to witness I shall think you ten thousand times more charming — I shall never forget what I then saw — I wish you had left it a little more open... O what a Dog I am.

He also found ladies of a higher tone. He aroused jealousy in an admiral, Sir Charles Nugent, whose wife Charlotte was close to the prince of Wales as well as to Ernest. A caricature shows her hugging Ernest and the admiral angrily reaching for his sword. Yet another indicates a tiff. Ernest, striding hand-in-hand with 'Mrs N——', says, 'You were full of your fun last night, you had a mind to teaze me, you almost made me angry.' She says, 'It was all your fault for putting yourself in a passion.'[14]

Prudent ladies preferred to avoid Ernest. Lady Susan Strangways writes in her journal about him at Weymouth in 1802, 'It's disagreeable to be the subject of HRH's conversation, who deals more in scandal & abuse than is very *edifying* & the less one is in his way the better.' Ernest generally felt free to speak as he liked wherever he was, whereas the other princes generally toned down their coarseness in mixed company. Their father enjoyed barrackroom bawdry. Mary Anne Clarke says in her memoir that sometimes the king's greatest amusement 'was to listen to all the tender and delicate stories that those two dukes [Ernest and the Duke of York] could collect or had the filthiness and obscenity enough to invent for him'.[15]

Some ladies admired Ernest for his vigour. 'There was life in him,' said William Pitt's niece, the eccentric Lady Hester Stanhope. She recalled a hot crowded party given by the Duchess of Rutland. 'Halfway up the staircase the Duke of Cumberland was trying to make his way... "Where's my aide-de-camp? Come and help me, for I am so blind I can't get on alone. Why, this is hell and damnation!" — "Here I am, sir." — "Give me your hand, there's a good little soul. Do help me into this hell, for it's quite as hot."' She describes him 'peeping about to right and left' through his monocular glass for his 'aide-de-camp', saying, 'Where is she gone to?'[16]

Ernest's involvement with Princess Caroline became so close in 1806 that it seemed more than political. This was the time of the Delicate Investigation, an inquiry (not public) into Caroline's loose behaviour and the birth, it was alleged, of one or two babies. The prince of Wales hoped the evidence would be enough to cast her out of his life. It happened that the death of William Pitt in 1806 brought in a coalition headed by the prince's old associates the Whigs. The Tories cynically took up Caroline's cause, and mischief-loving Ernest joined in the intrigue. The prince, his one-time 'dearest, dearest' brother, accused Ernest of hostile plotting. He was all innocence. He said George was accusing him of having 'invidiously attempted to do you mischief in a quarter to which I have had means of access [George III], & wherein I have mistated (sic) and misrepresented you. This I MOST SOLEMNLY & MOST UNEQUIVOCALLY DENY.' A solemn denial by Ernest did not convince those who knew him. The prince replied curtly, regretting that his protest 'has not had the desired effect'.[17]

The commission of investigators gathered copious sworn evidence about Caroline's indecorous behaviour, but they avoided finding proofs of fornication and pregnancy — which would have made the wife of the heir to the throne guilty of high treason. (No matter that *he* had been fornicating elsewhere for ten years.) The delicate report went in August 1806 to the king, the prince and Caroline.

The prince was advised that Caroline's behaviour had been bad enough to justify a divorce. Ernest worked with two leading Tories, Spencer Perceval and Lord Eldon (both lawyers), in shaping an exculpatory version, a case for the defence, and had it printed, a book of 156 pages. The prince knew Ernest was up to something. He wrote in October 1806 to the Whig premier, protesting at 'incessant communication' between Eldon and the king 'through the medium of the Duke of Cumberland'. The prince feared they would foil his hopes by persuading the king to receive Caroline at court. Lieutenant-General Ernest was meant to be in the west country, but came to London 'for the sake of mischief and to intermeddle in the business of the Princess of Wales', the prince said. He asked the Duke of York, commander-in-chief, to order Ernest to stay away.

He also wrote to his sister Amelia, suspecting that Ernest was scheming with her. In her reply she said, 'There are many things I highly disapprove in him.' They had 'never uttered' on the subject of Caroline. Then comes a curious passage of much wider significance:

> I do not think Ernest has been more if so much in my room as my sisters';
> I am grieved to think there should be a necessity for avoiding being left
> alone, but I fully understand you & you may depend on my remembering
> your kind injunction on the subject. I don't know how it has occurred, but
> that lately I have heard the offnest from him... I am very happy you have
> given me an opportunity of speaking out to you...
>
> Unless I *quarell* with Ernest I fear I cannot keep him out of my room, but
> I always can avoid being alone & of this be assured... My dearest dear G.P.
> [George Prince] ... ever remember your own child — Amelia [18]

Caroline told her brother in Brunswick that 'the dear Duke of Cumberland' was 'a true brother'; the Whigs were 'that infernal sect' and 'Jacobins'. Then a political reversal changed everything. George III broke the Whig coalition because it reopened the Catholic question. The Tories came back — with Perceval at the Treasury and Eldon as lord chancellor. What would they do now? Perceval had perhaps 2000 copies of The Book (as it was known) at his house, ready for the booksellers. The Tories drew back and advised the king to receive Caroline, implying innocence of fornication and childbirth, though with a warning to behave less imprudently. She still wanted The Book to appear. The prince was ready to retort with a counter-version; but then his own impure life would be raked up. In the end, politicians of both camps devised a truce to prevent the exposure of royal misbehaviour to the vulgar gaze. The books were burned. Perceval spent thousands of pounds of secret-service money to buy illicit copies, yet much leaked out. The game left Caroline and George undivorced, and both feeling foiled and ill-done-by.

Titled colonels of regiments generally performed an honorary role, but that was not Ernest's way with the 15th, a regiment in 1801 of 1068 officers and men. He took personal command for months at a time, says Colonel HC Wylly in his history of the regiment. The 15th wore hats with a two-foot white plume, blue jackets with silver braiding and scarlet collar and cuffs, gold cross-belts, red sashes and sabre belts, white breeches and black boots. Regiments vied, of course, in making a fine show. Ernest required every detail to be referred to him, even the horses' bits. When he converted the regiment in 1806 to hussars on the German model, he introduced Hessian boots and ordered everyone to grow moustaches. Lower ranks daren't disobey, but the officers used passive resistance. After leaves-of-absence they returned cleanshaven. Moustaches were countermanded.[19]

Far more serious was Ernest's despotic harshness. Officers of the 15th were 'throwing up their commissions and refusing to serve under him,' Lady Bessborough learned. 'The D of C's severity is so excessive that human patience cannot endure it. Surely, if the men are punished for disobedience to orders they *can* scarcely obey, the commander should not be exempted from punishment merely because he is a prince? It is whispered that to several of his own officers he has gone so far as to hold up his cane.'

She reports an incident when Lieutenant-General Ernest, inspecting militia regiments in the west country, told Viscount Hinton, colonel of the 2nd Somerset Militia, that his men were so bad that he must resign. 'Ld Hinton replied that if he did it should be to his father, who was Ld Lt of the county. On this the Duke rais'd the famous cane and said something which Ld Hinton interrupted by saying he was glad to perceive by this last action that the whole was a joke of his Royal Highness, as he well knew such language and action c^d not be seriously us'd to a gentleman.' Ernest was unwise to choose young Lord Hinton as a target of his pugnacity. Hinton could reply coolly because his father, the 4th Earl Poulett, was not only lord lieutenant of Somerset but also a Lord of the Bedchamber to George III.[20]

The regiment's senior captain, Henry Foskett, was so tyrannized by

Ernest that in 1810 he dared to present a petition to the Commons detailing 'grievous acts of injustice' and 'systematic oppression'. He could not win, and resigned; but set out his case in a 260-page book, *The Rights of the Army Vindicated in an Appeal to the Public*, which went into a second edition in 1811.

Ernest's enthusiasm for flogging and other brutal punishments was raised in the Commons by Sir Francis Burdett, the reformist baronet. He called for returns of punishments inflicted in all regiments over the past ten years When the 15th was under 'an officer who was not fond of inflicting corporal punishment', he said, during eight years there were only six such punishments. Under Ernest 'there had been no less than eighty punishments in less than half that period'. The regiment 'was likely to be spoiled'. Soldiers should not be left to 'the caprice or accidental character' of their commanders. Napoleon's armies used 'no such disgraceful punishments'. Lord Castlereagh, war secretary, objected that it would be a 'great evil' to have the subject 'agitated among the common soldiers'.[21]

A leading Whig, Samuel Whitbread, renewed the charge in 1810, and accused Ernest further over a torture, picketing, that had been used by the Spanish Inquisition. The victim was ordered to stand on a stool beside a tall post, fitted at the top with a hook. His right hand was fastened to the hook by a noose round his wrist, 'drawn up as high as it could be stretched'. A stump 'cut to a blunt point' was driven into the ground to match the stool's height; the stool was removed and the victim had to hang with one bare heel resting on the stump. This 'put him to great torture', but if he took his weight on the wrist 'the pain soon became intolerable'. He was kept in this agony for a quarter of an hour. Whitbread told the Commons that although picketing had been abolished by a general army order in 1806, it had been enforced in Ernest's regiment 'until very lately'. He had brutally flouted the ban.[22]

A lampoon, *The R[oya]l Brood*, said of Ernest:

> One Chick, in wantonness of mind
> Left all competitors behind.
> To punish for caprice and whim
> Seem'd pastime full of fun for him.[23]

5

Death in St James's Palace

A young man from Cagliari in Sardinia, Joseph Sellis, '*Perruquier, agé de dix-neuf ans*', obtained a laissez-passer on 11 January 1791 at the mayor's office in Marseille, permitting him to continue northwards to Lyon. The pass affirmed that at Marseille, *grace à Dieu, la Santé est très-bonne* (the city was free of pestilence). At Lyon eight days later, Sellis obtained permission to go on to Paris. These details are known because Sellis's laissez-passer survives in the British Library, London, as almost the only relic of this unfortunate man.

The 19-year-old hairdresser had reason to travel in hope. It was just eighteen months since the Bastille had fallen. A revolutionary national assembly had abolished many feudal powers of the aristocracy and had proclaimed new freedoms. France seemed a land of opportunity. Soon, however, Paris was torn by violent conflicts, dangerous especially for the families with whom a perruquier might have hoped to prosper. Besides, elaborate coiffures became politically unwise. Joseph Sellis moved on, perhaps with an émigré family, to London, Europe's richest city, where many great houses had foreign servants.

About 1796 he was established as one of Ernest's valets. He married a milliner named Mary Ann. They were given lodgings in an upper floor of St James's Palace, and won such favour that Ernest was godfather to their fourth child, a boy — baptized Ernest Augustus in the palace chapel on 7 February 1810.[1]

Within four months of that ceremony Sellis was dead, and in strange circumstances.

The evening papers of Thursday, 31 May 1810 carried a sensational report:

ATTEMPT TO ASSASSINATE THE
DUKE OF CUMBERLAND

The first account that reporters were given was that when Ernest was undressing to go to bed, Sellis 'made several desperate thrusts at his master' with a sword, but Ernest 'sprung upon' and 'grappled with the assassin' and 'the villain fled'. Later accounts varied. Of one fact there was no doubt: Sellis was lying dead in his room, his throat cut from ear to ear. It was also true that Ernest had some sabre wounds.

A turbulent crowd gathered round the palace. The reporter for *The Star* noted a troubled figure, the eldest Sellis child, a girl of about eight. 'The poor little creature was in the crowd ... a melancholy spectator of the bustle and confusion excited by the horrid catastrophe.' [2] She is sure to have heard people speculating that Ernest had murdered her father, for many thought so at once.

Throughout that day and again next morning, palace servants and others made sworn depositions for Richard Ryder, the home secretary, and James Read, the chief metropolitan magistrate. Read was much more than a magistrate. He was in charge of the London police, directly under Ryder, and had a generous secret-service fund for combating radicals. The depositions were brought before a meeting of the Privy Council, augmented by the attorney-general, solicitor-general and three judges.

Selecting a jury for Sellis's inquest was a sensitive matter, and not only because Ernest was an illustrious but controversial figure. St James's was at the heart of Westminster, a constituency most unusual in having nearly 14,000 voters, mainly shopkeepers and artisans. The most notable of their two MPs was Sir Francis Burdett, a rich fox-hunting baronet and yet a fighter for reform and against corruption. And just at this time, Westminster was hot with political protest.

For the past year, scandals and defeats had aroused nationwide clamour. The Duke of York, commander-in-chief in the war against Napoleon, was proved to have financed his luxury-loving 'dearest darling' mistress, Mary Anne Clarke, by conniving with her in a brisk trade in army commissions (major £900, captain £700, etc). George III pulled every lever to save York, but the shameful facts were too much for the government's usually servile MPs to swallow. Spencer Perceval, the premier, had a sad time reporting circumlocutionally to the king: 'Mr Perceval is sorry to say that he should inexcusably deceive Your Majesty if he did not add that he apprehends the prejudice against His Royal Highness ... still remains.' York had to resign. Further scandal followed. Mary Anne possessed many curious royal secrets, from his pillowtalk and from ninety of his letters. To buy her silence he granted her an annuity, but then (always in debt) he lapsed in his payments. So she wrote her memoirs. When 18,000 copies were ready for sale, Perceval bought her off with £10,000 and a better pension. She yielded up York's letters, and the books were burned.

Soon after came a military disaster: another royal humiliation, for George III had insisted that the illconceived Walcheren expedition of 40,000 men, aimed at capturing Antwerp, should be commanded by a favourite, the 2nd Lord Chatham, a man notorious for negligence and torpor. 'Incompetence and folly', *The Times* said, 'consigned thousands of men to lingering deaths.'

When the Commons came to debate the disaster in March 1810, Perceval enforced a secret session, hoping to save his weak and derided government from further obloquy. This spurning of press freedom and public accountability only put him in deeper trouble. A veteran radical, John Gale Jones, posted up placards announcing a *public* debate about the cover-up. For this flouting of parliament he was instantly jailed. Sir Francis Burdett declared the jailing illegal, and published a hot denunciation in William Cobbett's radical *Political Register*. Perceval's obedient majority found Burdett guilty of a gross breach of parliamentary privilege for which he must go to the Tower.

He defiantly locked himself in his mansion, 78 Piccadilly, making his martyrdom a drama. Protesters shouting 'Burdett forever!' ruled the Westminster streets, smashed ministers' windows (a British tradition), especially those of Lord Castlereagh, the war secretary, and maintained a mass vigil outside Burdett's mansion. Thousands of troops were drafted into central London, among them Ernest's 15th Hussars. Cannon were set up in Berkeley, Grosvenor and Soho Squares and in St James's Park. Guns at the Tower were loaded with grapeshot against mob attack. Terrified citizens fled to the country.

Perceval agonized. Did a Speaker's warrant empower them to 'break open doors' at 78 Piccadilly? After two tumultuous days and nights, James Read's police did just that on 9 April. 'By what power, sir, have you broken into my house?' Burdett demanded. He was seized and dispatched to the Tower in a coach, escorted by Read, four hundred of Ernest's hussars and a large force of other soldiers. Caricatures and verses denounced this Grand Ministerial Expedition:

> This is the cavalcade, mighty in power,
> Six thousand strong men to take one to the Tower...
> An Englishman's house is his Castle no more!! [3]

At the Tower thousands of demonstrators were waiting. They pelted the soldiers with mud and stones — the 15th especially, because the uniforms imposed by Ernest made people think they were Germans. The 15th charged, slashing with sabres and firing carbines and pistols. Several people were killed and many wounded.

Richard Ryder's agents reported the alarming treasonable words 'used in alehouses and written on the walls'. Here are a few that survive in his files:

Reform in Parliament and we shall then be Masters
Burdett forever and no King!
Soldiers, fight for Burdett!
The Good Old Cause and no King [alluding to Cromwell's republic]

Ryder ordered the Tower governor to send daily lists of Burdett's visitors to enrich his file of radicals. A visitor of a different sort was Lady Oxford, famous for being liberal in love as well as politics. Burdett had fathered one of her miscellany of children. His wife was a daughter of Thomas Coutts, the immensely rich banker, but it was Lady Oxford who solaced the Tower hero. 'She used to take pains to tell everybody of her going almost every day ... to pass two or three hours with him.' [4] (A few years later she solaced Lord Byron.)

The agitation went on through May. London was an army-ruled city. A mysterious death in the palace of the unloved royal colonel of the 15th was the last thing ministers wanted.

Organizing the Sellis inquest was the task of a lawyer, Samuel Adams, who held a sinecure, Coroner for the Verge of the King's Palace of St James's. He sent a clerk to Francis Place, master of a large tailoring establishment at 16 Charing Cross, who suggested, as Adams said, 'the names of many persons fit and eligible to compose such a jury'. In modern accounts of the case, Place is called 'the radical tailor', but he had long renounced his radicalism of the 1790s. He was no longer a poor tailor, but a flourishing entrepreneur, associated with Utilitarian gentlemen such as James Mill and Jeremy Bentham, reform-minded but sharply at odds with radicals who demanded universal suffrage. Campaigners of the left, contending over true beliefs and over strategy, have always been bitterly factional.

Adams's clerk walked up and down Charing Cross (the stretch of street now named Whitehall) summoning Thomas Noble, ironmonger, John Wall, bootmaker, John Thomas, butcher, Thomas King, tailor,

Thomas Woolbert, hatter, Stephen Tapster, victualler, and other shop-keepers from Place's list. Place arrived at the palace after twelve men had been empanelled, but persuaded Adams, he says, to add him and others to the jury. He, the latecomer, was made foreman.

Before the inquest, Place says in his memoirs, 'the prevailing opinion was that the duke had murdered his valet'. Several motives were rumoured. One was 'that the valet was the duke's minion, and that the duke had killed him to prevent a threatened exposure'.[5]

In such a sensitive affair it was most helpful to the government that Place arose as foreman. His being a non-Tory might counter suspicions of inquest-rigging. Perceval's government, though feeble in great affairs, was ready with stratagems. An apposite example: when Perceval needed a Commons motion to imprison Burdett, he persuaded a Welsh banker-MP, Sir Robert Salusbury, to move it, telling him, 'Being a country gentleman and not always voting with us, it could not seem to arise from ministerial influence.'[6] Salusbury soon regretted being used. He had to flee from London, and Burdettites concerted a run on his bank. Burdett fervour was found everywhere.

The result of the inquest, and the strong role Place played in it, exposed him to accusations that he was a government tool.

Ernest's bedroom was at the west end of a range of a dozen rooms. His curtained fourposter bed was in an alcove on the bedroom's south side. Directly adjoining that side was a room where a valet, Cornelius Neale, slept if on duty. About 100 feet to the east was one used by Sellis. On the evening of 30 May, Ernest attended a naval dinner, then changed to go to a charity performance, patronized by the king and queen, of Handel's *Messiah*. He missed the start, but went in time to hear *O Death! where is thy sting? O Grave! where is thy victory?*

In the following summary of evidence sworn in depositions and at the inquest itself, the significance of some details will emerge later.

Neale's account

He saw Ernest to bed about midnight, then went to bed. His room 'is separated from the duke's only by a thin ... wainscot partition'. He is 'very wakeful' but 'never heard any noise' until Ernest came to his door, bleeding from wounds and shouting, 'Neale! I am murdered!' In Ernest's room Neale found a bloodstained sword and wanted to 'pursue the assassin', but Ernest told him to rouse other servants and then to go down with him (bleeding as he was) to the porters' lodge to raise the alarm. On returning upstairs, Ernest told Neale's wife to call Sellis, and told Neale to find where the assassin 'could have been concealed'. In a closet, Neale said, he found a scabbard, a water bottle, a lantern, and slippers with the name Sellis in them.

Nine or ten months earlier, Neale said, Sellis had accused him of being a thief and made 'other charges' against him — all of them untrue. Sellis had 'an evil disposition' toward him, so he hung a loaded double-barrelled pistol at the head of his bed in a red bag. Sellis was 'quarrelsome', of 'a very malicious disposition', 'very irritable', 'will not be contradicted'.

[*Francis Place asks if Neale knows of any motive for Sellis to attack Ernest.*] 'No motive in the world.' Ernest had done more for Sellis than for Neale, 'who had been longer in his service'.

[*In reply to a juror, Neale does find a motive*]: 'My opinion is ... Sellis meant to murder the duke, thinking that the blame should be put on me... I have no more doubt he did it to cause me to be suspected than I have of my own existence.'

Mrs Ann Neale, *housekeeper to Ernest*
Sellis 'was very obstinate and quarrelsome and would not bear contradiction, not even from His Royal Highness... The whole royal family were particularly attached to Sellis, and on every court day [at St James's] they had his wife and children brought into the gallery to see them. On the last day the queen was in town, she had the young baby brought into the room to be shown to her.'

Ernest's sworn deposition
Two blows to his head awoke him. Starting up, he received two more blows to his head, 'which being accompanied with a hissing noise, it occurred to him that some bat had flown against him, being between sleep and waking, and immediately received two other blows. There was a lamp burning in the room but he did not see anybody.' Making for a door leading to Neale's room, he received a wound on his right thigh. He called to Neale 'and said there was a murderer in his room'.

Another door, leading from his room to the rest of the apartment, and 'always locked the last thing', was open. 'The man had fled through the yellow room which leads into the ballroom, through the other yellow room into the armoury, to the summer bedroom, through the dressing-room into Sellis's room.'

Several royal servants
Sellis was 'a very good-tempered man and not at all quarrelsome ...

a pleasant fellow ... always with his family, very attentive to them'. 'I am not aware of the least circumstance whatever which could have made him entertain the least ill-will against His Royal Highness.' 'Sellis was a very civil, well-behaved man.' He had been very unhappy on account of Neale, who he said 'robbed and plundered His Royal Highness'. He wanted to find another place because Neale 'was so great a scoundrel he could not bear to live with him'. A maidservant having looked at the lantern, said 'she never saw it before, and never saw Mr Sellis with any lantern'.

Sergeant, Coldstream Guards

A razor lay on the floor near Sellis's body. On the opposite side of the room 'was a wash-hand basin with some water in it, which looked as if some person had been washing blood in it'.

Mary Ann Sellis ('extremely agitated', reporters note)

The day before, her husband went to market, then walked with her and the children in the park. At supper he talked about dresses she was to make up for herself and the children from muslin given by the queen and Princess Augusta, in time for George III's birthday celebration (June 4). Her husband devoted all his spare time to her and the family. He sometimes talked of leaving Ernest's service on account of Neale. She urged him 'not to make her unhappy by talking of it again'.

He had been 'much gratified' by the sponsoring of their last baby by Ernest and Princess Augusta, and by presents they gave.

He desired her to 'roast the veal tomorrow'. He would remind her of it in the morning. After supper 'he shook hands and wished her a good night, and she never saw him more cheerful'. He was wearing shoes — 'scarcely ever wore slippers'. Never took any lantern or candle with him when going down to Ernest's floor: 'There are lights always burning'. He had only one lantern (she produces it).

The jurors went to see Sellis's body, lying back on his bed, partly undressed, in shirt, blue pantaloons (trousers) and grey worsted stockings, and drenched in blood. (When the carotid arteries are cut, blood spurts with great force.) Between his room and Ernest's, they saw smears of blood on doors or frames.

The coroner read out a letter found in Sellis's portfolio, addressed to one of Ernest's Bedchamber Grooms, Captain Benjamin Stephenson, 9 July 1809. 'I am extremely anxious to know His Royal Highness's decision concerning the evidence produced before you against Mr Neale,' it begins. 'Either His Royal Highness is not acquainted with what has been proved, or His Royal Highness has entirely forgiven him.' He asks Stephenson to tell Ernest 'of the roguery of this man'. Witnesses 'are all ready to take their oaths in a court of justice'. If Ernest has forgiven Neale, Sellis must ask Ernest 'to have the goodness to dispose of me as His Royal Highness may think proper'. It is a mortification 'to live and act in the same room' as Neale. If Neale had been taken to court he 'would have been transported at least for seven years; and what I am going to communicate now is, I believe, transportation for life. I have been told, sir, that Mr Neale cheats His Royal Highness in everything he buys... This man is as great a villain as ever existed.' Then comes this obscure but suggestive passage:

> No oath or promise is binding with him. He relates alike that which he must have sworn to keep sacred in his bosom as he would a most trifling thing, and slanders and threatens with public exposure and large damages his benefactor and only maker of his fortune, just as he would one of his own stamp. To serve His Royal Highness, I have always thought it as my greatest honour ... the greatest pride of my life; but no longer can I live with this monster.

Stephenson was not called. Ernest himself, who had been removed to Carlton House, the prince of Wales's palace nearby, was not questioned about this or any other evidence. Neither the coroner nor Place asked for the slippers and lantern to be shown to Mrs Sellis, or asked why only the Neales alleged a malicious Sellis. Nor did anyone query the motive Neale alleged, which required that when he, 'very wakeful', was sleeping in the next room, Sellis would have had to dispatch Ernest silently, retrieve his things from the closet, retire (bloodspattered) to his room and finally accuse an unprotesting Neale.

Place told the coroner that he need not sum up, as the jurors had decided a verdict. *He* had decided them. In his own account of the affair, he wrote, 'I looked at my notes and I summed up myself to the jury.' Verdict: suicide.[7]

Ernest's wounds had been treated, the first night, by a surgeon and by Sir Henry Halford, the royal physician. Halford detailed them for George III in a note timed 4.30 am: 'One upon the side of the head above the right ear, which bled profusely but is not dangerous — another on the back of the right hand — a third upon the left — and two or three others of less importance upon various parts of the body,' making five or six in all. 'There is no danger to the Duke of

Cumberland's life... A most providential escape.' Indeed, Providence was repeatedly credited with having saved the sleeping Ernest from mortal wounds when attacked with a cavalry sabre.

When being removed to Carlton House he 'walked down stairs with assistance', *The Times* reported, 'and got into a sedan-chair'. His removal was explained by a surgeon and devoted friend, Wathen Phipps: 'The idea of being in the rooms where the act was perpetrated, & under the *same* roof with the *body of the murderer*, kept him in such a state of agitation as you cannot imagine. If anyone moved or stirred he was full of apprehensions & calling out to know who it was.' Even with large doses of laudanum, he slept '5 or 6 minutes at a time, & that very disturbed'; but 'has made *no* complaint of his *head*'.[8]

Princess Elizabeth wrote to her friend Lady Harcourt: 'My brother, by all accounts, has been mercifully preserved by the interference of a wise & good Providence... When I rise in the morning I feel, what will happen before night?' The queen is frightened 'to a degree that is *not to be believed*... After a servant has lived with one fourteen years, how would one suppose him such a premeditated villain?'[9] This was indeed a difficult question.

Princess Sophia came to see Ernest several times in the first week.

When Queen Charlotte visited Ernest, the prince of Wales took the opportunity to show her his improvements to Carlton House. This moved her to write to her daughter Mary: 'There are very fine things to be seen, but indeed, my dear Mary, I could not help saying to myself, *Oh! vanity, vanity*, comparing what I saw below to what I had just seen above [Ernest in bed]... The house is not near finished & if it goes on in the manner it has done, it never will, for there is constant building up & pulling down.'[10] (In 1827 it was *all* pulled down.)

Sellis still lay in his room. Respectable persons were permitted to view the scene. A Christian gentleman, the Rev Robert Lowth, fox-hunting son of a bishop, was so stirred by Ernest's 'most miraculous escape ... most truly providential' and by viewing 'the disgusting body of the suicide' that he dispatched a letter to Richard Ryder:

> The general idea is that it is to be buried with a stake driven thro' it at Charing Cross... A most marked anxiety was very generally expressed by those who indignantly witnessed the bloody spot that some *signal brand of infamy* ... should be adopted which shall operate *on the other side of the water*... This Monster of Ingratitude, Treachery & Blood being a *fellow countryman of Bonaparte's* is a circumstance surely not to go unmarked.

Some thought Sellis was a Corsican, like Napoleon. Seize the opportunity, Lowth urged, to associate him with 'the Corsican usurper's foul system of Espionage and Assassination'. He suggested that 'the Assassin's Carcase' should be exhibited at Charing Cross 'impaled on a Stake to hold the head and body together'. 'Or more appropriately perhaps, exposed *in quarters* on the Turrets over St James's, & then instead of being simply cast into a hole at a crossway, if it were sent in a case to Bonaparte himself "with Great Britain's Compliments & Thanks for all his *intended Favours*", I think it would be a present well becoming an indignant country.'[11]

Unhappily for the ardent and reverend Lowth, the last thing Ryder wanted was any display to agitate the populace. The rules for suicides prescribed a midnight burial with no Christian obsequies, not literally at a 'crossway' but at a 'three-went way', a T-junction. This was expected to be at Charing Cross (where Whitehall now meets Trafalgar Square). On the Saturday night a large crowd waited, but in vain. Officials were trying to fix on an *obscure* three-went way, for fear of a demonstration of radical sceptics. They had to complete the task urgently, because the next Monday was George III's 72nd birthday, a time for patriotic ceremonial.

In the small hours of the birthday morning Sellis's body was buried, unannounced, 'with a stake driven through it bearing the initials of this self-destroyer', 'midway between the bottom of Northumberland-street and the gateway into Scotland Yard, about two yards before the door of the egg and potato warehouse'. (The creation of wide Northumberland-avenue in the 1870s altered the scene. Sellis lies near the Sherlock Holmes public house, where Northumberland-street joins the avenue.) Despite the secrecy and the late hour, about thirty people gathered. Come daylight, 'an immense concourse of people' came to view the spot.[12]

In the state rooms of St James's Palace that afternoon there was a nobler concourse. George III's birthday was marked in a ceremony attended by the queen 'decorated with the most costly jewels', four princesses in the wide-hooped dresses of a century before, still ordained for them for such occasions, and hundreds of the nobility (the ladies all in new dresses, each one described in next day's papers). Two archbishops gave orations. An ode by the unpoetic laureate Henry Pye, promising eventual triumph over Napoleon, was sung.

The queen and Princess Elizabeth were seen to cry. It was a sorrowful birthday, and not only because of tumultuous radicals and now the fear of assassins. The youngest princess, Amelia, was near death ('constant retching and exhaustion ... hysterical ... coughing ... pain in the head and side', Halford reports at this time, prescribing laudanum, hock and water, brandy and water, beef tea, grapes, cherries and more laudanum). And the king, sadly, was not on show: again showing 'feverish' symptoms. [13]

Several newspapers ranted about foreign servants. *The Star* said they 'place our royal family, our nobles and the best blood of the land within reach of an assassin's dagger every day and night of their lives! ...Send them out of the country — let the bread of England be eaten by her own children.' The *General Evening Post* alleged that Ernest was determined 'to discharge all aliens from his establishment' to avoid 'the fawning deceptions of foreign hairdressers, artful spies and designing imposters'. London had '*twelve thousand* of these dangerous domestics'. [14]

Some people in the best circles took a cooler view. Sarah Spencer, a niece of the famous Georgiana Duchess of Devonshire, wrote to a friend that people were saying Sellis had been bribed by the French, 'but this is extremely absurd, I think, because the Duke of Cumberland being only fourth or fifth son of the king, what could it signify that he should live or die to any but his family? ...However, HRH is not at all dead nor in the least danger, the wounds having all been insignificant.' [15]

What of the *first* son of the king, George, prince of Wales?

Gentlemen aware of his timorous nerves mockingly called him Big Ben, after a noted boxer. The news about Ernest inspired Lord Paget, the future Marquess of Anglesey, to send his brother Sir Arthur a jesting letter that begins, 'I write to you to inquire after *Ben*. I entreat you to let me know how *Ben* is.' The Pagets knew the prince well. Arthur had been a special favourite, and no doubt had amused his brothers by reading out the effusive letters that the prince sent to his 'beloved Arthur'. In one of these, of ten pages, the prince gives a long account of a fall from his horse, and says 'how nearly the life of me, of your very best Friend, my dearest Arthur & Well-wisher, was nearly gone', and he closes with this: 'It is out of the nature of human affairs for any one Man to love another with more true affection than you are, my dearest Arthur, by Your ever affectionate — George P'

Lord Paget's merry letter of June 1810 continues:

I pity him from my soul. I do not understand what precaution he *can* take
to defend himself. If such persons as Jouard & Du Pasquier [his Pages of
the Back Stairs] are not to be depended upon, what is to become of him?
What is he to do?

I am *really* distressed to the greatest degree at the poor Duke of
Cumberland's horrid misfortune, but I will *fairly* own to *you* that I have
had *Ben* more constantly present in my thoughts... Does he bolt his doors?
No — for then he might be burnt to death or be taken with an apoplexy. He
certainly cocks his pistols — that of course — they have been cocked these
20 years— But then he may be asleep. In short my dear Arthur, don't treat
this anxiety as a joke, but do tell me, what does he do? How is he? What
does he say? I can think of nothing else... Of course he will lock up all his
sabres & keep the keys himself. But that may not do — there are others—
In short, what will he do? If you have any mercy find out & tell me.[16]

The prince had certainly been thrown into a nervous state. But he kept
his French pages.

Speculation was not silenced by the Sellis verdict. An MP's wife who
moved in high society, Mrs Frances Calvert, wrote in her journal, 'I
hear the soldiers on guard say they wish he had been cut to pieces
instead of wounded. The business is a most mysterious one, and
endless stories are circulated.'[17] Gwyllym Lloyd Wardle, an MP who
led the 1809 Duke of York exposure, told Place that 'everybody was
dissatisfied' with the verdict, Burdett in particular. Burdett soon
denounced Place as a paid spy among the reformers, and refused to
speak to him for years.

Lack of a motive was a chief cause of suspicion. *The News* said it
could not discover anything 'to induce a man to imbrue his hands in
the blood of his benefactor and also to ruin his own family'. Captain
Stephenson, the Bedchamber Groom, was puzzled. He wrote to a
friend four days after the event that 'no motive whatever has been
discovered', leaving him 'so amazed & confounded' that he could not
form any opinion. He also commented on a report that the tassel of
Ernest's bellrope had been dropped behind the head of his bed so that
he could not summon aid: 'The bellrope story nonsense.' A few weeks
later came an odd development: Ernest dismissed him. He remained
in high repute elsewhere, for in 1812, promoted colonel, he was given
a senior post in the queen's household. This would not be 'very
agreeable to the D of Cumberland', Princess Charlotte commented, 'as

I daresay you remember how ill the duke behaved to him, & then turned him out of his family'.[18]

Visits to Ernest's apartments were stopped after a few days, disappointing 8000 applicants. The cool Sarah Spencer wrote, 'Can you imagine that the finest, most delicate ladies in town went in parties to look at those nasty rooms as a morning lounge? ...His Royal Highness is almost entirely recovered, so, thank heaven, we shall have no court mourning to keep us in black gowns all the summer.'[19]

The Times said it was happy to report that Ernest 'has not kept his bed since the third day'. By 8 June he was 'free from pain'; on the 15th he walked in the Carlton House garden; on the 20th he drove out in a carriage, alighted outside Buckingham House and greeted his father. He had his arms in slings, looked pale, 'but not so much reduced as might have been expected'.[20]

The next day, the Lord Steward's office paid an unusual bill: *'John Young, for himself & the other Beadles employed in the execution of the Warrant for the Interment of the Body of Joseph Sellis, £6 16s 6d'* (say £200, for unpleasant and politically sensitive night work).[21]

Sellis lay with a stake through his heart. Yet his ghost would not lie down.

6

The ghost of Sellis rises

The stress inflicted on George III by the Duke of York's disgrace, the Flanders débâcle, the Burdett conflict and the painful decline of Princess Amelia deranged him once again. It became too evident, unluckily, on the day he was celebrating the fiftieth anniversary, 25 October 1810, of his accession to the throne. 'As he went round the circle as usual it was easy to perceive the dreadful excitement in his countenance,' says Cornelia Knight, a lady of the court. The king said to her, 'You are not uneasy, I am sure, about Amelia... You know that she is in no danger.'[1] Amelia died a week later. Ladies conferred about mourning dress. Lady Charlotte Lindsay wondered 'whether I should get a Black Velvet Pelisse, or whether it ought to be Black Silk covered with crape. I suppose that a Black Crape Gown for evenings & a Black Bombazine for mornings will be the proper things.'[2]

Spencer Perceval's shaky government now seemed doomed. The Whigs, linked for so long to the prince of Wales, thought their time had come. The prince had to pass a year, however, before being given full power as regent. As the poet Thomas Moore made him say —

> A strait-waistcoat on him [the king] and restrictions on me,
> A more *limited* monarchy could not well be.

In truth he had no right to royal power, having married a Roman Catholic, Maria Fitzherbert, in 1785. This had been well publicized and unconvincingly denied, but Tories and Whigs, wanting power, kept equally silent about it. Eventually he spurned the Whigs and kept the Tories in, with the high-Tory approval of his mistress, Lady Hertford, and of two men close to him, her son, Lord Yarmouth, and Ernest. The prince's Whiggish daughter Charlotte grieved to see Ernest 'such a *favorite*', she told her friend Miss Elphinstone. 'I *know so much* about him that I quite hate the sight of him.'[3]

Although George, as regent, was very much a person to cultivate, Ernest could not control his mischievous tongue for long. In December

1811 the regent was laid up at the Duke of York's Surrey mansion, Oatlands, having sprained a tendon when trying to dance a Highland fling. Ernest went about saying his brother's malady was 'higher than the foot'. As Princess Charlotte put it, he spread a villainous lie, '*no other* than that he *was mad*', and 'It *has reached* the P's ears.'[4]

The regent's head was in fact not in a happy state. His crony, Lord Yarmouth, said he was taking as much as 700 drops of laudanum a day, twenty times the usual dose. The regent's factotum, Thomas Tyrwhitt, reported he was 'frightened about his head and thought the numbness had a paralytic quality'.[5] But of course Ernest's talk outraged him. Ernest went out to Oatlands to swear he had said no such thing. Then sharing a carriage back to London with the regent's aide-de-camp, Benjamin Bloomfield, he inveighed against whoever it might be who had spread such a lie. Bloomfield mentioned this to Princess Charlotte. She pumped him (her word) for more. Bloomfield '*never had* passed so *unpleasant* a journey in all his life,' she reported to Miss Elphinstone:

> He [Ernest] was *vociferating oaths* against the *person* that *could* set afoot such a *lie* about the prince. Declared if he could discover the person he would *destroy him* with his own hands, used the most solemn oaths to declare *his innocence*, in short worked himself up into a sort of frenzy, that B. said he hardly knew what he would do next, as there were firearms in the carriage... B. said to me, 'Poor unfortunate man, who would ever wish to be him or to have anything to do with him?' [6]

This is by no means a rare instance of Ernest erupting. He himself repeatedly reveals how he rages when thwarted or challenged. His fury in Flanders in 1794 — 'My heart by God is ready to burst' — is noted in Chapter 2. In 1815 we shall have 'My blood boils in my veins'; in 1836, 'My heart boils with rage', and so forth. This can be kept in mind when one is considering Sellis's violent end.

After his trip to Oatlands, Ernest drafted a 'very serious & solemn declaration' of his innocence, which he asked Yarmouth to deliver to the regent to put him 'fully at ease'. Ernest also used Yarmouth as his go-between to deny, at great length, an accusation that he, colonel of the 15th, had poached an officer from the regent's still more elite 10th. The accusation, he said, was a 'quite *monstruous*' attempt 'to injure me with that dear Brother'.[7] When he next saw the regent at Carlton House, shouting echoed down the corridors, but a truce was reached.

Princess Charlotte, not yet sixteen, was matured in the rough school of court life. She wrote to Miss Elphinstone, '*Why can* the prince wish to *temporise* so with him? There *must* be some *hidden* cause that we *cannot* find out.' In other letters at this time she says her Uncle Ernest (Prince Whiskerandos) is 'a pest to all society' and 'at the bottom of all evil'. 'He has *no heart nor honour*, but a *deep*, *dark*, vindictive & *malicious* mind, brooding over mischief, & always active in pursuit of everything that is bad.' A few years later she writes: 'The P.R. [regent] is somehow or other deeply committed to & in the power of Ernest. What it is I have no idea, but I fancy it can be *nothing good or fit for the light* of day... Some nefarious transactions can alone account for the unaccountable power he has over him.'[8]

In August 1812 the Sellis case was revived. A dissident weekly, *The Independent Whig*, published an open letter 'To the **** ** **********' (4+2+10 asterisks). Its author says he is not 'one of that servile herd who can venerate Adultery, or even Murder, if dressed up in erminal robes or covered with a coronet'. He raises many doubts about the inquest and says, 'It is at best a foul business... Longer concealment is out of the question.' The *Whig* followed up with further questions:

– A night-light was burning but Ernest 'did not see anybody'.

– When Ernest, wakened, stood exposed and defenceless, 'then, and not till then' the attacker 'throws down his weapon and flies for refuge to his own apartment'.

– Would an assassin hiding in a closet have brought slippers with his name in them, a bottle of water and a lantern? 'The lantern too was needless, since Sellis knew that the duke burnt a night-light.'

The paper declares, '*Sellis was not his own executioner.*'

An article signed Janus speaks of a secret that might explain the mystery. 'This is not the first time in the history of the world that midnight *Italian Orgies* have been kept in the purlieus of a monarch's palace.' Janus quotes from Sellis's letter about Neale, produced at the inquest, the passage beginning 'No oath or promise is binding with him' (*page 57*). Janus says, 'How important must have been that secret, that *private* transaction, the publication of which had been forbidden under the sanction of an oath *privately* administered!! Of how extraordinary a kind must be that exposure which could draw after it such "large damages"!'

Janus calls Francis Place a 'redoubtable champion' and 'well acquainted with, if he does not indeed fill a conspicuous PLACE in' an anonymous pamphlet, *A Minute Detail of the Attempt to Assassinate His Royal Highness the Duke of Cumberland*. It begins by quoting the inquest evidence but follows with pages of inventive vilification. To cope with Sellis's lack of motive, it devises two. First, revenge. Seizing on Neale's assertion that Sellis schemed to murder Ernest 'to cause me to be suspected', it says, 'How immense this lust of blood and revenge!' Sellis is made an Italian melodrama villain, 'this monster, calculating, weighing, dividing in the scale of horrors so much crime to procure so much vengeance'. Next, robbery. The pamphlet picks up statements by three servants that while in America about twelve years before (when Sellis was in fact serving Ernest) they had known a man named Sellis — the same man, they thought — who had been suspected of theft and who said such things as, 'Damn the English king and all the royal family.' These allegations were, rightly, not offered at the inquest, yet the pamphlet presents them as fact. It alleges that this hater of royalty and 'established order', having murdered his master, intended to rob his treasure-chest and (somehow undetected, and abandoning his family) 'go and enjoy his plunder in another country'.

It was odd that during Sellis's fourteen years of service neither Ernest nor anyone else had had a hint of his being this bitter enemy of the royal family, let alone a homicidal villain. Place filed away *A Minute Detail* and endorsed its content. 'Most of the facts stated' were given at the inquest, he says. As for the rest, 'the inferences are generally so accurately drawn that I have not thought it necessary to make any comment'. As Janus suggests, he probably helped to write it.

The *Whig* gave some news of Neale. It spoke of 'the cruel desertion of the poor widow ... struggling in penury and want, her infants and herself thrown upon the parish bounty who once were cherished by royal munificence', while Neale, ' *though promptly discharged*, notwithstanding his *ready attendance* in his master's need, is with his wife now doubly pensioned and living in indolent retirement!'[9]

It is relevant here to detail a valet's duties, for the benefit of those who manage without one. A good guide from Ernest's time is *The Complete Servant*, 1825, by Samuel Adams (a coincidental namesake of the coroner), who during fifty years had served as footboy, groom, footman, valet, butler and house-steward.

It is a caring role, performed in his master's bedroom. He waits on him as he dresses and undresses. He keeps his clothes in good order.

First thing each day, 'he will see that the housemaid has lighted the fire ... will prepare the washing-stand, fill the ewer with clean soft water and the carafe with fresh spring water'. He sees that the basin, towels and brushes are clean, hot shaving-water is ready, the master's dressing-gown and slippers are airing before the fire and his clothes laid out across the backs of chairs. 'Having attended his master while dressing, combed his hair, &c, the valet will take the first opportunity after he is gone to set the room in order... The dressing-stand must be wiped clean and dry, the basin washed and wiped ... and everything put in order as if immediately to be used again...'

A paragraph on how to strop razors helps one to picture the olden cut-throat kind: 'Laying it flat on the strop, draw it diagonally, from the heel to the point, the whole length of the strop ... half a dozen or half a score strokes backwards and forwards, as often as it is used.'[10]

The *Whig* published a letter from a bookseller, John Bone, defending Place's handling of the inquest. This brought a reply signed Clincher that throws light on Place. It tells how William Pitt's government, when breaking the radical societies in the 1790s, used rewards as well as prosecutions and jailings. Clincher writes, 'Surely, says I to myself, says I — this cannot be my old political friend John Bone' who was 'a downright Jacobin and sans-culotte', was jailed for three years, but 'on his liberation took a dashing shop in Fleet-street'. He had 'profited by his acquaintance with a journeyman breeches-maker and Jacobin of the name of Francis P——, who during my friend's imprisonment [1798–1800] contrived to get from a two-pair-of-stairs room into a dashing tailor's shop at Charing Cross, to become very intimate with Mr Enos Smith, clerk and keeper of the records of the Privy Council; and thus having become the *Government Jacobin* was in a position to assist my young friend if he would become tractable.'[11]

Place *had* prospered remarkably. His own memoirs say so: 'At Christmas 1800 we had thirty-two tailors at work and three or four leather breeches-makers. No such rapid increase of business had ever been known.' He displayed his goods in 'the largest plate-glass windows in London' and had many customers 'in the public offices'.[12] Clincher attributes Place's rise to a man he denounces as a spy among the radicals: 'Mr James P---ll (clerk in the C[usto]m H[ous]e, *Jacobin*, *spy* and *reporter for the government* and several times their *agent at Hamburg*) introduced the Government Jacobin to his situation.'

Hamburg was where British and Irish radicals and plotters took refuge and were pursued. This James Powell had been a spy among London radicals from 1795. Official records prove this. In 1798, a year of many arrests, he was at a meeting of radical United Englishmen that was raided. He alone 'escaped'. Place's version of the sequel is that Powell came to him in a 'very pitiful' state and Place fitted him out in military-style clothes and collected money to send him to Hamburg. In fact the chief organizer of Powell's flight was the Home Office spymaster, William Wickham. As an ostensible radical on the run, Powell was ideal to plant among refugee subversives. Wickham gave him a good sum, £55, for his journey, but before sailing he demanded £30 more. He promised to use 'every exertion in my power for the service of government'. When sending his reports via a fellow-spy in London, he would write them in 'the common cant of democrisy, viz beginning Fellow citizen and concluding with health and fraternity, and introduce as much of the jargon in the body of the letter as possible'. Thus he would 'give you every necessary information without any suspicion should the letter be opened'.[13]

Place's rise from humble tailor to entrepreneur began in that year.

In his hundreds of self-justifying pages in his memoirs about the Sellis case and his conflicts with radicals, he complains that they accused him of being 'in the pay of the government' and 'a spy — a perjurer — a suborner of perjury — a concealer of a murderer'.[14]

Powell was still doing his devious work in 1810. When Burdett was to be freed after ten weeks in the Tower, Powell headed a committee, with Place and Bone, to organize a procession to escort him to 78 Piccadilly. It was to be a glorious display: trumpeters, a band, horsemen and marching radicals escorting him in a triumphal carriage, streamers flying, bands and carriages following. Advertisements brought Burdettites from all over the British Isles. On the day, the route was lined with 'the largest assembly of people ever known in England', sporting blue cockades and 'Burdett forever!' banners. Twenty thousand soldiers were on duty, but the mood was festive.

Then anticlimax, to the government's delight. At the Tower the crowd was told, 'He is gone by water!' The day before, Powell had visited Burdett in the Tower and persuaded him the parade was likely to end in riot and bloodshed, so he renounced his day of glory and went up-river by boat and then to his country home at Wimbledon. 'Thousands indignantly tore the cockades from their hats and threw them with contempt into the dirt,' said a radical paper, *Alfred*. The day became a bitter farce and the radicals were thrown into disarray. In the *Whig*, two years on, Clincher names Powell, Place and Bone as 'the active *junto*' who 'called out the people' — but then stayed at home.

Could the *Whig* impute a high crime to an illustrious prince and go unpunished? The law officers constantly scrutinized newspapers. The *Whig* had already been in court several times. Its editor, Henry White, was serving three years for criticizing a decision of the implacable Lord Chief Justice Ellenborough. Two better-known prisoners were Leigh and John Hunt of *The Examiner*, both fined £500 (say £15,000 now) and jailed for two years by Ellenborough. Their crime was that when the *Morning Post* printed ripely unctuous praise of the prince regent, they mocked it by saying, 'This Glory of the People was the subject of millions of shrugs and reproaches... This Adonis in loveliness, a corpulent gentleman of fifty ... a libertine over head and ears in debt and disgrace, a despiser of domestic ties, a man who had just closed half a century without one single claim on the gratitude of his country.' And Ellenborough had recently jailed William Cobbett for two years in Newgate, fined him £1000 and required him to put up sureties of £5000 for his future 'good behaviour', all for denouncing in his *Political Register* the unjust flogging of some rural militiamen.

The law officers chose their cases carefully, however. Their thinking survives in Home Office files: a paragraph is too 'artfully' worded; another is 'certainly libellous, but we cannot say a jury would convict'; prosecuting a radical broadside would 'call it into further notice'.[15]

Was it prudent to call the Sellis mystery into further notice? The *Whig* was not alone in asking questions. The law officers studied an article in the *Political Review*, 'The Shade of Sellis to his Wife'. Sellis's ghost says his object is 'to give the deadly pang to prosperous guilt and pave the road to awful retribution — to visit the widowed heart with consolation, the *Murderer's with despair*... *I had no cause for murder*... I had done no injury, committed no offence, feared no discovery, *had no dark mischief to conceal or nourish!*' His last words are: '*I have proof that could appal the world!*' The law officers let this lie.[16]

They also refrained from acting against Sir Francis Burdett for an address 'To the Electors of Westminster' deploring the state of the nation: 'Nine hundred millions of debts ... an army of German and foreign mercenaries; an army of spies and informers; ... a phantom of a king; a degraded aristocracy; an oppressed people; ... irresponsible ministers; a corrupt and intimidated press; pensioned justices; packed juries; ... a host of failures of foreign expeditions, and the present crushing burden of taxation.' As for parliament, it was a '*low farce*'.[17]

After months of hesitation, the law officers did prosecute the *Whig*. Its acting editor, Henry White's son, was charged in March 1813 with 'most unlawfully and maliciously intending and desiring to traduce defame vilify and injure' Ernest, 'and to bring his said Royal Highness into great and public scandal disgrace hatred and contempt among all the liege subjects of our said Lord the King' by publishing a 'scandalous and malicious libel'. The next *Whig* made new points for Sellis, and said, 'We do not KNOW the murderer... All we have meant to say we still adhere to, THAT SELLIS WAS NOT, COULD NOT HAVE BEEN, HIS OWN MURDERER.'[18]

A few days later, the treasury solicitor received an unsigned letter naming men who 'propagated the story' and 'a fellow who has long lived by extorting money and other infamous means' who 'assisted with a view to making something of it'. The story 'thus became, as the *Whig* observed, common conversation in pothouses and night cellars — and dupes — fools — and rogues were all willing to believe there was something behind the curtain — each persuaded his comrade that the duke was guilty — that proof was at hand — and at length that a bill of indictment would be presented to the Grand Jury against HRH.' Some of the *Whig's* articles, the letter says, were written by two swindlers in Newgate. The writer of this letter is Francis Place.[19]

Some dissident journalists did have a shady side, but Place overdoes the denigration. Survival was not easy for outspoken editors. If the attorney-general was unsure whether a charge of seditious libel would succeed, he might issue an ex-officio writ that held the editor *in terrorem* and imposed heavy costs, though not brought to court. Pliant editors were rewarded, meanwhile, with subsidies, news handouts and other advantages. The press was 'thrown into the hands either of adventurers or of the servile sycophants of the party in power', as the historian Arthur Aspinall says in his *Politics and the Press*.

Men of the *Whig* were risk-takers but not riffraff. One, William Augustus Miles, was a foreign agent in the 1790s, then had £500 a year to write for William Pitt's papers and to attack the spendthrift prince of Wales. Being flexible, he was bought over to write in praise of the prince, who eventually put him on a £300-a-year pension. Nor were the *Whig*'s readers riffraff. One was the heir-apparent, Princess Charlotte. She wrote to Miss Elphinstone in 1811, 'Do you take in the Independent Whig? ...There is a sort of letter to the Prince [her father] in it which is *quite frightful* & I *fear shows* too much the *opinion* of people *at large.*' This was an attack on the regent for keeping the Tories in power. 'From you we were led to expect deliverance,' it said. 'Why did you tolerate the votaries of corruption? We did not expect much morality from you, but we looked for public spirit.'[20]

In King's Bench Court in May 1813, young Henry White was found guilty, as the judge put it, of 'atrocious and malicious libels against an august personage ... in charging him with no less a crime than having murdered his own servant'. The libel 'arose from a foul and base thirst of lucre'. White was 'ready to prostitute himself to the vilest purposes'. He was fined £200 and jailed in Newgate for fifteen months.

The pensioning of Cornelius Neale was not a malicious *Whig* libel. Francis Place preserved a newspaper cutting saying Neale had 'obtained permission publicly to assert that he never was convicted of any improper conduct during the whole 14 years that he had the honour to live with the Duke of Cumberland'. Sellis had brought various charges, but 'nothing wrong could be substantiated'. Neale 'was retained about the person of His Royal Highness till very lately; and on his leaving his service, His Royal Highness has been graciously pleased to order his wages to be continued to him, as a mark of his protection and a consideration for his long services'.[21]

Twenty-two years after Sellis's death, Neale would be brought forth to affirm Ernest's innocence yet again.

While the *Whig* case was running, Ernest figured in a political scandal. He was accused in the Commons of vote-rigging and bribery in elections at Weymouth, a place with four MPs and conveniently few voters. A standing parliamentary rule said if a peer interfered in an election it was a breach of privilege. Peers often flouted the rule; but as a Whig MP said, Ernest's crime was all the worse as he was 'a peer of the blood royal'. Ministers managed to get a 105–57 majority against condemning Ernest, but such a large opposition vote was rare in the unreformed Commons. It showed that feeling against him was strong.

Ernest decided to escape calumny by seeking fame. Napoleon looked beatable at last after his disastrous Russian enterprise. Ernest applied for a British command, but was not wanted. 'Being alas convinced that there did not exist a chance of my being so employed', he opted to offer himself on the continent. In April 1813 he sold sixteen horses and his store of wines to raise cash, and just before the sentencing of White he sailed away.[22]

Calumny pursued him. In a caricature, 'The Borough-Mongering Trio', he says as he steps into a boat, 'Will nothing but a trip to Germany save my royal limbs from prison?' A *razor* dangles from his ankle. Another electoral offender, the Duke of Leeds, a court favourite, stands in a tub enjoying a thorough whitewashing outside the House of Lords, which is labelled *Whitewashing done here and all sorts of dirty work*. Off to one side is the third of the trio, a woebegone man behind bars: a lowly currier jailed for having played a small role in another piece of noble electoral dirty work. He says, 'I do'ant like for this Mr Duke of Cumberland and this Mr Duke of Leeds to get away while poor Tom Croggan is in Newgate. It's a rotten shame.'[23]

Ernest was pursued too in a lampoon, *Midnight Dreams*, in which all the princes have apposite nightmares. Ernest's is among the dead:

> The worms clung round my legs, poor sinner,
> And seem'd to claim me for their dinner...
> I stoop'd and trac'd a letter'd plate,
> Recorder of some victim's fate...
> But ah, what horror chill'd my frame,
> For ------ was that victim's name! ...
> Zounds! It can't be, at length I said.
> In a cross-road the corpse was laid...
>
> *[A spectre rises]*
>
> His eyeballs wildly glar'd around;
> His throat disclos'd a gaping wound...
> And tenfold horror chill'd my blood...
>
> *[Ernest wakes, terrified]*
>
> I'll quit this saucy kingdom. Yes,
> Some sweeter spot on earth I'll bless,
> Where conscience all his taunts shall cease
> And vulgar tongues respect my peace.
>
> There soon some yielding fair I'll find
> To drive this goblin from my mind.[24]

He did find a yielding fair one, but she became the focus of a family conflict in which Ernest was painfully outplayed.

7

'My blood boils in my veins'

In pursuit of glory, Ernest went first to Sweden's newly-created crown prince, Napoleon's renegade marshal Jean Bernadotte, hoping he might employ Britain's rejected royal general. Britain had promised Sweden a million-pound subsidy to spur it to join the Russians and Prussians (even more richly subsidized) in rolling Napoleon back, but Bernadotte seemed more interested in seizing Norway. In a caricature about Ernest's visit, Bernadotte says he is 'going to drub Bonaparte directly the weather permits ... but pray send the money'. Ernest promises 'oceans of money'. The caricature's real bite is in Ernest's next words: 'Do but drive that capering fellow Bonaparte from Hanover & I shall be governor & out of the din of that Rascal the *Whig* who is always bothering me about Sellis & the Devil knows what. I'd sooner hear the roaring of a thousand cannon than be baited so.'[1]

In absentia he was further baited about Sellis in ominous verses:

> Of this ferocious Cock is told
> A tale that might appal the bold;
> By death and mystery conceal'd
> But fated yet to be reveal'd.

> The bats that flit at dead of night
> Were witness to the dreadful sight.
> They saw the frantic victim bleed
> And shudder'd at the horrid deed.[2]

Not only the satirists were talking of horrid deeds. A crime one hardly dared name was being alleged, according to the private journal of Keppel Craven, an ex-lover of the Princess of Wales (not a rare honour, certainly) and brother of the Earl of Craven, a former aide-de-camp to George III. He writes that when Ernest was leaving London 'he was advised never more to return' because reports were gaining ground that 'go as far as to make him the murderer of Sellis in consequence of a disagreement between them occasioned by this last's jealousy of another servant [Neale], thereby involving the duke in an additional charge of culpability of another, but to English eyes equally atrocious, nature'. The reports reached the continent 'as soon as he did', Craven writes, and he was 'very coolly received'.[3] The *Whig* had ventured to hint at sodomy. People of rank were going further. The word would eventually be spoken in open court.

Ernest was indeed coolly received. He proceeded to Neu-Strelitz, capital of Mecklenburg-Strelitz, Queen Charlotte's tiny native land (48 square miles), ruled by her brother, His Serene Highness the Grand Duke. Ernest wrote to Tsar Alexander of Russia and King Frederick William III of Prussia offering himself for a suitably high role. 'If they refuse I shall then join the Prince Royal of Sweden [Bernadotte],' he wrote to the prince regent. He must prove himself 'worthy of being a descendant of the Gwelfs, for to return without seeing a shot fired I should consider an eternal disgrace'.

Britain's envoy at allied headquarters at Dresden, Sir Charles Stewart, was working to unite the Russians, Prussians and Swedes. He wrote to the foreign secretary, Lord Castlereagh, his half-brother, that the tsar and others were hostile to Ernest. He was 'best kept out of this undertaking'. Castlereagh replied, 'He cannot have a command.' He suggested asking the Russians or Prussians to 'let him witness as a volunteer what is going on'. Ernest's final move was to urge that a corps be created for him to command. Castlereagh parried that by saying there was not enough money to create one 'suitable to Your Royal Highness's exalted military rank and station'.[4]

A consolation at Neu-Strelitz was his discovery of his 35-year-old first cousin Frederica, a daughter of the grand duke. His first sight of her in her palace, when a serenade was playing and Maytime scents were wafting in from the garden, 'was the most beautiful and happiest moment of my life', he told her. She was an almost available princess: her husband, Prince Friedrich of Solms, was suing for divorce.

She and Ernest quickly became devoted, even before he went off to Russian headquarters in south Germany as an unheroic 'volunteer'. He did see some shots fired in skirmishes in Bohemia ('amusing himself at the outposts', as one report said), and sent spirited letters to Frederica. She wrote to her treasured lady-in-waiting, Caroline Berg, 'The duke's letters are truly divine and you will not believe how they attach me to him... Oh God, oh God!!! How I was blinded, and how can I thank God that He has sent me an angel to save me... God protect him! I cannot describe my anxiety.' She hopes to be as happy in the autumn of her days 'as I have been unhappy in the spring and summer'. She is alluding to past affairs, of which more will be heard.[5]

Ernest returned to Frederica in early October, and thus missed the pleasure of observing the battle of Leipzig on 18–19 October 1813, a close-run victory over Napoleon in which about 60,000 men died. Now Hanover would soon be liberated after ten years under alternating Prussian and French rule. Ernest pressed to be made its governor. 'Then I shall forget all the unhappy & uncomfortable time I have passed,' he wrote to the regent. He begged him not to say a word about this unhappiness, as that would be 'nuts to MANY in England' ('nuts' was slang for delightful). He has enemies in London, some 'nearly connected with myself'. 'Many things have within these last five months come to my knowledge which have given me more pain than I can find words to express.[6] One can guess that Sellis is the topic.

Bernadotte was chosen to preside over Hanover's celebration of freedom. Ernest was told not to go. Another rebuff! He set off at high speed and arrived two days ahead of Bernadotte. A British diplomat dealing with these delicate matters reported that the Hanoverians 'lavished on the duke the huzzas, the illuminations and good dinners' prepared for Bernadotte, so when *he* arrived 'the candles were burnt down to their sockets, the applauding voices of the people were hoarse and the luxuries which were to have recompensed the toils of the fire-breathing Bernadotte had greased the innocent mustachios of his royal highness of Cumberland'. Bernadotte was furious.[7]

Ernest settled in at Hanover, even organized a regiment of Cumberland Hussars. His conquest was shortlived. A new blow: London appointed as governor his youngest brother, Adolphus Duke of Cambridge. The regent kindly sent Benjamin Bloomfield, his chief equerry, to inform Ernest in good time before Adolphus arrived. Ernest heard the news 'with a burst of tears & evident distress & mortification', Bloomfield reported. Adolphus was being elevated to field marshal, so Ernest was consolingly granted the same rank. Eleven days later, the burghers of Hanover had to welcome Adolphus with huzzas, illuminations, banners, bouquets... Yet Ernest still had hopes. 'Should the case be that Adolphus does not like staying, then think of me,' he told the regent. 'For many reasons I prefer living on the Continent.' Again we learn how troubled he is: 'Whenever I return to England, I hope my mind may be more at ease.' He is sending presents for the regent, shoes and sashes and 'a Circassian mare, a most beautiful creature'. He concludes, 'Excuse my hurry but I am grown very nervous from much anxiety of mind.' He retreated to Neu-Strelitz and Berlin. [8]

The spring of Frederica's life had seemed to begin most happily. In 1793 she and her sister Louisa, nieces of Queen Charlotte, were acclaimed as beautiful brides. Louisa married the future Frederick William III, and Frederica, not yet sixteen, his younger brother Louis. 'I could only compare them to two celestial beings,' wrote the courtly poet Goethe, 'whose impression on my mind can never be effaced.' But Frederica's prince died within three years. In 1798 she accepted an offer from Prince Adolphus, but George III ruled that he must wait until peace was declared. The young widow was not patient. She became pregnant by Prince Solms, as he was known. Queen Charlotte wrote with uncharacteristic compassion to her brother, Frederica's father, 'If we consider her youth, her beauty, the court where she was living, the sort of familiarity that they say has recently been introduced at Berlin ... the ridicule they bestow on everything serious ... if we consider all that, she becomes perhaps less guilty & more to be pitied, for at her age the passions are stronger.'[9] Solms married Frederica — belatedly. His chief pleasures were wine and hunting. She found men to console her.

As Ernest waited in the winter of 1813–14 for the Solms divorce to be decided, he knew there was a further barrier to overcome. Although his mother did not exclude notorious adulteresses from court (for example, the regent's former mistress, Lady Jersey), she forbade divorcées. This added to Ernest's anxiety. He alarmed his eldest sister Charlotte, queen of Württemberg in southwest Germany, by proposing to visit her. He was 'quarrelsome & dissatisfied', she wrote to the regent. Ernest had clashed with the tsar of Russia, whose brother and sister were about to visit her, so he 'would keep me in hot water ... as he allows himself to say everything that comes into his head'. And the wife of her stepson Prince Paul gave 'frightful accounts' of Ernest's having been 'sadly familiar with her'.

The regent asked the queen at Windsor for advice. As a result we have a mother's analysis of Ernest. She said if the regent tried to stop Ernest from going to Württemberg, 'with his disposition he would be more eager to go'. However, if he *did* go, and behaved badly and was rebuked for it, he would soon leave, 'for he hates to be found fault with'. He did not go after all; but he was still a worry for Charlotte of Württemberg. She feared he would 'obstinately persist' in marrying Frederica, 'which must be a source of pain to the whole family'.[10]

He seemed unlikely to desist. He was 'desperately in love', the regent's daughter, Princess Charlotte, wrote to her confidante Mercer Elphinstone. 'This handsome Princess of Solms ... is both clever & lovely & in *every way* calculated to *attract* & to enslave the D. of Cumberland.'[11] And then in April 1814 there was helpful news for Ernest. Prince Solms died — so fortuitously that wicked gossips hinted the death was not natural. Ernest wrote to the regent that the divorce was 'thank God *prevented* by the death of the prince... Thank God she is *not divorced* but a WIDOW.'[12]

The engagement was announced. Queen Charlotte sent good wishes, though with hints of concern. Nowadays in Britain, she said, 'every action of the great is liable to be criticized'. In accordance with what the queen called 'my *antique way of thinking*', Frederica agreed to pass a full year in widowhood.[13] To her brother, the queen wrote that life at Windsor was 'very limited' (George III being in deep seclusion) but she and her daughters would do their best to entertain Frederica. She asked her brother to pass on some further advice:

> It is not the fashion here to receive morning visits from gentlemen, to which she will be exposed by the circumstance of the Duke being colonel of a regiment, unless he himself introduces them to her. She should also be very circumspect in the choice of ladies with whom she associates, which will be all the more necessary as the Duke has acquaintances among our sex who, although not of bad conduct, might perhaps become injurious to her in point of policy.[14]

Here are hints about Frederica's reputation. As for Ernest's 'acquaintances', a lampoon issued just after his marriage gives a scurrilous picture. It makes him say:

> We are no more the giddy rake
> Anxious of lewdness to partake,
> Seeking t'associate out of doors
> With ready pimps and worn-out -------.
> The brothel's charms no more invite
> To wanton through the flying night...
> We have our fill of joy at home.[15]

Ernest's wedding was planned for April 1815, the moment Frederica's year of widowhood was over, but Napoleon the Corsican ex-usurper leapt out of his Elba exile in March and headed for Paris. Ernest wrote to the regent, 'I lose no time in *offering my services* and asking *your permission* to go & *join* the *army* in Flanders' (a field marshal to serve under Field Marshal Wellington). He begged for a speedy answer, for he wished to marry Frederica before going off to the war. Two weeks later he was still pleading: 'Unless I serve in this campaign I can never show *my face again.*' If there was no other way, he would command the Hanoverian hussars.[16] Even that was denied (fortunately for him, as they disgraced themselves and were sent to the rear by Wellington).

Rejected for Waterloo action: again Ernest has to digest a rebuff.

Worse was in store. Someone had sent the queen new 'particulars' about Frederica that made her decide, late in 1814, not to receive her at court after all. 'The whole affair has *shaken & shattered* the Queen most terribly,' Princess Charlotte found.[17] For Ernest and Frederica the queen's decision would be a shaming blow, yet instead of telling them herself she asked the regent to do so, and he cravenly put it off.

Just before Ernest's forty-fourth birthday he was married at Neu-Strelitz on 29 May 1815 to Frederica, a 37-year-old mother of several grown children. The ceremony was in the town's quaint old church. The diplomat Sir George Jackson, an 'attesting witness', records that the Mecklenburg-Strelitzes 'and a numerous train of German princes and princesses, relations of the bride, and a vast number of visitors ... all *en grande tenue*, made a very brilliant show' despite 'the slender resources of this little court' (which George III had subsidized for years). Frederica 'looked very handsome'; Ernest 'remarkably well'.[18]

He still had to apply to parliament to increase his allowance by £6000 (£200,000 now), the boon customarily granted a prince on marriage. On landing at Dover, 17 June, he was handed a letter from his mother: his first news that she would not receive his bride, 'painful as it is to my feelings as a mother and an aunt'. She mentioned the long-ago Adolphus affair, but a sharper point was, 'You are aware of the grounds upon which I was induced to decline receiving the Princess of Wales.' This allusion to the princess's wantonness amounted to an accusation of Frederica.[19]

Next day the regent confronted his mother and asked her to take back the letter, her '*démarche décisive*'. She flatly refused. On this day of victory at Waterloo the regent suffered inglorious defeat. He wrote to Frederica that he regretted he had not torn up the letter 'before her eyes' ... but he had forgotten to bring it.

When Ernest's £6000 request came before the Commons, the debate shared newspaper space with long lists of the Waterloo dead and wounded. Grants on a prince's marriage were usually nodded through, but not this one. An MP asked whether Ernest 'had rendered any services to his country that could entitle him to the grant'. Others spoke of 'rumours afloat' about Frederica. A leading Whig asked Castlereagh (manager of the Commons as well as foreign secretary) whether it was true that the queen would not receive her. Castlereagh refused to answer 'questions calculated to vilify the royal family'. In the penultimate vote, the majority for Ernest dwindled to eight.

Two days before the final vote, *The Times* said it must raise 'invidious topics'. Ernest's income was already 'near £20,000 a year, a sum much greater than is possessed by many sovereign princes [such as Frederica's father] in that part of Europe where it is understood he means to fix his future residence'. Wounding words for Frederica followed: if she 'might have afforded an example of dignified morality to the British ladies' there would probably have been no objection.

On the morning of 4 July 1815 the newspapers reported, next to further lists from Waterloo, the refusal of the £6000 by 126 votes to 125. A Whig MP wrote to Thomas Creevey, who was in Brussels, 'What an age we live in! We fare victorious here, as you do at Waterloo. Think of our triumph.'[20] The queen, too, was not displeased.

Ernest's burden of rebuffs was becoming unbearable.

The vote inspired a daring caricature. A speciality of the monthly *Scourge* magazine was its etched coloured caricature folded in as a frontispiece. The 22-year-old George Cruikshank, a rising successor to James Gillray, created 'A Financial Survey of Cumberland' (*plate* 2). A cannonball blasts Ernest away from the door of the Commons. The cannon is fired by an MP who says, 'Do you think we are not up to your hoaxing, cadging tricks? You vagrant, do you think we'll believe all you say or swear? Do you think that your services or your merits will do you any good here? ...You are cursedly mistaken, so set off and don't show your ugly face here again.'

Ernest, in hussar uniform, cries, 'Pity the sorrows of a poor young man.' He wears cuckold's horns, already; and in the background grotesque smirking soldiers line up for a coquettish Frederica, who says, 'Oh, who could resist such lovers as these?' One is reminded of the queen's warning about officers' visits. Beside her a little boy sings:

My daddy is a grenadier
& he so *pleas'd* my Mammy O
With his *long sword* and *broad sword*
And his *bayonet* so handy O.

In the foreground there is something far more wounding to Ernest. An anguished ghostly figure with a slash across his throat stands at a crossroad, holds up a dripping razor and says, echoing Macbeth, *Is this a razor which I see before me? Thou canst not say I did it*.[21]

The Scourge was published at the same address, 5 Newgate-street, as the *Political Review*, which was nearly prosecuted in 1812 for 'The Shade of Sellis to his Wife'. Was it prudent to have the ghost openly accuse Ernest? The *Scourge's* publisher, William Naunton Jones, was well aware of the fifteen months Henry White had served in Newgate: the jail and the *Whig* office were both a short walk from *The Scourge*.

Here is the place for a word about the British caricature trade, then unmatched for its fecundity and freedom. Political caricatures, chiefly published as independent prints but also inserted into monthlies, had managed for years to escape political prosecution. Tories and Whigs had often hired caricaturists, among them James Gillray and Thomas Rowlandson, to attack their enemies. A man wounded by a caricature was wise to seem ungalled, and besides, to become a public target could be gratifying to his ego.

The prince regent, though, was so sensitive to ridicule that he pressed for prosecutions. As a result we can find in his law officers' files a clear reason for the immunity of caricatures. Their scurrilous meanings would have to be spelt out in court and would be quoted far and wide. The truthtelling in their exposure of a grotesque corrupt world became their safeguard. A good example is a Cruikshank caricature, 'Princely Predilections', which was laid before the attorney-general and solicitor-general as soon as it appeared in *The Scourge* in April 1812. Its central figure is the regent, staggering and dishevelled, with a bottle of curaçao (a favourite drink) at his lips. Beside him stands a junoesque coroneted woman saying, 'You will always meet with a warm friend in *Hertford*,' identifying her as his mistress Lady Hertford. She holds the regent's Leading Strings, having helped to woo him from his 'predilection' for the Whigs. Her husband wears cuckold's horns. At her feet stands a leering cupid, clutching a phallic arrow and tickling her crotch with the tip of his wing (*plate 10*).

The law officers opined, 'This is a most indecent and impudent print but it would require so much of difficult explanation in stating it as a libel upon the regent that it does not appear to us advisable to make it the subject of a criminal prosecution.' Not 'advisable' to spell out that two of the regent's predilections are impudently alleged to be drink and an illicit lust for the 52-year-old wife of his complaisant Lord Chamberlain. In the same month the law officers looked at another caricature in *Town Talk*, 'National Pursuits', showing Lord Castlereagh and others enriching themselves, John Bull bearing a huge tax burden and the regent galloping towards 'Hertford Abbey', on which is the label 'Messalina'. Again the law officers found that 'it does not appear to us advisable... (etc)'. The following year four more caricatures were referred to the law officers, perhaps at the regent's insistence — with this result: 'We are fully sensible of the scandal of these and other similar publications, but they would require explanations of so difficult and delicate a nature ... that we do not think it advisable...(etc)'[22]

Ernest, though, might well be more aggressive over Sellis's libellous ghost. Jones was smitten by caution after a run of this caricature was printed and handcoloured for *The Scourge* and for people buying it as a separate print. He got his colourists to obliterate poor Sellis and his speech-bubble with heavy dark paint. If puzzled purchasers sponged some of this off, held the print up to the light and discovered Sellis, that added to the effect and still allowed Jones to argue, if prosecuted, that he had done all he could to correct the error of the heedless young Cruikshank. He was not prosecuted.

Ernest's defeat in the Commons inspired a lampoon, *Salms for a R[oya]l Duke!*, in which he speaks:

> O! Blot on my illustrious name!
> Confusion! disappointment! shame!
> ...Say why, of all the r---l brood,   [*royal*
> Your votes would *me alone* exclude
> From revelling in luscious pickings
> So dear to hopeful pr----ly chickens?   [*princely*

His elder brothers, Frederick and especially the prince regent, were voted large sums:

> Why thus with wealth, pray, sate and gorge
> The appetite of r---l G----e
> And leave poor me *to starve*, I swear,
> On twenty thousand pounds a year?

He concedes that he has been accused of election corruption and 'military tyranny'; but how is he worse than his brothers?

> Is there some *secret dark offence*
> That makes you deaf to my pretence —
> *Some deed* involved in *shades of night*
> That has not yet been brought to light?[23]

Thoughts about a *secret dark offence* certainly were in people's minds — and even in the prince regent's. The Royal Academy artist Joseph Farington notes in his diary that the regent, sitting to Thomas Lawrence at the time of the Commons debate, 'alluded to the unpopularity of the Duke of Cumberland and to the report of Sellis having been murdered by him which had been current with many, & remarked on the improbability of there being any just foundation for such a report'. In the context, 'improbability' is rather a weak word.[24]

Ernest returned to Germany to fetch Frederica without having dared to confront the queen. 'My Indignation was so rouzed by this unexpected Letter,' he told the royal doctor, Sir Henry Halford, 'that I did not trust myself that my Temper, being rather warm, might not have got the better of my Judgement.' He told the regent, 'I have now done all in my power to *bring her round* by *fair* means.' If she still refused, 'by the Lord, HER letters shall be made publick, and I think she never can be supported after that... My blood boils in my veins... If you find she is immoveable then tell her to *what* she will drive me.'[25] 'HER letters' are the early ones promising that Frederica would be welcome. Ernest had kept his aide-de-camp, Captain Charles Jones, busy making copies of all the correspondence.

Frederica wrote to the regent that she was 'dishonoured and covered with shame'. The king of Prussia, her brother-in-law, pressed the queen to give way. Frederica's brother, Duke Charles, wrote to the queen that he was suffering cruelly: '*Je dis rendez nous la vie, car l'honneur est la vie et la honte est la mort*' (...honour is life and shame is death). Frederica has been 'purified by sixteen years of unhappiness' (as Prince Solms's wife), and by *une conduite irreprochable* throughout those years, and is now being 'purified' by her marriage to Ernest.[26]

Ernest brought Frederica to London in August. Their first object was an English wedding to clinch the one at Neu-Strelitz. The regent summoned the Archbishop of Canterbury and Bishop of London, brought cabinet ministers from their country retreats, and set up a crimson-draped altar in Carlton House. For her wedding to a third husband, Frederica wore a gold-embroidered white satin robe with a five-yard train, and a bejewelled tiara and ducal coronet. The only royals to honour her with their presence were the regent and the Dukes of York, Clarence and Kent. The queen forbade Princesses Augusta, Elizabeth, Mary and Sophia to appear.

The royal warfare became grotesque. Duke Charles wrote to the queen, '*Votre Majesté ne dit pas quelles reproches elle fait ... et quelles sont les circonstances parvenus à sa connaissance*' (Your Majesty does not state *what reproaches* she makes and *what circumstances* have come to her knowledge). 'As mother, mother-in-law, sister and aunt' she must desire justice for Frederica. The accusations must be black calumnies, *des 'on-dit' sans fondement* (baseless tittle-tattle).[27] His elder brother George, heir to Mecklenburg-Strelitz, dared to come and confront her. Here is a description of the old queen by the Comtesse de Boigne, daughter of the French ambassador:

> She had never been tall, and in recent years she had become shrunken and completely misshapen. Her head was on an extremely short neck; her face was scowling, yellow and wrinkled; her hair powdered like hoarfrost... Despite her strange appearance, however, she did not lack a certain dignity... Towards divorced women she was inexorable...[28]

She told Duke George he need not come to Windsor again to attack her with '*l'insulte et la ménace*'. He wrote imploring pardon. He had been in a feverish state for three days, almost without sleep, '*tellement affligé par le spectacle de souffrance que me présente ma soeur, que je puis vraiment être considéré comme un homme déseseré et malade de corps et d'esprit*' (so afflicted by the picture of suffering that my sister presents that I am in truth a man in despair, ill in body and mind).[29]

The struggle was a plague for the government at a time when it had to cope with resurgent reformers, Corn Law rioters, an uncontrollably spendthrift regent, a vast national debt and the reshaping of Europe. The prime minister, Lord Liverpool, said Ernest was 'only increasing his own embarrassment as well as that of every branch of the royal family'. He asked two of Ernest's friends, Earl Bathurst and Lord Chancellor Eldon, to try to persuade the troublesome couple to depart. They failed. Ernest wrote to Bathurst that he was grieved 'that she acts so little up to the Doctrine of that religion she has been professing so many Years in which FORGIVENESS is one of the tenets... She is so totally altered from what I have known her.'

He carried out his threat to publish 'HER letters'. Royal leaking is nothing new. He sent extracts to the newspapers, to show her as deviously inconsistent. In November she published a riposte, drawn up by her secretary, Sir Herbert Taylor. Her chief point was that although she had undertaken to welcome Frederica, 'particulars' she later received from Germany made her 'hesitate as to the propriety' of the marriage. The particulars were presumably of adulteries.[30]

Ernest made a late attempt at reconciliation, proposing a meeting for a 'fair and honest pouring out of our hearts'. He might come, the queen replied, but he must avoid the 'painful' subject. Her refusal to see Frederica was 'insuperable'. This made the blood boil in his veins. Just before Christmas he dared to write that 'the *secret* informers of yours have *deceived* you'. She had refused to name Frederica's 'insidious accusers', so he was not able to challenge them. 'Must it not strike you that the sole and entire object of these secret informers was to sow the seeds of discord between the duchess and me?'[31]

A reply came. Ernest saw it was addressed in Sir Herbert's hand, not the queen's, so h e sent it back unopened. 'I am determined not to enter into a paper war with a *secretary*,' he wrote to the regent. Although he knew Sir Herbert had been composing the queen's letters, hitherto she had at least written them out — 'decency was kept up'. He was 'determined to be treated like a gentleman'.[32]

She did send the reply in her own hand. It was delivered to Ernest when he was at dinner with Frederica in St James's Palace on Christmas eve. The queen's messenger was Benjamin Stephenson — the man whom Ernest had dismissed after the Sellis affair, and who was now a colonel on the queen's staff. The queen wrote that her decision was unalterable, so 'this correspondence so distressing to us both' must cease.

This was the climax to two years of chagrin and defeat for Ernest —
　　Spurned by all for service against Napoleon;
　　Ousted as governor of Hanover;
　　Refused any role at Waterloo;
　　Denied his marriage allowance by the Commons;
　　Shamed and enraged by his mother's rejection of his bride.
Why should he be afflicted with such a weight of ill fortune? The queen's final letter threw him into a frenzy of bitterness and of guilt. He made a tormented confession. It will have its place later.

8

Sophia opens her heart

'I require time to restore my spirits,' Sophia wrote to Lady Harcourt in December 1800. A pregnancy and secret childbirth were indeed not quickly overcome by a woman 'easily overset' and subject to low spirits. She suffered years of recurring illness. Her inner conflicts — her self-doubt and passionate feelings, her sense of alienation and longing for intimacy — are shown movingly in two surviving letters.

In December 1805 she wrote to Lady Bathurst, whose husband, Earl Bathurst, was a cabinet minister and a friend of Ernest, to thank her for a kindness the Bathursts had shown 'to my DEAREST & best friend' (unnamed). This has 'endeared me more than I can tell you', she says. '*No one* (tho brought up at Court) is more sensible of friendship & affection than myself, & you are one of the few people I wish to be loved by.' She goes on (some punctuation is added):

> Tho I live away from every body still I can *cotton* (to use an odd expression which I love) but I cannot express what I feel & two or three times I had it on the tip of my tongue to say all this to Lord Bathurst but thought he would think me so impertinent that I thought it better to be silent. This is all in your *private ear* that I tell you this for I find silence in the situation I am placed in the best thing, for to one person who does understand me hundreds don't, & to a feeling heart it chills and kills you. See how mine expands now in knowing it is to a warm & friendly heart I am writing...
>
> I have often longed to take up my pen to tell you what I felt for *yourself* & how readily I would if in my power bear your pains. For me it would be of no consequence, having no home nor no blessings of husband & family. I cannot bear your suffering but as it is the will of Heaven it is for some wise end, therefore don't tell what I feel, for even my good wishes for you may be wicked. God bless you...   Your Aff^te Sophy

Next to her signature she adds a note about herself: '*She, dear L^y G, is well in health her eyes very poorly but we trust in God.*'[1] Lady Bathurst's 'suffering' was surely not financial, for the earl had great rent-rolls as well as sinecures. Sophia's fear that her good wishes might wickedly defy God's will is best left to theologians; or analysts.

The second letter is addressed to Sir Henry Halford, her chief physician. Here something should be said first about royal doctors.

They earned extraordinary incomes. Their most lucrative patient over many years was of course George III. Even his final hopeless immurement at Windsor, 1811–20, earned his medical attendants £271,691 in all, about £9 million in modern terms, surely a record for one patient. The rest of the family also yielded large fees. One of the biggest earners was Halford, who became president of the Royal College of Physicians. When he and Dr Matthew Baillie, in their formal black attire (coat, waistcoat, breeches and silk stockings), enlivened with white cravat, gold watch-chain and goldheaded cane, were sharing a carriage to Windsor in 1810 to attend poor Princess Amelia, they compared fees earned in 1809. Halford's totalled 9500 guineas; Baillie topped him with 9600 (£10,080, say £300,000 now).[2]

Halford soon far surpassed him. He flourished additionally as a royal go-between and occasional informer/betrayer. One of George IV's surgeons, James Wardrop, an inventor of nicknames, called him 'the eelbacked baronet'. He enjoyed such favour that when the regent had Charles I's coffin opened at Windsor in 1813, Halford felt free to pocket a cervical vertebra that had been cut through by the executioner's axe. At dinner with friends he would pass it round the table.[3]

Though he was a charmer with royal or titled patients, lesser ones might have to follow do-it-yourself orders. To a woman suffering from an abdominal strain: 'My Dear Madam ... I fear I must ask you to put 10 leeches upon the part strained, followed immediately after their dropping off [when sated] by a large bread and milk poultice.'[4]

Both Halford and Baillie (a blunt Scot, a noted anatomist) attended Sophia. Halford's visits became much more than medically comforting. She had found the longed-for 'warm & friendly heart'. In January 1811, when she was 33 and Halford 44, she wrote an ardent letter of about 1,500 words, which he kept all his life. She began it as soon as he left Windsor to return to his wife and children at his Mayfair mansion, 16 Curzon-street: 'My VERY VERY Dear kind Friend — As you so kindly assured me you would look forward with pleasure to a letter from me tomorrow I trust you will readily believe how I *treasured* up those *welcome* words and sat down as soon as I was left alone to begin a few lines. They will but *ill convey* how *much* I miss *you*.'

First she reports to him as a patient: 'I had my dinner at three, tried to eat the Chicken but it went down very *so so*... *Baillie* came but his

Glum Countenance did me not much good… I am afraid of him as I believe he *treats nerves* as *nonsense* and I cannot help being *low*… I only hope he will not scold me or tell *tales* out of *school* for my odious *low spirits* is always *a bone of contention* [with the queen] and God knows I cannot help it and those who have ever suffered from them can alone *conceive* what the suffering is.' The letter soon becomes a declaration of love. It displays so much of her vulnerability and also her artfulness that it must be quoted generously, after arduous deciphering of her slurry writing. (Some paragraphing and punctuation are added. Words capitalized are those she *treble*-underlined.)

…Now it is *just five*. I am trying to recover myself before a *Great Personage* [the queen] makes her appearance and to find comfort I shall write to you *My FINE kind Soul!* Would to God I had you *here* and could look forward again to *comfort* this evening.

I cannot tell you how I have felt all this day and how vexed I feel that our *DEAR ANGEL* [George III, deranged since October] is yet in the dark about all that is going on. Dear Lord! how he is tried and how striking it is when one thinks of his *Perfection* & sees how little happiness he has enjoyed. In his situation at best there is but little comfort to be looked for, but surely his Cup of adversity has been full; we may say about him '*The Lord Chast'neth whom he loveth*' for his fine mind & firm principles are such that if one Man was to be blessed and happy in this uncertain world one should suppose he is the one on whom any happiness should fall. But dark and unknown are the ways of Providence and whatever is, is right. Do not set me down as a *METHODIST* for I am no such thing…

Now I am better & hoping to revive since I have been talking to you; but I should do better still if *you were with me* and I am already counting the hours to *Monday* and in 46 you will I hope be by my side and I shall be *VERY VERY MUCH* disappointed if you are not here by the 1/2 hour after four and if you cannot *steal* an *additional* 1/4 when you come to complete a *FULL* & *FAIR* half hour with me. Now mind what I say as one *MINUTE SHORT* in these *CASES* is very hard.

I have thought of you a *great great* deal; I think till I make myself miserable & then I know you will scold me— No, I hope not, for I am sure you cannot *blame* my trying *to struggle* against *impossibilities*. I wish I had no *feeling. That's not true*; I wish not to lose a particle of what I possess but I wish I could call that *forth whenever I liked*, always in my own *Sanctum*; and that in *this house* I could *hide* it *all* when in company. My *foolish foolish Eyes*; what *tell Tales,* and then I am tortured with < — ? — > and no one ever makes allowances for my feeling low and weak after being confined [with illness], together with all the anxiety I must suffer about our *beloved Invalid* whose situation is *REALLY* so *VERY VERY* melancholy —

I stopped just in time as a *Great Personage* has been here. Very little was said and that *slightly* about this day's *Interview* [with George III]. She said *the Delirium* was there but made *lighter* of the whole than I expected. I fear she was angry at seeing me here [in her room] and that only makes me worse for if I was to be hung for it I cannot help it —

Well my dear dear Soul I suppose you are in Town by this time & perhaps have given me more thought on the Road for which I shall *BLESS* you. Oh! how any kind word is fixed in my heart that you ever say to me, but I wonder how you can so lose your time; yet I like to indulge the thought that our *feelings* are *so alike;* you are so kind, & affectionate, and then you asked me this morning if I had repented what I had said to you. *Sometimes I do;* now do not *be angry* ... for that would make me miserable, but I will tell you all I *feel* and that honestly. I told you how friendless I am, and that I believe you know to be true, and most *solemnly* now I declare that *except* my dear brother [the Duke of York] *you* are the only < ?creature > to whom I could open *my heart*; this I have found, as also explained to you how totally impossible it has been for me ever to *trust* any *Individual* of my family. I love them *ALL DEARLY* but ... those to whom I could most easily have spoken have always been *violent* on the subject of our forming *attachments,* thinking it < ?wicked >. I cannot divest myself of feeling & therefore all that can be done is to act with that degree of prudence as shall < – ?– > as far as I am able.

You know I am *VERY WARM,* therefore easily found out, and as some are imprudent I dare *not trust* nor indeed am I inclined at any time to be very *intimate with females* as they are not always true to each other, & this *house* abounding with them, all I can do is to *steer clear* of any *Intimacy.* This constant caution grown upon me from experience makes my *house uncomfortable* & from *real misfortune* I am afraid has given me a degree of *suspicion* and dread of people in general which I am ready to admit I may carry too far; but this shows you how highly I think of you, to have put myself *WHOLLY* in *YOUR POWER,* and from having *NO FRIEND* and now finding so kind & Affec^te a heart in you, My Dearest kind Soul, consider what I am drawing upon myself. Not having enjoyed the *Treasure* of a *warm friend*, I went on in my dull way, very wretched but not expecting kindness. How much the difference; since I have known you, *ALL* my *dormant* feelings have been rous'd and I have gain'd your friendship and kindness… Your feelings do so *consist* with my *OWN* and your attentions so kind and gentle that you half < ?kill > me.

Am I doing right in *annoying* what *makes me* so *HAPPY*, and which with my feelings must tend to *misery* when the time comes to part with you? You gain upon me *every day every hour* and how can it be otherwise for such kindness I never *BEFORE EXPERIENCED*. It is so *DIFFERENT* from any thing I have been accustomed to. All is now delight but how can that continue when I < — ? — > my Room and < — ? — > when the time must come that each daily *Interview* will < ?cease >? You are becoming more and more necessary to my happiness and I feel I am acting < ?shamelessly > by you my dear *KIND* and < ?best > *Friend*.

I have been thinking of you and am now going to try *TO STOP*. I assure you I feel still as I ought, for I <—?—> *THE WILL* not to wish to do any thing to prove how < sincere ? > my affection is— Can you forgive all this— You bid me not fear what I wrote & I have given you a proof of this promise. God bless you, forgive me all I have said. Remember I *CAN LOVE* & that not by halves, so *PITY* & forgive

     Your affectionately attached —— [*a curving dash; then she adds*]
     You shall surely have a letter by tomorrow's Post— I finish this at 1/2 past *TEN EXACTLY* and am thankful you are comfortable at home where you <—?—> my happiness. If you scold me I shall *DIE OF IT*— 5

She is *very warm*, yet friendless. Her vulnerability and self-rebuking confession of her desire for this forbidden man serve to woo him. One sees hints of how she was open to the 'real misfortune' of 1799–1800.

Halford's 'attentions so kind and gentle' make one speculate. The 'comfort' he gave was of course in part medicinal. Her flow of words and slurry handwriting remind one that physicians were enthusiasts for laudanum. A *Medical Guide* of 1817 says, 'When judiciously administered, opium no doubt is the most valuable medicine we possess.'

By the end of 1811 Sophia had 'grown *dreadfully* thin' and was so weak that 'everything *fatigues* her', Princess Charlotte reported. 'Yet she rides out every day & is as amiable & charming as ever.' Charlotte called Windsor 'the *royal menagerie*', and wrote (rising 16), 'No family was ever composed of *such odd people* ... & there *have happened* such extraordinary things, that in any other family ... are never heard of before.' Sophia however is clever and sympathetic: 'When I see her with the rest of the family I can hardly believe she belongs to them — so wholly different is she in thoughts, opinions, manners.'

Strife around the ageing illnatured queen afflicted Sophia: 'The constant scenes of intrigue, of tracasseries, she can but ill support... Her health is impaired by her acute feelings, not for herself but for those she loves... She has often fought my battles.' One day the queen, behaving 'infamously', so upset Sophia that Charlotte feared it would 'bring on a spasm'. A little later, Charlotte reports Princesses Mary and Elizabeth and the queen 'caballing shockingly against me'. There is 'a wheel within wheel about everything.' Sophia 'puts in a little comfort wherever she can'. Charlotte's sharpest remark about the queen comes in October 1810, when doctors are being summoned in the vain hope of reversing George III's final madness: 'Instead of throwing the money & time away, they had *much better take* the old Q—— *under their care & shut her up* with her *train of followers.*'[6]

Sophia avoided tracasseries by keeping to her room, sometimes for months. Ill health has its uses. She had a merrier side, however. She and her brother George, both good mimics, had fun making mock of court personages. She was noted for her exact take-off of her mother's German accent. She could write a comical letter. When George, as regent, managed to have the incomes of Augusta, Elizabeth, Mary and Sophia raised from £4000 to £13,000, although all housed economically at Windsor, Sophia sent a letter of thanks 'From the Nunnery':

> The only thing that frets and worries me is the idea that your kindness to *four Old Cats* [she is 34] may cause you any *désagrément* with the Ministers... *Poor old wretches* as we are, a *dead weight* upon you, *Old Lumber* to the *Country*, like *Old Clothes*, I wonder you do not vote for putting us in a *sack* and drowning us in *the Thames*. *Two* of us would be fine food for *the Fishes* [plump Augusta and Elizabeth], and as to *Miny and me*, we will take our chance *together*.[7]

The regent's kindness with the taxpayers' money in a time of war and distress raised the family's income to £1,668,000 in all (enough to maintain 60,000 labourers' families). This did arouse *désagrément*. Although George had repeatedly had huge debts paid off, promising each time not to offend again, he now had new debts of £552,000, yet ministers could not halt his architectural and other profligacies.

Again Sophia became ill, and dangerously. In December 1813 Princess Charlotte notes her 'worn-out delicate little frame'. A month later the Duke of Kent writes to Halford about 'my poor little suffering Favorite' and says, 'I perfectly understand all you say about the difficulty of making a certain quarter [the Great Personage] understand the real state of things, but when there is a natural lack of warmth it is difficult in the extreme to make a proper impression.' He feared Sophia might die. So did Ernest, who wrote to the regent, 'I feel very uneasy at the accounts of poor Sophy; this constant slow fever ... makes me fear there is little hope of her recovery, poor thing. I am positive that the constant scene of Windsor has done all the mischief.' One can only guess whether he felt guilty about an earlier mischief.[8]

Sophia survived, but in seclusion. Matthew Baillie's sisters assured the author Maria Edgeworth in 1818 that 'Sophia is not insane — only nervous and weak — this is the truth and *nervous* is not here used as a soft equivocal word.'[9] The queen was then dying of dropsy. Augusta and Mary saw her daily (Elizabeth had escaped the Nunnery by marrying at 47). Sophia stayed in her room and communicated by way of Halford. A note of his about the queen is addressed to 'My dear sweet Princess'. Sophia wrote daily letters to the queen for Halford to read out at the bedside. An extract from the last one, which the queen did not live to hear: 'I was very anxious indeed for an account of your night & am thankful that you got some sleep... I know how to feel for you dearest dear Mama on this score as I confess I suffer sadly from that cause myself & yesterday & even this day I have been at moments just oppressed which to me is worse than decided pain... I hope I may see Sir Henry this Evening as it will be a proof you are free from fear of that dreadful Spasm... It is impossible to say how happy he is when you allow him the privilege of being Your Nurse...'[10]

The queen bequeathed Lower Lodge to Sophia. It held too many memories for her, not least the conceiving of her son. She gave it to the regent. The death of her father in January 1820 freed her to escape the Nunnery after more than forty years. She arranged with George IV (as he now was) to have apartments in Kensington Palace, which also housed the newly-widowed Duchess of Kent, her baby Victoria and her handsome six-foot Irish comptroller, John Conroy. Thanking George IV, Sophia wrote: 'If *I know myself*, which is a doubt with me, as so few people do, I am not very difficult to please, having very few wants and only wishing for a quiet, snug home. Of course some thoughts of a serious and painful nature will at times occur, but when I consider, as I really do, how much I have reason to be grateful for, the prospect soon has a more cheerful appearance.'[11]

A cheerful royal gathering is described by Harriet Countess Granville, August 1820: 'The Duchess of Clarence [William's Adelaide], ugly with a good *tournure* and manner; the Duchess of Kent, very pleasing indeed and raving of her baby. "*C'est mon bonheur, mes délices, mon existence...*" Augusta, good-humoured and jolly, stuffing *filets de sole* and veal cutlets; and Sophia, very clever and agreeable. I had to go with each of them the usual course. "How many children has Lady Georgiana Morpeth [Harriet's sister]?" "Eleven, ma'am." "God bless my soul, you don't say so, it seems but yesterday," etc.'[12]

Sophia invited old acquaintances. One was Fanny Burney, who had served at Windsor during Sophia's girlhood. In 1821, when John Linnell was to paint Sophia's portrait, she asked Fanny to amuse her during 'the *odious occupation* of sitting still'. Fanny talked about the ten years she had spent in France in Napoleon's time, having married a General d'Arblay — a returned émigré, but who refused to serve against England. Napoleon naturally came into Fanny's reminiscences, having recently died. She noted Sophia's response: 'Only the name Buonaparte ... even without embellishment or admiration, was sufficient to make her open her fine Eyes in a manner extremely advantageous to the Painter [*plate 12*]; who himself was so enchanted to be in the room with anyone who had seen Buonaparte that in his envy of my great happiness he evidently began to look on me ... as a personage eminently extraordinary.' Napoleon, though vilified for years as the Corsican tyrant, still stood high in the British imagination.

Linnell's commission provided a royal lesson. Sophia was not the fairest princess of them all. 'I ventured to make my picture really like,' he recalled, 'though as favourable as truth would admit of, and I calculate it was on that account I had no more from that direction.'[13]

Fanny went for drives with Sophia, spent 'evenings tête-à-tête', and came to see Sophia 'in a fairer & fairer point of view'. This suggests that she spoke of her pregnancy. In 1835, after a long interval, Fanny paid another visit. Sophia eagerly looked forward to it: 'No words can convey my *happiness...* I think y^r *presence* after such a *separation* worthy of *Illumination...* I felt *sure* my kind dear friend would not forget— her Affect^{ly} attached Sophia'[14] There were certainly new secrets she might wish to disclose in a frank tête-à-tête, as Chapter 22 will show.

9

Hunting for the heir

Princess Charlotte, the regent's only legitimate child, died in November 1817 after agonizingly giving birth to a stillborn son. This left the royal family in disarray. George III and his queen had overfulfilled a primary need of a hereditary monarchy by begetting numerous children, but their parental management failed sadly in providing heirs-apparent. Consider the state of the family in that November of mourning. First, the seven sons who survive:

George, the regent, aged 55. Two wives living: Maria Fitzherbert, the unofficial one, comfortably at Brighton on £6,000 a year from him; Princess Caroline, wantonly in Italy. Probably two children by Mrs Fitzherbert; and several bastards.

Frederick Duke of York, 54. A childless wife; at least four bastards.

William Duke of Clarence, 52. Unmarried; ten bastards by the noted actress Dorothy Jordan, and at least one earlier one.

Edward Duke of Kent, 50. One bastard from 1789. Has lived since 1790 with the *soi-disant* Madame de St Laurent.

Ernest Duke of Cumberland, 46. His Frederica has so far had one miscarriage. One bastard known, George FitzErnest.

Augustus Duke of Sussex, 44. Marriage of 1793 declared invalid, son and daughter ruled out.

Adolphus Duke of Cambridge, 43, unmarried.

And the five surviving daughters:

Charlotte, 51. Wife of Friedrich of Württemberg. No children.

Augusta, 49. Probably a secret marriage. Children, if any, ineligible.

Elizabeth, 47. A long-ago secret marriage. Two or three children, ineligible.

Mary, 41. Married, 1816, to cousin, Duke of Gloucester; childless.

Sophia, 40. Unmarried. One child, Thomas Garth.

So the twelve have given the nation well over twenty illegitimates but not one child to continue the Hanoverian line. The princes, barred from choosing non-royal British brides, had gratified themselves informally. The princesses were pitiable victims of their parents. Part of Elizabeth's story was told in Chapter 1. Charlotte, Augusta and Mary deserve some mention.

The Princess Royal escaped the Nunnery in 1797 by accepting the grotesquely fat Duke Friedrich. He had cast off his first wife, a sister of Caroline Princess of Wales, for being too freely amorous. She mysteriously vanished (perhaps murdered). Napoleon quipped that Friedrich existed to demonstrate how far a man's skin could be stretched without bursting (his desk, with a front deeply incurved to accommodate his belly, can still be seen at Stuttgart). Charlotte had the consolation of living in a 365-room schloss. In 1806 Napoleon promoted Friedrich to king as a reward for helping to rout Britain's subsidized allies at Ulm and Austerlitz. Years before, Württemberg, a flexible princedom, had sold soldiers to George III to fight the Americans. Friedrich, a willing bonapartist vassal, put a gilded crown atop his schloss. He also married off a daughter of his first marriage to Napoleon's brother Jerôme; so George III's eldest daughter entertained the two Corsican upstarts, Jerôme and Napoleon, as guests and whist partners. She infuriated her mother by addressing her, according to queenly protocol, as 'sister' — '*Ma très chère Mère et Sœur*'. A sort of winner, perhaps.

The next, Augusta, was in love from 1800 with a handsome general, Brent Spencer, a royal equerry but ruled out as a husband. After 'suffering martyrdom' for years, she asked the regent in 1812 to persuade the queen to let her marry. But the queen used the king's madness as an excuse for violently denying any independence for the four princesses still at Windsor, then aged 44, 42, 36 and 35. Augusta is said to have married Spencer secretly.

Mary's husband William, being thin, was known before marriage as Slice of Single Gloucester. As he was so dire a bore that people were terrified of being cornered with him, he was abbreviated to Bore Slice. To Mary he was a domestic tyrant.

The day after Princess Charlotte's death, the *Morning Chronicle* said, 'It will be the earnest prayer of the nation that an early alliance of one of the unmarried princes may forthwith be settled.' Ernest was already in with a chance, so this amounted to a wish that William, now third in line for the throne, and Edward, fourth in line, would achieve an heir who would block any child of Ernest, fifth in line. Overnight, William and Edward, 50-plus and not noted for grace or charm, had become desirable matches for non-Catholic princesses willing for a gamble. Any wooing that began would be a great anxiety for Ernest.

The kingdom was deeply moved by the loss of Princess Charlotte, an acute and spirited girl who had seemed likely to preside over a court very different from her father's. In a pensive letter to her mother a month before her death she mentioned 'the sufferings of my early years' and said, 'A sort of premature experience has given me that insight into human life & human character which in ordinary cases & circumstances is the result of the study & observation of years.[1]

After the mourning, though, came the irresistible fun of the princes' sudden race to procreate. John Fairburn, one of the sharpest satirical publishers, offered *Who Can Get an Heir!!*

> No sooner had death stricken down
> The much-lov'd heir of En---d's C---n
> Than all her kin, their grief to smother,
> Debated how to *get another*.

The regent might do it, 'could they but get him *a new wife*'. (Still with divorce in mind, he was gathering evidence about Princess Caroline's amorous life in Italy.)

Ernest says he is sure he'll get an heir: Frederica 'has shown some breeding qualms'. But the regent chaffs him:

> And pray, what have you, since you married,
> With *amorous Salms* done but *miscarried*?
> The first thing you miscarried — zounds —
> Miss'd carrying the *six thousand pounds*...
> Then you miscarried with mamma...

William, being a sort of sailor-prince, speaks nautically of his potency:

> In *navigating river Jordan*,
> *Ten vessels* of the first-rate burthen
> I have obtain'd...
> Where 'mong our brothers, Georgy, now is
> A man can boast of equal prowess?

In 1811 he had cruelly cast aside Dorothy Jordan and in the hope of paying off his debts had wooed several heiresses (one was Princess Charlotte's friend Mercer Elphinstone) and even Tsar Alexander's sister. The wildness of his wooing inspired the quip that he might soon need the Willis mad-doctors. Now his potential had risen. Money was still his primary need. He told Queen Charlotte he had ten children to support, had debts of £56,000, would need a town house as well as his Bushy Park mansion (which had to be *'entirely* new furnished'). So 'it would be madness' to marry without knowing what increased grant he would get.[2] He obtained a government promise of a rise from £18,000 to £40,000 a year, plus an 'outfit' grant of £20,000. So he resumed wooing: first a Danish princess, then Adelaide of Saxe-Coburg-Meiningen.

Edward, also deep in debt through endless spending on ostentatious mansions and fine horses, had decamped with his mistress in 1815 to Brussels, where they could live cheaply and beyond the reach of bailiffs. Besides, it was a handy base for seeking a bride. Like William, he was an early runner in the marriage stakes, needing the extra revenue. He began secretly negotiating for a young widow, Victoire of Saxe-Coburg, a sister of Princess Charlotte's husband. Edward assured Madame de St Laurent that he had no thought of casting her aside, but she was soon distressed to hear rumours. He confided to the Whig MP Thomas Creevey, whose advice he sought, that he suffered 'infinitely uncomfortable moments', poor man, as he worked to deceive her with 'daily dissimulation'. He told an aide in London to send lying 'showable' letters to make him seem innocent.

But then Charlotte's death deepened Madame's alarm. She was soon aware of the desire in Britain that William and Edward should put Ernest into third place in the heir-getting race. Edward wrote to his aide that she feared that the government did not wish 'that the Crown of either E-----d or H---ver [*England; Hanover*] should depend on the issue of the D--- of C--b-----d'. (Edward often pointlessly used such dashes.) He asked for 'showables' to 'keep *up* the idea' that William would marry but *he* would not.

The Coburg widow accepted Edward. The wedding was fixed for May 1818. Edward's aide provided a showable requiring him in London. He went to arrange things, especially a £3000 loan from Coutts's Bank. Madame never saw him again. She went to a convent. His success made him the forebear of the family line now reigning.[3]

It was hopelessly late for the princesses to enter the heir-getting race. Princess Elizabeth had been longing to marry for years. When a friend, Augusta Compton, was engaged, she wrote to her, 'Thank God again & again that you have determined to quit that *vile class*, you know

J.ⁿ Gillray del.ᵗ & fec.ᵗ ad viv.ⁿⁿ

1 Ernest portrayed *ad vivam* (from life) by James Gillray in July 1799, when he was newly established in St James's Palace. As Gillray lived just up St James's-street at Hannah Humphrey's printshop, he had only to wait with sketchcard in hand until Ernest walked past. He unkindly records Ernest's *left* side, with his sunken eye. The print is laconically entitled 'A Portrait'.

2 **The Commons spurns Ernest** (*see pages 79-81*). George Cruikshank's caricature dares to suggest a reason: the lingering suspicion that he killed his valet. 'Thou canst not say I did it', says Sellis's ghost. In nearly every copy of the print, the Sellis area was blacked out at the last minute for fear of prosecution. *Wilhelm-Busch-Museum, Hanover*

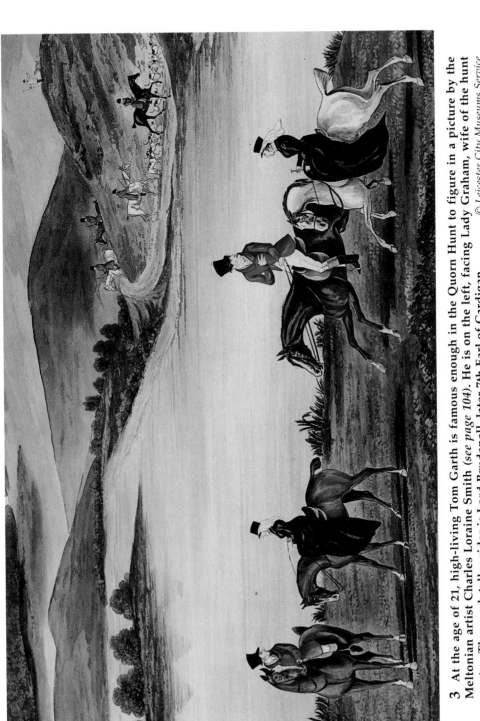

3 At the age of 21, high-living Tom Garth is famous enough in the Quorn Hunt to figure in a picture by the Meltonian artist Charles Loraine Smith (*see page 104*). He is on the left, facing Lady Graham, wife of the hunt master. The much taller rider is Lord Brudenell, later 7th Earl of Cardigan.   © *Leicester City Museums Service*

4 Lady Astley elopes from her Mayfair mansion. Caricaturist's licence has her descend by a 'Jacob's ladder' — a play on her husband's name. The 'To Sophia' missive in Garth's pocket shows that his royal origin is already public knowledge (*see pages 107-9*). A four-horse carriage is waiting. It drove off with them 'at a great rate', the parish watchman said in court.

Within the caricature:

ST JAMES'S HOTEL

JER MYN St.

Yes my dear, we have shewn
Sir Jacob some fun for the
Shilling!

this is a new method of
mounting guard my love

Come along my Girls.
I'll give you a treat to Night.
and we'll spend the Shilling
in Gin

ONE SHILLING DAMAGES

We all know Sir Jacob a bit of a Swell.
High ha says Rowley
He likes to go larking with Kitty or Nell
And he treats us to Night at the Sign of
the Bell.
With his Towley, fowley, gammon & spinnage
and hugh says Anthony Rowley.

ha. ha. 'ha

there they go.

5 Inspired by the
defeat of Astley in
his £12,000 suit
against Garth, this
caricature shows
the two noted
riders well
mounted: Astley on
three Leicester
'bonnet-makers',
Garth (as a hussar)
on Georgiana.
Astley hooks up a
girl's skirt with his
whip handle, as
described in court.
The lovers mock
him over his
shilling damages.
Georgiana wears
horns of cuckoldry,
but Astley's are far
grander.

*By permission of the
British Library:
frontispiece to Crim.Con.
Extraordinary!
(BL 1131.h.27)*

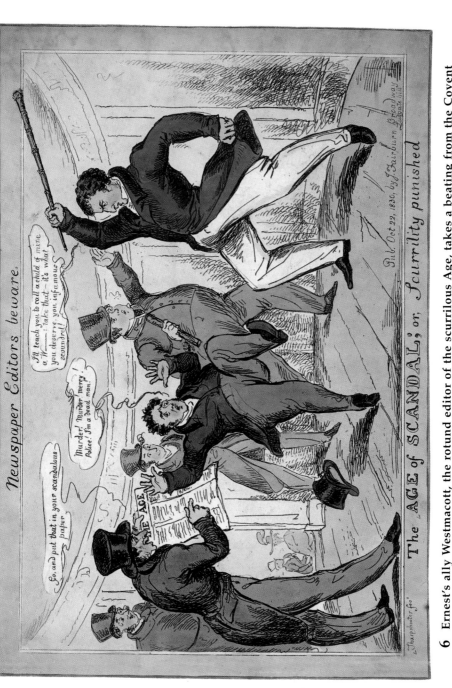

6 Ernest's ally Westmacott, the rotund editor of the scurrilous *Age*, takes a beating from the Covent Garden actor-manager Charles Kemble (*see page 192*). A man holds up a copy of *The Age* and says, 'Go and put that in your scandalous paper.' *by Sharpshooter; BM ref 1991-7-20-94 (not in BM caricature catalogue)*

7 Lord Graves, distressed by Ernest's affair with his wife, has cut his throat. Two accusing spectres terrify Ernest. One is Graves. The other, saying, 'What ——! another victim,' is Joseph Sellis, unforgotten 20 years after his death. Passages from Shakespeare declare Ernest's guilt.

8 The name Graves is a gift to caricaturists. Ernest has been spotted still visiting Lady Graves (*page 163*), so here he is as 'The Beast among the Graves again' with the unmourning widow. Graves's ghost rises, astonished, from his tomb (marked with horns). By this date Ernest is often caricatured as bestial.

what I mean [spinsters]. Don't let anyone know my sentiments for else
I shall bring a Hornet nest about me, but my language is that of *Truth*,
seldom spoke anywhere, particularly near the dwelling of HRHs. You
have set me a good example & I will follow it whenever I can. I hope
you will promise that the first person you write to after your wedding
may be *me* — I long for my piece of Cake.' In a postscript she sends
her compliments to the bridegroom and says, 'Dont make him wait.'
Earlier, when anticipating her friend's engagement, she offered her the
use of 'my dear pretty Cottage, which I hope will be the place where
you will pass your — [*she prints the words almost an inch high*]

'Honey Moon

Amen

&

A ——— Man'

Miss Compton sent her a Cupid figurine. Thanking her for 'the dearest
of all dear little creatures', Elizabeth says she instantly put it 'exactly
in the center of my Chimney piece & did nothing but look at it.'[4]

At last, aged 47, Elizabeth defied the bullying tantrums of her
mother and married the 48-year-old heir to the Landgrave (count) of
Hesse-Homburg — 'the monster of a man, a vulgar-looking German
corporal whose breath and hide is a compound between tobacco and
garlick', the Duke of Buckingham's informant unkindly reported.
'What can have induced her, nobody can guess.'[5] What induced her
was the tyranny of the Nunnery. This is movingly expressed in a letter
she poured out to her Saint, Lord St Helens, the man who ought to
have been her husband years ago. Here is just a little of it:

> God bless you do not hate me & dont change your opinion of me w[h] has
> been the pride of my life for many & many a long year— In accepting the
> P. of H.H. I did it from always wishing a home & I never should have
> done it if his character had not stood so very high... My Mother alas! from
> motives of delicacy to my Father will not give her consent as a letter from
> the P. of H.H. was never answered by him [George III] with the same
> proposal some years back — & this certainly has caused me much misery
> & distress but my Brother the P.R. has given his cordially... You may
> conceive the state I am in, nearly distracted but I hope the worst is over —
> for what I have gone through these last ten days passes all the misery I
> ever indured. When we meet ... you shall have my whole history in strict
> confidence... Promise me the continuation of your friendship, that you
> will not forget me & that you will write to me & still think as you have
> done of your truly attached ——— etc etc etc[6]

98

In 1821 she wrote from her Homburg castle, near Frankfurt, 'I have been now a *Year & three quarters* without a *line* from my Saint... Still, if you are not inclined to give me a thought, stop here, & throw this epistle into the fire ----- ' He did write, which put her into a 'sort of extasy ... at seeing Your handwriting again'. Returned to England in 1830 (aged 70; he 77), she writes of 'the extreme joy that I experienced in seeing You again, & seeing You so much better than I expected'.[7]

Elizabeth's marriage in 1818 inspired some bold satire. One caricature gives the couple this dialogue:

> *Elizabeth*: Where, my love, shall we *humbug* tonight?
> *Homburg*: Not at *Maidenhead*, mine dear Betty, for dat be too far off.

Another, George Cruikshank's 'The Hombourg Waltz', seizes the chance to mock the marital difficulties of the regent and his brothers, but the newlyweds, vastly fat, are the central figures. Waltzing, then thought a lascivious German import, serves to imply something else:

> *Homburg*: You do it very easy, my love!!! Is dis de first time you dance dis valtz?
> *Elizabeth*: First time 'pon honour — but 'tis a delightful dance & I knew we should soon get into it.

Ernest is visible, waltzing with his wife but *outside* the room. Queen Charlotte, a shrouded crone, says, 'This is rather late in the evening to begin Waltzing my little dears, but better late than never... As to Master *Earnest* ... he shant bring his partner to dance in *my room.*'

A John Fairburn lampoon, *Hunting for the Heir!!!* takes up a notion that the father of Elizabeth's babies in the 1780s was a court barber:

> She *hunting for the heir* must go.
> She's used enough to *hair*, you know.
> Witness the *barber*, who, they say,
> To dress her *wig* came every day.
> With him she had as pretty sport
> As ever had been known at C---t.
> *Two heirs*, 'tis known, they got together,
> *Hunting the hair* in May-day weather;
> Till Friz gave tongue, the foolish lad!
> And then we swore the rogue was *mad*.
> ...So still he in a *madhouse* lies
> And for his *boys* and *Betsy* sighs. [8]

A variant notion was that one of Elizabeth's lovers was a man named Stone with some modest role at court. Certainly a man of this name was sent to the Bethlehem Hospital (Bedlam) about 1788. The official account was that he was possessed by a wild desire to marry the Princess Royal. He was still in Bedlam in 1801, maintained by royal funds, as revealed in a cashbook of the Lord Steward's department that chiefly lists payments for such things as bonfire ale for the Guards, asses' milk for George III and 'muffins for the Duke of Clarence'. In January 1801 it records, 'A year's maintenance & clothing of Marg^t Nicolson & Thos Stone ... Bethlem hospital, £31 8s 5d.' Margaret Nicholson was a deranged woman who made a pathetic knife attack on George III in 1786. It is pleasant to find that two persons who had troubled the court were maintained by it year after year.

The First Book of the Royal Chronicles, a mock-biblical commentary on passing events, published 1788, tells of 'the daughters of George' who 'dwelt with their father, waiting for *consolation* from a far country'. It goes on: 'Lo! no man in those days dared to *look* at the damsels save two... One of these *royal lovers* was set up as an image on the wall of Bethlem, even a pillar of *Stone*. While the other moonstruck genius, being a barber, was sent to shave his brethren in Bridewell.'

While 'hunting for the heir' was in progress, Castlereagh came to the Commons with financial proposals. 'To excite some of the members of the royal family to marriage is now an object of much importance to the country,' he said in April 1818. 'A single marriage will not satisfy the anxiety of the people.' Nobody had thought to 'excite' the princes earlier, when all depended on Princess Charlotte.

The princes' basic allowance was £18,000 a year, plus various extras, chiefly for military near-sinecures. At first Castlereagh proposed to raise William to £40,000 on marriage and the others to £30,000. *The Times* denounced such 'profligate and scandalous grants in the present state of the country'. The postwar debt stood at £760 million, hungry labourers were rioting, radicals were ever more boldly demanding reform. Although Castlereagh could count on his well-disciplined, and rewarded, MPs not proposing serious changes in the running of the nation, they might refuse largesse for 'illustrious' princes with little lustre. He retreated to £28,000 for William, £24,000 for the others.

This climbdown was still not enough. The Commons had never

been able to stop the compulsive overspending of the regent, but they could show some spirit by trimming his brothers. They remembered William's treatment of Dorothy Jordan and his comically abortive heiress-hunting. Enough MPs disobeyed Castlereagh's whip to cut William down to £24,000. Castlereagh said this meant that William's proposal to marry Adelaide of Saxe-Coburg-Meiningen 'might now be considered at an end'. It was not. He married her on 11 July 1818, which happened to be the second anniversary of the funeral near Paris of an impoverished exile, Dorothy Jordan.

Ernest, being married, did not need to be 'excited', but Castlereagh said it would be unjust to make him an exception. The Commons would not want 'to force that illustrious person into exile'. An MP protested that ministers were not treating the Commons fairly by 'hooking the Duke of Cumberland in among the other princes' (*loud and continued cheers*). Another said, 'I see no reason for granting him now what was refused him in 1815.' Another noted that the queen still refused to receive Frederica. The second attempt in three years to give Ernest an extra £6000 was defeated by 143 votes to 136 (*loud cheering*).

'Humiliation upon humiliation,' said *The Times*. Britain was 'the only country in Europe in which the court expenses have not been permanently diminished'. What had been diminished here? Allowances to officers' widows.[9]

Thomas Creevey, during a long talk with Wellington that summer, mentioned the votes on the princes' money. Wellington's comment, often quoted, was, 'By God! there is a great deal to be said about that. They are the damnedest millstone about the necks of any government that can be imagined.' He softened this a little by putting the princes' unpopularity down mainly to royal bad manners: 'They have insulted — *personally* insulted — two-thirds of the gentlemen of England, and how can it be wondered at that they take their revenge upon them when they get them in the House of Commons?'[10]

Since 1815 Ernest had refused to leave England unless he was 'given *Hanover*', because retreating would imply Frederica's guilt. He told the regent, 'Am I *alone* to make a sacrifice? Have I not been most infamously used?'[11] But after the Commons again refused to grant 'that pitiful addition', he borrowed £10,000 from Coutts's and retreated to Berlin, where living was cheaper.

Frederica was pregnant. In Saxe-Coburg, where Edward had

settled, his duchess was also pregnant. He wanted his heir to be born in England, but had to find money to transfer his household there and set up a new one. Although deep in debt when he married, he had sunk deeper by lavishing thousands on stables for a string of thirty-six prime horses. Months passed while friends in England struggled to raise £25,000. At last the Kents and their entourage in a cavalcade of carriages journeyed over more than 400 miles of jolting roads to Calais. By the time they crossed to Dover on a rough sea, the duchess was within a month of her full term. She was lifted ashore without mishap. On 24 May 1819 in Kensington Palace a daughter was born: Victoria. She ranked one step higher than Ernest himself; and thus two steps higher than a son born to Frederica on May 27.

Edward's success in the heir-getting race was, one might say, a close-run thing. He died only eight months later.

The list of princes narrowed further in 1827 when the Duke of York died of dropsy at 63. George IV was by now a punishingly self-indulgent gentleman in his 65th year and not thought likely to live long. His Caroline had died in 1821, but he made no move to hunt an heir himself, being devoted to a 'new old lady', wife of Lord Conyngham, his Lord Steward. Ten years after the 'hunting for the heir' began, this was how the succession stood:

William, 62, looking forward to the crown, but with no legitimate heir (two girl babies did not live).

Princess Victoria, aged eight.

Ernest, 56, living in Germany with Frederica and their son George.

After George IV goes, only unstable William and little Victoria stand between Ernest and the throne.

10

The wild Meltonian

Horses to ride and horses to drive were the chief delight of young Tom Garth. He acquired the taste early, thanks to the indulgent General Garth at Ilsington House. Here is a first glimpse of the lad going at a cracking pace — in a *horseless* carriage: 'At eight years of age, the future driver of the barouche and four might be seen driving six goats in an open phaeton [light carriage] into Dorchester, threatening to break his own neck and everyone's else that came in his way.'[1]

When he was eleven he was placed among young gentlemen of the same bent. The general sent him to Harrow School, entered in the Head Master's House, the head being Dr George Butler (nicknamed Pomposo by Lord Byron), who reigned over Harrow from 1805 to 1829. A number of Garth's fellow-Harrovians were destined for cavalry regiments, the most memorable or notorious being Lord Brudenell, later 7th Earl of Cardigan, leader of the charge of the light brigade at Balaclava in 1854. Another boy of Garth's time, until expelled in 1813 for fighting, was John Mytton, who won fame on horseback in a different way. He is remembered in foxhunting circles for his daredevil feats, wild drinking and a terrible end in a debtors' prison ... where we shall find Garth himself coming to his aid.

The future that General Garth planned for young Thomas was in his own 1st (Royal) Regiment of Dragoons. The general, 'in great good humor', told Princess Charlotte his plans when she was visiting Dorset in November 1815. She writes to her friend Miss Elphinstone, 'The boy is come home & is going directly into the army. Next Gazette, look for his name in the *Royals*. Frederick [Duke of York, commander-in-chief] has given him a cornetcy in Garth's reg[t]. He has left Harrow & is to go abroad directly to learn French & German perfectly, then to join the reg[t] afterwards.'[2] The following June, aged nearly sixteen, the boy became a half-pay lieutenant in the Royals (six maturer lieutenants had Waterloo medals).

Being on half pay, he was free to go abroad. He certainly learned some French, for he headed for Paris, just as hordes of the better-off

British did in the post-Waterloo years. Garth wins two friendly mentions in the noted *Reminiscences* of Captain Rees Gronow, who tells of memorable times at the Café Tortoni and at Véry's in the Palais Royal, beginning with breakfasts of pâtés, game, fowl, fish, eggs, broiled kidneys, champagne and liqueurs. In the circle of young *milords* such as Lord Brudenell, 'you were sure to stumble upon the kind and excellent Tommy Garth, full of spirits and youth'. A place best to avoid was the Salon des Étrangers, a gaming hell. When 'the chief gambler of the day', Count Hunyady, was stripped clean at last, Gronow says, 'he actually borrowed £50 of the well-known Tommy Garth — who was himself generally more in the borrowing than the lending line — to take him back to Hungary'.[3] Tommy's serious borrowing days were some years later.

By 1818 he was with the Royals, but that did not last. The Duke of York inquired why he was taking a long leave. General Garth put off replying, then offered an excuse: 'I have not written on the subject of my Protegee [sic], fearing to intrude on the anxious moments' (Queen Charlotte was on her deathbed). About Tom Garth, he said, 'As I received a report of his being ill at Sligo with a fever I became greatly alarmed, and therefore applied to Sir G Beckwith [a colonel] for leave of absence for him as soon as he was able to travel, which was kindly granted till December, and he is now in Dorsetshire in perfect health.'[4]

Two words stand out here: 'my Protegee'. When dealing with the Duke of York, the general had no need to pretend to be the boy's father. York himself had arranged his surrogate role.

The general managed to return his cosseted protégé to a non-active half-pay life. Soon Tom was emulating the sons of opulent families, though his half-pay was a few shillings a day. He divided his time between London and, in the foxhunting months, Leicestershire, home of the Quorn, by far the most expensive hunt. Members whom he had known in Paris — Lord Brudenell, Lord Chesterfield, Lord Alvanley — probably decided his choice.

Tradesmen who dealt with the dashing Quorn men knew they must be wary. The name of General Garth, royal equerry, served Tom in obtaining credit. He could hint too at a benefactor at court, knowing or guessing that some funds came from Princess Sophia, whose grant was now £15,000 a year. To his companions he must have been an intriguing figure. In their world, rent rolls were the normal and most esteemed source of wealth. Men endowed with broad acres or with

choice parts of London could buy MPs, solicit titles, serve in government or at court. Perhaps Garth's anomalousness spurred him to
outmatch others in prodigality. Before long he was running up debts.

An attempt to curb him was made before he was 20 by a man high
in both the army and the court. This was General Sir Herbert Taylor,
private secretary successively to the Duke of York, George III and
Queen Charlotte, who probably knew as many court secrets as anyone
(*plate 11b*). He put pressure on General Garth and had the young
lieutenant transferred in August 1820 from the dragoons to the less
fashionable 37th (North Hampshire) Regiment of Foot, with the rank
of captain. Sir Herbert's reason for choosing the 37th was that it was
stationed abroad, at Montreal. His plan was that young Garth,
'removed from scenes and habits of dissipation and extravagance'
(Chapter 12 reveals more about this), would begin a serious army
career. He was to have command of a company, for such was the army
then. But he rebelled against exile, General Garth upheld him, and Sir
Herbert gave way. In October 1821 the unwilling soldier was gazetted
a half-pay captain in the 15th Hussars.

The 15th: the regiment of which Ernest is colonel. The teasing
prophecy of Princess Charlotte back in 1811, *I suppose he will be in the
army — in the 15th*, has come true.

It was a boon for Tom Garth that the decision came by October,
freeing him for the foxhunting season, November to April. He had an
establishment at Melton Mowbray, 'the celebrated resort of the wild
Meltonians', as Thomas Creevey put it. This was the 'scene of
dissipation and extravagance' that Sir Herbert deplored. By early 1822
Garth was notable enough to figure in a sporting picture by the
versatile Charles Loraine Smith, deputy master of the Quorn, MP and
artist. A print version of it (*plate 3*) is entitled 'The Rendezvous of the
Quorn Hounds at Grooby Pool, Tuesday, April 10, 1822'. Others in the
scene are Garth's fellow-Harrovian, Brudenell, and Lady Graham,
wife of the hunt master, Sir Bellingham Graham.[5]

Titled Meltonians were plentiful: the Dukes of Buccleuch, Montrose
and Cleveland; Marquess of Worcester; Earls of Chesterfield, Darling-
ton, Howth, Jersey, Lonsdale, Plymouth, Radnor, Stamford, Wilton;
Lords Alvanley, Belgrave, Elcho, Forester, Molyneux, Muncaster,
Rancliffe, Southampton...

'A winter in Leicestershire has ever been found to be the passe-partout that leads to the best society in the world,' says the *Sporting Magazine* in a special report in 1825 by its best contributor, Charles James Apperley, who styled himself Nimrod. He says of the Quorn, 'No poor man should ever go near it.'

His reports give some idea of what Garth was spending. A man must have fine horses, often costing 200 guineas, sometimes much more. To have only three or four would be laughable. A thorough Meltonian can hunt every day, Monday to Saturday (Sunday being a day of rest for foxes). If the Quorn is not going out he can ride with the Cottesmore or Belvoir (Duke of Rutland's). After each run a horse needs rest. The 'hard-riding Meltonians' cover great distances over Leicestershire's pastureland and challenge the most perilous fence or ditch, Nimrod reports, so 'it is useless to go out without a second horse (and many have three) in the field', ready to be handed over by one's 'second-horse man' when one's mount is blown or injured.

In a list of twenty-seven Melton studs where horses may be seen 'in perfection', Nimrod names Lord Plymouth with the most, twenty, and Lord Alvanley with sixteen. A few modest men have only six or seven. And here is Captain Garth, ranking well with ten horses 'in perfection'. They probably cost him several thousand pounds, and then comes their care and feeding. Nimrod tabulates the expenses for '12 hunters kept at Melton all the year round':

groom	£100
4 helpers at £70	280
1 boy	50
keep of 12 horses	500
rent of stables	50
saddler	50
taxes	50
shoeing	25
	£1000

Besides, there are a gentleman's personal outlays: lodgings, servants, carriages, fashionable clothes (the Pytchley men of Northamptonshire, Thomas Creevey reports, 'in dandyism are very second-rate to the Quorn'). Nimrod says Melton can 'produce more good cooks in a given space of ground than any other place in England'.[6]

A Meltonian must also have portraits painted — of his horses more often than of himself. A Meltonian of a later generation, Major Guy

Paget, says in his *Melton Mowbray of John Ferneley* that in the 1820s a picture by Ferneley, a prolific equestrian artist, 'seems to have been part and parcel of the perfect Meltonian's equipment, just as much as the latest hat or boot'. Sure enough, Garth patronized him. Paget quotes an account book of the artist starting in 1824 (a previous one is lost), listing paintings for many noble foxhunters, and the following for Garth:

December 1825. Portrait of a Chestnut Mare & Groom & Dog, £15 15s

April 1826. Portrait of Two Horses & Two Grooms, £31 10s

Portrait of a Chestnut Horse, £10 10s

Paintings come much cheaper than the horses themselves, but there goes another £57 15s. It is pleasing to find that although Garth was soon to be pursued by creditors, Ferneley was not one of them. As Paget says, 'He knew his Meltonians too well to give credit.' He was part of the social scene. On Sundays, the gentlemen's routine was a heavy lunch after church, followed by 'religious contemplation with their eyes shut', then a stroll to Ferneley's workplace to view canvases in progress.[7]

Gentlemen naturally found less innocent diversions. The courtesan Harriette Wilson tells in her *Memoirs* of a visit to Melton a few years earlier with her current rich keeper. Dining in the Quorn clubhouse, she sees 'wretched, squalid prostitutes' tap at the windows, luring some members to 'sneak out of the room ... *Mon Dieu! Quel dommage!*' She thinks the Meltonians in their evening dress (red, lined with white) 'never looked half so handsome as when, glowing with health, they took their seats at dinner', so handsome, indeed, that her keeper flies into a jealous rage, fearing she might offer herself 'as an indoor substitute for the dirty, shivering frail ones without'. She is in theory faithful to only one kind gentleman at a time, but she confesses that the thought 'did strike me very forcibly indeed'. After all, 'if women will tap at windows for the sole purpose, and beautiful young men will retire for the sole purpose, why, the idea is forced upon one'.[8]

Tom Garth will have seen plenty of girls at Melton and at Leicester, the county town, eager to supplement what they earned in the knitwear, millinery or Stilton cheese trades. Their high time was the hunt season. Garth began an affair in 1826, however, not with a wanton milliner but with a Meltonian's wife. This brought him into court as defendant in a case that offered delightful scandal. He was sued by Sir Jacob Astley, 6th baronet, possessor of a fine 17th-century Norfolk mansion, Melton Constable, set in a Capability Brown park. In the park was a tower up which he took guests to view some of his vast rent-bearing Norfolk acres. In Northumberland he had another mansion, Seaton Delaval, and thousands more acres. When he chose as his bride Georgiana Caroline Dashwood, of an eminent but less opulent family, this was seen in society as 'an immense catch' for her.

He sued Garth for 'criminal conversation' with her. An action for 'crim con' was a financial one, for damages. The law said a wife's seducer had trespassed upon her body, the husband's property. Compensation for that trespass could make a gratifying addition to a husband's fortune. In a famous case in 1770, Earl Grosvenor, ancestor of the Dukes of Westminster, sought £100,000, an all-time record, from George III's brother Henry. Grosvenor was proved, however, to have enjoyed 'kept women', which reduced the damages to a mere £10,000.

Astley sought £12,000 (about £475,000 now). Would *he* prove to be a tarnished husband?

Astley v Garth was heard on 19 February 1827 in the Court of Common Pleas, Westminster Hall, before Lord Chief Justice Best. The court was 'crowded to excess at an early hour'. 'Noblemen and gentlemen of rank' fought for seats. The excitement extended to royal circles. Georgiana Astley's elder sister, Marchioness of Ely, had been a maid of honour. Their father, Sir Henry Dashwood, baronet and MP, of Kirtlington Park, Oxfordshire, was a Gentleman of the Privy Chamber: a sinecure he retained despite a scandal more than thirty years before. Sir Henry had caused great distress to his wife, a Bedchamber Lady to Sophia and to other princesses, when 'the infamous Lady Wallace', as Fanny Burney called her, got Sir Henry in her clutches, sued for large sums and sent in bailiffs to seize goods from his house — even children's toys and clothes. Lady Dashwood fell ill, and died when Georgiana was only seven months old. It had been a stressful start in life for her.

Beyond all this was the fact of Garth's royal connection of a rarer kind. Well-informed people knew he was Princess Sophia's son.

Georgiana had eloped at midnight in July 1826 from the Astleys' London mansion in Grosvenor-street, Mayfair, abandoning sons aged 16 months and four years. Caricatures were soon on sale at printshops patronized by the best people. The caricatures' titles play on the fact that a celebrated equestrian entertainment, specializing in trick riders, was called Astley's. The Humphrey printshop in St James's-street issued 'A Scene for a new *Piece* at *Astley's* Theatre!'. Garth, in hussar uniform, runs off carrying Georgiana on his back. Astley shouts, 'Stop thief!' A placard advertises for a mare 'stolen or strayed': '*Chestnut mane ... has good paces ... capable of carrying any weight... The thief will be prosecuted.*' Two barristers look forward to 'a job for Westminster Hall'. It is already kown that Garth is in debt, for he is singing —

> How happy's the soldier that lives on his pay
> And spends half a crown out of sixpence a day.

(Half a crown being five sixpences.) And Georgiana sings —

> He fears not Sir Jacob nor warrants nor bum [*bailiff*
> But *soothes all my care* with a roll of his drum.

Another caricature, 'A Change of Performance at *Astley's*', from S W Fores of Piccadilly, goes further by alluding to Sophia (*plate 4*). It is a midnight scene in Mayfair. Georgiana, in beribboned hat and swirly garments, uses a 'Jacob's ladder' (an allusion to Astley's name) to descend to Garth from her balcony. A coach-and-four is waiting.

GARTH: Descend my Angel to these R---l Arms, & glory in the contemplation of so *Noble an Alliance.*
GEORGIANA: I do. I do, & to evince my independence I bring down *nothing but myself.* [Her weeping children plead, 'Pray don't leave us Mama.]

A mere captain speaking of his 'royal arms'! The print gives a clue. Sticking out of his coat-tail pocket is a letter addressed 'TO SOPHIA'. Labelled letters were a frequent device in caricatures. This one shows that the Sophia connection was known far beyond the court.

Both sides in Astley v Garth fielded costly teams of lawyers. For Astley, James Scarlett, King's Counsel (shortly to become attorney-general), with three barristers in support. For Garth, Mr Serjeant Vaughan, former attorney-general to Queen Charlotte (and a brother, as it happened, of Garth's mother's doctor, Halford, who acquired that surname with an inheritance). A serjeant ranked even above King's Counsel, with extra rights and a special wig to announce them. Vaughan too had three helpers, one being Henry Brougham MP, already famous for his dramatic defence of George IV's wife Caroline in 1820, and soon to make his way to the lord chancellor's woolsack.

Scarlett's theme was that from the time of Astley's wedding to Georgiana in 1819 at St George's Church, Hanover-square, the Archbishop of Canterbury officiating, when Astley was 21 and she 23, their marriage had been uninterruptedly happy until Garth came on the scene. In May 1826, when Meltonians and others came to London for urban pleasures, Garth called at Astley's mansion and was introduced to Georgiana. Soon afterwards a general election was held. Nominations, wooing of voters and the polling itself lasted for many weeks. Astley was absent a good deal, standing for election in Sussex and also casting his vote in Bedfordshire and Norfolk, as one did. Garth became Georgiana's devoted companion.

'Lady Astley is a woman of great beauty and agreeable manners ... a great favourite in society,' Astley's sister told the court. 'Mr Garth kept a close carriage, of chocolate colour' and an open phaeton, 'and appeared to have an establishment like a man of fortune'. He took Georgiana to parties and the opera. They drove in the phaeton in Kensington Gardens, where the fashionables paraded to see and be seen, to gossip and make assignations. They went on excursions to Greenwich and Richmond, and late at night to Vauxhall pleasure gardens.

People talked. 'Illnatured' people, as funloving ladies would say, alerted Astley's mother. She said Georgiana must leave London and retire into Norfolk. Georgiana seemed to agree, but after midnight, 24–25 July, she vanished. A watchman of St George's parish told the court he saw a carriage waiting and 'a lady looking out from the balcony of Sir Jacob Astley's house'. Soon after, she 'stepped into the carriage in a hurry and it drove off at a rapid rate'.

Butlers are called upon to serve in many ways. The Astleys' butler pursued the runaways to an inn. Georgiana, he said, was 'much affected and very low'. His evidence goes on: 'I said, "I hope your ladyship will return." She replied, "I cannot return." She repeated this twice. She spoke very low. I said, "I hope you will return for the sake of the children."' The butler, as it happened, had worked years before at Weymouth. In later evidence for the divorce court, he said that when Garth first visited Astley's London house, he remembered having often seen him as a boy at Weymouth 'under the care of General Garth' (*not* 'with his father General Garth').

When the crim-con case was heard, Garth was living in style with Georgiana at the St James's Hotel, Jermyn-street. A waiter told the court, 'Captain Garth keeps a carriage and saddle-horses. He has a valet, footman and lady's maid.' He also had a coachman, postilions and stable-helpers 'all living at the hotel', and had to pay for stables.

Astley's counsel, Scarlett, noted for his red face and aggressive pleading, brought Astley's mother, sisters and chaplain to swear he was a devoted husband. 'They appeared to be the happiest couple that could live,' said the chaplain. Scarlett said Georgiana had 'given way to the wiles of an artful seducer ... well versed in the scenes of fashionable life' who 'had gone about seeking whom he might devour'. Newspapers had cast aspersions on Astley's morals, Scarlett said, but he defied Garth's barristers 'to prove that a more affectionate husband ever found his way into a court of justice'. Mr Serjeant Vaughan welcomed the challenge. He said Scarlett had pictured the Astleys as having lived in 'happiness as pure as that enjoyed by our first parents before the fall'. How was it then that the lady had 'left the arms of this devoted, tender, faithful and unprecedented husband'? He would present another picture, but keep it 'as little disgusting as possible'.

Garth's lawyers had brought witnesses from Leicester and elsewhere. First came a scene at Leicester racecourse. Astley was there with Georgiana in his phaeton to see a horse of his run for £100 against the horse of a friend, Sir Edward Mostyn. Astley alighted to chat to several girls. Mary Ann Webster, self-styled bonnet-maker: 'The carriage was standing in sight with Lady Astley in it. He hooked our petticoats up with the end of his whip and said we were "gallows ones" and something else beginning with a b—.' (That is, 'gallows bitches', gallows being slang for 'fine, excellent'.) Lucy Burbidge, 19, bonnet-maker: 'He got out of the carriage and said, "Girls, I shall be with you tonight and give you a treat." He went to the carriage again, and blowed a kiss to us. Lady Astley was in front and could not see.'

'With you tonight': that meant at Mrs Mary Richardson's well-known house in Goddett's-place, Leicester. Lucy said she went upstairs with Astley, 'he took liberties' and promised a present, but she never got it. Astley's friend Mostyn said, 'Several of us went occasionally to Mrs Richardson's. There were generally three or four girls.' Astley was upstairs with Lucy for a quarter of an hour, 'but I don't think he had any connection with her. I think we all went there only for the purpose of making them drunk and kicking up a row.'

Lord Chief Justice Best: 'It was rather an odd way of kicking up a row, for a gentleman to retire into a separate room with a female and keep her there a quarter of an hour.'

Mary Richardson herself said she had twice paid visits to Astley at Leicester's Bell Inn, where many Quorn men stayed. Lady Astley 'lodged a few doors off'. Girls from Great Yarmouth in Astley's home county gave evidence that he made propositions to them at the races there in the very month of the elopement. A brief exchange with one of them adds to our image of both men. Girl: 'He is a small gentleman.' Scarlett: 'Captain Garth is a small gentleman too.'

How could Scarlett cope with such evidence (and there was more) against the pure, devoted husband? Lawyers have fast footwork. He accused Garth of having had a reprehensible motive for bringing the evidence. Astley had begun separate proceedings for divorce in the Consistory Court, which came under the Bishop of London (until replaced by a civilian court in 1858). A single adulterous lapse by a wife was enough to cast her out *a mensâ et toro*, from table and bed. The husband was excused a *single* lapse. However, if proved not to have 'clean hands' he lost his divorce suit. Therefore the evidence about loose women was doubly a danger for Astley.

Scarlett said Garth had 'dived into brothels to rake up mere suspicion' against Astley. And he took a line that was sure to distress Georgiana. No doubt Garth had promised to marry her, Scarlett said, but his object in vilifying Astley was 'to prevent him obtaining a divorce'. 'He first robbed the husband of his wife and then endeavoured to fasten her about his neck for life... He seduced, deceived and then betrayed his victim.' His 'disgraceful defence' ought to 'increase rather than lessen the damages'. Scarlett hinted at Garth's royal background — 'moving in the first circles, and esteemed, as it was said, by many and powerful friends'.

Lord Chief Justice Best told the jury that Astley's divorce hopes were nothing to do with them. Then followed a classic statement of marital rights and duties:

> Let it not go forth to the world that profligacy on the part of a husband gives countenance to a wife's retaliation. It is the duty of the wife to overcome evil with good — to endeavour by all means in her power to correct the bad habits which her husband may have contracted. The infidelity of a wife produces consequences far more fatal to her family, to the children which she has borne, than any crime of that sort which the husband may commit. But where the husband ... conducts himself in a scandalous, open and debauched manner ... he has no right to ask for damages in a court of justice... He has thrown away the jewel which he possessed.

The jury decided that Astley, 'not having come into court with clean hands', merited only one shilling.[9] Thousands of words in next day's newspapers (seven wide-measure columns in *The Times*) were followed by further shaming of Astley. A radical publisher, John Fairburn, retailed it all in a slim volume, *Crim. Con. Extraordinary!*, prefaced by a large coloured caricature that played on the two men's enthusiasm for riding. Astley, wearing cuckold's horns, is mounted on the shoulders of two of his girls, and confronts Garth, similarly mounted on Georgiana (*plate 5*).

The case gave the publisher of Harriette Wilson's memoirs, John Joseph Stockdale, an opening to mock the hypocrisy of his betters.

Harriette had made her deal with him in 1825 at the age of 39. After a quarter-century of amorous activity, she had enticing memories of dukes (Argyll, Beaufort, Devonshire, etc), marquesses, earls and scores of lesser gentlemen. Stockdale issued weekly instalments, bringing crowds to his shop in a St James's arcade. One of his printers said sales reached 17,000 a week. Fear of what each instalment might bring caused consternation in great houses. And here was a source of extra earnings for Harriette and Stockdale: they kindly gave potential victims the opportunity to pay hush-money. One who famously refused is the Duke of Wellington. Stockdale wrote to him:

> In Harriette Wilson's Memoirs, which I am about to publish, are various anecdotes of your Grace which it would be most desirable to withhold...
> I have stopped the Press for the moment; but as the publication will take place next week, little delay can necessarily take place...
> > Your Grace's ever-attached Servant —

Wellington's reply, either to this sensitive example of the blackmailer's art or to a letter from Harriette herself, is always said to have been 'Publish and be damned.' According to Harriette's friend and rival, Julia Johnstone, Harriette asked him for £300 and he sent back her letter 'with "write and be damned" written in red ink on the back'. Whichever it was, Wellington was *not* saying 'I don't give a damn'. He threatened to sue Stockdale. This allowed Harriette to mock him in the memoirs — 'my own Wellington, who has sighed over me and groaned over me by the hour... Is it thus he would immortalize me?' He did not sue, perhaps because she writes of his adulterous ardours teasingly but not too scurrilously.[10]

Various characters did sue, evidently backed by greater men, and

Stockdale was heavily punished with damages and costs. In one case, Lord Chief Justice Best denounced the *Memoirs* in court as 'a threat to all that is good and noble and amiable in the country'. This phrase rankled with Stockdale. By the time of the Astley case he was publishing a weekly, *Stockdale's Budget* (advertised above his shop with 'my flaming board, OFFICE OF STOCKDALE'S BUDGET, in large letters of gold on a ground of dark blue'). He printed the liveliest detail of the Meltonian licentiousness in the *Budget*, then hit back at Best by recalling 'the picture of the Melton Hunt drawn by the infamous Harriette Wilson'. He commented, 'Here at least one portion of the Memoirs is verified upon the oath of the "good, and noble, and amiable of the country", between whom, and Lord Chief Justice Best and his learned brothers, I leave the dilemma.'

He could have made a further and riper riposte if he had learned, later that year, that George IV sent his prime fixer, Sir William Knighton, to Paris to offer Harriette £300 cash and a £100 pension to suppress embarrassing letters written by a 'young gentleman' of his court that somehow 'wounded' the king.[11] Knighton, by the way, was known as the Accoucheur, having entered George's service years before on the high recommendation of Wellington's brother, Marquess Wellesley, whose mistress had benefited by his gynaecological care.

One past lover of Harriette appears in the *Memoirs* only in a favourable light: the ambitious barrister and MP Henry Brougham. He had paid up. In 1824 Harriette wrote to him, 'Your flaming love letters etc would certainly add to the value of the book... I leave it to your generosity as to what you will contribute.' She pursued him further in 1827, when he had his eye on high office. He signed an agreement to pay her £40 a year for as long as he was 'in *no shape annoyed*' by anything she published.[12]

While Astley's divorce suit was pending, Georgiana applied for interim alimony to support her 'in a manner befitting her rank' as she was 'without pecuniary resources'. Rich though Astley was, the Dashwoods had enriched him further with a £5000 dowry. Her lawyers backed her alimony claim by presenting a statement of Astley's wealth, giving high, middle and low estimates for each item. Here is the list with only the *low* figures:

At Melton Constable, 'mansion house ... and a Park, Pleasure
    Grounds and about one hundred acres of land', which if let would

yield at least £1500 net. Elsewhere in Norfolk, 'Divers Manors,
Messuages, Farms, Houses, Woods, Arable, Meadow and Pasture
Ground' yielding at least £10,000.

Mansion of Seaton Delaval set in about 100 acres — if let, £800.

Rent from manors, farms, etc, in Northumberland, £16,000.

Rents from other properties, £1000.

Money in the stocks or out on loan yielding £1000 per annum.

Silverware, jewellery, household goods, furniture, linen, china,
farming stock, horses, carriages and wines at Melton Constable,
Seaton Delaval and elsewhere — £16,000.

'Other personal estate' — at least £8000.

'Capital house in Grosvenor-street and very valuable furniture' —
sold for £17,000.

Besides being well provided with mansions and whatever else a
gentleman needs for comfort and pleasure, the baronet therefore has
an annual revenue of at least £28,000 (by the high estimate it is
£38,000, in modern terms £1,500,000), plus what the £17,000 would
yield in interest. Georgiana was granted £800 for that year.

The divorce hearing in June 1828 brought out more evidence about
Astley's Meltonian merriments. He was stated to have 'retired into a
bedchamber' at Mrs Richardson's with others besides Lucy Burbidge.
At the Bell Inn, too, he was guilty of 'great and indecent familiarities'
with them. Mrs Richardson swore she was not 'loose and abandoned'
but 'in the millinery line'. Her husband was a gentleman who had 'run
through his fortune'. The evening of the race, Astley had come to her
house with two friends and sent her out to buy a bottle of port. 'On
my return I found my house quite in an uproar. The two girls were on
the floor and Sir Jacob and Captain Ross rolling upon them and
Captain Rich sitting on a table and laughing at them... I would not
have such goings-on in my house.' Ross gave one girl, Charlotte
Spawforth, 17, a pound 'for pulling you about'. Lucy 'went into
hysterics because she got nothing'.

The court heard next about the eloping lovers. After Georgiana's
midnight flight they drove through the night about forty miles to a
Hampshire hamlet, Murrell Green, and 'retired to bed' at the
Wellesley Arms. The account continues, using the language required
by the Bishop of London, 'During the morning of Tuesday and on the
nights of the said Tuesday Wednesday and Thursday following they
... constantly lay naked and alone together in one and the same bed ...

and there had the carnal use and knowledge of each other's bodies.' They travelled on to the Bear Inn, Reading, and went to bed about 11 pm. A chambermaid affirms that she 'did not again see either of them until between 2 & 3 o'clock in the afternoon'. Garth had a valet and the lady had a maid. The maid asked for some things to be washed 'for Lady Astley', and told the chambermaid to ask the valet for 'Captain Garth's things'. This the chambermaid 'thought odd'. Either Georgiana's maid was inept or the lovers felt devil-may-care.

Carnal use and knowledge continued there until the end of July, when the lovers went to Calais (noted for fine cuisine at modest prices) and stayed at Quilliacq's Hotel. They were traced. A summons from Astley was served on Georgiana. They returned, and it was served again at Batt's Hotel in Mayfair. The charge was that 'not having the fear of God before her eyes but being moved and instigated by the Devil' she did 'commit the foul crime of adultery'.

Garth next took Georgiana on a sentimental journey to the scene of his birth and boyhood, Weymouth. He wrote to Mrs Elizabeth Cass, landlady of the Crown Inn for thirty-two years, to book 'his old apartments on the first floor' (the inn survives). Mrs Cass said she knew Garth from his infancy 'when he came with a nurse and General Garth to the said hotel', and 'for many years afterwards as he grew up'. In George III's time the inn would have been packed in summer, but now the crowds were at George IV's Brighton, so the Crown was able to take Garth and Georgiana for three weeks.

Counsel for Astley argued that his visit to Mrs Richardson's was 'unpremeditated'. 'He had rushed out of a tavern with seven or eight others and had entered the house on hearing that one of their party had been ill-used there.' But the judge noted that Astley ended up with Lucy Burbidge, and 'could not have a more ample opportunity of committing an act of adultery than at a house of ill fame — alone for a quarter of an hour in a room with a common prostitute'. And it was not 'one frail moment': there were others. The legal clincher was, 'A man cannot complain of the breach of a contract which he has violated.' Divorce refused.[13]

Astley challenged Garth to a duel. It was nearly two years since his wife's elopement. His grievance was over Garth's having been so ungentlemanly as to bring evidence about his immoral ways. 'Noblemen and gentlemen of high rank', *The Times* reported, were asked to consider whether his challenge was justified. They ruled that in the divorce action Garth ought not to have used his witnesses, because of the consequences to Georgiana. Garth reluctantly answered the challenge. An early-morning 'meeting' was fixed. Friends of both men tried to abort the duel by having constables posted outside the two men's houses and at the appointed place (duels were unlawful). But at dawn on 14 June 1828 in Osterley Park, then beyond London's western fringe, the two small gentlemen faced each other with pistols. 'On the first fire Captain Garth received Sir Jacob's shot, but declined returning it... The friends of both parties were consulting on the necessity of Captain Garth's giving his pledge to return the hon. baronet's next fire when the police officers interposed... Captain Garth and his companion were seized and compelled to enter into sureties, while the other parties escaped.'[14]

As soon as Georgiana eloped she had become vulnerable. Unprincipled gentlemen would see her as fair game, if they could turn her against Garth. Not long after the elopement, a Weymouth acquaintance of his tried to seduce her. This became public when this man, Sir Robert Steele, was tried at Dorchester assizes for sending Garth an insulting letter challenging him to a duel.

The trial, six months after Astley's crim-con defeat, also revealed that Garth's first response to the £12,000 suit had been to offer Astley a choice. Garth warned him that he would counterattack with evidence of Astley's wenching; but Astley could avoid that danger if he were content to divorce Georgiana and to settle a large income on her. Steele knew of this because Garth, staying with Georgiana at the St James's Hotel, asked him to come up and advise him. According to Steele, he urged Garth to be moderate and require Astley only to hand over 'the fortune which Lady Astley had brought [her dowry of £5000], together with her jewels and other personal property'. But Garth demanded that Astley allow Georgiana £4000 a year 'or he would exhibit such a case against him as would reduce the damages to a farthing'. This demand proved more than Astley could stomach.

Steele's attempt on Georgiana was at Christmas 1826. Garth had gone to Dorset to consult General Garth. 'A few hours only' after he left, she swore, Steele spoke of him 'insultingly and contemptuously', tried 'to assume a familiarity with her' and made 'indelicate proposals'. According to Garth's solicitor, Steele said to him, 'A man is not always master of himself in the presence of a lovely and accomplished woman.' Steele even accused Georgiana of having 'induced him to make the advances'. This was 'utterly false', Georgiana riposted. In the middle of the night Steele had 'attempted to force his way into her bedchamber', even though her maid was in the room.

Steele pleaded that he wrote his challenging letter to Garth, after Astley's crim-con defeat, 'under feelings of great irritation' over his 'betrayal' of Lady Astley. Here is a little of what it said:

> Having betrayed her because you could not get your price for letting judgment go by default — having, by criminating her husband, made it impossible for you to make the only miserable reparation in your power ... you lie in your throat if you say that I ever took advantage... Although you are a traitor to your mistress, and an assassin of my good name, if you will come half way to meet me you shall have an opportunity to show that you are not incorrigibly a recreant knave.

Steele deepened his offence by circulating copies in the town clubroom and 'among Captain Garth's friends in Dorsetshire'. For this breach of the peace he was given a month in the county jail, fined £100 and required to put up sureties totalling £900. [15]

Garth's notoriety brought out further allusions to his mother. The *New London Rambler's Magazine* quoted a horticultural saying, 'Bastard slips never thrive', and cited some exceptions, such as Dorothy Jordan's ten children by Sophia's brother William: 'All the plants from the banks of the river *Jordan* have flourished amazingly.' And then: 'Little Garth, who is also a prime bastard slip, receives from his royal mother, the Princess S-----, three thousand, and my Lady Astley's fortune is two more, so that he may truly be called in a thriving way.' [16]

Those figures, and especially Lady Astley's, are doubtful guess-work. Garth was not in a thriving way. As a cavalry half-pay captain he got seven shillings and sixpence a day, or about £135 a year — a decent income for a humble person but a pittance for a Meltonian. Whatever he was receiving from Sophia or General Garth, his burden of debt, swelled by lawyers' bills and the cost of keeping Georgiana in style, was so heavy by 1827 that creditors at Melton Mowbray and in London threatened him with arrest.

11

A just title to rank and fortune

Tom Garth's debts led directly to the opening up of the truth about his origin. He sent a plea for help to Princess Sophia, but was told he must deal with Sir Herbert Taylor, the man who had tried in 1820 to remove him from 'scenes and habits of dissipation and extravagance'. Sir Herbert no doubt greeted the wayward captain with an air of justified asperity. Tom's account of what happened is set out in a Chancery affidavit he swore in 1829. Here is its opening, with some repetition deleted and a few non-lawyerly commas inserted. (An Orator is a Chancery petitioner. The affidavit takes care not to name Sophia.)

'Your Orator Thomas Garth of Melton Mowbray ... being in the month of June eighteen hundred and twenty-seven in great pecuniary embarrassment and harassed by the unceasing demands of creditors ... was induced ... to submit the distressing state of his affairs to the merciful consideration of one who, he was directed to believe, although at that time he had no proof of the fact, stood with respect to him in the very nearest degree of relationship and who had, as he was also directed to believe ... frequently expressed towards him the kindest feelings of parental affection.'

Meetings with Sir Herbert followed. Garth's knowledge that Sophia was his mother was enough to win from Sir Herbert an offer of £1200 a year for life — but subject to harsh conditions. Tom must sign a declaration that he had 'no claim to that bounty' and would never 'presume again to make any similar application' or have 'any communication by letter or otherwise with the quarter from which such bounty proceeded'. Sir Herbert pressed him to sign instantly, saying he had urgent business in Downing-street. Tom signed, Sir Herbert left — and Tom at once regretted signing. He was gagging himself. His affidavit says he saw 'the great impropriety and disgrace of thus in substance renouncing his birthright'.

He quotes a letter he immediately addressed to Sir Herbert: 'The haste and confusion which distracted our meeting a few minutes since, as you said from some imminent call on business to Downing

Street, has I find on a moment's reflection betrayed me into an error which I beg at once to recall. You desired me to read and sign a most important document ... without thought, without being enabled to have a copy of the paper or even to consider its purport or serious consequences... It pledges me to disclaim ever seeking the happiness of seeing or even communicating with a beloved and venerable parent. She never can desire a pledge so revolting and unnatural.' He signs himself as Sir Herbert's 'unhappy friend TG'. Sir Herbert was not a man to be turned by pity. His role was to keep trouble at bay — by silence if that would serve. Months passed. Tom communicated with his mother again. In January 1828 he wrote to Sir Herbert:

> I have abundant proof that I am not estimated in that Noble Heart in the light of a formal pensioner. I know from her own authority that her feelings towards me are affectionate and liberal in the extreme... I will give you any pledge that can be justly asked of a man of honor and feeling, but I would rather beg my bread than purchase any income on the humiliating conduct of renouncing the inalienable right and paramount blessing of communicating with the only person on earth (with one venerated but, I fear, not long existing exception) to whom I can look for protection, and from whom I have hitherto received my whole support... What would that Illustrious Individual think of me? She would inevitably despise me.

The venerated person is General Garth, in his 84th year and ailing. When Tom says Sophia has 'hitherto' supported him, that word is significant. By 1827 she was lavishing great sums on the rapacious John Conroy, comptroller and much more than that in the Kensington Palace ménage, so her aid to Tom is sure to have been cut back. (The astonishing Conroy story comes later.)

Still Sir Herbert kept silent. After ten days Tom wrote, 'My present suspense is a state of infinite distress. Let me hear from you at your earliest convenience.' They met, but Sir Herbert refused to give way. That proved a misjudgment. Tom informed General Garth. He approved the stand Tom was taking, and he did much more. He asked Tom to see him at his London house. Ailing, lying in bed, he asked a servant to bring Tom a parcel of letters, receipts, vouchers, memoranda and other papers. They were a revelation. The affidavit says they were 'the indisputable and only proofs of his birth and parentage and of his just title to rank and fortune', and they related to the claims that he 'had and still hath upon certain persons' named in them.[1]

Forty years of court life had taught the general how rights could be flouted. It may be that he told Tom how his fellow-equerries, Colonel Charles Fitzroy and Colonel Brent Spencer, were treated over their affairs with Princesses Amelia and Augusta. He also had a personal motive to empower Tom against Sir Herbert: Ernest was not contributing to Tom (*see page 139*) and Sophia was diverting her money elsewhere, so an unjust burden was laid on himself. A more telling point about his decision is that it confirms that Tom was not his son but, as he himself had said, his protégé (*p103*). As the general had performed the role of father since 1800, the documents' point could not be that they showed he *was* the father. Nor could it be that they named Sophia: Tom knew she was his mother. What they put on record was his true father: a secret to all but a few since August 1800.

Tom could now expect Sir Herbert to be more helpful, but past experience made him reluctant to negotiate face-to-face. He needed advice. He revealed some of the documents' contents to several men 'who have enjoyed the intimacy of Captain Garth at Melton Mowbray and elsewhere', as the *Morning Chronicle* later said;[2] or as Sir Herbert was to put it, 'divulged the contents to many individuals'. Someone advised Tom to employ an agent. The choice fell on Charles Molloy Westmacott (*plate 13*), editor of *The Age*, a Sunday paper noted for saucily scurrilous items about newsworthy sinners (those, that is, who refused to pay hush-money). Perhaps Tom was advised that a knowing operator would be the one to make a good deal.

The Age had another side, however, to which young Meltonians would not have given a thought. In politics it was ultra-Tory, and especially an advocate of forceful action against the Irish Catholics, who were then threatening rebellion. Thus Ernest the ultra-Protestant was its illustrious hero. Tom had made a flawed choice.

Knowledge of how Westmacott had got his hands on *The Age* would have made Tom wary. The story ranges round the theatres, newspapers, law courts and clubs of late-Georgian London, where men of rank collided or colluded with humbler but often cleverer mortals.

Westmacott, born about 1787, claimed to be the illegitimate half-brother of the eminent sculptor Richard Westmacott, maker of monuments and of the controversial nude Achilles statue erected in Hyde Park to honour the Duke of Wellington. Here is an account of 'the great captain of *The Age*' by a colleague of his, Dr William Maginn, scholar, poet, wit and unreliably bibulous journalist: 'He may, we believe, blazon a baton-sinister in his arms as securely as if he were Duke of Grafton, Richmond, Buccleuch or St Albans [*all descended from bastards of Charles II*]... If we do not much mistake his history, he is the son of the late facetious Dick Westmacott ... and the pretty widow of Kensington, Mrs Susannah Molloy, who kept the King's Arms ... some forty-odd years ago. Old Westmacott reared him as his son, sent him to St Paul's [School] ... passed him through the Royal Academy and educated him as an artist.'[3]

Maginn is promoting his friend as an Illustrious Literary Character in *Fraser's Magazine*. Note his slippery 'we believe' and 'if we do not much mistake'; but his account is not entirely fiction. St Paul's School records reveal no Westmacott but they do have 'Charles Molloy, 12', enrolled in May 1800 by his father, 'Richard Molloy, merchant, Lambeth Marsh' (alleged to have been in fact a master chimney-sweeper, an employer of 'climbing boys'). The school, then in St Paul's Churchyard, was humbler than nowadays. The boys, taught in one large room, were often sons of shopkeepers and tradesmen.

Young Molloy had some art training (*not* at the Academy) and worked in provincial theatres. In 1819, when the actor Robert Elliston took a lease on Drury Lane, the self-styled Westmacott applied for 'the situation of Modellist, Decorator and Propertys', claiming 'considerable experience in the Invention & Makeing Transformations for Pantomime, etc'.[4] According to Maginn, Westmacott could 'boast that he wrote a piece, painted the scenes and played a part in it'. 'Transformations for pantomime' were valued at the chief theatres, Drury Lane and Covent Garden, as much as at minor ones. Every night's drama was followed by a comic afterpiece. When Edmund Kean was starring in *Othello*, *Coriolanus* and *Richard III* at Drury Lane, the climax of the evening was 'the new comic pantomime called *Jack and the Beanstalk or Harlequin and the Ogre*'. At Covent Garden (not an opera house then), Shakespeare starring William Charles Macready was backed by 'the new grand pantomime, *Harlequin and Don Quixote*'.

Westmacott did work at Drury Lane, but soon turned to journalism. He was well placed in the convivial district where theatre people mixed with journalists all along the Strand and Fleet-street — the liveliest thoroughfare of London. They exchanged news and gossip in taverns such as the Coal Hole, noted (Westmacott wrote) for its 'truly merry company of actors, authors, reporters, clerks in public departments, and half-pay officers, full of whim, wit and eccentricity'.

In 1822 he launched a weekly, *The Gazette of Fashion*, 'a publication *tout à fait nouvelle*'. One topic was the villainy of gaming-houses, the 'fashionable hells' of St James's. He soon revealed a tough, combative side. He was charged at Bow-street with assaulting a Mr Woodroffe, 'a gentleman who has lately been somewhat conspicuous,' said *The Times*, 'as the prosecutor of several gaming-house proprietors'. Woodroffe alleged that Westmacott called him 'a liar, a scoundrel, a villain and a common informer' and struck him with his stick. Westmacott retorted that Woodroffe called him a common gambler, so he demanded his card, wanting to sue him for libel. He struck Woodroffe because he was 'a cowardly fellow who could insult me and yet had not the courage to give me his address'. Woodroffe said the gaming houses had tried to deter him with threats and bribes, and implied that Westmacott was in their camp: 'Am I to fight with every vagabondizing assassin employed by the gaming-house keepers, because, after having been robbed of £18,000, I have proceeded against them?' The case ends in mystery.[5]

Westmacott wrote a musical farce for Elliston, *Nettlewig Hall*, which did well enough to be reprinted, with a preface describing him as 'a round little man with a dumpling figure and physiognomy; smart and lively as his farce'. He issued a *Punster's Pocketbook*, and wrote a 'NOVEL EXTRAORDINARY!!! ... a romance of the present times', *Fitzalleyne of Berkeley*, inspired by scandals in the noble Berkeley family. He claimed friendship with Thomas Rowlandson, whose attic rooms were near Westmacott's lodgings in Adam-street, Adelphi. Westmacott's *Spirit of the Public Journals for 1824*, a selection of 'choice, witty and amusing articles', has eleven illustrations 'by the veteran Rowlandson, whose facetious pencil appears to acquire additional richness with his lengthened years' (he was nearly seventy).

A monthly magazine that Westmacott launched in 1824, *The English Spy*, carried in its two-year run seventy-two coloured plates of London life high and low for which it is still valued. Most are by Robert Cruikshank; but one by Rowlandson (June 1824) shows a dozen Royal Academicians 'reflecting on the True Line of Beauty at the Life Academy' (drawing a female nude). Noted RAs such as Thomas Lawrence are there. So too, though never an RA, is little Westmacott, squeezed in next to Benjamin Robert Haydon. *The English Spy* retailed scandals in the theatre, a scene of frequent fornication and drunkenness, and in society. Westmacott reveals in passing that he is very short. Telling of a hussar colonel's amours, he says, 'As he is full six feet high, *and we are not quite five*, prudence bids us place our finger on our lip.'

By now Westmacott had his eye on *The Age*. There was money in newspapers. London had fourteen morning and evening dailies and a dozen Sundays. A few lines from 'The Newsmonger's Song':

> Run, newsmen, run, the papers now are publishing.
> Crowds of boys besiege the printing-office doors.
> Such scuffling and shuffling, their places each establishing...
> 'Buy, gemmen, buy, Sunday papers — here's Examiner,
> Bell's Messenger, Dispatch, Observer, Sunday Times and News.'[6]

Although newspapers were heavily taxed to make them expensive for the lower orders, they were available at inns and taverns, and were even hired by the hour. *The Times*, with the highest daily sale, about 10,000, had perhaps 100,000 readers, and strong advertising revenue. Its editor, Thomas Barnes, was paid £1,000 a year. Many journalists, said *The Times* in 1825, could 'live as gentlemen'.

That was Westmacott's ambition. *The Age* had been launched in 1825 by a man he knew, 29-year-old Alfred Bunn, stage manager at Drury Lane. (His name lives on as the librettist of *The Bohemian Girl* and other operettas.) *The Age*'s society scandalmongering was Bunn's idea. It could be a dangerous game. Some verses hinting at wantonness between Lady Fitzroy Somerset, niece of the Duke of Wellington, and Lord Alvanley, a pillar of White's Club, the most exclusive of St James's, so outraged Alvanley that he burned a copy of the offending *Age* at White's. The next *Age* said saucily, 'Now really we cannot conceive how a little innocent sally of this kind could so agitate his lordship's nerves.' Soon after, *The Age* reported a break-in: 'Papers of very considerable importance have been STOLEN.' Someone was trying to discover the cad who was selling secrets.[7]

Enter Westmacott, making mischief for his own ends. In another weekly, *The Telescope*, he gave White's Club some clues:

> Come all ye ragged needy crew
> Who deal in dull detraction.
> *The Age*, a Sabbath paper new,
> Invites your pens to action.
> Great AFB, a counterfeit
> From Brummagem's the leader,
> And Birkilee, in am'rous fit,
> With cash the lib'ral feeder.[8]

AFB is Alfred Bunn. Birkilee is Colonel William Fitzhardinge Berkeley of the Guards and of Berkeley Castle, noted for serial seduction, especially of actresses. Berkeley was indeed Bunn's 'feeder': he installed Bunn's wife in Berkeley Castle and paid Bunn handsomely, thus ensuring that he could not sue for damages. Cruelly lampooned for his cuckoldom, Bunn challenged Westmacott to a duel. At dawn on 30 September 1825 they met with pistols in the greenfield neighbourhood of Chalk Farm. The diary of a Drury Lane stage manager, James Winston, records that the first shots went wide. And then —

> Mr Bunn's pistol missed fire and Mr Westmacott's ball passed clean through Mr Bunn's coat pocket, blowing away in its progress the whole of the editor's manuscripts intended for this week's paper, upon discovery of which Mr Westmacott declared himself fully satisfied.

The damage is exaggerated, for two days later *The Age* appeared much as usual. Bunn's wad of paper was probably only a bullet-absorber.[9]

Westmacott's deep scheme was to mire *The Age* in costly libel cases and acquire it at a bargain price. His confederate was a dandyish peer, the Earl of Glengall, with great estates in County Tipperary, who dabbled in journalism and the theatre. At White's, Glengall accused Lord William Pitt Lennox, youngest brother of the Duke of Richmond, of feeding scandal to *The Age*. Lennox swore he was innocent. He pursued Glengall to Cowes, Isle of Wight — a fashionable resort thanks to George IV, patron of the Royal Yacht Club — and challenged him to a duel (again bloodless). Glengall had an interest in the *Southampton Town & County Herald & Isle of Wight Gazette*. He hired Westmacott, who wrote a piece branding *The Age* as 'a filthy weekly print which is a disgrace to the *age* we live in ... a conspiracy of unprincipled slanderers', and Bunn as 'that cowardly, lying, cuckold bully who pretends to have a knowledge of good society'. *The Age* retorted with a satirical bill posted up round Southampton:

> ONE GUINEA REWARD: Absconded — Charles Molloy Westmacott, said to be editor of the *Southampton Herald*. Description: two feet three inches high, bandy legs, knock-knees, broad thumbs (made for mixing up plaster of Paris), splay feet and square toes. He served in the capacity of a cad [errand-boy], scene-shifter, colour-grinder, moulder, reporter, spy, common informer, eavesdropper, sweep and deliverer of messages on the Liverpool stage. Whoever will restore him to his disconsolate father, Charles Molloy, chimney-sweeper, Drury-court, Drury-lane, shall receive the above reward.

Those were merry days for lawyers. Bunn sued Westmacott over 'cowardly, lying, cuckold bully'. Westmacott's lawyer quipped in court that he knew nothing about Bunn 'except that he appears to be a *hot cross* one'. He got a shilling damages, inglorious compensation, though 'cuckold' was true enough.

Bunn slid away from *The Age*. A journalist named Richard Downing Richards took charge. Five-foot-minus Westmacott mocked Richards, a tall man, as 'long Reach-yards, the fool', and made him the target of a libel-writ confederacy. Richards said in *The Age* that 'a GALL'd nobleman' intimate with Westmacott had set up a fund for 'a series of vexatious actions' by 'profligates' whom the *Age* had castigated. Several of these profligates won heavy damages. Richards could not pay, owed other debts, and was sent to King's Bench Prison. Working under the prison's 'day rules', he kept the paper going — until one Saturday in May 1827. He got everything typeset for the morrow's issue and trudged back to the prison, but then his pages of type were seized by a creditor, probably egged on by Westmacott. [10]

In a final libel case Richards was fined £200 for having called Glengall 'the greatest liar in England … this blinking puppy … this dirty lord' who had been 'in continual converse with a rascally sweep by the name of Molloy'. Henry Brougham, defending Richards, said Westmacott was Richards's 'inveterate enemy'. Westmacott had contrived a deal by which he deviously won full control of *The Age*, while making Richards believe he would retain a half-share. Richards was left 'completely destitute in King's Bench Prison'. He had learned it was dangerous to be up against Westmacott. [11]

As soon as Sir Herbert Taylor learned what had come into Tom Garth's hands, he became ready to negotiate. In the spring of 1828 Westmacott, as Tom's agent, began visiting him at St Katharine's Lodge, a Georgian-gothic mansion he had built (a questionable royal perquisite) in Regent's Park. Ernest was apparently alerted, for he arrived from Berlin on 21 April and the next day visited Princess Sophia at Kensington Palace. He was in England until August.

General Garth, being concerned in Tom's future, named a barrister, Charles Frederick Williams, King's Counsel and a Bencher of Lincoln's Inn, to represent him. This man soon played a double role, as Tom was painfully to learn.

Sir Herbert scarcely needed to read the documents. When the Duke of York had arranged in 1800 for General Garth to be the infant's surrogate father, Sir Herbert was York's secretary. He told Westmacott that he must have the papers, 'to be destroyed'. On what terms? Tom's affidavit records that Sir Herbert, Westmacott and lawyers negotiated over seven months. The deal that Sir Herbert offered (of course with George IV's approval) went far beyond £1200 a year. Tom's debts, rising to £10,000 (in modern terms more than £400,000), would be paid off and he would be granted annuities worth £3000 a year for life. No ordinary royal by-blow could dream of such a grant. A son of George IV, for example, George Crole, was pensioned on £300. In salary terms, £3000 was the reward for such imposing persons as the Lord Chamberlain or such valuable ones as George IV's Privy Purse, private secretary, ever-active go-between and keeper of secrets, Sir William Knighton. To produce £3000 a year required a capital fund, invested in 'the 3 per cents', of £100,000. This, plus the £10,000 to pay debts, made the price put on the destruction of Tom's documents nearly £4,500,000 in modern terms.

Now one can see why, when the outraged Sir Jacob Astley challenged Tom to a duel in 1828 just as a negotiation promising such riches was progressing, he tried to avoid the challenge. It was not a time to be unluckily shot.

Westmacott proposed his friend Glengall as a trustee for Tom. Legal papers to seal the deal had to be prepared. Meanwhile, Sir Herbert said, the documents must be deposited at a bank. On 24 November 1828 he achieved this first step toward attaining his desire. Tom brought the documents in a black tin box to Westmacott's house, 15 Adam-street, Adelphi, just off the Strand. Lieutenant-General Sir Herbert Taylor, Knight Commander of the Bath, Knight of the Royal Hanoverian Guelphic Order (motto, *Difficulties do not dismay us*), colonel of the 85th Foot, adjutant-general of the British Army and principal aide-de-camp to George IV, arrived for what he no doubt hoped was his last encounter with the journalist of dubious reputation and with the far-too-royal half-pay captain. Tom showed the papers, locked them in the box and kept the key. Westmacott bound the box round with red tape, and he and Sir Herbert affixed their seals.[12]

As Sir Herbert departed westwards, probably for his Horse Guards office, two short men, rotund Westmacott and the more elegant captain, walked the other way along the Strand, past the offices of journals that would have loved to know their errand — *Courier, Globe,*

Bell's Life in London, *Observer*, *Morning Chronicle*, to name a few — and past *The Age* as well, to deposit the box with Westmacott's bankers, Paul, Snow & Co, at 217 Strand, next-door to Twining's the noted tea merchants. Perhaps it seemed reassuring to Tom that the bank's head, the baronet Sir John Dean Paul, was a noted Meltonian. Tom waited outside. He got no receipt for his box. Westmacott said he was given one as Tom's agent and another for Sir Herbert.

Having missed several weeks of the hunting season, and now living in hopes of riches, Tom posted to Melton Mowbray. *The Sporting Magazine* reported that Melton was 'more than usually gay', enlivened with 'many ladies of fashion'. Soon, however, the gaiety was blighted for Tom. He was somehow alerted to the fact that the game being played was not Garth and Westmacott versus Sir Herbert, but Sir Herbert and Westmacott v Garth. The long negotiation had given Westmacott opportunity enough to reach a rewarding private understanding.

Tom dismissed Westmacott as his agent and went to his solicitor. They set to work on the Chancery affidavit, which is the source of much of the preceding detail. It ends by saying that Sir Herbert's financial promises were 'mere delusion', contrived to gain possession of the documents 'without any real intention of ultimately carrying any agreement into effect'. The object of 'Your Orator Thomas Garth' is to obtain a Chancery injunction to stop Sir Herbert, Westmacott 'and the rest of their confederates' from going to the bank and appropriating the documents.

Sir Herbert's offer of great sums to acquire and *destroy* the documents has shown that they held a dangerous royal secret. When the affidavit became public, Sir Herbert and Ernest worked hard to repel the questions it aroused. Their efforts only made it clearer that Ernest was at the heart of the secret.

12

Ernest's tangled web

By a pure chance of timing, a quite different matter of great concern to Ernest had also come to a head during 1828. The two ran in parallel.

Ireland was in crisis. By 1828 the campaign by Daniel O'Connell's Catholic Association for emancipation — the repeal of laws that made millions of Catholics second-class subjects — was growing ever more powerful. In July, O'Connell dramatically raised the stakes by standing in a by-election in County Clare. He could not *sit* in the London parliament (all Ireland, 6,400,000 Catholics and 1,500,000 others, had only Protestant MPs), but he was not barred from standing. Catholic voters marched to the poll with a great display of green flags and shamrock devices. O'Connell won overwhelmingly.

The prime minister, the Duke of Wellington, a son of the Protestant Ascendancy in Ireland, had always voted against emancipation, like most Tories, whenever the Whigs proposed it. Now he saw he must make concessions or else hold Ireland by force (meaning civil war). Among O'Connell's followers, he knew, were thousands of ex-soldiers: men he had been glad to enlist against Napoleon.

He risked splitting the Tory party, but his first obstacle was George IV. Constitutionally, Wellington could have drawn up proposals for parliament and laid them before the king, but as a concession he undertook to seek the king's consent first. In a long letter he asked him to accept 'coolly and dispassionately' that emancipation was a state necessity: 'We have a rebellion impending over us in Ireland.' As prince of Wales long ago, consorting with the Whigs (and on and off with Maria Fitzherbert, his secret Catholic wife), George had been for emancipation. In 1797 he sent a memorandum to Pitt urging him to repeal 'every *exclusive restriction* and *disqualification* on the *Irish Roman Catholics*'. But in 1811 he had deserted the Whigs, and now his inventive memory allowed him to think he had always taken the line of his 'revered father'. Would he be as intractable as George III was in 1801?

Ernest, the royal champion of the No Popery ultras or Bruns-wickers, was in close touch with them, though based in Berlin. The

Irish crisis gave him a public reason to come to London in 1828, just when Westmacott was privately negotiating with Sir Herbert Taylor over Garth. At Windsor, Ernest worked to agitate George IV with the notions that had overset George III: that emancipation would endanger the constitution and the English state church. Ernest's policy for Ireland was simple: put O'Connell down by force. He rallied ultra peers and MPs, established Brunswick clubs, was made Imperial Grand Master of the Orange lodges in Britain, Ireland and beyond, and promoted Orange recruitment. Orangemen, bound by secret oaths, signs and passwords, were united in devotion to 'King William III of pious and immortal memory' who had saved Britain from 'popery and arbitrary power'.

That Westmacott's *Age* was fiercely Orange was of course well known to Ernest. It very likely had Orange subsidies. It hailed the progress of his lodges and clubs, and said, 'The contest will be whether the king or a junto of priests is to govern the empire' — exactly Ernest's view. Here is Westmacott's declaration of principle: 'We are Tory of the Tories. No Popery, NO SURRENDER are our watchwords. Avaunt, rogues, swindlers, idiots, buffoons, who wish to trick us or rob us of the constitution of the country.'[1]

Ernest must have been happy that Garth had chanced to make this man his negotiator with Sir Herbert. Before he returned to Berlin that August, he could feel optimistic on both fronts. He boasted to his friend Princess Lieven, the Russian ambassador's wife, that he could beat O'Connell and his association.

Wellington had to spend months overcoming the resistance of the agitated king, who was frequently suffused with strong drink and heavy doses of laudanum. He would dodge the issue by talking for hours, chiefly in praise of himself, his wisdom, his probity, and sometimes of his imagined glories as a general or as a jockey. Wellington's tactic with the deviously rambling king was, 'I let him talk himself out, and then quietly put before him the matter in question so that he cannot escape from it.' The king would rant away afterwards, saying, 'Damn this King Arthur, he is king over me as well as over everyone else. Whether he'll send me to Hanover I don't know, but I am sure he'll go to hell.'[2]

Ernest wrote frequently from Berlin to the king's private secretary, Sir William Knighton. His anxiety is sometimes touching: 'Often & often do I feel myself as it were in a wilderness... Sooner or later it must come to a crash.' He is ready for a fight: 'God knows I am no political coward & have still pretty strong nerves.' He will never believe that Wellington will propose 'anything like *emancipation*'. And so said *The Age*: Wellington had no thought of 'betraying the constitution', and O'Connell must be suppressed 'with a strong hand'.[3] By January 1829, however, the ultras saw alarming signs that Wellington did have emancipation in mind. Ernest was wanted.

Just at this time, reports linking Ernest and Tom Garth 'floated through all the clubhouses', as *The Observer* put it. The friends to whom Garth had revealed part of his story had not all been able to keep silent. On 23 January, weeks before Garth's Chancery affidavit revealed Sir Herbert's proposals and other facts, Lady Cowper (later Lady Palmerston) wrote to Lady Holland, the noted Whig hostess, 'I suppose you have heard the story of Captain Garth & the Duke of Cumberland. I hope it may keep him abroad or at least destroy some of his influence here. It is a horrid story & one feels sorry it should come out except from the good result it may have in keeping him away.' Four days later she wrote ('but pray don't quote me'), 'It appears that Captn Garth is his son as well as P^{ss} Sophia's & he has been paying him 3000 a year. Garth who is a great vaut-rien wanted 6000 instead of 3, & to force the Duke to give it him, put his letters & papers into the hands of an attorney.'[4] Her informant had heard about '3000 a year' but was far out in thinking Ernest was paying anything.

The thought that Ernest might be deterred, though regrettably by a horrid scandal, was passed on by Lord Holland to the Marquess of Anglesey: 'Such things are always disgusting, painful and detestable — yet if Ernest is damaged, still more if he is frightened and kept away, can flesh and blood resist some comfort?'[5] Anglesey was in fact in need of some comfort. Wellington had just dismissed him as lord-lieutenant in Ireland as a concession to the king, who saw him as too favourable to the Catholic cause.

Earl Grey, the Whigs' leader, tried to tease something about Ernest out of Princess Lieven, his 'ever dearest princess' to whom he wrote letters scented with musk. In her pursuit of influence, this clever woman welcomed both Whigs and Tories to her mansion in Harley-street (she was Ernest's *très chère amie*, he her *très dévoué & sincère ami*). Grey said he had heard (probably from Holland) of 'some exposure ... which will prevent his coming to England'. Her reply (translated here from French) ends with some notably evasive words: 'I have heard talk of a horrible affair involving the Duke of C———. It concerns his sister ——— & they say a certain Garth is minded to publish proofs... Not having seen them, and speaking peremptorily, I judge this to be an infamous calumny, because I never believe horrible, revolting things (*horreurs révoltants*).'[6]

When Wellington had explained what emancipation entailed, the king exclaimed, 'Damn it, do you mean to let them into parliament?' Wellington knew that if Ernest came over he could overset the king. Yet whatever Wellington had heard of the scandalous reports, he could not make use of them. He wrote a statesmanlike appeal to Ernest, saying a royal duke should never be 'a leader of one violent party', and especially not if he might become king. 'Events which are in the hands of Providence ... misfortunes which in the course of nature may befall this country, could bring Your Royal Highness into a most elevated situation.' He was saying what Ernest well knew: George IV was declining. After him, only William and the child Victoria stood between Ernest and the throne. If he came to that elevated situation, it would be 'a great disadvantage ... to be considered the leader of a party in the state, rather than the impartial arbiter of its destinies'. On 2 February 1829 Wellington dispatched Sir William Knighton, incognito as *Monsieur Le Blanc, courier de Cabinet*, with this letter. But Ernest was packing for England. Unaware that Knighton was Berlin-bound, he dispatched a letter asking him to 'order *good fires* in my rooms'. He also expressed anxiety about the king: 'Alas if he continues this damnable practice of laudanum he must not only in the end kill himself, but previous to that palsy himself.'[7] A palsied king might be difficult to stir into anti-emancipation fervour.

The King's Speech to parliament on 5 February announced that Wellington was bringing in a bill to remove 'civil disabilities on His Majesty's Roman Catholic subjects'. A precondition was the dissolving of O'Connell's association. *The Times* said 'desperadoes or idiots' among the ultras talked of forcing Wellington out. 'A messenger may be sent to Berlin, and a steamer come back freighted with a certain pair of mustachios, and a Hussar-Government may be found ... but how long would it endure?' *The Times* hinted that it held damaging information: 'Does that personage suppose, if the public knew what it may yet know, that his influence could endure for even a single day?'

Ernest was on his way (in bitter weather — the contents of Berlin chamberpots froze), eager to fight as 'leader of one violent party'. He did not encounter *Monsieur Le Blanc*, as they took different roads. He crossed by steam-packet to Dover on 14 February. That morning *The Times* (far and away the leading newspaper) asked whether George IV, now pledged to the bill, could allow Ernest to incite its opponents. *The Times* added a sly second hint of private knowledge: 'The visit of the duke may only be on private affairs. The health of his sister the Princess Sophia is said to have become more unsettled lately. It may be to comfort and support her that he is undertaking the journey.'

Sophia's health was indeed unsettled. Just at the time when Ernest was setting off for London, the appointment notebook of her physician, Sir Henry Halford, shows that she summoned him to attend her on 3, 4, 5, 9 and 12 February.[8]

When Ernest was on the road from Dover in his carriage, London-bound, Thomas Creevey, the Whig politician and memoirist, was sitting in Brooks's, the famed St James's club, writing to his constant correspondent, his stepdaughter Elizabeth:

> Brooks's, February 14 ... Your paper does not deal with this distinguished prince [Ernest] as many of the others are doing. Are you aware that Cap[t] Garth is the son of this duke by Princess Sophia? It is as true as your name is Elizabeth, accompanied with circumstances on his part that in a court of justice would hang any man. Gen Garth, at the suit of the old king, consented to pass for the father of this son. The latter, in every way worthy of his villainous father, has shown all the letters upon this occasion, including one of the king's. The poor woman has always said that this business would be her death & it is said she is dying of it.

To enhance the value of the letters, Creevey says, Garth 'shows the worst part of them'. Creevey's informant at Brooks's, Lord Kensington, 'knows all the contents'.[9] For Kensington's source one need seek no further than his sons William and George Edwardes, Meltonians of about Garth's age (George also a member of Brooks's), who lived at Edmundthorpe Manor near Melton Mowbray.

Early next morning Ernest sped out to Windsor to renew his exhorting of the king. That evening Wellington invited him to dinner to put all the points he had made in his aborted letter. They talked for hours, and again next day. Ernest promised 'to keep himself quiet' and not plot against the king's ministers.[10] He instantly did the opposite. And the king duplicitously allowed him to haunt Windsor and inflame him with the very notions that had overset George III in 1801.

Ernest declared in the Lords that the question was whether England was to be Protestant or Roman Catholic. 'The very moment we admit one Roman Catholic into this house or into the other house of parliament, I maintain that this becomes not a Protestant parliament.' He told his wife he was 'the only one of the Royal Family except the King ... faithful to the holy cause', and must stay on. 'If I quit, all is finished... Adored angel of my heart, you know your Ernest.'[11]

Wellington persuaded the agitated and often weeping king to write a letter to Ernest asking him 'to make a great sacrifice for me' and go back to Germany — but then the king would not send it. 'The Duke of Cumberland has worked him into a state of frenzy,' Charles Greville, secretary to the Privy Council, wrote in his journal. (Halford was being summoned to Windsor daily, sometimes even twice daily.) Greville summed up the king: 'Narrowmindedness, selfishness, truckling, blustering and duplicity, with no object but self and his own ease and the gratification of his own fancies and prejudices.'[12]

At last Wellington forced a showdown by resigning. Let Ernest see if he could contrive an ultra government. The old warrior calculated that though the ultra peers, plus many Anglican bishops, were a danger in the Lords, the ultras were too weak in the Commons. The diary of one of his ministers, the 2nd Lord Ellenborough, tells what happened next:

March 1: The reports are that the king is ill, if not mad. In fact, the excitement in which he is may lead to insanity, and nothing but the removal of the Duke of Cumberland from his presence will restore him to peace.

March 3 (*Wellington gives the king his ultimatum*): The king ... spoke of abdicating, and said he should retire to Hanover with his present income.

March 4 (*Wellington, Lord Chancellor Lyndhurst, Robert Peel*): The king talked for six hours. The duke [Wellington] says he never witnessed a more painful scene. He was so evidently insane. He had taken some brandy and water ... and sent for some more, which he continued to drink... During six hours, they did not speak fifteen minutes. The king objected to every part of the bill... It is impossible not to feel the most perfect contempt...[13]

Wellington's great love Harriet Arbuthnot wrote in her diary, 'To have his heels tripped up by such a wretch as the D of Cumberland ... and the *king's conscience*, too, to be made the bugbear! when everybody knows he has no more conscience than the chair he sits in.'[14]

Next day Wellington called a cabinet. Ellenborough assumed it was 'to announce the king's insanity'. No: Ernest's attempt had failed. The king had to recall Wellington. He wrote, 'My feelings of distress in consequence are such, as I scarcely know, how to support myself under them. *1/4 past 7 from my Bed.'* Ernest still went on browbeating him, until he said, 'My dear Ernest, do not talk to me any more about it.'[15]

At last the bill could be published. It is summarized by Daniel O'Connell in a letter to his wife: 'Whoever thought we could get such a bill from Peel and Wellington? Catholics can be judges, mayors, sheriffs, aldermen, common counselmen, peers of parliament, members of parliament, everything, in short, everything... I tread on air.'[16] In fact Catholics would still suffer many disabilities affecting marriage, bequests, worship and so forth; besides having to pay all their tithes to the Anglican church, which in Ireland had three archbishops and twenty-two bishops with the easeful task of governing 2000 clergy. When the Tories were opposing reform of this tithing injustice a few years later, the satirical *Figaro in London* made Robert Peel sing a parody of the Cockney song 'All Around My Hat':

> Old Mother Church vas a rich-un and a good-un,
> And Old Mother Church had a goodly store of pelf...
> There's thousands of clergymen, their wives, sons and darters,
> There's dozens of the bishops, and fat old rectors too,
> Would be starving in the streets or a harning of their livings,
> And arn't that a hard thing for a gentleman to do![17]

When emancipation was debated during March 1829, the Lords were the ultras' last hope. They organized gangs at the door to intimidate peers. 'The word is given to cheer or hiss,' Ellenborough says. 'It is a Cumberland trick, but others in the opposite faction are sent down, and he got some hisses today.' Ernest had a scheme to get 'a mob of 20,000 men to go down to Windsor & petition the king & frighten him', says Harriet Arbuthnot's journal. Wellington told her that if he tried this, he would send him to the Tower: 'One can never be safe with such an intriguing villain.'[18]

While Ernest was intriguing at Windsor and skirmishing in the Lords, the Garth question came to a head. The ultra *Age* accused 'that abominable journal' *The Times* of printing 'insinuations at once dark, horrible and revolting'. *The Times* replied with stronger insinuations. Just after Wellington had outfaced the ultra bid for power, it spoke of fears about the 'mischief' Ernest might still do: 'It is true, he might be checked by disclosures; but then what a scene for the British nation! — for any Christian nation! ...The bankers, respectable bankers, dare not surrender the Œdipodean box; and if they do, there is another Œdipus in the next-best legal evidence. What a heap, too, of living as well as documentary testimony!'

This was still a week before Garth's affidavit became public but *The Times* had advance information and was firing warning shots. 'Another Œdipus' seems to imply another case of incest. *The Times* deplored the fact that Sir Herbert Taylor, 'hitherto of untainted character, and now with a religious office attached to his name' (one of his perquisites), was involved with Westmacott. 'O Secula! what an AGE! Is it not shocking that honourable men should be tainted by their unavoidable intercourse with the person alluded to?'[19]

Another ultra paper, *The Standard*, accused 'the Whigs and Papists, and Whig and Popish newspapers' of libelling Ernest to hunt him out of the kingdom. It ventured to declare that Ernest 'on the day of his landing in England did not, we have reason to believe, know that such a person as Captain Garth had ever existed. Everything connected with that person's story, as affecting the Duke of Cumberland, IS FALSE AS HELL... Let the villains who threaten do their worst; they can offer to the Duke of Cumberland no favour which he would prize so highly as to go with them before twelve Englishmen as sound-hearted, as fearless, as honest and as manly as himself.'[20]

Then the *Morning Chronicle* published, under the heading THE MYSTERIOUS AFFAIR, extracts from Garth's affidavit giving its essence. *The Times*, catching up next day over many columns, said it had held back to avoid causing 'general disgust by sad disclosures'. It added in a gesture to Sophia, although she was not named, 'Our pity is most unfeignedly bestowed where pity is due.' It summed up the story like this: 'Sir Herbert Taylor had agreed — as the agent, no doubt, of some more important person — TO PAY GARTH'S DEBTS *and settle on him an annuity for life of* THREE THOUSAND POUNDS a year, as a recompense for the mysterious contents of a certain box.' Garth's object, 'originating in a suspicion of his quondam friend Westmacott's faith, is to prevent him from going with Sir Herbert to the banker's and claiming the box before the stipulated price has been paid'.

The Times let it be known that it had private information about General Garth's role as surrogate father. In reply to a letter signed 'G' defending Ernest, it challenged G 'to *prove* what he asserts in behalf of the accused', and it asked whether he knew of a letter written by the Duke of York to his mistress — that is, to Mary Anne Clarke. As commander-in-chief, York had made the Garth arrangement in 1800, and he told Mary Anne many royal secrets. *The Times* said, 'If G knows nothing of that letter, we do.' Nothing more was heard of G.[21]

The sums agreed by Sir Herbert showed the public that a great secret was at stake. For one man at least they also caused resentment. The painter Benjamin Robert Haydon, a troubled supplicant for royal patronage for his ambitious pictures, wrote in his diary, 'The Duke of ――――――――is getting exposed about this child of his by the Princess Sophia... When I consider the sincere purity of my own views, and have the duke say he cannot afford to *devote* public money to art, while thousands are devoted to stop a royal bastard's mouth!'[22]

Another telling remark occurs in the diary of a highly-placed man, Sir George Seymour, a cousin of Lord Hertford and formerly secretary to Lord Castlereagh. Serving at the Berlin embassy from early 1828, he frequently played billiards with Ernest (beating him), dined with him and his duchess, played whist with them and sat up late exchanging ghost stories. On 21 March he noted, 'The English papers are full of allusions to Capt[n] Garth, who it appears is miscreant enough to demand a large annuity for the suppression of some proves [*sic*] of his double connexion with the House of Brunswic.'[23]

Sir Herbert worked to counter talk of incest. He made use of a cabinet minister, Earl Bathurst, a friend of Ernest since the early 1800s, to spread the word that General Garth 'certainly is the father'. Bathurst said so, for example, to Charles Greville (his former private secretary) — who commented in his journal, 'which I believe he certainly is not'.

If the begetter of Sophia's child was an equerry who was not disgraced but promoted, what need could arise to destroy Tom Garth's documents at enormous cost? To cope with that difficulty, Sir Herbert went so far, privately, as to make Ernest guilty of something only *verging* on incest. Thomas Creevey heard a hint of this as early as 16 February. A story was 'afloat' that 'the scandalous matter affecting the duke [Ernest] arises out of letters from the Princess Sophia to General Garth stating the conduct of the duke and her horror of him'. Bathurst went further. He told Greville that according to Sir Herbert, Sophia's letters said Ernest had 'made attempts upon her person'. In his journal

Greville follows this with, 'It is notorious that the Old Queen forbade the Duke's access to the apartments of the Princesses.' One is reminded of what Princess Amelia wrote in 1806 (*page 47*) about avoiding being alone in her room with Ernest.

Court ladies were active in declaring the general to be the father. The Marchioness of Bath told Greville that her sister-in-law, Lady Caroline Thynne, 'had no doubt that Genl Garth was the father, for the princess was so violently in love with him that everybody saw it. She could not contain herself in his presence.' The Bath family, the Thynnes, had long enjoyed royal favour and salaries. Lady Caroline's mother, the previous marchioness, had served Queen Charlotte for fifty-seven years. In 1829, Lady John Thynne was a bedchamber lady to Sophia and another Thynne served Princess Mary (as did a Bathurst daughter). Court ladies could not thrive without some skill in dissembling, and Lady Caroline made Greville feel 'disposed' to accept her assertion. Although the general 'was a hideous old devil', he reasoned, the princesses were 'ready to fall into the hands of the first man whom circumstances enabled to get at them'. This last thought might however also apply to Ernest.

Greville's journal continues, 'As to the D of Cum^d, everything about him is mysterious, but there must be some cause for the universal and deep execration in which he is held, especially by his own family... Lord Bathurst told me that the only time he ever nearly quarrelled with the Duke of York was about Lady Bathurst's visiting the D^{ss} of Cumb^d... He [York] said, speaking of the duke, "If you knew—" and then stopped.'[24]

Sir Herbert's intimation about 'attempts' put him in a new difficulty. If the general *were* the father, Sophia had no imaginable reason to write (either to him or to her brother, York) about attempts by Ernest. Her only motive for doing so could be that when the general was being made the ostensible father, she palliated the guilt of having yielded to Ernest by telling of his having begun with attempts.

As for 'horror' of Ernest, that was certainly not seen at Weymouth in 1800, and they remained on sociable terms. When Ernest was in Berlin, they corresponded. A letter of 1827 from Sophia, being a rare survivor, is worth quoting. It is clearly one of a series. First she felicitates him over a successful cataract operation on his remaining eye. Then she refers to mementoes she had sent him of the Duke of York (an ultra like Ernest), who had recently died of dropsy.

Your kind letter my dearest Ernest gave me the greatest possible comfort, as it was a more decisive proof of the improvement in your health, & also of your sight! God be praised *all* has succeeded so well! I am very much gratified at your appearing so satisfied with the *offerings* I sent you as having belonged to & constantly used by our dear Frederick; & herewith I forward by your desire the *Pamphlet,* which is I believe a perfect copy of that written by Sir H^t Taylor.

She turns to 'the *Monstrous changes* in the Political World', meaning the formation of a government under George Canning — *monstrous* because it included pro-emancipation Whigs. She too shares Ernest's ultra-Protestant views.

She has had 'a violent cold' for three weeks. 'It fell in my eyes and disabled me from writing or reading, & confined me to the house. I am now better, but still a prisoner, & shall I hope mount my *Nag* the moment the weather is a little warmer.' Her next news is that their sister Charlotte, Queen of Württemberg, though enormously fat and in decline, is undertaking a journey to England after thirty years' absence. Sophia says, 'I am sure you are greatly surprized at the visit we are to have from Old Royal!'

Sophia closes with this: 'I hope dearest Ernest that your dear Boy is well & that he continues as < *illegible* > as he was to his father. I dare not write more today as my eyes are still so weak, but I was resolved you s^d hear from me by return of post; & believe me Ever —

Your Affec^{ly} attached Sister   Sophy' [25]

One of the first persons Ernest visited when he arrived in London in April 1828, and again in February 1829, was Sophia.

The dust-laden parchment pages of Tom Garth's affidavit in the Public Record Office are the primary source for the account in the previous chapter of his dealings with Sir Herbert and the deposit of the sealed box. And they reveal much more. Many details did not reach the newspapers and are now published for the first time.

Garth entered letters which, though unflattering to him, served to show how Sir Herbert and Charles Frederick Williams KC went to work. When the terms were being negotiated, Williams visited the general in Dorset, who then sent Garth a letter, 'actually composed [Garth says] by the said Charles Frederick Williams': 'My Dear Tom, I do not wish to remind you of the pain and anxiety you have often occasioned me, but I am encouraged in the hope that although I might suffer from your imprudence you would never embitter the remnant of my life by your committing or contemplating an act of frightful dishonor that would consign me to a premature grave.

'I learn that your pecuniary embarrassments distress and overwhelm you and that your personal liberty is endangered and that ... you have been led to reject an offer made to you through the mediation of our best of friends Counsellor Williams which was at once honorable and fair. You are making the papers a pretext for conduct which affects me in proportion as it dishonors you. Those papers were confided to you in a moment when my life seemed at its close, with a solemn and I supposed at the time a deathbed injunction that you would never descend to make a bad use of them.'

Was it 'a bad use' to assert his claims? Tom Garth responded by making a point about Ernest. The general had told him how little money had been contributed since August 1800 by a person *not* Princess Sophia. Garth wrote to Williams:

> You may easily conceive that a prison is not an enviable residence, but I candidly tell you I would sooner submit to incarceration than surrender those documents which ought to have given me a claim to affection, protection and tenderness, and not the treatment that I have hitherto experienced. I am in possession, as you well know, of the amount of the pitiful assistance General Garth received through the hands of *<here is a run of dots long enough for 'the Duke of Cumberland'>*, upon which act of liberality I shall decline making any observation, considering that it was the sum-total received from August 1800 up to the present hour.
>
> In conclusion I beg once more to repeat that the correspondence of *<a string of dots probably concealing Sophia's name>* as well as all the other documents relating to my birth were committed to my charge by General Garth unasked-for.

Sir Herbert had spread a story that Garth obtained the documents 'surreptitiously'. Garth quotes a letter from the general condemning this as 'slanderous'. Other falsehoods 'have been industriously circulated'. One is that he threatened to publish the documents. Here he hits at Westmacott. 'The editor of a weekly publication remarkable only for its calumnious charges, with whom your Orator unfortunately was at that time on terms of intimacy which he has ever since regretted', urged him to publish, but he refused.

The affidavit shows him finding he cannot trust anyone. When he broke with Westmacott before Christmas 1828 he also broke with his 'alleged friend' Williams, who 'then acted as the adviser and agent' of

Sir Herbert. The affidavit also shows that as soon as Sir Herbert had the box safe in the bank he began to retreat from his promises. Garth quotes a letter Sir Herbert wrote to the general, 31 December 1828, complaining that Garth had not broken up his extravagant Quorn establishment and that the general had failed to persuade him to seek 'professional advancement': 'I am anxious to be able to report at W—— [to George IV at Windsor] what has been the final result of my appeal to you... You must excuse my asking whether Captain Garth's military services, or whether his recent proceedings with respect to the letters and documents affecting the honor and the peace of the Royal Family which have been so indiscreetly dealt with by him, have established any claim to consideration.'

Sir Herbert refers to his efforts in 1820 to have Garth posted far away. He denies having had any thought of posting him to the West Indies 'in order to get rid of him': 'The regiment in which he obtained a company was the 37th, then in Canada, considered one of our most healthy stations... I urged you to allow him to join that corps and represented the advantage he would derive from being required to give his attention to military duties ... and from being removed from scenes and habits of dissipation and extravagance to which you had lamented he was exposed here. You admitted the justice of my observation but said you could not bring yourself to part with him or call upon him to make the sacrifice.'[26]

When Garth refused service with the 37th, he did have reason to fear a West Indies posting that might 'get rid of him'. The 37th had served there (one of many regiments used to suppress uprisings of slaves) and was soon posted there again — both times losing hundreds of men to yellow fever, malaria and smallpox.

The newspaper war grew fiercer. Ernest's advocates, *The Age*, *Standard* and *Morning Journal*, furiously asserted his innocence. Their line was that the Garth affair was opened up only to calumniate Ernest for political reasons. The sequence of events refutes this. Yet upholders of Ernest have ever since uncritically or cynically taken this line.

The Standard was founded in 1827 with £15,000 put up by the ultras. They further subsidized its editor, Stanley Lees Giffard, by paying him to insert their anti-Catholic, pro-Ernest articles. This is shown in a letter from a leading ultra, the Duke of Newcastle. Sending an article, he asks how much he owes 'for this & former publications'.[27] The

Standard's assertion that Ernest had not known that Garth existed was inept, as Garth had appeared in the *Army List* since 1822 as an officer of Ernest's 15th Dragoons.

Ernest quickly set the *Morning Journal* in a different direction. It opened a column-long attack by ranting about 'the malevolent insinuations of the two leading ministerial journals, the *Morning Chronicle* and *The Times*, which have been so fiendishly directed against an illustrious duke'. It called Garth 'a person whose exploits upon town, and with the wife of Sir Jacob Astley whom he seduced, have yielded a vast fund of materials for the gossip of the day'. And it asked three questions:

'Who is Captain Garth? To whom else other than General Garth is he related? And by what circumstances comes he to involve his private relations with those of the royal family? These, we confess, are exceedingly delicate questions... But when we see this notorious rake and unprincipled seducer put forward as the tool of a faction, to heap slanders on the innocent, we sink all minor considerations and advert to facts which ... we should much rather not allude to. This Captain Garth, then, is the reputed son of an illustrious princess who, by every religious and moral tie, was the wife of General Garth.'

When Lord Ellenborough read this, he wrote in his journal, 'That infamous man ... gives up his sister altogether, says she was married to General Garth, that Garth is her son, that the Duke of C^d is innocent.' By 'gives up' he means that Ernest makes official what other papers have refrained from saying, that Princess Sophia is the mother of Garth ... 'this notorious rake and unprincipled seducer'.

The *Morning Journal* went on to say that '*ministerial* slanderers' insinuated that a letter in the handwriting of Garth's mother contained 'accusations of the most repulsive kind against a royal duke'. Two gentlemen, 'a distinguished member of His Majesty's government' and 'an Irish Catholic holding a high office in Dublin' (O'Connell?) were reported to have seen the letter. A violent denial follows: 'We now declare, in the most solemn manner, and on undoubted evidence, that there is not the slightest ground for the accusation. We believe it has its origin in the most foul and infernal conspiracy that ever disgraced public men... The persons who conduct the ministerial papers practise the arts of heartless scoundrels... Malice is their weapon, private reputation their victim, revolution their object.'[28]

How perplexing for Ernest to present a coherent case! It is a foul lie to say the princess made 'accusations of the most repulsive kind', yet just at this time Sir Herbert has been telling important people that Sophia had complained of 'attempts upon her person' by Ernest.

Next day *The Observer* said, 'We trust that a regard to public decency will prevent all further disclosures. If the Illustrious Duke cannot triumphantly repel the slander and punish the slanderer, we trust that he will depart our shores and never return.' On the same day Westmacott's *Age* made a furious assertion of Ernest's innocence: 'The leading Popery journals, *The Times* and *Chronicle* ... ought to blush crimson deep with shame at their own credulity in giving currency to the foulest insinuations against the Duke of Cumberland, who, we openly and *authorizedly* state, is as free from even the suspicion of any criminal knowledge of Captain Garth's birth or circumstances as the child unborn.' Garth is 'the most contemptible of human beings' who has '*violated* his sacred word as an officer and a gentleman' by exaggerating his debts and refusing to reduce his Melton establishment. Ernest is 'the most injured man in His Majesty's dominions'.[29]

The Times dismissed this *authorized* statement as 'wild ravings'. Garth's affidavit, though 'guarded against all avoidable disclosures [naming neither Ernest nor Sophia], has driven some people to a state which borders on insanity... Desperate denials of facts have been attempted.' *The Times* asked questions going to the heart of the matter:

> Will somebody be pleased to inform us how Captain Garth's demand of a large sum of money, and an enormous pension, came to be listened to even for a moment? People do not nowadays bind themselves for nothing ... for no dread of infamy or other paramount evil, to pay the debts of those who importune or threaten them — debts amounting to very many thousands of pounds, and to pay besides annuities of £3000 per annum ... if they have nothing to fear... What secret was to be kept? Tell that, or say nothing.

The *Morning Chronicle* recalled *The Standard*'s assertion that Ernest had not known that 'Captain Garth had ever existed'. 'And yet Captain Garth is the son of the duke's sister, by a solemn but illegal marriage! These two accounts do seem hardly reconcilable with each other. We pretend not to know so much of these matters as our contemporary, or so little as the Duke of Cumberland; but we may almost say we know that whose son soever Captain Garth is, *he is not the son of General Garth*.'[30]

Two days later George IV accidentally demolished all the assertions that his sister was the wife of General Garth. At a cabinet meeting in the royal bedroom, Ellenborough records, the king raised 'the business of the Princess Sophia' and 'spoke of turning the two Garths out of his service' (the general and the young captain). 'The D. [Wellington] told him that would only tend to convince everyone that the story was true; there was no ground for turning out the Garths. The king said, "Why, the affidavit!"' The general had helped to open up a painful scandal, it is true, by handing the captain the documents, but the king would never have thought of dismissing him if he were really Sophia's husband.[31]

No answer came to *The Times*'s question. Nor did Ernest venture, as *The Standard* had promised, to bring anybody to trial before a jury as fearless, honest and manly as Ernest. His advocates managed, instead, to add a new tangle to the web they were weaving. They claimed that he had an alibi. The *Morning Chronicle* quoted 'the adherents of the Personage in question (for such there are)' as saying 'the imputation which formed the gravamen of the charge is clearly established by the stubborn evidence of dates, and facts, and distances to be a *physical impossibility*'. *The Globe* said the 'gratuitous zeal' of Ernest's '*soi-disant* friends of the No Popery party' created difficulties for him. In a nicely convoluted sentence, it said, 'Not satisfied with a plain denial ... they went on to declare that it was *physically* impossible that he could have been guilty, he having been out of the country at the time when, if in it, he might have been, if every natural and moral tie had been set aside, a guilty party, and they added that immediate proof would be offered... It has not been given.'[32]

In the face of all this, Sir Herbert again assured Charles Greville that General Garth 'is the father'. As for the promised money, Sir Herbert's word now was, 'He shall as far as he is concerned be against paying any money, as the object of the payment was to avoid publicity.' Sir Herbert rated Garth as 'an idiot as well as a scoundrel', whereas Westmacott 'has behaved well to him and he has never given him any money'. Greville comments, 'Money however of course he has had, for he is the editor of the Age and a great villain.'[33]

Ernest's zealous friends did not offer evidence for their geographical alibi. They could not. Nine months before Garth's birth, Ernest was not somewhere far distant from Sophia, but spent eleven days at Windsor (*pages 28–9*). Newspapers with files preserved from 1799 could have demonstrated this (files survive even now). It is likely that

Ernest escaped open refutation of his culminating lie only because editors shrank from a too direct exposure of the unhappy Sophia.

All the contradictory twists and turns and the final lie are compelling indicators of Ernest's guilt.

Emancipation was meanwhile progressing through parliament. On St Patrick's Day 1829, Daniel O'Connell, traversing the humble London district of St Giles after attending a Roman Catholic chapel, was hailed by hundreds of elated Irishmen, 'each with a large shamrock in his hat', shouting 'God bless you, Counsellor!' and 'Huzza for the Juke of Willington!' and all trying to shake O'Connell's hand. 'By my soul,' said one, 'we are all terrible dry with shouting. I wish the Counsellor would open his heart and give us our Patrick's pot.'

A few days later Wellington was up at dawn for a duel in Battersea Fields, pistols at twelve paces, against one of Ernest's wildest ultras, Lord Winchilsea, who had refused to apologize for accusing Wellington in *The Standard* of 'insidious designs for the infringement of our liberties and the introduction of popery into every department of the state'. Both shot wide. Winchilsea apologized at last, most grudgingly.

In the Lords on 11 April, Ernest's brother, Augustus Duke of Sussex, the sole Whig of the family, turned to Wellington and said his emancipation victory 'would far eclipse any of those he has gained in the tented field'. Millions of people had been 'restored to their place in society by his intrepid patriotism'.[34]

Even then Ernest made a final attempt to kill the bill. In a long letter he urged George IV to refuse to give his royal assent, and undertook to 'take upon my shoulders the responsibility of giving that advice'. The king wept when he read the letter, Ernest said, 'but alas! he did not have the resolution to do that which would have immortalized him'. The king agonized. 'What can I do?' he said to the ultra Lord Eldon. 'What can I now fall back upon? I am miserable, wretched... If I do give my assent, I'll go to the baths abroad and from thence to Hanover. I'll return no more... Let them get a Catholic king in Clarence.' Like his father in 1783, he thought better of abdicating, but he went on raging against Wellington. Angry over his long ordeal, Wellington summed up the king: 'The worst man he ever fell in with in his whole life, the most selfish, the most false, the most illnatured, the most entirely without one redeeming quality'.[36]

At his next levee the king turned his back on bishops who had voted for emancipation, and when he saw O'Connell he said, 'Damn the fellow! What does he come here for?'[35] Nine months later O'Connell was sitting in the Commons.

As emancipation was passing its final stages, the king wrote to Sir William Knighton that he was 'very much worried & distress'd *indeed*, in *body* and *mind*, with *all* that is passing in the busy & clamorous scene'. Besides politics, there was 'the other most distressing affair'. He told Knighton, 'I sincerely hope that the Chancellor will persevere, with as little loss of time as possible, to get possession of *all* that is *necessary* to prevent its ever again being brought into notoriety, & which if so, may still possibly be the means of preserving my poor Sister's Life.'[37]

What must never again be brought into notoriety?

It cannot be the fact that Sophia is Garth's mother, for that has now been openly declared. It can only be the truth about his father. To achieve the speedy destruction of Garth's documents, the king looks to the lord chancellor. He is, after all, head of the Court of Chancery.

13

A still more tangled web

The Court of Chancery was notoriously well designed for defendants who wished to foil plaintiffs. It was a scene of torment for litigants, and of profit for lawyers and the Masters in Chancery, registrars, clerks and clerks' clerks (hundreds in all, far more than in great departments of state). In an attempt at reform, an inquiry commission was appointed in 1826. One fact that emerged was that in endlessly-delayed suits over property, more than £40 million worth (at 1826 values) was immured in Chancery. The inquiry report, more than 1,300 pages, was dismissed by *The Times* as 'an apology for the abuses'. It tried to 'conceal the greater evils which abound there by unveiling the lesser ones'.

Every litigant's solicitor had to deal with a 'clerk in court' who was meant to smooth his way. It was common for the same clerk to act for the other side. Some clerks, besides, were rather odd. A witness told the inquiry, 'Mr Shaddick was a good clerk in court even when he was a lunatic... His successor has doubled the charges.' A constant complaint, *The Times* said, was 'the delay in hearing causes which are ripe for hearing'. By the time Garth sued in 1829, the number of cases in arrears had grown from 300 to 348.[1]

Sir Herbert, in preparing his answer to Garth, had the help of Garth's flexible ex-friends, Westmacott and C F Williams, and also of Lord Chief Justice Best, a high-Tory friend of Ernest. Best was ennobled later that year as Lord Wynford, causing John Cam Hobhouse, a reformist Whig, to write in his diary, 'The rogue Best is a peer — this the Duke of Cumberland got.'[2] Best, noted for harshness and suspected of corruption, had been refused a peerage by Wellington.

Sir Herbert knew Garth to be in peril of duns. He did not hurry to produce his answering affidavit.

The Examiner carried an amusing item, 'A Tale of the Court', which begins, 'The king is inordinately fond of gossip... One of the most favoured caterers of news is Sir Thomas Tyrwhitt [a Bedchamber

Gentleman] who, in consideration of his accomplishments in fetching and carrying, has the entrée of the bedchamber before His Majesty rises, and entertains the royal ear with the scandal of the day. The Duke of C. is admitted to the same honour.' A short time ago, the report goes on, Tyrwhitt brought news of a scandal in the west of England: a brother and sister, children of a baronet, had eloped. 'Brimful of his news and forgetful of all other circumstances' (the presence of Ernest), Tyrwhitt began 'the strange tale':

'At the very first mention of brother and sister, the royal bedclothes were strangely agitated. The courtier, unthinking, went on with the story ... but the king hemmed and hawed, and fidgeted about prodigiously, while the Duke of C. strode up and down the room as if walkng for a wager. Sir Thomas persevered, and the king knocked the counterpane about with his legs at every word... At last the truth flashed upon the courtier's mind, and looking from the monarch floundering in the bed like a fish out of water, to the annoyed peripatetic prince, he exclaimed, losing his presence of mind with the sense of his blunder, *Oh! — the Duke of C* ——— *!* The curtain falls on the rest.'[3]

Ernest, staying on in England for the sake of politics as well as of Garth, instructed Frederica to join him, bringing their ten-year-old son Prince George. There was a financial bonus. Parliament had voted in 1825 to grant £6000 a year for the boy, but only if he lived in England. In the debate on the proposal, Henry Brougham said the previous refusals of an increase for Ernest arose from 'a rooted dislike ... felt by man, woman and child' [*hear, hear!*]. He lived abroad to please himself 'where his income of £19,000 per annum is equal to £30,000 in this country'. Other MPs condemned the grant as 'a juggle', helping Ernest 'by a side-wind'. It passed by only 120 to 97.[4]

Shortly before Frederica was due in London, an unpleasant report about Ernest began to circulate in high society: that he called on the wife of the lord chancellor, Lord Lyndhurst, and tried to ravish her. Lyndhurst's lady was thirty-four, more than twenty years younger than he, and noted for her coquetry. 'She has beautiful eyes and such a way of using them that quite shocked Lady Louisa [Molyneux] and me,' Creevey noted a few months earlier. And the novelist Maria Edgeworth wrote, 'I never in my life was in a room with any lady that *flirted* so atrociously as Lady Lyndhurst. She is vulgar and bold and shows legs and arms &c beyond all that I could have conceived.'[5] She certainly went beyond coquetry. Ernest had some excuse for being tempted. But now he had to repel the gossip. When Frederica was actually on her way, an item about him and Lady Lyndhurst appeared in *The Age*, Ernest's mouthpiece. This may seem surprising — until one notes how it was presented:

> We copy the following absurd paragraph, the falsehood of which it is unnecessary for us to contradict, from the *Dublin Freeman's Journal...*
>
> 'The Duke of Cumberland. — It is stated that this person was turned out of Lady Lyndhurst's house some few days ago. Having acted so as to incur Her Ladyship's displeasure, she ordered that he should be turned out ... and turned out he was. On retiring, it is said that he exclaimed, "*I shall make the Chancellor pay for this!*"'

The Age says no lady exists 'of more polished manners, of more dignified affability or more amiable disposition' than Lady Lyndhurst. It is 'really astonished' that the Dublin paper could print 'such trash'.[6] It is an item planted for Ernest's use. He instantly followed it up. He wrote to Lyndhurst that he had ignored 'idle reports', but the appearance of newspaper paragraphs made it necessary to request a contradiction.

Lyndhurst replied that he regarded the article as 'one in the series of calumnies by which Lady Lyndhurst has, through the medium of a portion of the public press, been for some time assailed, & which she has at length learnt to despise'. Ernest again demanded the contradiction — 'I have a *right* to expect it.' Wellington helped Lyndhurst to draft his next reply: Ernest had no right to require anything of him, and he did not think he needed to annoy Lady Lyndhurst by asking her 'what passed' during Ernest's visit two months before.

Charles Greville, the constant diary-keeper, gathered some details: 'The duke called upon her and made a desperate attempt upon her person, which she resisted, and told him that she did not intend he should have her. He said by God he would, on which, after a scramble, she rang the bell... He said, "By God, madam, I will be the ruin of you and your husband, and will not rest till I have destroyed you both".' Later Greville learns more, direct from Lady Lyndhurst. Ernest's manner and language were 'brutal and indecent', and he would 'never forgive her for putting him to so much pain'. In the end he 'went off upon politics and abused the whole administration, and particularly the chancellor ... for two or three hours'.[7]

Here Ernest can be said to be maintaining a royal quirk. The

Duchess of Devonshire's sister, Lady Bessborough, tells of the prince of Wales, back in 1809, making a passionate assault on her. 'He threw himself on his knees, and clasping me round, kiss'd my neck [genteel for 'bosom'] before I was aware... I screamed... He continued, sometimes struggling with me, sometimes sobbing and crying.' He vowed eternal love and promised to break with Mrs Fitzherbert *and* his mistress Lady Hertford. The prince, 'that immense, grotesque figure, flouncing about half on the couch, half on the ground', persisted for two hours. Then he 'kept me two more telling me stories'.[8]

To return to Ernest: on the day that Frederica was to arrive, he again demanded a denial. Lyndhurst replied that if anything had been 'imputed or insinuated unfavourable to the conduct of Lady Lyndhurst ... no one who knows Lady Lyndhurst can for a moment doubt that such reports are utterly false'. *Her* conduct: not much help for Ernest there. He made what use he could of the letters. He showed them to Frederica, of course with his commentary, and sent copies to possible supporters such as Princess Lieven. He mocked Lyndhurst's *'digne et chaste épouse'* and scorned Lyndhurst's replies as 'the most shuffling performance, *et qui ferait honneur à un* pettifogging attorney'. He and a crony, Sir Henry Cooke, went about alleging that Lady Lyndhurst 'had begged him to call upon her, then to dine with her, and upon every occasion had encouraged him to make love to her', but 'he had not the least inclination'.

Greville resisted an attempt by Ernest to enlist his support, and in his journal called Ernest 'the most audacious villain in the world and totally without fear or shame'. He recalled George IV's having said, 'In anything in which a woman is concerned there is no believing a single word that he says,' yet now the king was taking his side: 'Good God, what a set they are!'

With Ernest's age (fifty-eight) in mind, Lord Holland wrote to Grey, 'That's no age to ravish, say the poets, but not it seems the statesmen.'[9]

Lady Lyndhurst certainly preferred younger men. Holland's 27-year-old son Henry could vouch for this. A few months later Henry was at Brighton at the same time as the Lyndhursts. His journal touches first on politics: Lyndhurst feels precarious. 'The D of Cumberland has vowed his fall — every day the influence of the D increases at Windsor.' Next day: 'The Chancellor is gone. Before he went she received another anonymous letter from London threatening to expose her to him and accusing her of an embrace with me on the steps leading to the Chain Pier.' But on *that* day he was in London. 'This takes off any apprehension we might feel, for it proves the ignorance of our enemies.' Lady Lyndhurst showed her long-suffering husband the letter and also a paragraph in *The Age*. Lyndhurst advised her 'not to allow the avarice of blackguards to harass and torment her'.

Henry was a great-nephew of Charles James Fox, the Man of the People, yet when blackguards exposed upper-class fornication he wished there could be despotic censorship: 'Great God what a dreadful country this is to live in and how much better for the peace of society and for the *agréments* of life is the despotism of one man than the inquisitive tyranny and insolent exactions of a whole nation.'

A few days later he is enjoying the *agréments* of Lady Lyndhurst: 'I stayed there till late. X.' Next day, 'In the evening to Ly L when I played at écarté and then X.' Next day, 'Lady L — twice.' And the next, 'Passed a delightful hour with L L. X X.'[10]

Frederica had a warmer royal welcome in 1829 than in 1815. Queen Charlotte was fourteen years dead. George IV set the serviceable Sir Herbert to work to put his sisters into a hospitable mode. 'There has been a negotiation, through Sir H. Taylor, with the Princess Augusta, and she has consented to receive the Duchess of Cumberland,' Lord Grey wrote to Princess Lieven. 'This, I suppose, means the whole family,' Augusta being the senior princess.[11]

Frederica found a letter awaiting her from Princess Lieven, an old friend, and replied instantly (in French), 'Dear, dear friend! I owe you so many thanks for your dear letter and all it contains. I await tomorrow & the moment between 1 & 2 o'clock with the greatest impatience. I shall not really believe I am in London until I hold you in my arms!'

George IV invited Frederica to Windsor, the previously unattainable castle. Afterwards she told Princess Lieven delightedly about her reception by the king '& *les Princesses*'; her introduction to Wellington; her tour in a landau with the king; her visits to 'the park, the belvedere, the ruin, the Chinese temple, the tents and several delicious views'; and finally a *déjeuner à la fourchette* with the king at Frogmore. As she left, the king showed her 'the great courtesy of leading me himself to my carriage'. Next day she is going with Ernest and their son to see another princess, Sophia, and the Duchess of Kent at Kensington Palace. The whole family is so welcoming, Frederica says, 'that I can truly say that I forget the past' (*je passe l'éponge sur le passé*). She found Sophia 'extremely good & obliging'.[12]

Frederica's long experience of courts helped her to cope with these first days. Some idea of her character and appearance is given in the *Chronique* of the Duchesse de Dino, niece and intimate companion of the great Talleyrand, about a year later when Frederica was 52: '*Elle a de l'esprit, de l'instruction, les plus belles manières ... de la grace, de la douceur, des restes de beauté, surtout dans la taille.*' (She is clever and well-informed, has the most beautiful manners ... charm, sweetness and remains of beauty, especially in her figure; *and see plate 16a.*). A less positive picture appears in correspondence between Princess Lieven and Lord Grey. The princess says her 'two most intimate woman friends' are Lady Cowper, a noted Whig hostess, and Frederica. Grey says he cannot understand the princess's fondness for Frederica — 'Her manners appear to me those of a great lady on the stage.' Princess Lieven concedes that she has 'the appearance of a stage-queen', and that 'everything goes with her at a snail's pace, it is so long-drawn-out, formal and particular, and yet with all this ... she is so excellent and faithful, so appreciative and devoted in her friendship, that it is impossible for me not to love her.'[13]

Ernest was still intriguing with rebellious Tory ultras to undermine Wellington. One of his bought editors, Stanley Lees Giffard, wrote in *The Standard* that Wellington was suspected of 'indifference to the interests of the established church'; of wishing to be 'the *sole* minister'; and of 'wishing to perpetuate his power by dangerous designs connected with the succession to the crown'. Wellington asked the attorney-general, James Scarlett, to consider prosecuting this, but he replied that although *The Standard* and *Morning Journal* were conducted 'with a hostility unqualified by the least regard to honour or to truth', newspapers often escaped paying fines and damages by employing 'a scapegoat who has no objection to earn moderate wages in prison'.[14]

Ernest angered Wellington, too, by scheming behind his back with George IV to have Frederica's brother, Prince Charles of Mecklenburg, made king of newly independent Greece. Wellington stamped on this. Soon after, when the king had caused yet another 'distressing scene', Wellington wrote to Sir William Knighton, 'If I had known in January 1828 one tithe of what I do now, & of what I discovered in one month after I was in office, I sh^d have never been the king's minister, & sh^d have avoided loads of misery! ...I believe there never was a man suffered so much; & for so little purpose!'

The king was still wasting Wellington's time with his drugged ramblings. Creevey reports, 'Prinney must be mad. He tells almost daily how he won the cup at Goodwood by *his own* riding. "I kept the old mare back till I was within fifty yards from home, and then, by God! I made such a rush with her," etc, etc.' He has also told Wellington that he, Prinney, 'gained the battle of Salamanca' (a Wellington victory in 1812) by bringing up the heavy cavalry *'when things were looking very ill indeed'*. Or sometimes Prinney's victorious charge is at Waterloo, moving Wellington to remark, 'I have heard you, sir, say so before, but I did not witness this marvellous charge.'[15]

Fantasy of a different sort appears in Sir Herbert Taylor's eventual answer in Chancery about Garth's documents in the black tin box. He swears that they tend 'in some manner to affect or throw imputations on the characters of certain individuals' in whom he takes an interest, but they do not in any way relate to Garth's fortune. They are 'of great or considerable importance' but not of any 'just or legitimate value' to Garth. He follows with a still more surprising statement. 'Never having perused the said documents ... nor been made acquainted with the contents thereof', he cannot say 'to what the same relate'. Yet in this state of ignorance he can swear he is 'seriously apprehensive' that Garth is disposed to publish them, which 'might be injurious to or might wound the feelings of certain individuals'.

The funds promised to Garth for these documents of no 'just or legitimate value' to him (£10,000 for creditors, plus the lifetime £3000 annuity), Sir Herbert says, were to have come half from palace sources and half from General Garth. The documents were to be given up 'to be destroyed'; so were any copies; and anyone who had seen them 'should contract a solemn obligation to maintain a strict silence' about them. Yet their content was an entire mystery to Sir Herbert.

Sir Herbert persists in his allegation that Garth obtained the documents 'improperly'. His chief assertion is that because Garth did not 'give up his expensive style of living' at Melton Mowbray or furnish a proper list of his debts, and because he divulged the contents of the documents 'to many individuals' and made copies of them, he has 'lost all right' to have the agreement performed.

Just before the box was deposited at the bank, he says, he personally drafted the wording of the receipt he wanted — ominously for Garth, a single one saying the box was to be produced only on the 'joint order' of himself and Westmacott. Next day, Sir Herbert says, Westmacott gave this receipt to him.[16]

Westmacott too puts in an affidavit. He cannot swear ignorance of the documents (they were in his hands for some time), but he manages to swear that he does not believe they relate to the claim that Garth made 'upon certain persons' named in them. Westmacott's affidavit adds one item to our small inheritance of Garth correspondence. It is a note Garth sent him early on 23 November 1828, when Westmacott was about to see Sir Herbert to finalize the handing over: 'I have sent the gig early as I should like to see you ere your interview. For that purpose I should be happy to see you at breakfast at 9.' The next day, the trusting Garth gave up the black tin box.

Westmacott denies that he intends to join Sir Herbert 'in demanding the said box', but Sir Herbert does intend to prevent Garth from regaining possession. A brief statement entered by Sir John Dean Paul and partners says they must not part with the box 'except by the joint order' of Sir Herbert and Westmacott.[17]

Sir Herbert's and Westmacott's affidavits were published in November 1829. They showed, *The Times* said, that 'the celebrated Garth case has not been compromised'. Garth 'is determined, it seems, to make his antagonist bend to him, and recover his box of papers — the mysterious, awful, or, as the result may prove, the damning papers — which a desperate effort no doubt will be made to destroy or suppress, that some colour may be given to the next step in the transaction, viz, the maintaining solemnly that such papers exist not, and never have existed'. *The Times* asks again, as it did in March, why Sir Herbert offered so much money:

> We wonder who the man might be whose 'feelings' or 'reputation' could be wounded to the extent of such enormous sums by the publication of papers recording the birth and parentage of any person living. Circumstances of extraordinary guilt and disgrace must unavoidably be inferred.

People are 'as much in the dark as ever', says the *Morning Chronicle*. 'The momentous question "Who are the real parents of Captain Garth?" remains unanswered.'[18]

That evening's *Standard* offers an answer on Ernest's behalf. It says Garth's father is the general, who is 'the husband of an Illustrious Lady'. Their marriage was '*politically* invalid', however, under the

Royal Marriage Act. 'It was therefore deemed proper to withhold any public declaration of it, though no attempt, we believe, was ever made to conceal it from such of the immediate connexions of the parties as were of discreet age.' Then what *are* the papers for which Sir Herbert had to offer so much? *The Standard* says they are letters that passed between the general and Sophia 'in the confidence of married life — letters which we know contained nothing but what would naturally and innocently pass between persons in that close relation — nothing that was not honourable to that Illustrious Lady — nothing in the slightest degree reflecting upon any member of her family'.

Not throwing any wounding imputations on anyone, then; yet they must be destroyed. *The Standard* strives to explain this:

'The Lady whose dreadful misfortune it is to have given birth to such a son was at the time [when Sir Herbert offered the money] in extremely delicate health'. Publication was feared — 'the shock of such a cruel threat alone would kill her'. The marriage was against the law; there was concern over 'the gluttonous curiosity of the public'; and George IV 'felt it his duty to put an end to the perplexing difficulty at any reasonable sacrifice'. Besides, *The Standard* says, the king perhaps thought 'that silly and profligate as Garth had been, he was a young man and might reform'. As a member of the royal family, 'he was entitled to some respectable provision'. No longer, however. Owing to his 'shuffling and incorrigible folly', the deal is off, and 'there is not much chance of its being renewed'.[19]

The Times points out next day how weak this all is. 'Everybody has, for these last two- or three-and-twenty years, received the most industrious and positive assurances that it *was* a real, though not a lawful, marriage', it says (royal guidance for editors has a long history). But now, 'after this alleged marriage had been talked about as long as most of us can remember, it was to be henceforth kept a dead secret, by virtue of a bribe of some tens of thousands of pounds! What amiable simplicity, what infantine nonsense in this ingenious version!'[20]

On the very day, 16 November 1829, that *The Standard* declared General Garth to be 'the husband of an Illustrious Lady', he died, aged 85, at 32 Grosvenor-place, a fine mansion (just behind Buckingham House) that he had bought from Wellington's friend Sir Henry Hardinge. News of the death reached Sir Herbert Taylor from a professional colleague of many years, Charles Greenwood of the army agents Greenwood, Cox, Hammersley & Cox, in a note beginning,

'The name of Garth must be hateful to you.' The general 'expired in his son's arms', Greenwood reported. 'He embraced his son with the greatest tenderness, told him he had left him all he had, and was sorry it was no more. This intelligence comes to me from a person that was present.'[21] All the efforts and lies of Sir Herbert had not estranged the general from the young man.

Not quite 'all' went to Tom Garth. The general left some property in Northamptonshire to a nephew, also named Thomas Garth, a retired Royal Navy captain. To Tom he bequeathed an annuity of £1500 a year, the Grosvenor-place mansion and its contents (furniture, silverware and personal effects), and also the contents of Ilsington, the manor-house he had rented for years at Piddletown.

In the next *Age* after the general's death, Westmacott printed a coldly disparaging comment: 'We shall not violate the sanctuary of the tomb by saying all we might on the departed general. He is dead — gone to his account — and his ingratitude to the illustrious family who made him what he was is the only relic he has left for after-times to judge him by.'[22] Yet this was the man who, if *The Standard* was to be believed, had left a mourning royal widow. Ernest's newspapers were imperfectly coordinated.

The general was conveyed to 'the sanctuary of the tomb' (the crypt of St Martin-in-the-Fields) in a cortège rather modest for a royal equerry of forty years' standing — a six-horse hearse and two coaches of mourners. Ernest, who had once shared many a royal staghunt with him, was at Kew, 'indisposed with a slight cold'. Brief newspaper paragraphs said Captain Garth was the chief mourner.

The Standard printed not a word, so avoided having to report that the Illustrious Lady, the alleged widow of the general, had unaccountably failed to attend his last rites.

Further evidence pointing at Ernest is to come, but enough has now been produced to demonstrate beyond reasonable doubt (to adopt the strictest legal requirement) that Ernest was Tom Garth's father.

Courtly or kindly or negligent historians can no longer declare him innocent.

14

Ernest, a razor and The Thunderer

The happy establishment of Frederica in London did not inhibit Ernest for long, despite her 'charm, sweetness and remains of beauty'. Soon after the Lady Lyndhurst embarrassment, high-society gossip linked him and a lady slightly younger than Frederica: the 46-year-old wife of Lord Graves, comptroller for Augustus Duke of Sussex, and for many years a Lord of the Bedchamber to George IV. The affair's violent climax exposed Ernest to yet more execration.

Graves owed his title to his father, an admiral who served in George III's war against the Americans and who later gained an Irish barony for a victory against the French. The son and heir, born 1775, married in 1803 Mary Paget, aged twenty and a great beauty, one of the lively family of Pagets.

Her eldest brother, Henry, a noted cavalry commander, was made 1st Marquess of Anglesey after serving as Wellington's No 2 at Waterloo. A few years earlier he had figured in a scandal. An affair with the wife of Sir Henry Wellesley, Wellington's brother, became so flagrantly passionate that they left their spouses, causing turmoil in several great houses. The runaway wife's brother, a Cadogan, challenged Henry Paget to a duel. Lord Graves stepped in as a go-between. Thus we have a taste of his language. After talking to Wellesley and Cadogan he reported that they 'vote that stinking Pole Cat [Lady Wellesley] not worth the shedding blood. Damn her! How Paget's stomach will heave in the course of six months when she seizes him in her hot libidinous arms.' Another brother-in-law, Lord Enniskillen, declared, 'I wish I could get some huge Paddy to satisfy her lust and outdo Paget.'[1] (Irishmen, and Scotsmen too, were credited with special vigour.) The affair cost Paget £20,000 in crim-con damages. By means of a questionable arrangement of the sort available to the rich, Paget married his libidinous love (Graves was wrong to believe his stomach would heave) and his ex-wife married the Duke of Argyll.

Lady Graves had an anxious flurry in 1808 when a writer of royal exposés, Thomas Hague, published a lampoon about the Duke of Sussex and his household. She wrote to another brother, Sir Arthur Paget, 'I hope he has not dared to place me improperly. Pray send me his Poem — that I may see what he makes of me … the vile abominable Brute!' It is noticeable that she is concerned only about 'me'; but she finds she is not even in the lampoon. Graves himself figures as the harassed comptroller of the debt-ridden Sussex, fruitlessly seeking ways to raise cash. Sussex is satirized over his friends ('bad boys, who gamble, drink and wench, paupers, dupes, drunkards'), his devotion to the ageing, fat and still amorous singer Elizabeth Billington —

> Whose *scale* of voice three octaves neat trills out;
> Whose *scale* of person — is *three* yards about —

— his fondness for bracelets, flashy rings and gaudy clothes —

> Flesh-coloured trousers, all to show the shape,
> Adorn'd with frogs and fasten'd by pink tape.
> His slippers purple; yellow too his hose.
> *Ten* sorts of snuff regale the royal nose —

— and his 'book of prints, exposing ev'ry vice'. A footnote says, 'The Duke's collection of prints is of a singular sort.'[2] If so, he shared the tastes of his eldest brother. George IV's 'drawers full of *free* prints and drawings' were got rid of after his death — ostensibly destroyed, but allegedly sold, very lucratively, by his librarian. According to Sir William Knighton, 'Graves had a mind stuft full of the vice of conversation & few men had dipped deeper into the scenes (in early life) of immorality. One of his accomplishments was to recall them at the king's table.'[3]

Graves was a butt of jokes. He amused Lady Boringdon when he was a guest at Saltram, her Devon mansion: 'Ld Graves is beyond anything excellent in the extraordinary stories he tells, & the scrapes he is sure to get into in the midst of the recitals, & when he is floundering … it is excellent to hear Ld Fortescue pretending to get him out of them but in reality sinking him still deeper.'[4]

He was enormously fat, yet liked to figure as a dancer and a rider to hounds. By the age of thirty-five he was so vast that he bought a gigantic horse. Another brother-in-law, Berkeley Paget, wrote to Sir Arthur wishing that the supreme caricaturist James Gillray could depict him 'mounting this huge beast', but this was in 1810, the year Gillray had lost his reason. 'If Gillray wasn't raving mad,' Berkeley wrote, 'I should send him down to be present at the ceremony.' When Graves soon took a fall, Berkeley said he had 'so seriously shaken his huge carcase that he could never hunt again ... a fortunate event not only for himself, but his horse'.[5]

The Graves marriage was troubled. Some shocking folly committed by Lady Graves in 1826, a year after she had her twelfth child at 42, put her husband into an anguished state. He wrote, *Most private and confidential*, to Sir Arthur Paget (a diplomat by profession), imploring his help. He must ask her to show him 'two letters I wrote her today & one yesterday', and then give his advice. She must place 'her honor & her happiness' in Sir Arthur's keeping. 'I am not quite myself,' Graves says. 'It is impossible she can have acted but under the most extraordinary but uncontrollable illusion.'

Lady Graves, in a letter to Sir Arthur, says her husband is 'worked up to a pitch of indignation & rage'.[6]

Before long the Graveses were living apart, he in lodgings off Hanover-square, she in a grace-and-favour apartment at Hampton Court Palace, not far from Ernest's Kew residence. During 1829 she and Ernest became lovers. In January 1830 Charles Greville writes in his journal, 'The king is horribly annoyed about the story which has come out of the Duke of Cumberland and Lady Graves. They have been detected by Graves in an amour at the house of old Lady Lansdowne at Hampton Court.' That is, he caught them together. 'Graves went to the king... The story is all over town.'[7]

Newspapers picked up this intrigue of 'an illustrious personage' with a lady connected to the royal household. Caricatures showed them as lovers. In 'Romeo and Juliet — The Resurrectionist or Violator of Graves!!!', she echoes Juliet's words: 'Oh! C———d, C———d, wherefore art thou C———d? ...Be but my sworn love,' etc. A scrap of paper beside Ernest reads, *Thou shalt not covet thy neighbour's wife*.

Graves was worked up to a pitch of indignation too painful to bear. On Sunday, 7 February, when he was expected at dinner with Lord Anglesey at 1 Old Burlington-street, he went to his bedroom and stood facing a looking-glass lit by two candles; but he did not dress for dinner. He cut his throat with a razor. Blood jetted over the glass.

During that Sunday night an inquest was arranged with unparalleled speed. It was held early next day before any newspaper heard of it. Someone with shorthand was there, however, for several papers obtained reports. Graves's doctor, his landlord and his servant all said he had been very depressed. The servant said the depression had increased 'particularly of late'.

A juror: Can you inform us what has caused that depression of spirits?

The question aroused 'the greatest interest among the jury' and 'all eyes were turned towards the witness'.

The coroner: It is not necessary to put such a question.

Juror: Are we not bound to investigate all the circumstances?

Still the coroner objected, but the juror pressed for an answer.

The servant: I cannot take upon myself to state what was the cause.

So the words 'Duke of Cumberland' remained unspoken. Verdict: Graves killed himself 'in a sudden fit of delirium'.[8] This qualified him for Christian burial, but he was in any case not at risk of being buried like Joseph Sellis at a three-went way with a stake through him. That ancient law had been amended as a humane sequel to the suicide in 1822 of 'carotid-artery-cutting Castlereagh', as Byron called him. (The comment then of the radical journalist William Cobbett was, 'Now a minister may cut his throat without being either *mad* or a *felon*. That is lucky, at any rate.')

The general report was that George IV, aiming to counter the gossip about Ernest's affair, had persuaded Graves to forgive his wife and be seen in her company, but Graves had been fatally worked up when people sent him caricatures, newspaper cuttings and anonymous letters suggesting that Ernest had paid him to be complaisant.

The rushed inquest, Ernest's sinister reputation and a death by *razor* combined to rouse *The Times* to such a height as to imply that Ernest killed Graves. This, oddly, was the origin of the paper's long-cherished sobriquet, The Thunderer.

It opened its attack by saying Graves had dispatched a letter to his wife, and then, 'if he be the author of his own destruction, perpetrated the fatal act'. If! It asked, 'Is it possible that they [the jury] can have found their verdict without demanding a sight of that letter? ...Is it possible that they can have failed of requiring Lady Graves to be summoned, that she might give a description of the feelings of her husband and the causes which produced his irritation? ...Is it thus that a British nobleman can be passed out of life into eternity? ...The causes of the murdered man's death must be further inquired into!'

Murdered! True, this might be 'self-murdered', but a few sentences further on came an allusion to Joseph Sellis (unforgotten after twenty years): 'It is impossible not to connect this fearful act with a rumour which has been for some time in circulation, and to recall the public attention, however painfully, to another suicide — an inexplicable and mysterious suicide — with which a name that has been so often mentioned of late [Ernest] was also connected.'

Next day *The Times* backtracked, but tortuously. 'It is most unfortunate,' it said, 'when people of unpopular characters are in that rank of life that they can, of necessity, obtrude themselves where they please and drop in upon those whom they may choose as associates at will.' (In effect, 'Ernest might have called upon Graves unannounced.') It said it accepted a statement by the Pagets that Graves's letter to his wife was 'the most tender and affectionate she ever received from him in her life'. Then why the suicide? In a wonderfully convoluted sentence *The Times* blamed Ernest's reputation: 'But how miserable, if the lady (as we now conscientiously believe) be innocent, her lord convinced of her innocence, and only unable to bear up because the world unjustly thought he put up with that injury which it would have been base in him to suffer tamely, but which he himself knew he had never sustained! And all this because one man is ——— what he is!'

A proper inquest, *The Times* said, would have shown whether Graves's 'mental torture' was caused 'by false and scandalous imputations ... or by the knowledge of facts which injured his honour'. And now comes *The Times* as thunderer: 'We thundered out that article in Tuesday's paper, which created so great a sensation. And what did we do in that article? What we do now — reprehended the coroner and his inquest.' [9]

The credit for inventing the Thunderer sobriquet goes to the *Morning Herald*. It mocked *The Times*'s claim to be the Leading Journal of Europe, saying it was 'otherwise *The Thunderer* — but more commonly called *The Blunderer*'.

In the same issue in which *The Times* wrote of having 'thundered out', it thundered at Ernest in Latin. 'Our readers will see the application of the following passage addressed to Catiline,' it said, and gave an extract from Cicero's first oration against the conspirator, beginning, *Quousque tandem abutere patientia nostra*? Westmacott's *Age* was so eager to condemn this as a libel that it printed a translation — hardly a service to Ernest, for non-latinists could now judge the appositeness of Cicero's invective. A small sample:

Where will thy unbridled audacity end? What delight canst thou find in this city, in which there is not one but dreads thee, not one but hates thee? What brand of domestic shame is there that is not stamped in fiery characters on thee? ... Does not lust pervade thine eyes, perpetual crime thine hands and unceasing infamy thy whole body? ...Betake thyself to exile.

This alludes, *The Age* helpfully told its readers, 'to a Royal Duke whom we will not mention by name'; and 'unless libel loses its sting by being in Latin, this is as libellous a paragraph as ever disgraced the columns of a public print'.

The Age ascribed the whole affair to Whig malevolence: 'A lady of high birth was sedulously maligned and slandered — her reputation blasted — the honour of her family tainted — the peace, and at last the life, of her husband destroyed — for what? In order to gratify party spite... The Duke of Cumberland was the victim intended by the same party which has for years organized a system of slander of the basest dye... The profaned pencil was employed as well as the polluted press, and the windows of our caricature-shops abounded with pictures, the obscenity of which was their smallest crime.' In its zeal, *The Age* added a double-edged defence of Ernest: 'Suppose it true, suppose that the Duke of Cumberland had intrigued with a lady, how is he worse than Lord Holland? Did not Sir Godfrey Webster kill himself?' (Webster had divorced his wife for adultery with Holland.) *The Age* names other Whig adulterers — Lord Grey, Sir Francis Burdett — and says, 'It is ill throwing stones from glass houses.'[10]

In Princess Lieven's opinion, Graves's suicide was rather bad form. She wrote to Lord Grey, 'You must admit that the duke has had very bad luck in coming across a husband who goes and cuts his throat for a matter of this kind. Why did he not get a separation...? Why did he not call out the Duke of C [for a duel]? Anything, in fact, except this horrible suicide.'

Grey, a long-ago adulterer with the Duchess of Devonshire, told the princess that Lady Graves's sisters were 'abstaining from all intercourse with her', which accorded with 'the general opinion that there was something particularly atrocious in the case'. Yet he adopted the cool Lieven view: 'What is there more in this than in any other intrigue where no seduction has been used?' Ladies who 'declaim so loudly against the D. of C.' have not banished the many lovers of Lady Ellenborough from their society. 'And yet what difference is there ... except that Lord Ellenborough did not shoot himself?'[11]

The Times's allusion to Sellis was followed up by a caricature, 'A VOICE from the GRAVES!!!' (plate 7). Two ghostly figures terrify Ernest. Graves, holding dripping razors, says, 'Behold these gaping wounds! / Then shall thy own devouring conscience / Gnaw thy heart...' The other, Sellis, says, 'What ——— ! another victim.' Ernest utters lines from Macbeth, 'Avaunt! and quit my sight! Let the earth hide thee! (etc)' and from Richard III, 'Oh! tyrant conscience — how dost thou afflict me!' Near him, a book entitled Life of a Libertine serves as a paperweight for a cluster of Billet Doux from Lady G——.

Ernest, secluded at Kew, asserted his innocence in a stream of letters. His old friend Lord Eldon alone got six of them. They are in his usual style: 'The greatest lies ... vile scoundrels... I treat the whole with the contempt it deserves ... the most infernal lie that ever was invented... Do they pretend to say that my calling repeatedly at an old and sincere friend's house, drinking tea there, with all doors open, and never remaining there later than 11 or 11½, that for that reason I and she are to be suspected?' Like The Age, he blames political enemies: 'That party thought to frighten me and make me leave the country, but by God nothing shall. It is but a repetition of their tricks last year... Anonymous letters I received daily but chucked them into the fire.'[12]

What of his Frederica? First the Lyndhurst drama, now this! Surprisingly, she gave Princess Lieven the impression that she was unaware of the affair; even of Lord Graves's death. 'La duchesse ignore, je crois, totalement toutes ces circonstances et même la mort de Lord Graves,' the princess wrote to her brother. 'D'après ses lettres, que je reçois presque tous les jours, je n'ai pas vu le moindre altération dans son humeur.' ('... In her letters, which I receive almost daily, I have seen not the slightest change in her mood.')[13] Perhaps she was 'in denial', as therapists say.

One lady managed to think the lovers innocent. Harriet Countess Granville, daughter of the Duchess of Devonshire, wrote to her sister, Lady Carlisle, 'I am convinced of poor Lady Graves' innocence.' She thought that Graves 'had been goaded to suspect and tax her with what is certain he never discovered ... and that his misery has been the having by his accusations ruined her character'. Lady Graves 'has not had a moment of consciousness since she heard; in fainting fits, and delirious at times', Lady Granville declared. As for Ernest, 'I hear the nervous horror of his manner is dreadful.' The police have told him 'they cannot answer for his life if he goes about'.[14]

He reappeared after four weeks. He and Lady Graves overcame

their nervous horror and delirium. Harriet Arbuthnot's journal, May 17: 'The Duke of Cumberland is still *going on* with Lady Graves, & her children have in consequence left her.' Moustachioed Ernest was so distinctive that he defeated Lady Graves's efforts to be discreet. Grace Tew, of a Tory family on social terms with Ernest, wrote to her sister, 'Lady Graves goes by the name of Mrs Grey and has a snug cottage at Eltham' (a village then, beyond Blackheath). Ernest had been seen by a family friend, frequently coming from the cottage 'on horseback early in the morning, attended by a single groom'.[15]

Before long, the Kensington ratebooks show, Lady Graves bought a mansion in the Brompton district. This move to a less out-of-the-way scene proved unwise. Ernest's visits became known to the calumniating press. John Fairburn's printshop on Ludgate Hill published in June 1831 'R——L VISITS RESUMED; or, the *Beast* among the *Graves* again. Scene – A Rural Retreat at Upper Brompton'. Ernest is a hairy creature with bestial clawed hands and feet, seated on a grave and embracing plump Lady Graves, perched on his lap. Behind them Graves's ghost rises, saying, 'What, wouldst thou *pollute* my *Graves*?' A lightning bolt, *VENGEANCE*, strikes Ernest (*plate 8*).

For a Valentine issue in 1832, *Figaro in London* showed Ernest, an aged Cupid with a quiver of 'envenomed arrows', stabbing a heart labelled *Graves* on an altar of *Lust*. Some verses say —

> Sure, in your dreams, before your eyes
> At times a victim raves;
> And often you must hear the cries
> Of vengeance from the *graves*.[16]

Nothing deterred Ernest. A writer for *The Satirist*, an anti-Tory rival to *The Age*, reports that he often sees 'that illustrious pattern of Tory virtue, the Duke of Cumberland, wending his thoughtful way down Brompton-lane, as we at first conceived on some mission of divine charity'. Ernest alights each time at a particular house. 'Curiosity led us to ask whose house it was. "Lady Graves', sir!"' Ernest is 'a daily visitor to the house of the widow of the man who, in his passion of grief for the seduction of his wife, destroyed himself!'[17]

Lady Graves, shunned by her sisters and her children, and probably at last by Ernest, died in 1835, aged 52. In *The Satirist*, Ernest speaks:

> Oh! is it true? and is she dead? Another victim gone?
> Oh! tell me for what other deeds must I, the fiend, live on?[18]

15

The menacing Captain Ashe

Two scandalous affairs and an inconvenient suicide were not the only things on Ernest's mind in 1829–30. A manuscript of 321 pages entitled *Osphia or the Victim of Unlawful Affections* was posted to him in October 1829, with a letter from its author, Captain Thomas Ashe, at once self-accusing and threatening. Ashe wrote that when Ernest 'raised the Protestant standard', Daniel O'Connell and his associates 'collected materials' for *Osphia* and bribed him to write it, promising him £100. But he is a tormented man. 'He has ever entertained a romantic attachment for his Prince. What a Monster of Iniquity! to be at once an ingrate, a traitor and a barterer of principle for bread.' His excuse is that 'he is steeped to the lips in poverty'.

Instead of taking O'Connell's £100, Ashe 'casts himself upon the humanity of the Royal Duke'. Ernest need only pay him £100 and he can keep the manuscript. Ashe adds a little self-praise: 'The author is no vulgar character, he is a remarkable man well known to every branch of the Royal Family.'

Ernest did not scornfully cast this peculiar piece of blackmail into the fire. Soon he received a follow-up letter, in similar style but more threatening. It offered Ernest three choices: he can 'prosecute for an attempt at extortion, or he can wait the publication of Osphia & prosecute all the parties for conspiracy and libel, or he can say, "Damn the poor wretch, I really pity and will a second time snatch him from beggary and corruption." A second time, yes...' Ashe the one-time soldier claims that when he was 'returning naked thro' Hanover' in 1793, 'Prince Ernest took him by the hand and sent him on his way refreshed and rejoicing'. This 'grateful recollection' made him send *Osphia* to Ernest instead of 'to the parties bribing him to write it and whose agent is J J Stockdale of London'.

John James Stockdale: the man who wounded many great men by publishing the memoirs of Harriette Wilson. Ashe tells Ernest: 'Stockdale the publisher of Hariet Wilson dares to print and publish any calumny and he is in treaty with the author's employers to bring out the first edition of Osphia in Paris and a second in Ireland.' In a postscript he says, 'Should the MS be sent back to the author, he entreats the carriage money may be paid as he has scarcely wherewith to meet the exigencies of the day.' Steeped in poverty indeed!

Half-cracked Ashe might seem, but the Stockdale threat and above all the content of the manuscript were potent enough to make Ernest pass it and Ashe's letters to his friend and lawyer Lord Wynford; who sent them to the Duke of Wellington; who sent them to the treasury solicitor, George Maule, with a note saying, 'The book is an atrocious libel upon the king and the whole royal family, particularly the Princess Sophia and the Duke of Cumberland.' It might not be 'prudent' to prosecute, Wellington said, as *Osphia* would probably have to be produced in evidence. 'Shall we send it back to him, leaving it to him to publish it at his peril; or shall we pay him the Hundred Pounds? I am decidedly against the last course.' It is, though, 'a course to be considered'.[1]

None of Wellington's ministers or legal advisers dismissed Ashe as a beggarly contriver of calumnies. Neither Wellington nor Ernest nor anyone else said 'publish and be damned'. *Osphia* put them in a quandary. Over many months they agonized and consulted, sometimes at cabinet level, as Ashe dispatched increasingly dramatic letters from his distant haven, Rickerby Lodge, Carlisle.

Ashe, born near Dublin in 1770 of an Ascendancy family in decline, became a picaresque adventurer and, according to his own *Memoirs and Confessions of Captain Ashe* (1815, 3 vols, 915 pages), a spendthrift, peculator, seducer ('in love's wanton mazes'), soldier (erratically), debtor (occasionally imprisoned) and flexibly inventive journalist. His publications ranged from *Travels in America* to a three-volume novel, *The Charms of Dandyism, or Living in Style*, recounting 'a life of uproar and confusion, licentiousness and guilt'. More significantly, he wrote about, and sometimes on behalf of, royal personages.

In 1812 he sent the prince regent an outline of an allegedly imminent three-volume work, *The Claustral Palace, or Memoirs of 'The Family'*, about the blighted lives of Princesses Augusta, Elizabeth, Sophia and Amelia. His sole object, he said, was the repeal of the Royal Marriage Act, 'that most illegal and unrighteous law' which compelled the princesses 'to consume their lives ... in the stagnant Slough of Claustral Celibacy'. The outline offers a medley of fact, guesswork and fiction. Sophia, 'indued with a dangerous Sensibility', acquires 'a disorder which is contagious in Courts — a Dropsy grows upon her — the Air of the Sea is recommended...' Elizabeth resolves 'to drive her Chariot right through the Royal Marriage Act', and marries. Amelia gives her hand to 'the gallant Fitz Rex — a dropsical disorder ensues'. The queen 'falls upon Amelia and causes the miscarriage of her Complaint — the brutal Shock destroys the principles of Life...'

The attorney-general and solicitor-general studied this attempt at extortion but could not suggest 'advisable' steps to suppress it. If they paid Ashe off, they told the home secretary, 'What security could there be that the author, being such a man as he is ... will not threaten such a publication next year?' The outline is filed away in the Royal Archives, however, so Ashe was presumably paid.[2] He also wrote a 64-page version in rhyming pentameters, *The Claustral Palace, An Ovidian and Political Poem*, dedicated to Princess Charlotte, which as recently as 1999 came up at Sotheby's (unsold at £450).

Ashe had made what he could of the contention in 1806–07 between the prince of Wales and his estranged wife Caroline over the Delicate Investigation and The Book. He wrote a pro-Caroline work, *The Spirit of 'The Book' ... a Political and Amatory Romance*; but then was paid generously — or so he claimed — to write against her. When George IV put Caroline on trial in 1820 for adultery, Ashe wrote to her lawyers to offer help. He had been 'seduced at a time of deep distress', he said, to abandon Caroline in 1807, traduce her and 'elevate the husband', for which he was paid 'upwards of a thousand guineas'. The information thus acquired becomes his selling-point: he has evidence of the means used for years to 'write her down', and 'much more which I can put into your brief'. As ever, he is short of cash: 'PS ... My expenses to town and the means of getting a suit of clothes are all I require to repair to town the instant I hear from you.' He only wants to atone for his 'prostitution of his principles and his talents'. 'I *alone* can serve and SAVE Her Majesty... Have faith!'[3]

Ashe's past involvement in royal affairs, being known to the law officers, reinforced their need to take *Osphia* seriously. Wellington, in the midst of dealing with rebellious Canadians, restive West Indies slaves and relations with the Ottoman empire, as well as the usual annoying supplicants for titles and sinecures, was plagued with this

threat to Ernest, who had so often plagued him. Here are a few of the official exchanges (often marked *Secret*) in the course of one month:
— Wellington to Wynford, 17 October: Lord Chancellor Lyndhurst thinks Ashe could be prosecuted for libel, but advises against it.
— Wynford to Wellington, 20 Oct: has advised Ernest against prosecuting Ashe for attempting 'to extort money by threatening to publish a book charging him with murder' (*so Osphia also deals with Sellis*). [4]
— Ashe's solicitors to Ernest's aide-de-camp, 31 Oct: The manuscript was sent 'on the express understanding that it was to be immediately returned unless His Royal Highness should consider it worth a place in his library'. They describe it: royal octavo in green covers with yellow edges. If it is not returned they will take legal action.
— Wellington to Wynford, 5 Nov: James Scarlett, attorney-general, says if they prosecute, the libel will become public. 'Is it worth while to prosecute in order to punish him with transportation, with the certainty of bringing forth the libel?'
— Ashe to John Conant, Marlborough-street magistrate, 10 Nov: 'Silence is the policy of Sir Herbert Taylor. Believe me, it will answer no good purpose. Besides, those who despise the man should dread the dagger. The Duke of Buckingham and the Minister Perceval have taught the world this lesson.' (*Men with grievances assassinated Charles I's favourite, Buckingham, in 1628, and Spencer Perceval, prime minister, in 1812.*) Wellington thinks this threat 'goes very near the wind'. [5]
— Sir Robert Peel, home secretary, to Wynford, 13 Nov: Ashe's letter may be 'nothing more than an idle menace', but he has sent orders to Carlisle for Ashe to be watched, and 'will have a watch kept upon him should he arrive in the neighbourhood of London'. [6]
— Lord Ellenborough's journal, 16 Nov: 'Long talk about Ashe' in cabinet. The manuscript details 'all sorts of scandals of the Royal Family, and of horrors of the Duke of Cumberland'. Still no action decided, for fear it would 'bring out the case'. [7]

Ashe stayed quiet for six months, perhaps having run out of cash for postage. In May 1830 he came to life with a letter to Richard Mayne, chief of Peel's new Metropolitan Police (established 1829). It is in his usual style: 'I am an unfortunate Public Writer by Profession & after wasting a rather lengthened career in the uses & abuses of the Press, find myself a solitary individual of the world, a vagabond in appearance & a beggar in fact.' He would sue Ernest, but his solicitors demand their fee in advance. Must he 'repel cruelty & contumely by such means as Fenton & Bellingham [*the assassins of 1628 and 1812*] were driven to employ?' He implores Mayne to get him justice and so prevent the crime. 'Bellingham wrote a letter of this nature' which 'was regarded as an imbecile threat, & it cost Mr Perceval his life!'[8]

In July, Ashe came south (watched by Peel's men), found a room in Kensington and wrote to Mayne, 'I have travelled 300 miles on foot ... a man with famine in his heart & blood upon his mouth', seeking justice 'before he is goaded into acts of desperation & illegality'. He does not want to 'plunge the Royal Family into a state of unqualified mortification & sorrow'. Two days later (Ashe's 60th birthday, 15 July) he made an offer to Ernest's ADC, Lieut-Colonel Pöten: 'As I am most anxious to return to the Mountains of Cumberland, I entreat that an early hour may *be appointed* to set at rest & for ever a question which should never have been agitated.' He revives the Daniel O'Connell story, only to extol his own goodness. 'Better that *I* was employed than any *other* person whatever', because he put the manuscript in Ernest's hands. 'Who else than myself would have acted thus? And without keeping copy of a single page.' Ernest has kept him 'in a continual state of suffering & excitement'. Yet 'I never appealed to the press! No, never' — and he could have had thousands of pounds.

In return for this magnanimity, and for coming all the way from Cumberland, and for having written 'fifty letters', he requests 'a consideration'.[9]

Legal brains were still puzzling, ten months after Ashe's opening move, over how to act. Wellington became angry. Peel's under-secretary wrote to Maule that Ashe had become 'a serious annoyance' to Wellington: 'something must be done without delay'. Maule replied that despite Ashe's threat to assassinate, the attorney-general 'does not see for what offence he could be indicted'.

Peel had set his New Police to work, however. Thomas Quick, Constable No 114 of I Division, on surveillance early on 17 July outside Ashe's lodgings in Kensington, saw him emerge at 7 am and go for some breakfast. Then PC 114 shadowed him westwards, over Hammersmith bridge and on, six miles in all, to Ernest's place at Kew Green, and watched Ashe 'walking for an hour and a half in front of the palace gate'. He reported to Sir Richard Birnie, chief metropolitan magistrate, 'He kept looking very earnestly in at the gate, and when a carriage drew up he looked very attentively in at the window.' At the gate Ashe demanded to see Ernest. The ADC, Pöten, came out. Ashe said, 'It is very easy for you, who dine every day, to wait, but I have not eaten for five days' — forgetting that morning's breakfast. Pöten took pity: 'As you are in such distress I'll give you five shillings.' Ashe walked back to Kensington.

The cabinet again debated — inconclusively. Peel acted. That evening, constables watched Ashe spend some time in the King's Arms and the Wheat Sheaf in Kensington High-street. Then a police superintendent 'proceeded' to Ashe's lodgings (already, police *proceeded*) and arrested him. Ashe said, 'You can do nothing to me until you have given me back my property.' The superintendent produced Ashe's letter to the Metropolitan chief, threatening assassination. Did he write it? 'Yes.' He was escorted to a lock-up. [10]

What to do next? Ernest's friend Lord Eldon, the former lord chancellor, proverbial for being afflicted by doubts, wrote to Peel, *Most Private & Confidential*, to say Ashe might be able to argue in court that he was provoked to send his threats 'by the Matters of alleged Misconduct in the several parties alluded to' (*meaning incest and murder*). Ashe's lawyers, he feared, might 'irregularly' bring out enough to accomplish 'a Mischief' affecting many people named in *Osphia*.[11]

The treasury solicitor's office drew up an indictment for the felony of sending Ernest 'an atrocious libel upon their late Majesties King George 3d and Queen Charlotte and the Royal Family and particularly on Her Royal Highness the Princess Sophia and the Duke of Cumberland'. That was discarded: it would open up too much. Ashe was charged instead over letters 'threatening to kill and murder' Ernest.

Remanded to Middlesex House of Correction in Clerkenwell, he set to work writing appeals blending self-pity and effrontery. He asked Sir Richard Birnie to free him so that he could catch the next steamer to Newcastle upon Tyne, helped by 'a small purse to ... allow me time to look around me in Cumberland, and see, *having a little time afforded me*, whether I cannot produce a *good*, in place of a bad book. Could I get back to the mountains & sustain myself 4 months, I could engage to redeem myself & become, instead of a mere slave in the mine of Literature, a rich merchant & dealer in its wealth.' He suggests £10 in hand and £10 monthly for four months — totalling half what he had sought from Ernest, which itself was surprisingly moderate. Then a threat: 'I shake & tremble at the idea of going destitute out of this prison & being compelled to prostitute my pen... To pursue & yet to abhor crime is a fearful destiny! A destiny ever mine.'

To Ernest he wrote an immense petition headed 'Thomas Ashe, a Pariah & Prisoner'. Extracts must suffice. 'He implores HRH to apply the Roman adage to him — *Quem Deus vult perdere, prive dementat* [badly misquoted] — the gods, willing to ruin him, first made him mad.' In view of 'the losses, disappointments, sorrows and sufferings of the Petitioner *for the last 12 months*' he asks Ernest 'to have the great goodness to dispose Sir Richard Birnie to act the part of the Good Samaritan towards him, & to allow the poor Lazar to cast away his Crutch & run to the Mountains rejoicing'. He promises 'every possible atonement for his sins'. 'He will make a legal assignment of the Copyright of his Manuscript to any person appointed... He will never revert to the Manuscript, nor in any shape meddle with the concerns of HRH, his relations & connections or friends.' He is 'the most destitute & forsaken character this day on earth... Good God! Good God! ...Is no Good Samaritan ever to pass? Like the woman detected in the act of Adultery, everyone is ready to lapidate him — but no great character to stoop & write Mercy on the earth... What a lost solitary individual of the world. *And such his condition for 40 years!!!*'[12]

He says the manuscript 'is Romance from end to end'. Nobody involved, from Ernest down, ever treated it as romance. Four days later Ernest summoned Eldon, Wynford and Maule (with '*all* the letters and correspondence') to a conference at St James's Palace. Ernest showed them Ashe's petition. The question was, still, how to avoid 'a disclosure of the libel'. Maule reported to the Home Office: 'Long talk — Duke of Cumberland against being party to any compromise.' Eldon and Wynford agreed that 'either alternative was but a choice of evils, but that upon the whole the refraining to prosecute if it could properly be accomplished would be the lesser of the two'.[13]

Compromise prevailed. Maule had Ashe moved to the Newgate jail infirmary and advised him how to solicit mild treatment. Ashe said he would not employ counsel, thus removing Eldon's anxiety about a lawyer introducing 'the Mischief' in court. He promised not to name the manuscript in court, 'nor shall I utter a single word or sentence that can possibly hurt the feelings of your Royal Client or any of his illustrious Relatives'. His conduct will recommend him 'as an object of mercy'. As ever, he is a victim: 'I am now 60, am covered with wounds, besides 2 fractures in the head, & I have ever been misunderstood, misreported & misused.' Then he offers to 'be sent to New South Wales under instructions to the Governor not to be suffered ever to return'. Copies of all this were sent to the attorney-general and to Peel and Wellington.[14]

Still the attorney-general was unsure. He wished he could 'get rid of the thing without further public notice,' he told Maule, 'but I know not how to do it.' Being out of town, he sent Maule the key to his library bureau, where *Osphia* was secreted 'second drawer from the top', because Ashe's trial judge might want to see it. 'On no consideration ought it to be shown to the jury.'[15]

The case ended strangely.

Mr Justice Bayley presided at the Old Bailey, 18 September 1830. Ernest himself sat in court, no doubt to concentrate Ashe's mind. Evidence was given about Ashe's having threatened to 'act the part of Fenton or Bellingham', his being shadowed out to Kew, his arrest and his admission that a death-threat letter was his. Yet Bayley told the jury, 'Although the prisoner has acknowledged the letter to be in his own handwriting, no witnesses have been brought forward to prove that to be the case. Consequently they must acquit the prisoner for want of proper evidence.' (The law officers of course had many letters in Ashe's hand.) Verdict, not guilty. Ashe bowed and said he had 'no malice against His Royal Highness'.[16]

A pretence of incompetence got rid of Ashe. The public never heard of *Osphia*. Ashe was transported not to New South Wales but to the mountains of Cumberland with 'a small purse'. That month's Jail Delivery Record lists 'Thomas Ashe / sending a certain Letter threatening to kill & Murder a person / Not Guilty'. It also lists men transported to New South Wales for seven years, fourteen years or life for common larcenies.

16

Grave and alarming charges

A year after Garth filed his first affidavit in Chancery, he achieved something, or rather an illusory promise of something. The court ordered Sir Herbert to produce the receipt that the bankers Paul, Snow & Co had given 'for a Black Tin Box', and also to produce 'books letters receipts papers vouchers mem^da & writings' of late 1828 and early 1829, so that Garth's lawyer could 'inspect & peruse' them and make copies. Among these items was 'a statement of the terms proposed'. All these Sir Herbert had refused to produce.[1]

Sir Herbert was in no danger of having to comply instantly — if ever. As the recent inquiry into the Chancery Court had noted, 'Every order of the court must have its writ of execution served. In case of disobedience to the writ of execution, there must be an attachment. After the attachment, the course will vary according to the nature of the order. If the order be to deliver possession, and if that injunction be disobeyed, there is ultimately a writ of assistance directed to the sheriff... [*and so forth*].'

Sir Herbert's dealings inspired a critical article in *The Times*, signed Detector. It complained of 'glaring instances of high military rank and honours having been obtained by men whose only service has been one of subserviency to all above and of insolence to those below them'. In the *Army List*, Detector says, 'The first name that strikes my eye is Lieutenant-General Sir Herbert Taylor.' He lists his posts and titles, and asks, 'Can you or anyone tell where Sir Herbert won this rare compound of civil and military emolument and honour? What field of glory is associated with his name? Or how many scars he bears about him?' Detector concludes:

> Surely we can find better commanders and better examples to the army than those to be supplied by mere interest. It matters not whether it be borough interest, petticoat interest, or any other description of interest... Some recent exhibitions in Chancery savour more of the courtly intriguer than of the chivalrous soldier, and may afford a clue to his multitudinous honours and profits.

Friends of Sir Herbert wrote to *The Times* protesting over this 'most unwarrantable attack' and praising his 'urbanity, kindness and attention ... to everyone who has ever had business with him' and his 'strict integrity ... conciliatory demeanour, kind and amiable disposition', etc.[2] Sir Herbert no doubt saw himself as only doing his duty by the nation. In that unreformed time, any royal scandal was an alarming gift to inciters of disaffection and riot.

In Chancery, Westmacott provided some light relief. Garth's opening affidavit had said this editor of a paper 'remarkable only for its calumnious charges' had wanted to publish his documents. In reply, Westmacott alleged that he had had to talk Garth out of publishing (a course that could never have enriched him). Westmacott added a puff for *The Age* and its politics. It *is* remarkable — 'for the expression of spirited and fearless comments upon subjects which concern the moral and political safety, welfare and happiness of the community and for the utterance of such opinions as become free men'.[3]

Sir Herbert, the gentleman of 'strict integrity', swears again, in a new affidavit of June 1830, that he does not 'know suspect or believe what are the contents purport or effect' of the documents. His chief point now is that Westmacott and Charles Frederick Williams have told him that before Garth handed over the documents, copies were made. Sir Herbert has the box safe in the bank (or may already have presented his receipt), but the copies are a danger.[4]

The following month, Williams wrote a dramatic letter to Ernest's lawyer and friend Lord Wynford urging the absolute necessity of obtaining and destroying 'at once' the copies made by the 'infirm' and 'malign' Garth. The copies, Williams says, are in a locked box held by 'Mr Howard'. This is Garth's solicitor, Edward John Howard of Sackville-street, Mayfair. A second drama of a box is developing. Among the copies, Williams writes, are letters of Princess Sophia. His anxiety is not however about her. Ernest's case, Williams says, transcends hers 'a thousandfold'. Indeed it does. It always has.

It will be remembered that when *The Times* and others first asked why astonishing sums were offered to Garth, Sir Herbert ventured to whisper to influential people that Sophia had written of 'attempts upon her person' by Ernest (*page 136*). Now Williams, working to win control of every last dangerous document, goes so far as to take Ernest's guilt to that point, not in a whisper, but in writing. His letter to Wynford says, 'Several of the letters convey grave and alarming charges against HRH in the most unequivocal terms — charges of a description that would awaken and direct an overwhelming burst of popular Indignation against the illustrious Duke, which explanation, denial or natural improbability would perhaps ineffectually stem or control.' And Williams sets out the charges:

> An accusation by a Sister that Her Own Brother had more than once attempted to violate her Person rouses such horrible Emotions that Reason is generally overpowered & explanation or refutation are either heard too late, or rejected!

One must wonder what 'explanation or refutation' even a King's Counsel might have devised against the illustrious Sophia's word.

Someone is intriguing to obtain the copies, Williams tells Wynford. It is a matter of supreme urgency to obtain and destroy them 'at even a considerable sacrifice' (of money). Wynford passed the letter to Wellington, who was still prime minister. That is why it has become known, when so much was destroyed. Wellington was a careful filer of letters. When Elizabeth Lady Longford was writing her life of Wellington in the late 1960s she found it among his papers. It now seems, most oddly, to have become unavailable.

Its significance was certainly grave and alarming. At a simple level it confirms, from Ernest's side, that the contested documents were far from being innocent letters between Sophia and her alleged husband General Garth, as comically claimed by Ernest's advocates. It rules out any attempt to make Ernest a cruelly calumniated innocent, 'the most injured man in His Majesty's dominions'. And it goes much deeper. The letters of Sophia at issue here are part of a set of documents about Thomas Garth's parentage and birth. If the begetter of Garth were any man *other* than Ernest, Sophia would have no reason to write about his having 'more than once attempted to violate her'. She would do so only in telling what led to her becoming pregnant by Ernest.

Elizabeth Longford, dealing briefly with the Garth story, errs on details and makes assumptions that favour Ernest. Most seriously, and surprisingly, she proposes that Williams's letter frees Ernest of the 'terrible charge' of incest. He 'attempted', she says, 'rather than achieved his object'. She manages to conclude that General Garth is left 'in the undisputed but unenviable possession of Thomas'.[5]

Although Williams does not speak of actual incest, it must be remembered that his letter is to Ernest's own lawyer. To write about attempts was perilous enough. He ventured to go as far as he did because his urgent purpose was to obtain approval and money for the crime of suborning Garth's solicitor.

Wellington's first concern was, were there copies of the Garth papers besides those held by Howard? He had heard, he told Wynford, of 'copious extracts' held by another person (very likely Westmacott). Paying hush-money was often self-defeating. 'If it is given with facility and in large Sums it is almost certain that the Copies of these Papers will be multiplied; and as all these payments of Money are at the least of doubtful Legality we should at last have to pay Money in order to conceal the fact we had paid any for the suppression of these Papers.' Before he will consider paying, Wellington says, all other means 'should be resorted to'. He will want to be 'quite certain that all Vestige of these Papers is destroyed'. [6]

Sir Herbert had swung Westmacott and Williams to his side. Could he also turn Howard, the solicitor? Garth would learn what means could be 'resorted to'. He and Lady Astley were hiding from his creditors, Sir Herbert was unyielding, and Howard was inexplicably slow releasing cash from the general's estate to fend off Garth's creditors. In October 1830 a Middlesex sheriff's bailiff arrested Garth. This was gratifying news for Sir Herbert. Garth's debts had led to his Chancery suit and its revelations, so distressing to Sir Herbert, but now they were sending him to debtors' prison.

Garth's life in prison is told in the next chapter. His betrayal by Howard comes here. Working from prison, Garth twice took legal action against him. The first case was over some of the general's silver. Garth testified that when he was in hiding, Howard told him two creditors had discovered his address, so he must flee to Scotland. Howard then collected two chests of the general's silver in Dorset and more from the general's town house. All this he pledged at a pawnbroker for £200. Howard argued that Garth had given him power to manage his affairs, and quoted letters in which Garth urged him to get money 'in some way or other'. Once he asked Howard to send 'some blunt' (cash) urgently so he could get his boots mended. Garth won his suit, but Howard reversed that on a legal technicality.[7]

The second case, much more important, was over the box of papers at Howard's Mayfair office. In March 1832 Garth sought a Chancery order requiring Howard to produce it. Besides legal correspondence it contained 'other documents' (presumably Garth's copies) and 'sundry articles of jewelry'. Howard, he says, has no claim on the box: indeed, he owes Garth £570 in money advanced to him. Sure enough, the names of Sir Herbert and Williams arise. When trying to regain the box, Garth testifies, he found that a notice had been served on Howard not to part with it. He has reason to believe that Howard, 'acting in concert with Charles Frederick Williams', Garth's former 'adviser and pretended friend', became Sir Herbert's adviser and 'procured the said notice to be served on himself'.

When Sir Herbert is at work, whom can one trust?

The court ordered that Howard 'do forthwith deliver up' the box to a new solicitor appointed by Garth, so that Garth (on 'day rule' leave) could inspect it. On 17 March 1832 Garth had disturbing facts to report in Chancery. The key he was handed was not the original key. When opening the box he found 'that an attempt had been made to saw the lock (he supposes before the spurious key was obtained)'. And he reports a serious theft: correspondence between himself and Howard is missing, and so are 'divers copies of letters of importance'. Garth has 'no knowledge how and when and by whom or at whose instance ... the key produced to him was obtained'. He requests that a Master in Chancery should inquire 'when & by whom & under what circumstances' it was done, '& what is become of the papers'.[8]

When was the box rifled? Soon after Williams's urgent letter of July 1830 about Ernest's 'attempts'. This is shown in a letter of that month from Ernest's friend Lord Eldon to Sir Robert Peel, the home secretary. Eldon says, 'Wynford is convinced that there are no other copies of the papers of Mr G—th than such as he [Wynford] understood to be in the possession of a Person who, I was yesterday informed, had given them up to Sir H Taylor.' For 'Person' read Howard. This paragraph is an addendum to Eldon's *Most Private & Confidential* letter about *Osphia*, quoted in the previous chapter.[9]

No record can be found of a Master in Chancery doing anything to pursue the guilty men, to recover the stolen papers or to uphold Garth's rights in the black tin box.

17

A most royal prisoner

Sir Herbert and the Chancery machine had succeeded in foiling
Garth's plea for an injunction since March 1829. At last his creditors
struck. On 28 October 1830 he was arrested by that much-feared
officer, a bailiff, who if true to type was a sturdy fellow carrying a
stout club, backed by a sturdier assistant. As Westmacott's colleague
William Maginn wrote parodically in his careless youth —

> My heart leaps up when I behold
> A bailiff in the street.
> 'Twas so since from one first I ran...

Garth was escorted to a sponging-house, a lodging in which debtors
awaited committal. After five days there, he was taken across the
Thames to Southwark and the most famous debtors' prison of all,
King's Bench, known as Banco Regis.

Where was Georgiana Caroline, Lady Astley? More than four years
had passed since she eloped with Garth; nearly two years since he had
reached a deal with Sir Herbert that promised to bless them finan-
cially. Then came the anxiety of her lover's struggle against the court
of Windsor and the court of Chancery. If tempted to leave him, where
could she go? She was a social outcast. Astleys and Dashwoods were
united against her. Undivorced, she could not remarry. For some
erring ladies the role of kept woman had to serve. One gentleman at
least tried to win Georgiana (*pages 116–17*).

She did not abandon Garth. She could stay in lodgings near the
prison and visit him, as permitted by the prison's civilized rules.
Whether she did so from the start is not known, but it is certain that
she was visiting him in 1834, as a coming event will prove.

Garth's confinement in King's Bench Prison (a fact hitherto un-
discovered) was to last five years. He entered a community of nearly
500 inhabitants, within twenty-five-foot walls topped with spikes.
Rooms were a shilling a week. Debtors able to pay extra could lodge
less shamingly in approved houses nearby, 'within the rules'. They

could work and thus pay off their debts. One remarkable resident 'within the rules' was the author, journalist and comic poet William Combe, who was so content with his life at 12 Lambeth-road, half a mile from the prison, that he lived there from 1800 until his death in 1823, aged 81. He refused to pay off his creditors, saying their claims were unjust. For many years he was paid a retainer by *The Times* (a short walk away across Blackfriars Bridge), contributed hundreds of articles, and for a time was its acting editor. From 1812 onwards he wrote the verses for the *Tours of Doctor Syntax* and for *The English Dance of Death*, works famously illustrated by Thomas Rowlandson, and still in demand.

Inmates of the prison itself could buy a day of freedom for four shillings, so long as they came back before 9 pm. In 1827 Westmacott's victim, Richard Downing Richards, used this 'day rule' to edit *The Age* until he was defeated. He left Banco Regis just before Garth arrived, so they missed a chance to compare notes on Westmacott. Another inmate just before Garth's time, and again later, was the troubled painter Benjamin Robert Haydon, who wrote in his diary on a Sunday in June 1830, 'Passed the day in all the buz, blasphemy, hum, noise & confusion of a prison... Such language! Such jokes!' He prayed for his wife and children, but then 'to hear those poor fellows, utterly indifferent as it were, was really distressing'.[1]

A shilling book of 1823, *A Description of the King's Bench Prison*, gives a positive account. The author lived within the rules (11 Borough-road), so was unwilling to offend the prison marshal. He provides good firsthand detail, however. The prison has 225 rooms, up sixteen sets of stairs. Two prisoners, and sometimes three, are 'chummed' in each room. Eight select rooms in the State House are allotted to 'those who by their good conduct or gentlemanly behaviour have entitled themselves to this indulgence' on payment of an extra shilling a week. 'In this house have lived lords, members of parliament and colonels; not forgetting Mary Anne Clarke, who was sentenced for a libel.' Mary Anne, the Duke of York's ex-mistress, confined in 1814, complained to the lord chief justice about her discomfort and was promoted to the State House.

The beer in the State House tap-room, Messrs Barclay & Perkins's, 'is considered particularly good'. The cook in the prison kitchen 'is so good that many people send in their provisions to be cooked'. Prisoners can have 'a very excellent bason of soup for twopence' and hot water 'a penny a tea-kettle'. They can cook their meat and vegetables there, and find bacon, eggs, herrings, boiled ham or 'mutton pies all hot' in the prison shops. Enterprising prisoners are at work — 'Boots soled and heeled... Shave for a penny, hair cut for twopence... Children taken in to nurse'. There are work-benches. 'Pianofortes have been manufactured.'

For exercise, prisoners play rackets and fives against the courtyard walls. (Westmacott's *English Spy* magazine tells in 1826 of Harriette Wilson's latter-day associate, 'Colonel' Rochfort, '*rusticating* in Surrey, beating the balls about in *Banco Regis*'.)

A prison has class distinctions. One tap-room, The Brace, ranks 'between the *vulgarity* of the common tap of the prison and the *tip-top* of the coffee-house. Its frequenters are the semi-genteel ... between the canaille and what are familiarly and quaintly called the *nobs*.' Between 4 and 5 pm nobs dine at the coffee-house for half a crown (30 pence). The canaille, those who have sworn they are 'not worth £5', take turns standing at the prison gate with the poor-box ('Pray Remember the Poor Debtors'), and also get charity beef, bread and coal.

For prisoners such as Garth, dealing with lawyers and courts, there is a postal service exactly matching the one that so excellently serves all of London: five dispatches of twopenny letters between 10 am and 8 pm, and seven deliveries between 9 am and 10 pm. Wives or friends on visits to prisoners are warned by a crier going round at 8.30 pm, ringing a bell and calling, 'Strangers, women and children, all out!' and finally at 9 pm, 'All strangers out!'[2]

Although King's Bench was less oppressive than other London prisons, partly because many inmates were well-informed and occasionally titled gentlemen, it had its ugly side. The year before Garth's arrival, an Irish inmate named Robert Sterne Tighe petitioned the lord chief justice to inquire into abuses. The prison had become 'the most extensive and pernicious brothel in the metropolis' and a scene of 'drunkenness, gambling and robbery'. He accused the prison marshal of breach of rules and of extorting 'vast emoluments' from prisoners. But when an inquiry judge was appointed, *The Times* reported, 'The inmates, conceiving that the charges impeached their moral character ... got up a counter-petition ... signed by upwards of 400.' The petition rejected 'sweeping assertions' about debauchery and praised the marshal's 'humanity and kindness'.[3]

A few months later *The Times* reported that 'Miss Cynthia Little, an antiquated damsel on the wrong side of 40, dressed in the most fantastic style ... rouged up to the eyes', was charged with hawking obscene prints and immoral poems in the prison. A turnkey testified that, having noticed a poem, 'Encounter of Venus with a Mad Actor', he stopped Cynthia at the gate and seized 'a great number of prints of the most disgusting nature' and 'poems of an amatory nature'. There was 'contamination enough in prison without books of that kind'. The magistrate looked at the exhibits and named a few — *Cynthia among the Gods, Cupid Attacked by Satan, The Passion of Love Discussed*. He gave the damsel four months in the Southwark house of correction.[4]

Newspapers obtained stories direct from the prison, by way of journalist-inmates or others earning a few shillings. When Garth had been inside for seven months, a story headlined FRACAS IN THE KING'S BENCH, about an ugly scene in which he was involved, appeared in the *Morning Advertiser*. It so wounded Garth that he sued the paper for libel. It said a prisoner named Deacon was visited daily by his wife. Someone sent her 'an amorous epistle' signed XYZ, 'begging an assignation' and asking her to reply at the prison post office. She told her husband. They left an answer for XYZ. The messenger who called for it, the paper said, 'was employed by Captain Garth'. Deacon 'provided himself with a small pocket-whip used by sportsmen for their dogs, called a flogger. This he placed in the crown of his hat along with the love-epistle, and he accosted Captain Garth on the racket-ground at a time when it was thronged.' Garth allegedly acknowledged the letter. 'Mr Deacon instantly knocked him down with a blow of his fist ... and before he could recover himself, began to exercise the use of the flogger.' The marshal confined Deacon for a month in the prison strongroom.

The eminent Serjeant Wilde, counsel for Garth, said, 'Whatever might have been his misfortunes or his errors, he is not a fit subject for every calumny.' The editor seemed to feel it was a serious case, 'for he has brought the attorney-general [James Scarlett] here to defend him'. In a jibe at Scarlett, whose usual concern with newspapers was to prosecute them, Wilde said, 'The jury will no doubt hear an eloquent eulogium on the liberty of the press from my learned friend. It is not often that attorney-generals are blessed with an opportunity of expatiating on that topic.' Garth, he said, was not the author of the letter. He had been 'held up to the world as an object of ridicule and odium'.

A prisoner, brought as a witness, said, 'I can't say whether he [Deacon] struck him seventeen or eighteen blows with the whip, but he laid it into him.'

Scarlett professed to be bewildered by Garth's suit: 'Why has he not brought an action against the man who inflicted the flogging?' The jury, 'knowing what they did of this plaintiff', should award nothing. They awarded a farthing, and costs. But gaining the verdict mattered. Wilde said Garth had risked being 'excluded from all the comforts of society in a place where he could not select his companions'.[5] More important, though, was Garth's need to challenge the report for Georgiana's sake.

A remarkably detailed record of life in the prison, with frequent mentions of Garth, can be found in official memorandum books that survive, beginning in January 1832.

16 January, Garth pays his overdue room rent.

12 June, applies to have Sir Edwin Sandys's room if Sandys is discharged.

26 June, 'Captn Garth complained that a charwoman had beaten carpets behind the State House [evidently he is one of its privileged tenants], and was very impudent when he complained.' She promises 'not to do the like'.

14 July, a prisoner dies of cholera. An inquest jury of prisoners recommends having a doctor on duty at night, and 'that hot water sh^d be constantly kept ready and that the dustbins might be emptied every morning'. (*Cholera had reached Britain in November 1831.*)

18 July, the bins and the staircases are washed with chloride of lime.

The Times of that date reported having received many complaints of 'the filthy and neglected condition of this prison'. Several prisoners had died of cholera and the prison inquest juries 'have been *packed*'. Next day, a letter signed 'A prisoner' said a protest about 'accumulations of filth and stench ... a cause of terror under the existing visitation of cholera' had moved Lord Melbourne, the home secretary, to order an inspection. Soon after, 'A prisoner' wrote that publicity in *The Times* had won 'a sort of pledge' that the inquests would not be 'a screen for the neglect or misconduct of the keeper and his officers'.[6]

Garth could divert his mind from cholera by coping with day-to-day problems. He complained that a woman who sold provisions in the prison had overcharged him for the past year — '1s7d butter instead of 1s1d, cream 2d instead of 1d and everything else in the same proportion'. She admitted her guilt. He complained to the chief warder that another woman, who was dunning him for 25 shillings 'for greengrocery &c &c', had written him a letter threatening to expose him to 'ridicule in the *Satirist* newspaper unless the debt was paid this day'. The woman denied knowing anything about the letter.[7]

Garth was indeed topical enough for paragraphs in *The Satirist*, as will be seen later in this chapter. This Sunday paper, founded in 1831 as a rival to Westmacott's *Age*, was similarly spiced with items about blackguards, toadies, adulterers and mistresses, but generally those of a Tory complexion. Its staff had to beware (as did Westmacott) of beatings. In August 1831 *The Times* reported that 'two gentlemen connected with the *Satirist* newspaper' staggered to the police with 'blood upon their faces and clothes'. Five men had arrived on horseback at their office. 'While two of them kept the door, the three others attacked them with the ends [handles] of their whips, which were loaded with iron'. At the *Satirist* office, windows were broken 'and the floor covered with blood'.[8]

The prison's chief paperwork was to record the commitment of debtors, the creditors' claims, the discharge of each debt (marked with the abbreviation 'Dis') and the debtors' eventual release. The books list more than forty of Garth's creditors. The grand total that kept him in King's Bench was, before legal costs, about £7600 (other creditors had been quieted in 1828 when Garth was given an advance of £3000).

A search for his creditors' names in commercial directories yields some tradesmen of the sort one would expect: Burghart, Frederick, tailor, 17 Clifford-street, Mayfair, £340. Boutall, John, veterinary surgeon, North-row, Grosvenor-square, £100. Edwards, Thomas & Son, tailors, 52 Conduit-street, Hanover-square, £200. Giblett, William, butcher, 110 New Bond-street, £200. Moore, Jabez, breeches-maker, 136 New Bond-street, £26. Raven, Ebenezer, chandler, Bishopsgate, £266. Tilbury, John, coach and harness-maker, South-street, Grosvenor-square, £145. Watson, Jonathan, printseller, Vere-street, £143. In a different class are a colonel owed £427 for 'a guarantee on an annuity' and solicitors claiming £500. (Tilbury was the creator of the gig of that name. So he was no doubt the supplier of the one that Garth sent for Westmacott's breakfast-time visit in 1828: *page 153*.)

It was not until the spring of 1833 that 'Dis' began to be written beside any names in Garth's list. Why did he have to wait so long to benefit effectively from his inheritance? One must guess that his original solicitor, Howard — suborned for Sir Herbert in 1830 and exposed by Garth in 1832 — took his time about handing over the necessary paperwork to a new solicitor.

As Garth began to have hope of daylight, cholera struck again in August 1833. The prison memo-book says, 'Capt G suggested that the staircases should be sprinkled with chloride of lime.' This was done. Someone else suggested whitewashing the walls to a height of sixteen feet. During the next week three prisoners died. And Garth's occasional troubles continued:

14 August 1833: 'Capt G compl^d of of an attack ... by Mrs Bruere who he thought was the worse for liquor.' Her husband used 'most violent language towards Capt G, calling him a liar & threatening to pull his nose'. Mrs Bruere is ordered to be locked out.

9 September: a sword-cane is seized from a prisoner, who says Garth gave it him to repair. Another prisoner, Sir Nathaniel Peacock, complains that when his servant brought his dinner in a basket, it was inspected (probably for banned liquor — previously, Sir Nathaniel had complained that his health suffered for lack of the sherry 'he had always been used to').

1 February 1834: Garth wants the match-girls locked out because they are going up the staircases and 'stealing whatever they can'.

7 February: he sits on an inquest jury.

11 February: complains of dirty privies.

22 February: an inmate to whom Garth gave his razor strop to repair pawned it for four shillings and passed the ticket to another. This man redeemed the strop, saw 'Capt G's crest & cypher on it', and pledged it for six shillings. Garth recovers his royal strop.[9]

During the first three months of 1834 Garth was much concerned with the fate of a prisoner in a desperate state. This was John 'Mad Jack' Mytton of Halston Hall, near Oswestry, Shropshire, born 1796, heir to an ancient landed family, scholar at Westminster School 1807–11, then at Harrow School 1811–13 when Garth was there (expelled for fighting), and inheritor at twenty-one of an estate yielding £10,000 a year. He was a hussar officer (briefly), MP for Shrewsbury (briefly), high sheriff of the county, major in the Shropshire Yeomanry, master of foxhounds (owning 124 hounds), winner of racing gold cups, and performer of such reckless feats of horsemanship and of drinking that he figures still in the annals of foxhunting and other country sports.

In the *Sporting Magazine*, its correspondent Nimrod (Charles Apperley) reports on a visit to Halston Hall in 1826. He looks at Mytton's ale and wine cellars. 'In the first we saw hogsheads of ale standing like soldiers in close column; and in the other, in bottle and in cask, wine enough for a Roman emperor... Mr Mytton makes his own malt, and the words JOHN MYTTON, LICENSED MALTSTER are painted in large letters over his malthouse door.' Then just thirty, Mytton, a powerfully built man, was still in good shape. On a cold morning, wearing only shirt, dressing-gown and slippers, he took Nimrod to his racing stables to see 'his filly that is in the Oaks'. He began playing his 'harlequin tricks', says Nimrod: 'He laid himself down at full length under her belly, with his naked head toward her heels — playing with her tail, tickling her about the legs, &c, &c. "I cannot stand this," said I... One of these days *he must drop short*. Indeed, what with falls from horses — runaway gigs — upsets in carriages — swimming his horse over the Severn (though he himself cannot swim) ... it is next to a miracle that he is now alive.'[10]

Nimrod in his *Memoirs of the Life of the Late John Mytton* (1835, 1837 and often reissued) says Mytton was *'mad half by nature and half by wine'*. He recounts many 'harlequin tricks'. When a friend, with him in a gig, a light two-wheeler, was unnerved by his furious driving, Mytton said, 'Were you ever much hurt, then, by being upset in a gig?' Friend: 'No... I was never upset in one.' 'What! *never* upset in a gig? What a damned slow fellow you must have been all your life!' Mytton ran the nearside wheel up a bank and 'over they both went'.

It was the drink that killed him. Many sportsmen were hard drinkers. A noted Leicestershire master of foxhounds, Thomas Assheton Smith, tried to set an example of moderation by announcing that his daily quota was one pint of wine (probably port). But Mytton, says Nimrod in the *Memoirs*, drank 'from *four* to *six* bottles of port wine *daily*' (good port, however, eight years old). He would start on a bottle while shaving.

By 1831, pursued by creditors, he fled to Calais, a frequent refuge. Nimrod happened to be there for the same reason. Mytton knocked on his door, 'a decrepit, tottering *old-young* man ... a mind as well as a body in ruins'.[11] By then he had moved on from port to 'brandy, brandy, brandy, morning, noon and night'. Tormented with a persistent hiccup, he said, 'I'll *frighten* it away,' and set fire to his nightshirt. He wrote to his long-suffering agent at Halston, Walter Broughall, 'I'm badly burnt. Come over to me here QUICK as I have much to do with you... Have no fear, I shall live they say now though they were frightened damnably... Bring me £200 or £300 if you can from my tenants but be quick... I have often been afraid of Mr Fire. He caught me sharply at last. Bring any pheasants that can be killed, as far as 20 brace.' He returned to Halston, was arrested for debt, and was escorted back to King's Bench by the governor of Shrewsbury jail, a friend named Griffiths whom he had appointed when high sheriff.

So in 1831 Garth was reacquainted in prison with his famed fellow-Harrovian. One can imagine them exchanging stories of hunting and other exploits. Mytton obtained his discharge before long, but in the next couple of years he became more and more alcoholically turbulent. In January 1834 he arrived back in King's Bench, decrepit and tottering, and with few possessions. The prison memo-book notes a box of his, brought from his lodgings, containing 'a pack of cards, dominoes, two or three French games and a dicebox'. These were admitted, except for the dicebox.

Mytton's first wife had died long before and his second wife, with five children, had left him, but his mother stood by him to the end. Some time before this she had written to Mytton's agent, 'I am half crazy about your poor master... Don't let him walk or hurt himself or ride. I *know* you will be tender to him... Pacify him and make him more content if possible.' The prison memo-book of 1834 says the mother wrote to Garth, who 'interested himself on his behalf'.

Nimrod says Mytton was a man who could never be made to take prudent advice. In his last known letter, from King's Bench to his agent, 8 February 1834, he has come to the point of confessing this dangerous trait, half-humorously: 'My position is such that I am OBLIGED occasionally actually to OBEY ORDERS.'[12]

Spirits were prohibited in the prison, except 'medicinally'. Six entries in the memo-book record the last three weeks of his life.

7 March: A doctor issues a certificate to allow Mytton '$1/2$ pint of brandy daily' and '2 bottles of stout each day if he required it'. Mytton is 'not actually insane' but 'incompetent to manage his affairs' (he has delirium tremens).

8 March: Garth reports that several gentlemen are in Mytton's room, 'about to prevail on him to sign some deed ... for the assignment of Mr M's property for the benefit of his creditors'. (This seems to have been foiled.)

22 March: Very ill. Garth is asked to suggest anything that can be done.

27 March: Mytton's mother and his Shrewsbury friend Griffiths have come. The mother asks that Griffiths be allowed to stay in the prison that night, as Mytton might die before morning.

29 March: '*Died* this Evg, $1/4$ before 6.' He was 37.

31 March: inquest verdict, natural death.[13]

Nimrod's *Memoirs* add to this spare account. They tell of Garth, in his fourth year out of the great world, devoting himself to Mytton, and praying with him.

Nimrod writes: 'A brother sportsman and a brother prisoner (well known at Melton Mowbray) who, as I have before mentioned, had been extremely kind to my poor friend during his first and second incarceration, and who was a constant attendant on his sickbed, wrote me — unsolicited — some interesting particulars... In the opinion of his friend, he [Mytton] took much to heart this second confinement in the King's Bench ... and he thought it hastened his end... He had the church service read to him nearly every day, and more particularly on Good Friday, when he held a long conversation with his brother prisoner on the sacrament'. Here is a touching glimpse of Garth, changed by misfortune.[14]

Even when he was in his fifth year in Banco Regis, journalists had not forgotten him — and his parentage. *The Satirist* made bold references to Ernest and Sophia, often in the form of dialogues:

> 'Why, Garth, I perceive that the Duke and your mamma visited the disconsolate Mary [their sister, recently widowed] on Sunday last — have they been of late to see you?'
>
> 'No, it is against the rules of society and good breeding for such parents nowadays to visit their offspring.'

William IV's bastards by Dorothy Jordan were then in the public eye, acquiring good incomes and titles. They are the peg for a daring jibe:

> 'Why should you, Garth,' asked a fellow-bencher [in the prison], 'be excluded the moral privileges of other lefthanded scions of royalty? Your blood is more pure than either the Fitzjordans or the Fitzmurrays.'
>
> 'It is the *exceeding purity* of my blood, and the moral *impurity* of my parents, that is my curse,' replied this living evidence of royal infamy.

A dialogue between a 'Fitzjordan' and Garth is headed NO MYSTERY:

> 'There's mystery in your birth, I hear!'
> Said Jordan's cub —
> 'Or rather,'
> Cried Garth, 'say now it's more than clear
> That CUMBERLAND's my father!'

The Satirist makes someone put a question to Ernest himself: 'Why not do something for Garth?' The 'enemy of mankind' replies, 'Because I did too much for his mother.'[15] If Ernest or his lawyers read *The Satirist*, they deemed it ill-advised to prosecute. Nor is there any sign of these slurs having provoked a visit to the editor by men with horsewhips.

As Garth's day of freedom drew nearer he made frequent 'day rule' exits. Some were no doubt on business, but most of them will have been to Georgiana at a house 'within the rules'. For she was pregnant. And here a doubly tragic end to their romantic or reprehensible affair is about to be revealed.

In *The Times* of 30 June 1835 this announcement appeared:

> DIED: On Sunday, the 28th inst, of scarlet fever, Georgiana Caroline, the wife of Sir Jacob Astley, Bart.

Nine years had passed since she ran away with her royal but illstarred lover; years that can have given her little joy. She was 39.

Newspapers did not then have the staffs or the space for copious follow-ups of high-society dramas. The *Morning Herald* of 2 July carried a short item: 'We have to record a melancholy termination to an unfortunate career, in the death of Lady Astley, which took place in the King's Bench this week.' It said 'this unhappy person' had married Sir Jacob Astley, who was 'eminently qualified to render her lot a fortunate one'. Her elopement with 'the well-known Captain Garth' was followed by 'vicissitudes of fortune', until he was imprisoned in the King's Bench, 'where Lady Astley has also lived, until the scarlet fever has suddenly put an end to her sufferings'. In fact she was not 'in' the prison: her name does not occur in its records. Next day *The Times* merely copied the item, between a paragraph about an illegal gaming-house and one about an MP's wife falling into a cellar.

What these papers did not learn was that a few days before Georgiana died she had given birth to a girl. Research for this book has discovered this, as indeed it has revealed the fact of Garth's imprisonment. He had been assumed to have disappeared by 1830, perhaps paid to retire to the continent, but the *Army List* showed him continuing on half-pay year after year in the 15th Hussars. It also gave a London address, enabling a check in census returns — which showed him declaring a daughter named *Georgiana*, a promising clue.

The church records to be searched first were those for St George the Martyr, Southwark, a short walk from the prison. They do not list Lady Astley's burial, but the 1835 register of baptisms has a rewarding entry: '*August 19th, Georgiana Rosamond Caroline | Dau^r of Sir Jacob and Georgiana Caroline Astley | Melton Constable, Norfolk | Father's occupation: Gent., Bart.*' It is understandable that Garth avoided giving his own name. Still, a noted baronet as the father must have astonished the curate, the Rev Mr Horton. In the same page, other fathers are a silk mercer, distiller, carpenter, boot-closer and chair-maker.[16]

'Scarlet fever' would also be Garth's invention. Several months later, one newspaper did learn of the birth — *The Satirist*. It says the 'much-to-be-pitied Lady Astley ... died of what is termed milk-fever, five days after giving birth to a girl'. This paragraph is strongly anti-Garth, calling Lady Astley 'the victim of the monster-child of royalty' and alleging he 'expressed but little concern ... and suffered Sir Jacob Astley to defray the expenses of her funeral!' Garth seems to have protested, for a fortnight later *The Satirist* gave a slightly less hostile picture. 'The infant granddaughter of the Princess Sophia ... is with its nurse at the lodgings of that left-handed "illustrious", Captain Garth, in the plebeian regions of St George's-fields. The captain, who possesses, as all the world knows, an overabundant share of the milk of human kindness, intends bringing up and educating this second-hand "brilliant" himself.'[17] This indeed was what he did. The daughter whom he gave his lover's names remained with him all his life.

What *The Satirist* said about the funeral was also untrue. According to Sir Jacob's direct descendant, Edward Delaval Astley, 22nd Baron Hastings, neither the birth nor Georgiana's place of burial was ever known to the family. Where Georgiana was buried is a mystery. It is not recorded at the Dashwood parish church in Oxfordshire.

In royal courts, the birth of even a distant cousin is punctiliously noted. Princess Victoria will not have learned, however, that just after her sixteenth birthday she gained a 'first cousin, once removed', born in plebeian Southwark, to add to the roll of casual cousins produced over the years by her Uncle George, Uncle Frederick, Uncle William, Uncle Augustus, Uncle Ernest, Aunt Elizabeth...

Five months after Georgiana's death Garth satisfied his last creditors. On 2 December 1835, after more than five years, he was free. Perhaps he made a point of wishing luck to people he had come to know as they passed through the portal on day rules: a diverse lot, such as William Jerdan, editor of *The Literary Gazette*; Clement Joseph Philippe Baron de Bode; Sir Edwin Sandys, Bart; and the unconvincing Dame Fanny Parker, 'commonly called Lady Hyde Parker'.

18

The rewards of chicanery

No trace of a conclusion to Garth v Taylor can be found in the Public Record Office's Chancery files. Garth did not obtain his injunction. George IV's urgent command that the Chancellor should 'get possession of *all* that is *necessary*' is sure to have helped to open the way for Sir Herbert Taylor to go to the bank with his receipt and extract the black tin box. When? Garth, even before his arrest, was conveniently out of the way, evading bailiffs. The seizing of his copies was in July 1830, so it is safe to say that Sir Herbert already had the originals. All were certainly burnt. Caricature prints can dare to be truthtellers. 'An old SATYR in Retirement' (*plate 14*) shows a shaggy, bestial Ernest crouching beside a box of Garth Papers destined for the Land of Fire.[1]

The blaze itself was a small one in a long series of royal burnings, heartbreaking for historians. Sir Herbert had had years of practice. After Queen Charlotte's death he burned all letters to her from George III, from her sons William and Augustus and from Princess Amelia, as well as the king's letters to Amelia. Earlier he had burned nearly all letters to the queen from Sophia and the other princesses.

Other bonfires served George IV. When regent, he dismissed his alcoholic Privy Purse, Sir John McMahon (also known as Privy Pimp), then found that many sensitive papers chronicling his early dissipations were missing. He sent Sir William Knighton, his physician, in pursuit. 'I found him very very feeble in Body, and his Head *quite* gone,' Knighton reported. His doctor had ordered 'entire absence of all Stimuli'. Knighton fed McMahon 'strong Brandy & Water' and 'his Mind, though feeble, gradually returned'. A five-hour negotiation, no doubt with further strong medication, succeeded: 'All Your Royal Highness's private Letters, early Correspondence and other Documents are now safe in my possession.' Sorting the lot, Knighton was free to learn many useful secrets. A few papers were kept, the rest he burned in the regent's presence.[2] McMahon died within four weeks. Knighton's rise to power began. The regent rewarded him with two rich sinecures, and as king made him his Privy Purse and secretary.

After George IV died, 'notes and letters in abundance' were burned at Windsor; also 'trinkets and trash ... a prodigious quantity of hair ... of all colours and *lengths* ... heaps of women's gloves'.[3] Hundreds of letters to and from George and his unlawful wife Maria Fitzherbert were gathered at her Mayfair house and expired together in a fireplace, with a pause when Wellington said, 'We'd better hold our hand for a while or we'll set the old woman's chimney on fire.'

Much purging of the royal literary heritage remained for Sir Herbert to oversee. Most of the papers of the scandal-prone Duke of York, whom Sir Herbert had served for years as secretary, were deemed unfit even for the obscurity of the royal archive. So were most of William IV's papers. Incineration continued into the 20th century. Diaries kept by Queen Victoria during sixty years were burned by her daughter Beatrice after she had shaped a new version with continuous cosmeticizing and filleting (the emaciated version still makes 111 manuscript volumes). Nearly all Edward VII's papers, political as well as those 'of very delicate private character', vanished in smoke.[4] The story of later royal blazes remains to be told.

Sir Herbert's rich rewards for discreet services aroused comment. In 1834 a letter to *The Times* signed Scrutator said the public was agitated about 'profligacy, corruption and favouritism'. He offered an example. 'It is everywhere asked, are there more than two individuals of the names of Sir Herbert Taylor and Lady Taylor? Or can these names upon the pension pauper-list be intended to designate the hitherto much respected names of the king's private secretary and lady?' Scrutator says they enjoy various 'wealthy pluralities':

Master of St Katharine's	£1200 per annum
Home [house in Regent's Park]	600
Regiment [colonel's profit]	1200
Private secretary to the king	2000
House and Table [Civil List allowances]	1200
Pension to himself	900
Pension to Lady Taylor	800 [5]

These total £7900 per annum (about £370,000 now). Sir Herbert's first perquisite is a fine example of the conversion of a charity for the poor into a benefice for the rich. The Royal Hospital of St Katharine and its church, founded in the 12th century for 'poor brothers and sisters', survived at Wapping until 1825, when it was demolished over strong protests. Queen Charlotte had made Sir Herbert its Master (a sinecure) but he did not fight to save it. He had a profitable alternative. At a more agreeable site, two acres on the edge of recently-created Regent's Park, he built a new 'Royal Hospital', a Georgian-gothic mansion with stables and gardens, a residence for himself and his lady (it was here that Westmacott saw him to work out their deal). A few reverend gentlemen and court ladies also had grace-and-favour apartments. Besides the Master's allowances, the Taylors enjoyed pensions derived from ground-rents at Wapping that had once benefited the poor.[6]

Scrutator says 'instances of rapacity' such as the Taylors' £7900 bring the court into disrepute. It would be hard to find another functionary of the 1830s with similar rewards.

Westmacott's reward for his special services to Sir Herbert was often stated at the time to have been £5000 — a good deal cheaper than paying Garth £3000 a year for life. In 1830, the year Garth went to prison, Westmacott was satirized in *The Devil's Visit*, an imitation of *The Devil's Walk* of Coleridge and Southey. The devil, busy round London, comes upon the office of *The Age*:

> While lounging one day along Catherine-street
>   His *Highness* was seized with the vapours,
> Beholding the type of himself at the door
>   Of a shop where they vend Sunday papers.
>
> He cross'd o'er the street, and with whisk of the tail,
>   Bowing ask'd, 'Don't you know your own brother?'
> 'By my *Age*!' exclaim'd W . . . . . . .tt. 'You must be I,
>   'Since one is the stamp of the other.'
>
> 'Why surely,' said Nick, 'you're the same little man
>   'That sold *Captain G - - th* and his *letters,*
> 'And who squeez'd a *fat Duchess* to make her disgorge.
>   'Your motto, *I'll work all my betters.'*
>
> 'And you,' quoth the Man of the Age, 'as I live
>   'Are my idol. So come — shake hands — hearty!'
> 'You're a trump, by my soul,' answer'd Nick. 'Here's my arm,
>   'Let's off to a *tête-à-tête* party.'[7]

It is striking to see the selling of 'Garth and his letters' by devil-Westmacott stated as early as 1830. The 'fat duchess' is the former actress Harriot Mellon, mistress and then wife of Thomas Coutts, who bequeathed her his fortune. The squeezing was probably when she, a widow of 50 with a lively past, was marrying the needy 9th Duke of St Albans, aged 26. She was unkindly labelled Duchess of St All-bum.

A good account of the precautions taken by scandal-vending editors against being horsewhipped is given by an editor of the time, James Grant. They employed large men with cudgels, usually 'natives of the Emerald Isle'. He tells of 'a colonel full of martial fury' coming to the *Age* office, 'burning with revenge and grasping in his right hand the riding-master's whip of the regiment', and demanding to see Westmacott. 'In marched an individual of the Brobdingnag species, clad in a thick white frowsy greatcoat, his chin buried in a red cotton handkerchief, with a broad oilskin hat on his head and a most suspicious-looking oak stick under his arm... "I am the editor, sir — at your sarvis." ... "Indeed!" ejaculated the colonel, edging away towards the door. "Oh, another time." "Whenever you plaise, sir." ' [8]

Away from his office Westmacott was vulnerable. The Covent Garden actor-manager Charles Kemble gave him a dramatic beating for having unkindly mocked Kemble's two latest attractions, the romantic piece *Black-eyed Susan* and his 20-year-old daughter Fanny, heavily puffed for her debut as Juliet. They were not good enough, *The Age* said, to save Kemble from being 'dished' by the rival Drury Lane:

> *Your* defence lies on two wenches,
> Black-eyed Susan, black-eyed Fanny...
> Prythee change them, Charlie Kemble:
> If you don't, you well may tremble.
> Soon you'll find your two pet doxies   [*trollops*
> Will leave you nought but empty boxes.

Kemble, on-stage a few nights later, spotted Westmacott in a dress box. As soon as the play was over, Kemble, still in costume, seized a stout stick, went round to Westmacott, dragged him into the lobby and beat him, exclaiming, 'You villain, I'll murder you, I'll teach you to call my daughter a whore!' He was no doubt enraged not so much by 'doxies' as by *The Age*'s opinion of Fanny's 'red and coarse' arms and 'decidedly bad' legs; and most cruelly, 'Her squat figure ... judging from her mamma's, will rather grow worse with her years.' While Westmacott lay begging for mercy, people crowded round egging Kemble on and 'insulting me in every possible way', he said in his account of the affair. A police superintendent refused to intervene. The incident inspired a caricature (*plate 6*). An unloved editor, it seems.

A surgeon, JF Clarke, tells in his memoirs of Westmacott turning

London Publyfhd by E.Harding May 19. 1806.

9 Princess Sophia aged 19: a print after a painting by Sir William Beechey, one of a series of royal portraits he showed at the Royal Academy in 1797. He had the art of making like-nesses that won favour with the family, yet with a touch that revealed character. His Sophia (a sufferer from spasms and low spirits) has an air of introspection and stress.

10 George, as prince of Wales, regent and king, makes so many appearances that he deserves a portrait. Here he displays his predilections for women and drink. His ruling mistress, holding Leading Strings, says he will always find 'a warm friend in Hertford' — being a marchioness of that name. A lewd cupid attends her. George's Privy Purse, John McMahon (feeding him curaçao), wears horns in tribute to his wife, the little woman caressing George. Behind McMahon stands Ernest, labeled 'AM I NOT A MAN AND A BROTHER?'

The regent's law officers found this 'a most indecent and impudent print' (*see page 80*) yet did not prosecute. *Cruikshank's 'Princely Predilections,' April 1812 (detail)*

11a Another of Beechey's portraits dating from 1797: Princess Elizabeth at 27. She has not asked him to flatter her full figure. He brings out a character far stronger than Sophia's. Her ruff may allude to her love of amateur theatricals.

11b The court's ruthless fixer, Sir Herbert Taylor, he of 'strict integrity', who coped with many royal embarrassments and outplayed Tom Garth. As Elizabeth said of the court, 'Poor Truth has a bad life of it.'

By courtesy of the National Portrait Gallery, London

12 Princess Sophia in 1821, aged nearly 44, painted at Kensington Palace by John Linnell. It is a miniature, exactly of this size. To pass the time for Sophia during 'the odious occupation of sitting still', Fanny Burney reminisced about her years in France in Napoleon's time. The mere mention of his name made Sophia 'open her fine Eyes in a manner extremely advantageous to the Painter'... as one can see. *The Royal Collection © 2002, Her Majesty Queen Elizabeth II*

13 Charles Molloy Westmacott, the self-pleased 'great captain of *The Age*' and blackmailer, in 1834. In the desk are 'communications many and strange, destined no doubt in due time to see the light of day'. Note 'the knowing horsewhip in the hat ... copied from the *life*'; though he is more likely to receive a whipping than give one. The artist is Alfred Forrester, a friend of George Cruikshank. *By permission of the British Library (BL 10855.h.10)*

14 Westmacott's *Age,* Ernest's ardent defender, figures in 'An old SATYR in Retirement', published with prudent anonymity when Sir Herbert Taylor and Westmacott defeated Tom Garth. The placard echoes *The Age*: '... injured character ... universally beloved ... infamous libels ... Garth hush-money all humbug - bow wow wow!!!' Garth's seized documents are packed ready to go to the Land of Fire.

15a At the height of the 1832 reform battle, radical pamphleteers use wood-engraving for cheap mass-produced satire. This permutation of Ernest is captioned, 'This is the Dog, a thorough BLOODHOUND... that hunts down his victims from their homes to their GRAVES.'

15b Reform has passed. Brougham thrusts Wellington and Ernest into hellmouth (an ancient image). Eldon weeps. A detail from 'The Tories' Chaunt'. Their song is, *We are all going, going, going, and we're all going to the shades below.* But they soon came back...

16a Frederica, Ernest's duchess, in 1830, displaying dramatic hat, curls and pearls, as published in a fashionable journal, *La Belle Assemblée*. Her friend Princess Lieven conceded that she had 'the appearance of a stage-queen'.

16b Ernest as king of Hanover, in his preferred right profile. Had he become King Ernest of Britain (and managed to stay in power), this would have been the head on our coins and stamps, 1837–51.

Both by courtesy of the National Portrait Gallery, London

up late at night 'in a sad plight', saying he had fallen down. Writing some years later, Clarke links this with the Kemble beating, but on that occasion Westmacott's own doctor attended him — so this was after a different beating. 'I gave him a lotion for a black eye and some medicine,' Clarke writes. 'The fellow had the impudence to fling a shilling on the table' (far below the rate). Clarke: 'What is this for?' Westmacott: 'Why, for yourself. I could not call you up without giving you a fee.' 'Oh, take up the shilling. I'll place you on the pauper list.' Westmacott 'laughed heartily, took up the shilling and departed'.[9]

Self-assurance was his style. James Grant recalled him on a Scottish tour in 1830, 'remarkable for the vivacity of his movements and for being on good terms with himself'. Years later he was remembered as 'the impudent, self-satisfied, rosy-gilled little journalist'.[10]

The author Edward Bulwer, later Bulwer-Lytton, later Lord Lytton, lashes him in 1833 in the name of Sneak, who 'keeps a Sunday newspaper as a reservoir for the filth of the week ... a *cabinet d'aisance* [privy] for any man who wishes to be delivered of a lie. No trader of the kind can be more obliging or more ill-savoured. His soul stinks of his profession... Sneak writes to you, "Sir, I have received some anecdotes about you, which I would not publish for the world if you will give me ten pounds for them." ...No man has been so often kicked as Sneak, no man so often horsewhipped.' Bulwer's venom was fed, one must add, by *The Age*'s exposing of his agitated love-life.

Westmacott, enriched by blackmail and by his royal reward, built a villa near Richmond with sculptures in its grounds. Bulwer mocks it: 'Sneak has stuck up a wooden box ... for all the world like a temple which a cit erects to the Roman Goddess of Sewers', where 'his soul sits at squat'. A special point of the cloacal imagery is that Westmacott was understood to be the son of Molloy the master chimney-sweep, of a trade that also performed the nightly collection of ordure.[11]

He cultivated titled people, gave great dinners, took a share in Drury Lane Theatre. High life led him deep into debt. In 1837 he tried to extract money from the Whig prime minister, Lord Melbourne. 'I would fain believe that two notes of mine delivered at your private residence have not reached you,' he wrote. 'I can hardly think it possible that your Lordship would wholly neglect to notice the respectful application of anyone, much less one who has been honored with your thanks.' He will not state his 'claims' in this letter because 'detail in matters of such delicacy ought to be made known to you by your confidential agents... If upon consulting them you should think that past services ought to be forgotten — so be it — but at least let me have your own authority for adding the name of Lord Melbourne to those who have treated me ungratefully.'

This must be a sequel to the sensational case of 1836 in which Melbourne was lucky to survive a charge of adultery with his friend, the author Caroline Norton. Westmacott presumably claimed to have helped the defence case in some way, but he probably played a double game, for his old associates, Ernest and Lord Wynford, were accused of having instigated the suit. *Figaro in London* said, 'The whole thing has been a beastly conspiracy, and it has been said in many quarters that that thoroughgoing old sinner Wynford is at the head of it.'[12]

Westmacott had to sell *The Age*. He migrated to Paris, where he survived until 1868. An obituary in *The Bookseller* says he was born Molloy, 'the son of a respectable master chimney-sweeper, whose shed and premises still remain in that narrow strip of a street ... which runs from the lower end of Drury-lane to the Church of St Mary le Strand'. On Garth, it says discreetly that Westmacott 'became acquainted with certain correspondence' about a court scandal, for which he was paid 'something like £5000'. It was then he built his villa and 'made a grand display of himself, his talents, his intimacies with titled characters'.[13]

In December 1868 the book auctioneers Puttick & Simpson announced a sale including a run of 'C M Westmacott's manuscript notebooks' in oblong octavo 'containing curious particulars relating to the secret history of George III and Family'. Some of the titles are, 'Curious Histories of the Offspring of Royalty ... Miss Jane Burnett, the natural Daughter of the late Duke of Kent ... The Banishment of Sir John Conroy, the Queen's Foster Father ... The Princess Amelia and her Offspring ... The Royal Cottage in Windsor Park.' Then comes Lot 321:

> Letters and Extracts of Correspondence in the Iron Box — From HRH Princess Sophia, General Garth, Miss Goldsworthy, the Duke of York, Capt Thos Garth, etc, with Explanatory Notes

Westmacott was certainly the man to have kept copies. An annotated catalogue shows the earlier lots going for modest sums, but the alluring Lot 321 is marked 'pass'. Usually this means unsold. Here it is likely that a successor to Sir Herbert made a deal with Puttick & Simpson and Lot 321 ended in the royal archives or was sent to the Land of Fire.[14]

19

'We shall have a revolution'

During Garth's years of seclusion the most significant national event, following the death of his Uncle George and the crowning of his Uncle William, was the bitter contest over parliamentary reform. Ernest and his friends naturally figure in this drama.

Ever since the French revolution of 1789, attempts at reform, however mild, had been repelled as dangerous jacobinical 'innovation'. Reliable majorities of MPs were sent to London from boroughs owned by great peers or otherwise corruptly controlled. Their subservience to ministers was reinforced by the granting or the promise of titles, sinecures, pensions and other rewards. Ministers and the crowd of beneficiaries insisted that the system (labelled The Thing by William Cobbett) 'works well'. But the millions who paid heavy taxes on daily necessities to maintain The Thing were becoming more and more restive. Could the old ways go on? A king-figure who much resembles George IV raises the question in a radical lampoon:

> We can play ten thousand pranks,
> We're the *sovereign mountebanks*...
> We can make a strumpet chaster
> Than a lump of alabaster...
> Bishops dare not call us sinners,
> We can take away their dinners...
> We love women that are fatter
> Than the puddings on our platter...

But this is the age of the March of Intellect. It is ominous for kings:

> Mobs, *hélas!* are now at college,
> Where they gain the accursed knowledge
> Of their left hand from their right one,
> And the SCUM thus learn to fight one.
> Servants read the Sunday papers...
> The rank and file use pen and ink,
> The radicals begin to think.[1]

The gulf between the opulent and the half-starved became dangerous. Wellington, a fierce anti-reformer, was reproached for denying there was 'distress', the official term for dire poverty. The point is made graphically in a caricature, 'Blind Man's Buff with the Poor'. Encircled by starving people, he says — his eyes tight shut — 'I can't see you.' A ragged, emaciated man says, 'Pray open your eyes.'

An unexpected witness against Wellington is a man with a rent-roll of £160,000, and with eight MPs in his pocket, the unsentimental 6th Marquess of Hertford. (His mother had much enhanced the family fortune during her years as the regent's *chère amie*.) In January 1830 Hertford wrote to his high-Tory friend John Wilson Croker, 'In Beddenham [Bedfordshire], a parish a few miles off, we had like to have had a rebellion, the labourers threatening to help themselves [to food stocks]. When once the poor rise, it will run over the country & the revolution will begin.' He says Wellington had repeated at Lord Westmorland's (another great landowner) that there was no distress, '& in proof, that in coming from Hatfield he had seen 13 new farmhouses building; and then the Arbuthnots [Wellington's friends] told him there was none in Lincolnshire!! Nobody pays my mother [rent] there, where she has a very good estate.'[2] Some great lords smelt danger.

Wellington's leadership was questioned on the right as well as the left. Ernest and his embittered ultras contrived plots to undermine him. In January 1830 Harriet Arbuthnot was outraged when 'the *Standard,* which is the Duke of Cumberland's paper,' said Wellington was out '& that the Duke of Richmond was commissioned to form a government *all Protestant'*. It was intolerable that Ernest was 'inundating the country with assertions that the ministers are dismissed'. His being 'constantly at the king's ear' gave weight to the assertions.

By that date, Ernest was not going to have the king's ear much longer. For years people had marvelled at George IV'z power to survive gluttony and other excesses. He went on punishing his gross half-ruined body to the end. He was drinking spirits 'morning, noon and night', Wellington learned. His doctor, Sir Henry Halford, feared the spirits would 'drive him mad', so as an antidote prescribed large doses of laudanum. Sir William Knighton retorted that the laudanum would drive him mad.

In April 1830, a few weeks before the royal gourmand's end, he began his day bravely. Wellington reported to Harriet Arbuthnot: 'What do you think of his breakfast yesterday morning for an invalid?

A Pigeon and Beef-Steak Pye of which he ate two Pigeons and three Beefsteaks, three parts of a bottle of Mozelle, a Glass of Dry Champagne, two Glasses of Port, a Glass of Brandy! He had taken Laudanum the night before; again before this breakfast...'[3]

When he died in June (making his brother William IV), the poet Thomas Moore wrote in his diary, 'Never saw London so excited or so lively.' People were ready for a political shift. A month later, an upheaval in Paris cheered all those who yearned for change. The Bourbon would-be absolutist, Charles X, and his premier, Polignac (Wellington's friend), abolished press liberty, dismissed a hostile parliament and were thrown out in a three-day mass rising, the *Trois Glorieuses*. Nearly everybody in London approved, Princess Lieven found, except for 'a few ultras, with the Duke of Cumberland at their head, who would have liked to go to war'.[4]

The news came in the midst of an election (one always followed a king's death), and benefited the Whigs. Wellington noted that in nearly every contest Paris was discussed, and 'even in a corrupt borough' candidates were called upon to give pledges 'to vote for reform, reduction of expenditure, etc'.[5] Yet in parliament that November he declared that the existing system could not possibly be improved. He would always oppose all reform. His colleagues were dismayed. The nation was soon in ferment. Menacing letters — often signed 'Swing', for the farmworkers' fabled leader, Captain Swing — were delivered day after day at Wellington's London home, Apsley House.

> I beg your Grace pardon but I have to inform you that this day Week at 12 o'clock at night your Mansion will display a prime Blaze.

> You are guilty of every evil you lobster-looking son of a Bitch... Look at the poor starving country people and ask your own consince if you are going on as you ought to do. It is my intention to shoot you or stab you & if possible burn your house down.

Cavalry, marines, New Police were all put on alert. A supporter sent Wellington an idea for a weapon that would be as good against a mob 'as a cannonade of grapeshot': an armoured troop-carrier, 'constructed as to shield the soldiers when assaulted with stones or other missiles', pulled by a steam-powered road vehicle (a recent invention). It would 'force its way through all opposition'.

Citizens of the most solid sort, as well as lowly radicals, deplored Wellington's declaration. 'A *terrible* bad spirit is rapidly spreading amongst the lower orders,' one wrote from Manchester. 'They are ripe for anything. Can you depend upon the military?' A former 'steady admirer' at Birmingham said it was monstrous 'that such towns as Birmingham, Manchester, Leeds and Sheffield should be unrepresented when such rotten boroughs as Old Sarum & many others should return members'.

A poor labourer made clear why many were desperately resorting to arson and machine-breaking. A small extract from a long letter:

> I may as well be hang^d as starved to death… You tax horses & why not Machinery — we mean that Machinery that only Bennefits the few Proprietors, to the starving of us poor Mechanics… After walking about all day seeking imployment I go home at Night weary & wanting — my poor little Children hang around me & cry father have you got any work — no my Dear is the reply. Then out they all burst a Crying & say then have you got a bit of bread in your pocket for we have not had a bit today — this is true by god… We wish to see you live in Splendor — but then live & let us live is all we want…[6]

Wellington went out. Lord Grey came in. This freed Wellington to go into action as lord lieutenant of Hampshire, organizing the pursuit of rick-burners and machine-breakers. In that county alone, 286 were convicted, of whom three were hanged and 107 transported to Van Diemen's Land.

In great towns with no MPs, 'political unions' for reform sprang up. The phrase 'the working classes' became current. Radical printing flourished. A new edition of a compilation of abuses, *The Extraordinary Black Book*, surveyed parliamentary corruption, listed the sums paid to royals, sinecurists and others, denounced 'oligarchical luxury, folly and profusion', and justified the rick-burners: 'The rural population is exactly what tithes, game-laws, the country magistracy, Church-of-Englandism and a luxurious non-resident priesthood have made them. And what do we behold? The people have resorted to nightly outrage and revenge — the last resort of the oppressed.'

Earl Grey, a great landowning Whig with a cabinet entirely of peers and other titled men, was persuaded to go beyond minor reform. His Reform Bill, published March 1831, proposed to abolish more than 100 seats in rotten and semi-rotten boroughs, give MPs to unrepresented towns, and create a voters' roll of about half a million on a household basis that ruled out men below the middle rank. It was a cautious half-measure, but many Tories saw it as a perilous revolutionary concession to popular clamour. Wellington, and Ernest too, predicted the destruction of the Lords, the Church of England, the monarchy itself. Wellington wrote to Harriet Arbuthnot, 'It may be relied upon that we shall have a Revolution... I told you years ago that the people are rotten to the core. You'll find that it is true. They will plunder, destroy and annihilate all property in the country.' The Upper Orders were demoralized, timid and 'excited alone by a thirst for Popularity'. A little later he had a more optimistic thought: 'If we are in luck we may have a civil war.'[7]

William IV had won early popularity. Any change after the dis-ordered, reclusive George IV was welcome. He delighted in being king and showing himself about, often in unseemly ways. Some of his wilder flourishes were fortunately not too public. At a great dinner attended by all his ministers, by ambassadors and other notables, he made a rambling speech in French, climaxing with a ribald toast (perhaps dating from his days of bliss with Dorothy Jordan):

> *Les yeux qui tuent,*
> *Les fesses qui remuent*
> *Et le cul qui danse —*
> *Honi soit qui mal y pense.*

Grey 'was ready to sink into the earth', says Charles Greville. The French ambassador, impassive old Talleyrand, who had seen and survived everything, murmured, *'C'est bien remarquable.'*[8]

Ernest was a constant attender at debates in the Lords. A good picture of him at this date, aged 60, is given by the journalist James Grant. It was not only Ernest's large white whiskers and moustaches that made a striking impression. 'His brow is ample enough ... but his eyebrows protrude, and are made more remarkable by his large prominent eyelashes. His eyes are small but quick, with a somewhat unpleasant expression... His complexion has something sallow about it... His figure may be said to be handsome... He dresses with much simplicity — he is never foppish. A plain brown coat, light vest, light small-clothes [trousers] and a white hat is the kind of attire to which he seems most partial.

'The Duke of Cumberland is no speaker... He emits certain sounds, it is true, but they are altogether unlike the ordinary tones of the human voice. The words have a sort of yelping or growling sound.' However, unlike some ultras such as the Duke of Newcastle, he is not a ranter. 'He stands quite motionless: there is no emphasis in his voice nor the slightest appearance of warmth about him. He looks a perfect model of political moderation.' And furthermore, 'A day or two after Lord Brougham, in one of his furious attacks on him, had called him "the Illustrious by courtesy", I saw His Royal Highness lean across the table and converse for some time with his lordship with as much apparent kindness and cordiality as if nothing had happened.'[9]

Grey stung Ernest by saying he prided himself on his opposition 'to any consolidation or extension of the rights of the people'. Ernest protested that Grey had accused him of being 'adverse to the liberties of the people'; and he made a bold claim: 'No member of this or the other house would fight more strenuously for the liberties of the people.' Grey repeated his point: every measure for 'the *extension* of either religious or civil liberty has uniformly met with the decided opposition of the illustrious duke'.[10]

The Lords, known as the House of Incurables, rejected Grey's bill in October 1831 by forty-one votes. Wellington was reviled, especially by fringe papers such as *The Radical*, selling for a penny by evading the fourpenny stamp tax:

> *'Duke' of Wellington.* — This detestable anti-reform 'thing' called 'lord' was well pelted with mud, and we regret to say with stones, on his way to the House of Noodles... His carriage was (like his political conduct) covered with filth.[11]

Ernest too was thoroughly pelted, and was even pulled off his horse. The windows of his ultra friends' mansions were shattered. He and Wellington were burned in effigy at Tyburn, the ancient scene of executions. The mob stoned nearly all the windows of Apsley House. Wellington installed steel shutters and posted army marksmen, ordered to open fire if the mob tried to storm the house.

The year before, Ernest had turned down his glass when a toast to Wellington was drunk at a dinner given by William IV. The crisis overcame his hostility. He wrote to Wellington to urge the creation of a national guard because 30,000 radicals were reported to be in arms. Wellington replied, 'I think that we are already in London stronger than they are. I would engage to get the better of them with what we have... I am much more apprehensive of the lingering but near certain mischief of Revolutionary Legislation.'[12]

Riots erupted. The most violent was at Bristol, touched off by the arrival of Sir Charles Wetherell MP, a supremely violent anti-reformer, to preside at the autumn assizes. He was a great crony of Ernest, who in after years recalled having spent 'many and many an hour' at Kew in late-night causeries, 'my greatest delight', with Wetherell, 'Black Billy' Holmes the Tory whip, and Theodore Hook, editor of the Tory *John Bull*.[13] Wetherell was notorious for his slovenly dress as well as for his ultraism. One of his furious anti-emancipation speeches had inspired the jest, 'The only lucid interval was between his waistcoat and his breeches.' The Bristol riot sent him fleeing in disguise (the jest then was that the disguise was a *clean* suit). In a three-day rampage, the mob devastated the city centre, destroying prisons, the bishop's palace and much else. Bishops were a target because their No votes had clinched the defeat of the bill.

Ernest's colleague, the Duke of Newcastle, was eager for battle. This large unwieldy peer was a prime example of Old Corruption, having nine MPs in his pocket. He was notorious for having declared, after evicting tenants who had voted the wrong way, 'Have I not the right to do what I like with mine own?' The 1831 rioters set fire to one of his properties, Nottingham Castle. He feared an attack on his great house, Clumber Park, twenty miles away in The Dukeries. He wrote to Stanley Lees Giffard, the London *Standard* editor whom he subsidized, to say it was time to stop 'passively yielding to the diabolical efforts of our enemies'. The political unions were arming. If the 'Conservatists' (new name for Tories) did not wish to be 'driven out of their houses & homes & to be tyrannized over by an armed body of revolutionists' they must 'unite themselves also in an armed body. If no one else will, I will offer to head the attempt. I care not whether *my head* is jeopardized by it.'

This was not mere rhetoric. 'In the report of the Birmingham Union,' he said, 'I see that mention is made of my armament here. The cannon which I have, I have had for *above 15 years, they were bought for an ornamental fort*. I can assure you positively that I am not safe in my house without this armament & that I am obliged to surround my house with sentinels... People are found lurking about at night.'

A little to the south in Leicestershire, the Duke of Rutland also had cannon. Sir Henry Halford, the royal doctor, learned that the duke 'had obtained from the Master Gen[l] of the Ordnance an experienced Gunner who was going down to Belvoir Castle to instruct some 25 trusty people of the Duke's establishment in the management of the Guns mounted about this splendid abode... Alas! that it should have come to this necessity!!!' A few weeks later the duke reported, 'I am having all my labourers and servants drilled to the use of the great guns here. I have an artillery sergeant residing here for the winter and we have drills every day. Last week I obtained a large supply of shot... I am determined to make a good defence.'[14]

Lord Hertford, who enjoyed shooting partridge and pheasant, could not even protect the game on his estates. Hertford to Croker: 'I hear the Woodbridge [Suffolk] magistrates refuse to convict poachers... I suppose I had better submit, discharge the keepers & night watchers, & relieve myself from vexation. My eggs will of course all be taken now in sight of the keepers & I shall be laughed at.'[15] One would not think this submissive marquess was the model for Thackeray's Lord Steyne in *Vanity Fair*.

Libels on Ernest became dangerously impudent. *The House of Reform that Jack Built* made him a bloodhound pissing on the gravestones of Sellis (marked with a razor) and of Lord Graves (*plate 15a*). *Figaro in London*, a radical-Whig weekly, devised some anagrams and said it regrettably had no control over the 'unfortunate coincidence' that 'certain letters, composing certain names, make up certain sentences singularly characteristic of certain individuals'. For example:

> Dear mad Londonderry —
> *Damn'd dreary noodle.*
>
> Ay! when Peel spouts —
> *Why one's put asleep.*
>
> Oh! Ernest Cumberland did —
> *Behold incest and murder.*

Punch in London said: 'A volume of Shakespeare is preparing for the use of the family of a certain royal duke, from which all indelicate and offensive passages are to be expunged. Of course, one portion of the Ghost's speech in Hamlet will be wholly omitted.' This wicked weekly says (slightly misquoting), 'We allude to that beginning, "Yes, that *adult'rous*, that *incestuous* beast".'[16]

The Lords, dominated by Tory peers created in record numbers during George III's reign, threw out the bill yet again in May 1832. William IV refused to create new peers for Grey. Charles Greville wrote in his journal, 'All the Royal Family, bastards and all, have been incessantly *at* the king … his womankind particularly.' Grey resigned. The king 'deserves to be deposed', said the Marquess of Anglesey, no radical. 'He has deceived his servants [ministers], & unhappily it is in the Blood.' Greville called him 'one of the silliest old gentlemen in his dominions; but I believe him to be mad.' The Tory *John Bull* exulted prematurely that Grey had 'gone, fled, run away … this lofty hypocrite — this grim and haughty peer'.[17]

Wellington did a volte-face. Having declared against all reform, he tried to form a government that *would* bring in a reform bill. 'The commander-in-chief of all the anti-reformers of the kingdom,' said *The Times*, was displaying 'humiliating and shameful' inconsistency. Work almost stopped. Mass meetings at Birmingham, Manchester and elsewhere threatened to pay no taxes until Grey's bill passed. Radicals talked of Paris-style barricades. A rumour spread that Wellington was planning a military coup. It was a plausible fear. Thousands of troops had been subduing disaffected citizens for years. Ernest's 15th Hussars had helped to suppress the Luddites in 1812, and in 1819 they and the Manchester yeomanry used their sabres with terrible effect against a reform meeting in St Peter's Fields — the action known ever after as Peterloo. Wellington wrote of the radicals then, 'It is very clear to me that they won't be quiet till a large number of them "bite the dust", as the French say, or till some of their leaders are hanged.'[18]

Wellington's attempt was doomed. His chief in the Commons, Sir Robert Peel, knowing he could not achieve a majority there, kept aloof. William IV had to bring back Grey. When the news reached Birmingham, the leader of its political union, Thomas Attwood, witnessed 'a scene that I never saw equalled … men shedding tears of joy… I have read of the tears of valiant men. I never saw them until then.' *John Bull's Picture Gallery* caricatured despairing Tories, and wrote:

> Cheer up, Duke Ernest, why that sorrowful mien?
> You look as frightened (pray, where have you been?)
> As if the ghost of Sellis you had seen.[19]

The king, too, was in an emotional state. He made a 'ridiculous and nonsensical' speech to the Jockey Club, Greville says, 'such a mass of confusion, trash and imbecility as made one laugh and blush at the same time'. Again Greville thought he was going mad.[20]

An alternative to creating Whig peers was devised. The king's secretary, Sir Herbert Taylor, wrote to Wellington, to Ernest and to dozens of other Tory peers asking them to abstain. Ernest kept Sir

Herbert's letter. Its key sentence reads: 'All Difficulties & Obstacles to the Arrangement in Progress will be removed by a Declaration in the House of Lords this day, from a sufficient number of Peers, that in Consequence of the present state of things they have come to the Resolution of dropping their further Opposition to the Reform Bill so that it may pass without further delay.' Sir Herbert asks Ernest to pass this on 'to Lord Wynford and any other Peers you may think fit' (that is, to the rest of his ultra friends).[21]

Two of these violently denounced Grey in the Lords. Kenyon accused him of following a 'rash, wild and atrocious' course and of preparing 'the destruction of the monarchy'. Grey rebutted this 'with the utmost scorn, contempt and indignation'. Winchilsea accused Grey of having sanctioned 'seditious and treasonable' addresses to the king by reformers. Again Grey hit back sharply. These clashes moved Ernest to urge peers to 'tranquillize themselves' and 'not to let their passions get the better of their judgment'. Ernest as tranquillizer! The caricaturist John Doyle depicted him as Placid, a comic stage figure — '*His first appearance in that character*'.[22]

On the day of the final vote, June 4, he was far from tranquil. He was ill from political anguish — '*si souffrant, si malade*', Frederica wrote to Princess Lieven when he set off for the House of Lords. She completed her letter at 10.15 that evening. '*C'est fini, le Bill vient de passer*', and Ernest had come home '*très malade*'. Only twenty-two diehards had voted against the bill. Ernest had abstained as requested. His abstention was a *sacrifice*, said Frederica, not a *defeat*. He had wanted to explain himself, but was too ill to stand: '*Il a essayé de se lever mais il ne pouvait se soutenir.*' Knowing the princess to be a frequent correspondent of Grey, she adds, '*Votre Grey est pour moi un Enigme!*" Ernest retired to his bed and took four days to recover.[23]

The Times said, 'A race of usurpers have been ousted from the field of their usurpation, and a great empire reconquered by its own people, without the shedding of one drop of blood.'[24] More than 120 years later, Ernest's chief eulogizing biographer, Geoffrey Malden Willis, was able to declare of the reform measures, 'No one will deny that they involved the destruction of all that had meant England.'

To combat revolution, Ernest sought a rapprochement with Wellington. He wrote (*Most private & confidential*), 'As far as I possibly can I am *desirous* to go *hand in hand with you* ... The *Revolution* has not only already begun, but has lately advanced more than I could have *expected.'* The first election on post-reform rules had given the Tories 150 seats, the Whigs 320. Alarmingly, among the 320 were sixty *'Radicals* and *Repealers ... pledged* to vote for anything or everything to overturn the Country & her sacred Institutions'. He urged 'the absolute necessity of *an immediate private meeting of the leading Tories'* to establish *'one Conservative party'* to 'stem the torrent of Destruction'.[25] This was when the Carlton Club was founded.

Ernest promoted his counter-revolution in great houses such as Hatfield, home of the high-Tory 2nd Marquess of Salisbury. Lady Salisbury, in her diary, reports an ingratiating Ernest, September 1833: 'I must say he has made himself very amiable in this house — endeavoured to be civil to everybody, said nothing disagreeable and swore very little, comparatively... I suppose he wishes to make himself a footing in good company.'

The hostess of Hatfield had a difficulty however over Ernest and his cousin, the Duke of Gloucester. Whenever they were at Hatfield, Wellington refused to come — 'he cannot stand the bore of either of the Royal Dukes'. Some months later, 'Their surprise at *never* meeting him here increases every time they come. It is difficult sometimes to find an answer to their very pointed questions.'

Lady Salisbury records snippets of Ernest's conversation. 'Boasting of his attachment to the Church, he said, "By God I'd be damned for religion!"' (this was then shocking as well as comical). And the Archbishop of Canterbury was honoured with a stronger affirmation: 'By God, my lord, I am a damned infernal sinner, and I know it, but I think it right to go to church for the sake of example.'

One day Lady Salisbury remarked that some people 'had at least one good quality, they were zealous Tories'. 'Ah!' said Ernest, 'that covers a multitude of sins. That is the reason you all bear with me. There is not a sin in the calendar that I have not been accused of.'

Lady Salisbury comments in her diary, 'True enough.'[26]

20

The black secret of his guilt

Doubts about the suicide verdict on the valet Sellis had persisted ever since 1810, and not only among readers of radical sheets. When Charles Greville wrote in his journal in 1829 of 'the universal and deep execration' in which Ernest was held (*page 137*), he also noted, 'Sellis's affair was never cleared up... Everybody believes that there is some mystery of an atrocious character in which he is deeply and criminally implicated.'[1] Public misgivings deepened when only an infirm William IV and little Princess Victoria stood between Ernest and the throne.

In March 1832 a book with no named author, *The Authentic Records of the Court of England for the Last Seventy Years*, rich in accounts of scandals and unworthy actions, went on sale for a guinea. Pages 93 to 106, on the Sellis drama, pointed so accusingly at Ernest that he instructed his barrister-friend Sir Charles Wetherell to prosecute the publisher, a young man named Josiah Phillips, for criminal libel.

An attempt to dissuade Wetherell came from an unexpected quarter — from Francis Place, the controversial inquest jury foreman in 1810. In a long letter to Wetherell he argued that the prosecution of the *Independent Whig* in 1813 'induced multitudes of people to believe the calumnies', money was collected by 'highly reputable men' to pay young Henry White's fine and to support him in prison, and suspicions of Ernest's guilt were 'more and more generally credited'.[2] Place evidently did not want such ideas to be stirred up again.

Wetherell went ahead. He thus enabled 'multitudes of people' to read newspaper reports of the book's allegation that Ernest had a motive to kill Sellis (one that had been suggested from the start): 'A short period before this dreadful catastrophe the duke had been surprised in an *improper* and *unnatural* situation with this Neale by the other servant, Sellis, and exposure was expected. A brother of the duke had also received accommodation in those very same *suitable apartments*... He [Ernest] looked down upon mankind as creatures of an inferior species that existed only for his pleasures and purposes, and through whose medium his unnatural inclinations might be gratified.' Of Sellis's death, the book said, 'The general opinion was that the duke was the murderer.'[3]

A private prosecution for criminal libel instead of a civil action for damages was unusual. Wetherell had to obtain leave in the Court of King's Bench, which meant presenting an explicit case: that the book made 'a charge or insinuation against the illustrious individual of having either committed the detestable crime of sodomy' (for which the punishment was death, and remained so until 1861) 'or some attempt or design to commit that crime, or some practice of an improper or indecent nature connected with that crime'. And that it alleged that Ernest 'either murdered or was accessory or privy to the murder' of Sellis 'in order that he might remove him as a witness'.

For some time, Wetherell said, there had been 'vague allusions, mysterious insinuations and various modes of assailing the character of this illustrious individual'. They had not been worth noticing; but no man could ignore charges that he committed 'a crime on which the law of England has justly inflicted death', and that he murdered 'a witness to the asserted or supposed crime'.

The libel law favoured Ernest. He must swear an affidavit that the allegations were *not* true, yet Josiah Phillips was barred from pleading in justification that they *were* true (this rule was eased eleven years later). Ernest duly swore 'that he never did commit, nor had any intention or design of committing, the said detestable crime of sodomy or any other unnatural or indecent offence or practice' with the valet Cornelius Neale 'or with any other person whatsoever'. On the second point, that Ernest 'either murdered or was accessory or privy to the murder' of Sellis, it was curious that he swore only that he *was not in any manner accessory or privy to* Sellis's death.

Neale, Ernest's pensioned ex-valet, came forth, twenty-two years after the event, to swear he had never been 'in an unnatural, indecent or improper situation' with Ernest 'or any person whatsoever ... nor ever had any design, intention or thought of permitting the said offences'. His 'actual real name' was stated to be McNeale, 'of Brompton-row, gentleman'. Here was a servant elevated to 'gentleman', and revealed to have a fashionable address in Kensington.

Ernest found he had little to fear from Phillips's barrister, Daniel Wakefield, a young man of 'humble station', as he himself put it. Just before the hearing, Francis Place had intervened again. Having failed to deter Wetherell, he had meetings with Wakefield, offered advice, then wrote a long letter making points good only for undermining Phillips. It began, 'Dear Dan, The rascals who have put up the calumnies against the Duke of Cumberland deserve nothing in the way of assistance ... but criminal informations for libels should be perplexed and embarrassed as much as possible.' He urged Wakefield to 'make his name' by presenting an argument that the Sellis inquest ought to have been held according to a law of Henry VIII's time — a point of no value to Phillips. He even pressed Wakefield to say that his clients, 'concocters of the libel', were bad characters. In court, Wakefield attempted little more than to argue that pursuing the case would 'spread the slander': 'The illustrious prosecutor should remember that though he may stop the printing presses he cannot stop the tongues or the ears of Englishmen.'[4] Ernest was given leave to prosecute.

Tongues were not stopped. Nor were some presses. The *True Sun* newspaper went so far as to say that in the Phillips book 'transactions are detailed which have long been considered as the blackest stain on the present royal family... A deeply injured man the Duke of Cumberland must be if the imputations against him, so long believed by a great portion of the public, should turn out to be groundless.'

A revised edition of the *Authentic Records*, entitled *Secret History of the Court of England*, was published, not by Phillips. It named as its author Lady Anne Hamilton, sister of the 10th Duke of Hamilton and a former lady-in-waiting to Princess Caroline. Lady Anne later professed to be indignant that someone had obtained material from her and published it. This edition declared that in giving an account of the 'mysterious murder of one Sellis' in the *Authentic Records*, 'we did what we conceived to be our duty as historians — we spoke the TRUTH!' It cautiously cut the passage about the sodomy motive. Instead it raised questions about the 'very contradictory evidence' at the inquest, and said, 'Enough is set forth to make us receive the evidence of Neale with *caution*, if not to render him *unworthy of belief altogether*.' Besides, 'affidavits from interested persons are not worth much'. It affirmed its right 'to expose vice and castigate mischievous follies, even though they may be found in a *palace*!'[5]

A penny satirical paper, *Asmodeus*, carried a front-page illustration, 'Fatal Curiosity or the St James's Tragedy' — 'fatal curiosity' alluding to Sellis's having 'surprised' Ernest with Neale. Sellis lies dead in his bed and a man, tall and lean like Ernest (but masked, prudently), washes his hands in a basin, thus recalling one piece of inquest evidence.[6]

At Phillips's trial, June 1833, Wetherell raised a question never aired before. He denied that Ernest 'endeavoured, by inflicting wounds upon himself, to induce the belief that the deceased valet had attempted to assassinate the duke'. Such a stratagem would have been 'worthy not only of a Machiavel, but of the most wicked of the human race'. That Ernest wounded himself was 'utterly untenable'. Sir Wathen Waller (formerly Phipps), Ernest's surgeon-friend, testified, 'I saw the pulsation of the arteries of the brain... The suffering of the duke was such as I have not ever seen equalled.' In June 1810 he had reported very differently: that Ernest made '*no* complaint of his *head*' and suffered less from his wounds than from 'the idea of being ... under the *same* roof' as Sellis's body (*page 58*).

Sir Henry Halford, reporting to George III after dressing Ernest's wounds, had listed five or six, none dangerous. Now Ernest told the jury he had seventeen wounds. And dangerous ones: 'I was in a state of agony, I suppose, from six weeks to two months... It was not, I believe, till the beginning of August that I was able to leave the house.' If so, he had not ventured out for nine weeks. In fact he left his bed after three days and appeared in public after twenty days.

Ernest's deposition in 1810 said, 'There was a lamp burning in the room but he did not see anybody.' Sceptics wondered at this. Now he said he saw the flash of a sword in 'a faint light from the window-shutter'. The lord chief justice asked: 'There was no light in Your Royal Highness's room?' Ernest: 'I think not.'

In the *Authentic Records*, Phillips wrote, 'We hope our efforts in the best of causes, TRUTH, will be crowned with success ... though we may pay the *price* of *liberty*.' His barrister, Wakefield, did not cross-examine Ernest or anyone else. He resorted to deprecation of his 22-year-old client, saying he was 'ignorant' and the book was 'one of the weakest publications that ever issued from the press ... so extremely clumsy that no man could believe it for a moment'. It was beneath Ernest to prosecute. Phillips was found guilty — a second man condemned on the word of Ernest — and given a six-month sentence. Ernest's advocate, *The Age*, said Phillips was convicted of 'nauseous and abominable libels ... which have been repeated so often as to pass in the minds of the vulgar as truths'.[7]

Ernest's chief latterday eulogist, G M Willis, says the prosecution 'had a very salutary effect': the libels 'suddenly ceased'. They certainly did not. The cut-throat razor appears more often than before, in word and image, as the accusing emblem of Ernest. A weekly series of caricatures by Charles Jameson Grant, *The Political Drama*, launched in 1833, has a dozen examples. 'Billy's Birthday' shows Ernest and others bringing gifts for William IV. Ernest says, 'Here Bill I've brought you a nice *Razor* made by *Sellis* and *Graves*.' In another, Ernest is leading a Tory attack on the Whigs' municipal reform bill. He hacks at the 'villainous bill' with a razor and says, 'I'll see the *Graves* open and *Sellis* and *the rest* appear first.'

Neither Phillips nor Ernest knew that far away in north Germany a former officer of the 15th Hussars, Captain Charles Jones, held a 2500-word document that could have vindicated Phillips and might have finished Ernest forever. It was Jones's record of a confession by Ernest.

It is important to know what sort of man Jones was. He came of a well-to-do family with property in Suffolk and Essex. Soon after 1800 he obtained a commission in Ernest's regiment. In 1805 Ernest made him his aide-de-camp, a role he filled for years except when the 15th were abroad. When the regiment joined Wellington's campaign in the Peninsula in 1808, he was made adjutant. His brigade commander, Lord Paget, wrote home about an action in which they gave 'a good licking' to a superior force of French cavalry: 'It was with those lucky rogues, the 15th, who always happen to be under my hand when there is anything to be done.' Jones was wounded and his horse was killed under him. In 1813, in action again in Portugal, he was brigade major for the 15th and two other hussar regiments. Again a horse was shot under him. His last action was as a brigade major at Waterloo, when Paget was Wellington's cavalry commander and earned the title Marquess of Anglesey. Just before the battle, Jones wrote in his journal of Paget as 'the cleverest cavalry officer in the British Empire' who inspires his men 'wherever he appears'.[8]

Jones, then, was a gallant officer and highly valued by his superiors. His regiment was at the heart of his life. As aide-de-camp he became, by his own statement, devoted to Ernest: 'My affection for him had become so habitual that his very likes & dislikes had become also mine.' He was 'ready at any moment to venture my life in support of his person & reputation'.

Ernest was driven to make his confession in December 1815. As chapter 7 brought out, he had suffered more than two years of chagrin and defeat: rejected again and again for action against Napoleon, ejected from Hanover, spurned by the Commons, and then painfully shamed and enraged by Queen Charlotte's barring of his wife. The climax came when Ernest dared to accuse the queen of having been deceived by *'secret* informers'. She replied that her rejection of Frederica was 'for ever unalterable'. To deliver this reply she sent Colonel Benjamin Stephenson, the officer whom Ernest had strangely dismissed from his staff soon after the Sellis affair.

It was Christmas eve. Ernest, Frederica, Jones and others were at dinner. The scene that followed was one that would remain sharp in anyone's memory. Jones's memoir records it in vivid detail. 'The duke in great agitation took me with him to the library & said, "Jones, you shall reply to this letter directly," then throwing himself into a chair he with much bitterness begun to upbraid his mother.' He went on for three hours 'in a gloomy phrenzy'; then 'having become more calm', he went up to Frederica's room for an hour.

'He returned in nearly a state of phrenzy, declaring that he believed he had not one sincere friend in the whole world.' After 'many imprecations against certain persons', Ernest began his confession. Jones sets down his words 'as accurately as I can describe them':

> My dear Jones, you see how I am treated. I believe I have not another friend besides yourself who feels for my situation. I am perhaps justly dealt with, for I have much on my mind — more than I can bear. I want to unbosom myself but I know not whom to trust, & the Duchess ... she feels only for herself.

I am perhaps justly dealt with... I want to unbosom myself...

Jones tried to calm him, 'declaring that I would freely sacrifice my existence upon the spot if it could procure him the slightest of his wishes, & indeed I felt most perfectly ready & willing to do so, for the state in which I saw H.R.H. gave me the greatest pain, but had I known what was to follow, no power on earth could have induced me to have heard the dreadful confession.' Ernest, 'with extreme vehemence', said, 'Swear to me, my dear Jones, that you will never divulge what I am going to say to you, for my mind requires relief.' Jones swore on his word of honour.

Then Ernest said: 'You know how I am treated & you can feel for me more than I deserve. You know that miserable business of Sellis's, that wretch, I was forced to destroy him in self defence, the villain threatened to propagate a report & I had no alternative.'

Jones had often faced death in battle, but Ernest's confession overwhelmed him. 'Thunderstruck & breathless I could scarcely hear the remaining statement & will therefore not set it down.' But Cornelius Neale came into it: 'H.R.H. continued some time and mentioned much of a fellow of the name of Neale.'

Ernest took note at last of 'the dreadful impression his words had made upon me'. 'For some minutes probably I could neither hear nor see for I remember that the first thing that struck me on recovery was the bust of Mr Pitt which stood opposite to me, & the next was the duke looking amazed. I was literally stupified & stammered out that if H.R.H. had done the act in self defence it was justifiable before God & man... The duke seeing the state of my mind said, after a pause, "You swear solemnly that this rests buried in impenetrable secrecy." I answered, "Upon that, sir, you have my oath."'

A maid knocked: Frederica wished to speak to Ernest. He went 'in apparent tranquility' and left Jones in the library 'in a state not to be described'. It was nearly midnight. He waited an hour, 'expecting the duke would see me again that night', then went to his lodgings and passed the night 'under the most distressing sensations'.

Next day Jones was 'in the utmost state of anxiety' over what Ernest might say after his confession. 'It was with much trepidation that I entered his dressing room for my morning audience.' Ernest began with 'many questions on indifferent matters'. Then 'turning to me with great earnestness', he said 'very emphatically', 'Of course the conversation we had last night remains buried in eternal oblivion.' Again Jones promised. Ernest shook his hand and began 'a conversation on various subjects'.

He had eased his mind but imposed a grievous burden on his loyal aide-de-camp. This was painfully clear to Jones: 'H.R.H. ever afterwards appeared to me more cheerful and to have lost a certain weight which appeared to be hanging on his mind... I can most justly affirm that he had transferred it to me, for from that fatal night ... I have never known peace of mind since. In fact H.R.H. had thrown the black secret of his guilt from his own into my breast. From this time I became gloomy, lost all spirit & energy, was unwilling to meet the duke and invented all sorts of excuses to be absent from his table.'

He looked for a way to leave Ernest's service. He thought the opening had come when Ernest and his duchess were leaving in 1818 to live in Berlin. 'I represented to the duke that having married, I trusted His Royal Hss would excuse me from attending him to the Continent.' Jones had married in 1817 the daughter of a Kentish landowner. Ernest 'was not willing to leave me behind him' (one might guess why) and 'prevailed on me to accompany him to Spa', the Belgian resort. At Spa they 'had a fresh altercation'. Ernest prevailed on Jones to come on to Berlin. Jones's wife joined him, a son was born in January 1819, and Ernest was his godfather, an honour hard to refuse. The boy, Ernest Charles Jones, proved to be of some note.

At last, 'worn down with ill health for which none of the physicians could find a cause', Jones left Ernest's service in April 1821 and retired with wife and child to a small estate at Reinbeck, near Hamburg, 250 kilometres from Berlin. Still he was not free of the dark secret. His health grew worse. In September 1827 he made a will, 'believing from my present state of health', he says in it, 'that I have not long to live'. It was witnessed by the British consul at Hamburg. In the same month he wrote his memoir. At its head he printed the Sixth Commandment,

THOU SHALT DO NO MURDER

In the memoir's opening page he says, 'He has laid on me a weight that is pressing me by degrees to the grave... I find it impossible to quit this life with the secret of a murder upon my conscience... A thousand contending reflections place me upon the rack. I must destroy the little reputation which remains to a man to whom I had devoted my very existence.' He wants the world to understand why he has 'secreted him from justice'. He had sworn his oath of secrecy, and he had felt for Ernest 'an attachment which knew no bounds'.

'Let it be also remembered that at the period the author of the crime made himself known to me, the murdered wretch had slumbered for more than five years under the common causeway, a grave which had been awarded him by the sentence of a coroner's court. I say a wretch because the author of his death declared that he freely lent himself to the most infamous practices.'[9]

Was Ernest's allegation that Sellis too had 'lent himself' to 'infamous practices' the truth? The evidence available about Ernest and his valets has pointed only to Neale, but it is possible that Ernest asserted his will with one and then the other. The Duke of York's ex-mistress, Mary Anne Clarke, says in her suppressed recollections, dated 1813, that Ernest should help Sellis's widow and children. 'The Duke of

Cumberland knows best *why* he should *immediately* provide for them — he has for Neale. And it is also well known in his own family; where, and at Carlton House, his affair with Sellis was called the *shirt dance*.'[10] However, those who had talked about the 'shirt dance' may have confused Sellis and Neale.

When Jones left Berlin, he was not sorry to see the last of Frederica. He says he had been loud against Queen Charlotte's ban, but having been told certain facts in Berlin 'by a man of the most revered character', he wondered that the queen 'shewed her detestation of her daughter-in-law within so small a boundary'.

He closes the memoir with these words: 'To that Being unto whom all hearts are open and from whom no secrets are hid I commit myself' and 'pray for forgiveness for this tardy confession, and I hereby enjoin my heirs & executors to make this memoir public as soon as convenient after my death'.[11] Thus he found a way between the guilt of shielding a murderer and the guilt of breaking his oath.

Disburdening himself of the black secret did restore his health. He devoted himself to his son, engaged two Lutheran clergymen to teach him English, German, French and Italian, then sent him to a college. In 1838 the little family moved to London. The date is significant: Ernest had left London in 1837 on becoming king of Hanover .

Jones renewed old associations, notably with the 7th Duke of Beaufort, who was an aide-de-camp to Wellington in the Peninsular war when Jones was a brigade major. (In Beaufort's hot youth he had been sent to the front to stop him from marrying the courtesan Harriette Wilson.) He presented Jones's son Ernest to Queen Victoria at a levee in 1841, and the young man attended royal receptions. He had literary as well as social pretensions, wrote romantic poetry and plays and frequented the soirées of a society novelist, Lady Stepney.

About this time the ageing Charles Jones became ill, and in September 1842 sent an appeal for aid to Ernest King of Hanover: 'In the moment when it has pleased Almighty God to restore your Majesty to health and happiness — suffer me Sire to appeal to your Majesty from my sick bed — perhaps my bed of death, and to pray your Majesty to grant me such pecuniary succour as will prevent your Majesty's old and devoted servant from sinking in *deep distress* to the grave.' Jones says Ernest's representative in London, Count Kielmansegg, 'is acquainted with my misfortunes and promised to make them known to your Majesty'.[12] Ernest's response is unknown. It may be that Jones, remembering the years of suffering that Ernest had caused him, felt justified in asking for some belated succour. He died about six months later. His will bequeathed to Ernest Jones the Reinbeck estate, a house and its contents in Chelsea, and about £1600.

Soon afterwards it happened that King Ernest visited London. The diary of his godson has a brief entry, 4 June 1843, 'I called on the King of Hanover.' Young Jones had evidently not come upon the record of Ernest's confession among his father's papers. His diary merely notes three social calls on Ernest.[13]

The inheritance seems to have unsettled Ernest Jones. There are dangers in having been a prized only son. He bought a fashionable house, had a 'dashing wedding' (his diary says) at St George's, Hanover-square, and bought a Kentish mansion. Then he seems to have been a victim (like many others in the 1840s) of railway promoters. By 1845 he was bankrupt. The disaster had a surprising sequel: he joined the Chartists, then campaigning for social justice and for such exorbitantly radical rights as manhood suffrage, the secret ballot and equalized constituencies. He became one of their leaders, a maker of rousing speeches and heartening verses.

Soon after Sellis's death, a lampoon had foretold (*page 73*) that the truth about the 'horrid deed' was 'fated yet to be reveal'd'. It took some time. In 1899 a Manchester bookseller bought some of Ernest Jones's papers, found Charles Jones's memoir among them, and loyally passed it to the royal library at Windsor. (Whether someone showed it to Ernest's 80-year-old niece Victoria is a piquant question.) It lay unrevealed until in 1970 the historian Arthur Aspinall, near the end of his laborious and praiseworthy editing of seventeen volumes of royal letters, put it in an appendix to volume 7 of *The Correspondence of George, Prince of Wales*. In publishing this piece of evidence, however, he abandoned scholarly rectitude and strived to absolve Ernest. He showed bias even in his heading to the appendix, 'Documents Relating to the Attempted Assassination of the Duke of Cumberland', which rather prejudged the question.

In his introduction to volume 7, Aspinall devotes several pages to undermining Jones's evidence. First he summarizes 'the facts' presented at the inquest, but selectively and with arbitrary comments. For example, Sellis had 'obviously' washed Ernest's blood off his hands in the bowl of water in his room; he had 'clearly' been trying to conceal evidence of his guilt; suicide 'was the only means of escaping justice'. At the inquest, 'It was indeed a fortunate thing that Francis Place happened to be chosen foreman of the jury' (having in fact 'happened' to nominate the jurors). As for Henry White, he is the 'malignant' editor of the 'disreputable' *Independent Whig*.

Aspinall is most inexcusable in his analysis of Jones's memoir, which he calls 'a curious document'. His verdict is, 'As a piece of evidence on which to found a charge of murder the document is valueless.' Then how to explain it? Perhaps, he ventures, it was 'nothing but malicious invention'. Or if 'written in good faith ... the explanation may be that Jones misunderstood the duke, who was trying to convey that he felt partly responsible for driving Sellis to making his criminal attack through failing to lend a sympathetic ear to his grievances'. Besides, Jones 'might well have put words into the duke's mouth'.[14]

Thus Aspinall offers a choice of ways to dismiss the confession:

a) It was malicious invention. He suggests no motive; and what malicious purpose could Jones serve by inventing this circumstantial narrative and hiding it away?

b) Jones was mistaken in thinking that Ernest said, 'I was forced to destroy him in self-defence, the villain threatened to propagate a report', etc. When Jones reacted with horror, thunderstruck, breathless, stupefied, Ernest did not say, 'My dear Jones, what the devil's the matter?' or try to clear up, as one would, anything Jones had 'misunderstood'. No, he made Jones swear, *three times in all*, an oath of strictest secrecy. If innocent, why would Ernest do that?

Any doubter who reads the memoir cannot help being convinced that everything in Jones's account of that December night in 1815 is true. In the full context of the Sellis affair, Aspinall's efforts to exculpate Ernest can only be seen as shameful and sad. It may be that he yielded to pressure from Sir Robin Mackworth-Young, then Queen Elizabeth's librarian in charge of the Windsor archives, to shield the honour of a royal duke. His attempt is soundly negated by its self-evident sophistry.

It is now possible to propose a sequence of events on the night of 30–31 May 1810.

Some time after midnight Ernest and Neale go to Sellis's room.

Neale seizes Sellis (a small man). Ernest cuts his throat. What he has not foreseen is that when the carotid arteries are severed, blood spurts out in jets of at least four feet (information courtesy of the Association of Police Surgeons). Ernest is drenched in blood. He washes some off in Sellis's basin and hurries back to his room, leaving smears of blood as he goes. He has to account for his blood-drenched state. He slashes himself with his sabre and invents the assassination attempt. Before morning, Ernest and the two Neales have agreed their stories.

Of course it is long before the use of fingerprinting or blood tests.

A final word about Cornelius Neale, the chief denigrator of Sellis. His inquest evidence in 1810, his rise to 'gentleman' and his appearance as an affidavit-swearer for Ernest all cohere. By giving his address as Brompton-row he shed light on his life as royal pensioner. The early Kensington ratebooks, which record house-owners and assessed values, reveal that the Neales, converted or reconverted to McNeales, were established at Brompton, a desirable neighbourhood of Georgian houses, early in 1816. In the name of Cornelius's wife they took a substantial house, rated at an annual rental value of £50, in Michael's-place, now part of Brompton-road west of Yeomans-row. Such a purchase could not have been made unaided. Some time before 1832 they moved to an even better house, rated at £54, in Brompton-row, which is now 78–188 Brompton-road. A directory of the time lists a hundred 'nobility, gentry and clergy' at Brompton, as well as lawyers, journalists and actors. Not far from McNeale, in a superior house rated at £120, the ratebook reveals a person well known (heterosexually) to Ernest: Lady Graves. It was here that the visits of 'the *Beast* among the *Graves*' were detected.

In Brompton-square, a few minutes' walk from McNeale's house, a resident from 1825 on was of direct interest to him: Francis Place himself, living in well-to-do retirement with his second wife, a gin-loving ex-actress. During the 1810 inquest the two men had spent a day face-to-face. At Brompton they must have encountered each other. Did Place wonder at the other's prosperity? Or need to wonder? In 1832–3, did they confer about Ernest's libel prosecution?

After McNeale's appearance for Ernest in 1833 had revealed his address, he and his wife vanished from the Brompton ratebooks.

21

Ernest aims at the crown

Wellington fought shy of Ernest's offer to go hand in hand with him politically, but Ernest already had a bolder scheme to 'stem the torrent of Destruction'. He set to work expanding his Orange lodges in Ireland, Britain and the colonies. The enemy was not only popery. His hope was to halt and even reverse the reforms that imperilled the foundations of British life. Emancipation and parliamentary reform were already calamitous. With *Radicals and Repealers* invading the Commons, what might the old and unstable William IV have to concede next ... and after him, Victoria, a mere girl? Repeal of the union with Ireland? Orangemen must save the Empire.

Ernest the Imperial Grand Master, a field marshal as well as an Illustrious Prince, already had many Orange lodges in the army, in defiance of a general order making them a court-martial crime. One reason for the order was that Orangism caused dissension. A graver reason was that the oath Orangemen swore, kneeling, with orange sashes round their necks, pledged only a conditional loyalty to the crown. If, in their view, it failed to maintain the Protestant Ascendancy, their allegiance ceased. In August 1832 Ernest sent out 'our trusty, well-beloved and right worshipful brother, Lieutenant-Colonel Fairman', on a mission round England, Scotland and Ireland 'to communicate to the brotherhood the signs and passwords of the new system ... to open new lodges ... to expel refractory members'. Above all, he armed Fairman, his Deputy Grand Secretary and Treasurer, with warrants for creating still more lodges in army regiments.

Fears arose that Ernest had daring schemes in mind, the deposing of William IV and the ousting of the heir-apparent, Victoria. In view of his perturbing reputation, and at a time of revolutions and king-creatings on the continent and hazardous political conflicts at home, the fear was far from absurd. In 1835 the Commons ordered a select committee inquiry, at which Fairman and Ernest himself were accused of having promoted treasonable ideas.

William Blennerhassett Fairman had an erratic past. In 1809–10, as a captain in the lowly 4th Ceylon Regiment, he solicited the commander-in-chief himself for promotion. ('I feel I am entitled to promotion. I am not in the habit of overrating my claims.') His highest claim was that after the capture of Curaçao by the British he served briefly as aide-de-camp to the governor, 'with the colonial rank of lieutenant-colonel'.[1] His plea failed. In 1813, still a self-promoter, he wrote to the prime minister 'From Storey's Gate Coffee House' (by St James's Park) proposing an 'unprecedented system of offensive operation', the use of militia units for an invasion of Normandy.[2] Postwar, he declined to half-pay captain. That did not stop him from being 'colonel' whenever he wished.

He turned to journalism. In 1825 he launched an ultra-Tory weekly, *The Palladium*, and sent sample copies to the home secretary, Sir Robert Peel, soliciting a subsidy.[3] At the time that Westmacott was ruthlessly acquiring *The Age*, Fairman went beyond his depth in rival scandalmongering, was sued for libel by Colonel Berkeley, Lord William Pitt Lennox and Lord Hertford, could not pay damages, owed stamp duty and was sent as a debtor to Fleet Prison. In a plea from his cell he said his last shilling had been drained from him, he could not afford a lawyer or even food, and furthermore, 'injurious paragraphs' in *The Age* were accusing him of 'cowardice and military delinquency'. He got free in 1828 by selling his captain's commission for £800.[4] This is the 'Colonel' Fairman, now not even a captain, who found a berth as Ernest's Deputy Grand Secretary at Orangism's London headquarters, 9 Portman-square, the mansion of Ernest's Grand Deputy, Lord Kenyon. Fairman displayed his wit and zeal in an idea he put to Kenyon:

> That filthy concern, *The Times*, which spares neither age nor sex, public
> bodies nor private individuals, which at a less degenerate era would have
> been burnt by the common hangman, ought to be forthwith checked in its
> flagitious course of unparallelled infamy. This can only be done by the aid
> of an uncompromising journal of opposition principles for the intrepid
> exposure of its vile fabrications.[5]

Orangism was already backed by the evening *Standard* and the Sunday *Age*. Kenyon proposed funding Westmacott to set up a morning daily to counter the filthy *Times*. This came to nothing, perhaps because Westmacott knew Fairman too well.

Enrolling Orangemen was the supreme task. By the time of the Commons select committee inquiry, their membership was estimated at 220,000 in Ireland, many of them armed, and over 100,000 in Britain.

The committee, headed by a radical MP, Joseph Hume, obtained a copy of a letter Fairman wrote in July 1832 to Lord Londonderry (heir of the late Lord Castlereagh), urging direct action. 'When the altar and the throne are alike assailed ... when, indeed, we have a popish and democratical ministry [Grey's] who, having given birth to a monster they can no longer control ... and are the abject slaves of a ferocious, revolutionary and subversive press', they must lay aside 'non-resistance', Fairman urged. 'By a rapid augmentation of our physical force we might be able to assume a boldness of attitude which should command the respect of our jacobinical rulers.' To the Duke of Gordon he wrote, 'We shall be assuming such an attitude of boldness as will strike the foe with awe.'[6]

At lodge meetings he went further — too far for some members. One gave evidence that Fairman said William IV had had no right to sanction the 'revolutionary' Reform Bill. The time had come to make a stand: 'If any "row" [open conflict] took place, would they rally round the Duke of Cumberland?' According to a pamphlet, *The Orange Exposure*, Kenyon excommunicated thirty-two senior Orangemen in Yorkshire and Derbyshire because they 'refused to participate in an Orange conspiracy to depose the present monarch'. The pamphlet quoted a letter that one of the expelled men, Hayman, wrote to Kenyon about Fairman: 'Did he not act under His Royal Highness's and Your Lordship's directions ... to sound the brethren how they would be disposed, in the event of the king, William IV, being deposed, which was not impossible on account of his sanctioning the reform of parliament; and if so, it would become the duty of every Orangeman to support His Royal Highness, who would then, in all probability, be called to the throne?' Kenyon called this 'pure fabrication'. Unluckily Hayman died before he could testify before the Commons committee.[7]

Ernest openly spread the idea that William IV was unfit to reign. He went about saying he was mad. William's bizarre actions had indeed sometimes qualified him for the word. In 1828 Wellington had had to force him to resign as Lord High Admiral because, inspired by this honorific title, he tormented real admirals with flurries of impossible orders. Wellington told Princess Lieven that for a fortnight William was kept in a straitjacket; and in 1834 she wrote that William *'me paraît être en bon train de devenir fou comme son père'* (seems well on the way to becoming as mad as his father). He behaved oddly in public, made ridiculous speeches, erupted in rages and revelled still in giving orders. The Duchesse de Dino, companion of her uncle Talleyrand, the French ambassador, says in her journal, 'He goes to the barracks ... gives the most absurd orders ... exposes himself to the soldiers' mockery.' The royal family are alarmed — except for Ernest, that is, who 'goes to the clubs and says straight out that the king is mad exactly like his father, which is hardly either brotherly or filial. Some people think already about who will be regent if this sad state continues.'[8]

Ernest certainly thought about it. Victoria was only fifteen.

Hume's select committee invited Ernest to give evidence. He refused. He sent the newspapers a denial that he had 'countenanced and even issued warrants to various regiments'. When warrant-issuing was proposed, he claimed, he instantly refused, as it was contrary to army regulations, 'and I therefore know of no lodge in any regiment'.

A few days later the Sunday *News* said the inquiry had revealed a vast confederacy of men 'initiated with a mysterious ritual — governed not by the laws but by Grand Lodges — armed, organized and presided over by a Prince of the Blood ... near the Throne'. It mocked Ernest's 'lapses of memory': 'He has never heard of Orange lodges in the army ... poor ignorant man.' Next week Ernest partly overcame his memory-loss. He *did* know of such lodges. He published an instruction to his followers that 'all warrants held by any person in any regiment' were illegal, null and void. Army lodges had been created without his knowledge. He blamed the 'indiscretion and negligence' of Lord Kenyon and others.[9] Daniel O'Connell called Ernest 'a mighty great liar'.

Fairman had a set-to with the committee. It had obtained a letter-book from Portman-square that went as far as 1833, so it asked him to produce the next one. He refused, was summoned before the Commons, admitted the book contained letters to and from men in the army, but still refused. This was declared a breach of privilege. A warrant was issued to send him to Newgate. The serjeant-at-arms went to arrest him, but he had gone into hiding with his book.

A pamphlet, *A Letter to the Duke of Cumberland*, quoted the select committee's condemnation of the effects of Orangism: 'To make the Protestant the enemy of the Catholic and the Catholic the enemy of the Protestant ... to excite to breaches of the peace and to bloodshed ... to raise up other secret societies among the Catholics in their own defence ... to interrupt the course of justice' (all effects that were to prevail until the present day).

The pamphlet told Ernest he should be prosecuted; 'and though the Deputy Grand Master of Ireland traitorously proposed to proclaim you as the "*nearest to the throne*", you may be assured that the people will never permit you to ascend that throne... Your Royal Highness's plot against your niece has exploded.'[10]

Wellington, though politically far removed from Joseph Hume, was concerned that Ernest might mount that throne. Two otherwise unrelated events in the autumn of 1835 brought out his misgivings. Princess Victoria was dangerously ill; and Tsar Nicholas made a speech in Warsaw raging about the Poles' uprising of 1830–31 and warning them to abandon 'dreams' of independence. 'On the smallest insurrection,' the tsar said, 'I will have the city cannonaded. I will destroy Warsaw... It will not be rebuilt. I say it for your good.'

Wellington had seen some cannonaded towns. He deplored the speech, he wrote to his niece, Lady Burghersh, and 'principally on account of the impression it has made on the mind of the D of Cumberland. He admires it mightily; and would willingly imitate it if he should have the opportunity... Among other evils with which this country is threatened is that of the loss of the Princess Victoria. We shall witness a scene here in that case which I fear will afford ample opportunities for pranks of this description.'[11]

That is, Ernest as king would mean civil war.

An equally serious thought had struck Charles Greville, the Privy Council secretary, as early as 1831: 'The king is ill. I hope he won't die. If he does, and the little girl, we shall have Cumb[d]... That would be a good moment for dispensing with the regal office.'[12]

Figaro in London's caricaturist, Robert Seymour, drew Ernest as 'The Devilish Royal Brigand', perched in an *orange* tree, threatening William IV and Victoria with a carbine. A quarrel within the Orange 'gang', *Figaro* said, had revealed that 'this dreadful set' were aiming not only at the king. 'It was intended to knock out the delicious little Princess Victoria from the line of succession.'

A radical sheet pictured Ernest, labelled The Wolf, trying to steal the crown. He says he wishes he could get rid of this 'sprig of royalty' (Victoria, The Lamb) 'as well as someone else I did for'. Soon *The Satirist* went further. It showed a man, unmistakably Ernest, smothering someone in a bed. The victim's identity is indicated on the bed-hangings with a V and a coronet. Beneath, verses denounce Ernest as an unpunished spiller of blood. An extract:

> Will a proud people yield their mighty throne
> To that base, heartless prince, whom all disown?
> Blest day, when their loud voices shall decree
> This land from such a monster shall be free!
> When rank like his no more shall shelter guilt
> And blood no more shall unreveng'd be spilt.

The next week's *Satirist* printed a conversation under the heading 'Cumberland's Sunday Dinner Parties':

Cumberland — A brother's brat between me and the crown!
Bishop [of Salisbury] — Yet there are means.
Cumberland — By Beelzebub, there *shall* be means.
Billy Holmes — Poison, for instance.
Wetherell — Or a razor.
Cumberland (with a fiendish laugh) — Aye, a razor, if nothing better serve.
   I should know something of its use.

William 'Black Billy' Holmes, for years a Tory whip, and like Wetherell a crony of Ernest, was described by Greville as 'the greatest rogue unhung'.[13]

In the Commons, Joseph Hume said he refrained from asserting that the lodges 'are in a conspiracy to alter the succession', but he would call Ernest 'a dangerous man' with 'the power of assembling a body of 300,000 men'. Sir William Molesworth, an MP for Cornwall, urged that 'the illustrious Grand Master', his noble lieutenants and the Bishop of Salisbury should be sent to New South Wales like the Tolpuddle Martyrs, the farmworkers transported in 1834 for swearing oaths of mutual support. 'A few years residence on the shores of the southern ocean,' he said, 'would teach the titled criminals that the laws of their country were not to be violated.'[14]

The Commons voted for measures for 'the effectual discouragement' of religiously exclusive societies using secret signs and symbols. The king immediately reaffirmed the army's ban on lodges. Ernest instructed all his lodges ('painfully', he said) to dissolve themselves. *The Age* proclaimed that they would live on: 'The flag of the Death's-head and Cross-bones was not unfurled in vain... THEY BIDE THEIR TIME.' A week later it said the lodges need only discard secret symbols and 'an unmeaning formula of mummery'. Then 'like a phoenix from the ashes ... let a Protestant Union of the Empire arise!'[15] Orangism was indeed not dead, and proves it still.

In the Lords, Ernest protested that he had been 'abused, accused and treated in the most cruel manner that ever a human being was treated'. If the allegations of a plot against Victoria were true, he ought to be tried in the Lords for high treason. Who could suppose he 'could have been such a madman as to have entertained even a thought of such an act?' He would shed his last drop of blood for his niece.[16]

He wrote to Frederica, 'My heart boils with rage at all these attacks of Hume and company.' As for Fairman, his 'trusty and well-beloved' Deputy Grand Secretary and Treasurer, with whom he had worked for years, he became an unperson. Ernest told Frederica, 'I never had any connection with that man, never received him at my house, never was in company with him in the whole course of my life, except when he brought me as secretary warrants to sign or at the great meetings.'[17]

Poor cast-off Fairman threatened to expose Ernest. 'Circumstances will at length compel me to seek a compensation from royalty for my services,' he said in a letter that became public. Should that appeal fail, 'I shall enforce my claims through the medium of the press, both in pamphlets and papers, when a dread of exposure may prompt them to do that which ought to have emanated from a sense of gratitude.'[18]

But that is the last we hear of Ernest's Deputy Grand ex-friend, the Curaçao colonel.

22

Sophia and the amazing Conroy

Princess Victoria's girlhood was troubled by equivocal relationships among the adults nearest to her in Kensington Palace. One might speak of a ménage not *à trois*, indeed, but *à quatre*.

When Victoria's father, the Duke of Kent, died in January 1820, his handsome and ambitious Irish equerry, Captain John Conroy, took a commanding role as comptroller of the household of the widow, who was a self-doubting character, and self-deceiving or worse. In the same year, Princess Sophia came to live at Kensington Palace. Conroy became her comptroller as well. The fourth in the ménage, Conroy's wife, was a pliant person who counted for little.

In 1820 Conroy and the Duchess of Kent were both 34. Their relationship soon inspired talk. This six-foot-tall captain with persuasive Irish charm was seen to treat a royal highness without deference; more as an intimate equal. Some years later Wellington told Charles Greville that Princess Victoria had 'witnessed some familiarities' between her mother and Conroy, which was the cause of Victoria's 'alienation' from her mother and hatred of him. When Greville asked Wellington whether he thought they were lovers, he said, 'I suppose so.'[1]

More remarkable, and of greater interest here, was the alliance that Conroy established with Sophia. In the words of the duchess's son by her first marriage, Prince Charles of Leiningen, Sophia 'stood in close-linked friendship' with Conroy. In 1827 Sophia persuaded George IV to knight him. She served as his 'spy' at court (his own word), intriguing on behalf of his Kensington System ('We shall see what I have to report tomorrow... God bless you! ...Your name carefully avoided...'). The plots and power-plays of these years are detailed in Cecil Woodham-Smith's *Queen Victoria*, Elizabeth Longford's *Victoria R.I.* and (for Sophia especially) Katherine Hudson's *A Royal Conflict*: *Sir John Conroy and the Young Victoria*. Conroy's 'system' required that, having made himself master of Kensington Palace, he would prevent interference by George IV (and William IV) and their court, and would control Victoria's upbringing. Through the duchess he would command Victoria. When she became queen he would be the power behind the throne, as her private secretary and Privy Purse.

Sophia was 42 when the 'close-linked friendship' began. Years earlier, she had declared to Sir Henry Halford her need for a *'warm friend'* to whom she could open her heart. How intimate was she with Conroy? The question must be asked when one sees how she rewarded him. He was ruthlessly milking the duchess's income, but that did not sate him. Sophia lavished extraordinary sums on him. This went on for nearly thirty years. Elizabeth Longford calls him 'an intriguer, a vulgarian and a scamp'. She might have used a harsher word than scamp.

As Sophia had always lived reclusively she must have accumulated large savings from her Civil List revenue (£13,000 a year from 1812, £15,000 from 1818), whatever she was allowing to Tom Garth. If her brother Frederick Duke of York had not been a criminally outrageous squanderer she would have been further enriched by his death in 1827, for he made her his residuary legatee. She wrote to her bed-chamber woman, Lady John Thynne, 'What a *loss He is*! ...So kind a brother, so affec^te and sincere a friend... Of course there is *nothing* to inherit, but the naming me in such a manner has made me feel I am Heir of his *affection*.'[2] So kind a brother: dating from 1800, when he made the Garth arrangements. And 'what a *loss*'! Indeed: above all to creditors whom he owed over £200,000 (say £8 million) and who were still being fobbed off years later by his executor, Sir Herbert Taylor.

Besides creditors, there were claimants of a more intimate sort, Sir William Knighton reported in February 1827 to Wellington —

Two mistresses of the early 1800s, Mary Anne Clarke and Elizabeth Carey, both anxious not to lose long-standing annuities;

A woman at Hampstead 'by whom he had two children', applying for her pension to continue;

'A natural daughter of the D of York applies to His Majesty for relief... I have also had a visit from a natural son';

'Another female friend' presents a bond for £1000, 'so that you will see the disbanded troops are rather numerous'.

Actions still less worthy of an Illustrious Prince are revealed by Knighton. York's duchess bequeathed jewels worth £11,000 to her old servants. He sold them, 'put the money ... into his pocket' and gave the servants a bond 'which is now of course become the value of waste paper'. George IV must find the money or else the servants will sue for it, which would be 'the most afflicting blot' on York's character. Such royal swindles are not 'blots' if concealed. Many of York's servants, furthermore, 'had been without wages for a long time, and from many of them HRH had borrowed the savings of their whole lives'. This contribution of York's servants was a mere supplement to his borrowings from Coutts's and other banks, borrowings so vast that the annual *interest* came to £45,000 (say £1,800,000). Yet in his declining days he raised further huge sums for an 'unprincipled foolery' (Knighton's phrase) — building a great mansion.[3]

Sophia's kind, affectionate, sincere brother, devoted lifelong to profligate ways exceeded only by George IV, had not set her a prudent or moral example.

Her gifts to Conroy apparently began in 1823. Her first substantial payments were in 1826. She was so charmed or dominated by the 'intriguer and scamp' that in that year she bought him a house for £4000, a few minutes from Kensington Palace, and contributed £18,000 toward his purchase of an estate at Llanbrynmair in Wales.

Here we have new light on Tom Garth's difficulties. It is likely that by 1827, when he asked Sophia for aid, she had been reducing her contribution, so he hoped to establish a satisfactory figure. That he was told to apply to Sir Herbert was no doubt the doing of Conroy, who had a strong motive. Sophia's gifts to Conroy grew. Katherine Hudson, using Conroy papers at Balliol College, Oxford, quotes Conroy's grandson John (Sophia's godson) as saying Sophia contributed a further £10,000 to Llanbrynmair and £20,000 to buy a Berkshire estate, Arborfield Hall. Until her death in 1848 she also paid him an annual sum, ostensibly for handling her affairs, amounting over the years to £96,000. The grandson's reckoning brings Sophia's gifts to a grand total of £148,000 (over £6 million now), but it was certainly more. Katherine Hudson quotes Prince Albert's private secretary, Sir Charles Phipps, as saying that Conroy protected Sophia from the 'bullying importunities' of Garth. But as she indulged Conroy with sums vastly greater than what her son needed to save him from prison, a fairer phrase would be 'desperate entreaties'.

Many facts show Sophia's closeness to Conroy. Near to the Kensington house that she had given him, she bought another, creating a retreat unobserved by Kensington Palace staff. 'She and the Conroys were frequently in and out of each others' houses', says Katherine Hudson. In March 1838, when Queen Victoria and her treasured prime minister, Lord Melbourne, were looking for a way to get rid of Conroy discreetly, the queen wrote in her journal, 'Spoke of SJC [Conroy] and Princess Sophia with Lord Melbourne for some time, and *how* it happened that Princess Sophia was quite in the power and *à la merci* of Sir JC, at which Lord Melbourne was quite horrified.' One is left to guess the meaning. Victoria told Melbourne that 'Princess Sophia used to court him more than anyone'. Charles Greville wrote years later that Sophia was thought to have let her apartments in Kensington Palace be used secretly by the Duchess of Kent and Conroy — safe there from the eyes of Victoria and of her loyal governess, Baroness Lehzen. [4]

Wellington said Victoria had not a particle of affection or respect for her mother. This is confirmed in Victoria's journal notes of a talk with Melbourne: 'Talked of my dislike of Mama. Lord M. said that she was a liar and a hypocrite. "I never saw so foolish a woman," said M. Which is very true and we both laughed.' [5]

Melbourne, who had seen (as well as enjoyed) enough liaisons not to be easily amazed, said of Conroy, 'What an amazing scape of a man he must have been, to have kept three ladies at once in good humour.' [6] Sir George Anson, private secretary to Melbourne and later to Prince Albert, said Sophia was Conroy's *chère amie*. The third lady was not Conroy's almost invisible wife, but Lady Flora Hastings, a lady-in-waiting to Victoria from 1834, and in Conroy's camp.

One can see how it was that Mrs George Villiers, who was close to Sophia as well as to Princess Amelia in the early 1800s, came to disapprove of Sophia. In 1847 she wrote to her daughter, Lady Theresa Lewis, 'At first my *intimacy* was chiefly with the Princess Sophia, who seemed to place the most unbounded confidence in me and excited my sympathy and compassion to an unbounded degree in return, as I thought her more sinned against than sinning [in the matter of the pregnancy]. My general impression of her character was much changed afterwards, as you know.' [7]

An episode in which Sophia did a service *not* for Conroy has some interest because it brings out a little of her private correspondence (otherwise rare), and Ernest's name comes into it. In October 1829 the widow of Warren Hastings asked Sophia to help her to obtain a pension. She wrote that she was struggling 'to maintain the station becoming the widow of that revered character Warren Hastings, who saved an empire to our beloved Sovereign'. Hastings, years before, had spent heavily in a long fight against impeachment for his crimes as governor-general in India, so he did not leave great wealth. The widow asked Sophia 'to solicit His Royal Highness the Duke of Cumberland ... to be so gracious as to mention my name to our glorious King and to beseech His Majesty to place the name of the widow of Warren Hastings on the pension list'. (The fulsome wording will have been designed for the king's eyes.) That she asked Sophia to promote her appeal through Ernest shows that she knew them to be on good terms — in the year when the court had alleged her 'horror' of him.

Sophia suggests to 'dearest Mrs Hastings' that a better approach would be 'a *direct appeal* under your own *hand* & seal'. If she will write a letter addressed to George IV, Sophia will see that he gets it, with some supporting words.

This correspondence reveals one of the sensual pleasures of the half-blind Sophia. She asks Mrs Hastings whether the perfume of her writing-paper is 'a *Pot Pourri* of *Flowers* or a mixture of *Scents* in liquid'. 'Never did I smell anything to come up to it — as the ingredients appear to me so sweetly powerful of Rose < illegible > & Jassmine... I'm too passionately fond of perfumes *well* mixed.' Mrs Hastings takes the hint. Soon afterwards Sophia thanks her for a '*precious* little Bottle': 'So *luxurious* a *perfume* I never possessed before.' She fears she had '*done wrong* in asking what perfume you used'. She reports that the king has spoken to Wellington about the pension.[8]

Ernest and Frederica had cherished a hope that their son George, born three days after Victoria, might marry her, as royal cousins often did. Then Ernest might be a power behind Victoria. On his visit to England in 1828 Ernest brought the boy with him and presented him at court. 'The chit-chat of the day is about the young prince of Cumberland, the supposed *futur* of our young Queen Victoria,' Lady Holland told her son. 'He is a lively, pretty boy ... remarkably inquisitive about the state of the Royal Family, the succession, etc.' Wellington's friend Harriet Arbuthnot was concerned about the boy's 'rude boisterous ways', so different from the 'very *posée* & well bred' Victoria. The boy behaved 'as if he was crazy' at the Drawing Room (palace reception): 'The whole room rung with his shouts of laughter, when the judges passed, at their grotesque dresses, & when his tutor passed by dressed in his canonicals, he said, "What, you are come to make a fool of yourself too, are you?" What a Royal Family ours is!!'[9]

Ernest himself was depicted as a more serious objection. In a caricature entitled 'The *Betrothing* interrupted by the GHOST of SELL—HISS!! — HISS!!!', Victoria's mother is shown (falsely) as promoting a betrothing. Sellis's ghost rises up holding a bloody razor and saying, once again, 'Thou canst not say *I* did it.' Ernest, terrified, cries, 'Oh! hide me — screen me from this vision.'

Whatever hopes Ernest had were dashed when his son was 13. He became blind. A few years earlier he had lost his right eye as a result, it was said, of 'inflammation'. He seems to have inherited a weakness from Ernest. In September 1832 an illness affected the other eye. Frederica wrote to Princess Lieven that she and Ernest were *'plongés dans les plus vives inquiétudes'*. Over six weeks, George's sight came and went uncertainly, then faded entirely. The Duchesse de Dino gave a touching picture of the boy two years later: 'A pleasant and handsome young man ... without impatience, without regrets, without ill-humour... Improvising on the piano is his chief amusement. His melodies are always sad and grave, but when he hears his mother's steps he passes to a gay, animated theme.'[10]

Conroy developed his Kensington system by working on the Duchess of Kent's anxieties. The alarm over Ernest's Orangemen was useful in persuading her that they must always be on guard. How much Conroy believed in a plot is a question; but Baroness Lehzen 'recognized a need to guard Victoria every hour of the day and night', Elizabeth Longford writes. Until Victoria became queen, just after her eighteenth birthday, she was required to sleep in her mother's bedroom.[11]

When Victoria had been forty years on the throne, the wife of Conroy's son Henry, a Guards colonel, sent her a manuscript account of an alleged conspiracy by Ernest 'aimed at the youthful life of Your Majesty'. As Victoria read it, she added comments. It must be noted that she had hated Conroy and might discount what his son said.

On the manuscript's allegation that Ernest 'was seized with the terrible temptation to remove the only life that then stood between him and the throne', she commented, 'He never showed the slightest symptom of this.' A statement that Ernest urged George IV to remove Victoria from her mother's care because 'the Duchess of Kent was too much attached to Sir John Conroy' brought this puzzling comment: 'All Sir John's invention and Pss Sophia's fearful falseness.' The manuscript accuses Ernest of having spread rumours about Victoria's health (she was in fact seriously ill in 1835). It says his plan was that, having removed her from Kensington, he would surround her 'by persons in his own pay', and either by neglect or by poison bring about her death, which people would think 'a very natural ending to a frail and delicate life'. Victoria's comment is '*Utterly* false.' But this was forty years on.[12]

On the very day that William IV died in 1837 and Victoria became queen, Conroy put in a claim to Lord Melbourne for the reward he expected for his years of service: a peerage, the Order of the Bath and a pension of £3000 a year. When Melbourne read this, the paper dropped from his hand and he exclaimed, 'Have you ever heard such impudence?' Victoria forbade Conroy to come near her court. Baron Stockmar, one of the soundest men in her early entourage, said to her that he was 'a man whom Your Majesty knows best to be one of the most immoral and unprincipled men in your kingdom'.[13] Yet he was consoled with the £3000 pension and the next-best thing to a peerage, a baronetcy.

A small part of the roguery of the scamp was soon exposed. The Duchess of Kent's revenue had been raised to £30,000 a year to enable her to clear her debts (debts caused by him), but this money too slipped sideways. Debts of more than £70,000 remained. *The Times* congratulated Conroy on the 'happy state' of her affairs. The scandal cast a shadow over the queen's first year. In April 1838 a large body of creditors, chiefly Kensington tradesmen — butcher, saddler, coach-maker, baker, grocer, fruiterer, tailor, coal merchant, etc — were summoned to receive large cheques drawn on Coutts's: not from comptroller Conroy, however, but from a concealed source which *The Times* learned was the Department of Woods and Forests.[14]

More about Conroy remained to be revealed, some of it only after Sophia's death.

23

His most moustachioed majesty

A consolation for Ernest when Victoria came to the throne on 20 June 1837 was that he instantly became king of Hanover, where a female ruler was barred. Hanover, a troublesome continental annex of Britain since 1714, ceased to be under the British crown. If any of Victoria's subjects felt regret at the loss, it was outweighed by the departure of King Ernest.

When William IV was dying, Ernest had asked Wellington for advice. 'I told him the best thing he could do was to go away as fast as he could. Go instantly, I said, and take care that *you don't get pelted*.'[1] Or in another version, 'Go before they pelt you out.' He departed amid still sharper jibes. *Figaro in London* called him 'THE FIEND KING ... his most moustachioed majesty, Ernest the First, King (thank God) of Hanover'. This genially mordant weekly was the creation of Gilbert à Beckett (soon to be a founder of *Punch*). William IV's death, it said, 'gets rid forever of *Cumberland*, commonly called the Demon Duke'.

> The Duke of Cumberland hurried off, on Tuesday morning, to his apartments in St James's to pack up for Hanover. He secured his dressing case and, of course, did not forget his *razors*. His dukedom is now at an end, and His Majesty was greeted as he passed with the sincere howls of the populace.[2]

Before he went, Ernest made an obeisance to Victoria. On June 21 all privy councillors swore allegiance to the new sovereign. Ernest and his brother Augustus were first in line. 'As these two old men, her uncles, knelt before her, swearing allegiance and kissing her hand,' Charles Greville noted, 'I saw her blush up to the eyes, as if she felt the contrast between their civil and their natural relations, and this was the only sign of emotion which she evinced... She kissed them both.'[3]

Figaro in London celebrated Ernest's departure with a caricature of him as a devil flying away. 'John Bull has in fact been possessed of a devil,' it said, 'and Victoria has been mercifully sent to *cast him out*.' It offered a Royal Anthem to be sung by Ernest's Hanoverian subjects:

> Deuce take our precious King —
> Deuce take the horrid thing,
>   Deuce take the King.
> Send him, the wicked wretch,
> On straightway to Jackey Ketch,   [*the hangman*
> Who ought his neck to stretch.
>   Deuce take the King.[4]

Sir Herbert Taylor, who had loyally served Ernest, or rather had served the royal family's name, now felt free to speak frankly, at least to the foreign secretary, Lord Palmerston. One of Sir Herbert's aides, named Hudson, having been appointed to Ernest's Hanoverian legation in London, Sir Herbert wrote to Palmerston, 'It is my duty to mention to you that I have for some years been very much in the black books of the King of Hanover, and that Hudson … has come in for his share of the scowl. I do not imagine that this will injure either of us in your opinion.'[5] The scowls will have occurred *after* Sir Herbert had got Garth out of the way. As private secretary to William IV, Sir Herbert had to cope with highhanded manœuvres by Ernest over colonelcies, horses and so forth; and more seriously, with his Orange plotting in the army. Sir Herbert no doubt faced something worse than scowls. His well-rewarded life was not all roses.

The north German kingdom Ernest inherited at the age of 66 measured 11,000 square miles and had a population of about 1,300,000. Since 1813 his younger brother Adolphus had been its viceroy, but power was chiefly in the hands of near-feudal landowners, served by a rigid bureaucracy. Adolphus was no modernizer, and besides grew so eccentric that Wellington called him 'mad as Bedlam'. During his time, liberals here, as elsewhere in Europe, were agitating for reforms. The early ideals of the French Revolution were not forgotten. In 1830–31 the old system was challenged by an insurrection led by Ernest's one-time university, Göttingen. The army quelled this, but a new constitution was conceded, creating an elected assembly with modest powers.

As soon as Ernest had settled into his Hanover palace a few years later, he revoked the constitution, which he said would have made him 'a mere cypher'. His people must obey him: then they would be happy. In London the reaction to his coup was that Britain had had a lucky escape. *Figaro in London* said, 'His Majesty King Ernest the First can only be at present addressed in the emphatic language of Sam

Weller to the cabman: "You're a-going it, old feller".' (*Pickwick Papers* was the book of the year.) *Figaro* said we now had 'some idea of the games Cumberland would have been up to' if he had become Britain's king: 'His first step would have been to declare the Reform Bill all my eye, and dissolve the House of Commons without issuing new writs for another.' *Figaro* developed its devil image: 'His Infernal Majesty hereby tramples the legislative house under his royal hoof and snaps his tail at it.' It sardonically recalled the Graves affair: 'His Majesty intends to grant a royal dispensation making suicide no longer criminal, particularly in cases of injured husbands who, when their wives prove false to them, cannot do better than cut their own throats.'[6]

Greville wrote that Ernest's 'violence' in Hanover made him 'still more odious here than he was before, and it would be an awful thing if the Crown were, by any accident, to devolve upon him'. *Figaro* made the same point: 'The life of Victoria is more precious than that of any sovereign that ever sat upon the throne of England.'[7]

Again the University of Göttingen rebelled. Seven professors, among them the famous folk-tale collectors, the brothers Jacob and Wilhelm Grimm, stood by 'the constitution, truth and justice' and refused to swear allegiance to Ernest. He dismissed the Göttingen Seven and exiled three of them. Liberals round Germany hailed them as martyrs; defenders of the true state, as one protest put it, 'against monarchic caprice'. The elected assembly showed fight, but Ernest managed to make every member swear allegiance under Hanover's old, unliberal constitution, then offered small concessions.

'*All* has gone off most *admirably*,' he reported to his old friend Princess Lieven, though 'the Radicals tried their Tricks'. He has had 'messages from most of the Princes of Germany saying they look upon me as the Champion of Monarchical Principles'. To Sir Henry Halford he wrote that he was able to outwit the 'Radicals and Malcontents' because after '39 Years Apprenticeship in an English Parliament ... I knew what I was about'. Now he is 'assailed with Congratulations from every quarter' and is told he is 'the only *King* who could have stemmed the democratic spirit here on the Continent'.[8] Yet democratic disaffection persisted. He wrote to Halford in 1840, 'Oh how often do I sigh after dear Kew & my little Cottage there. There is a great deal of Glory but little Enjoyment in a King's life, & as the Duke of Cumberland I was much happier & more my own Master than I now shall ever be again, but my *Heart*, my *Principles* remain the same.'[9]

He asserted himself against Victoria by claiming that a quantity of royal jewellery, dating from the time of George II and George III, was Hanoverian property. The claim caused outrage. Lady Cowper, Lord Melbourne's sister, wrote to Princess Lieven (now living in Paris), 'I imagine it will make his accession to the English throne absolutely impossible in any circumstances. I think its only effect will be to redouble the state of tension ... until the queen is married and has heirs to preserve us from danger.' His claim led to years of argument, ending in the handing over of £150,000 worth of jewellery — but only after his death.

He was certainly wrong in another dispute, over his refusal to give up his St James's apartments for the use of Victoria's mother. 'Domineering insolence,' said Greville. 'It was a gross insult to the queen to refuse to give up to her an apartment in her own palace,' but Lord Melbourne, prime minister, 'preferred knocking under ... which is always as contemptible as it is useless'.[10]

'Heirs to preserve us from danger': in 1839 Victoria chose for a husband Prince Albert of Saxe-Coburg and Gotha, her first cousin (her mother's nephew) — 'excessively handsome, such beautiful eyes, an exquisite nose, and such a pretty mouth with delicate mustachios ... a beautiful figure, broad in the shoulders and fine waist; my heart is quite *going*'.[11] Her delight in him inspired the wilful young queen to insist that he should be given precedence second only to herself. This son of a scandal-ridden marriage in a German dukedom, population 131,000, must rank above George III's sons. The junior ones, Augustus Duke of Sussex and Adolphus Duke of Cambridge, were persuaded to agree, but Ernest, with justification, refused. 'The princes of the blood royal being in the *straight* line of succession,' he wrote, 'you cannot admit that a royal highness (N.B., a *paper one*) can claim precedency to those *born* so.'[12] Luckily he did not discover that Albert (as Melbourne revealed to Greville) 'wanted to have the title of king'.

The Tories opposed Victoria's demand. This aroused the spitfire in her. 'I was quite furious and raged away,' she wrote in her journal. Melbourne tried to soothe her, in vain. 'Vile, confounded, infernal Tories... I'll never forgive these infernal scoundrels.' Melbourne advised her to yield the point. Never! 'I was perfectly frantic... I cried with rage... Poor dear Albert, how cruelly are they ill-using that dearest Angel! Monsters! ...Revenge! Revenge!' Her rages made Greville say to Melbourne, 'Everybody knows her father was the greatest rascal that ever went unhung, and they will say it is the bad blood coming out in her.'[13] A compromise title was found, Prince Consort.

Ernest saw Prince Albert as 'a terrible liberal, almost a radical ... still more dangerous than a Roman Catholic, being a sort of free-thinker'. In February 1840, just before Victoria conceived her first child, Ernest wrote to Princess Lieven, 'Oh how different are the present times to what they were when we first knew each other... England was at the pinnacle of its glory, respected by all Europe, and now what is it alas descended to!!! It really makes my heart bleed.'[14]

Since June 1837 he had been heir-presumptive, but that ceased on 22 November 1840 when Victoria's firstborn arrived. Disappointingly, it was not a boy, but as Lord Clarendon, Lord Privy Seal, wrote to our ambassador in Paris, 'What the country cares about is to have a life more, whether male or female, interposed between the succession and the king of Hanover.' Or as Lady Cowper put it, 'The general public is mad with joy at this happy event, this new barrier against the king of Hanover.'[15]

Ernest's Frederica died in June 1841, aged 63. The Duchesse de Dino, who was visiting Germany, says in her *Chronique* that Ernest was thrown into despair, and his blind son George, then 22, suffered even more. 'Not being able to *see* his mother, he could not convince himself that she was dead, and asked to be allowed to touch her body. The moment that his father put the mother's cold hand in that of the son, the poor blind man was seized as if with an attack of madness. They sent him away to the seaside.'

To Princess Lieven, Ernest writes of his 'broken and torn heart'. From his window he can see the vault where his 'beloved Angel' lies: '*There* my eyes dwell and dwell till my tears blind me.' Indeed, many words in this letter are blotted. 'Now I cannot write, my tears prevent me, *write* pray pray, it is an Act of Charity, and I disdain not Charity ... write pray...' He tells Sir Henry Halford, 'The Anguish of Soul and anxiety of Mind I have gone through, & living between fear and hope, all has made a deep ravage in me, & I begin to feel I am giving way.' To another friend, Viscount Strangford, he praises Frederica as having had the soundest judgment 'of all the women I have ever known', and besides 'she knew how to soothe and tranquillize my mind when irritated and disgusted at all the ingratitude and hostility I met'.[16]

Hostility, indeed, was never-ending. In the same letter he says he has dissolved his parliament because 'seven to eight Radical attorneys' blocked a vote on the budget. He has made a proclamation 'exposing all their infamy'. Two months later he had to accept a new cabinet despite 'the number of *Waverers*' in it. To Lady Georgina Bathurst (Georgy) he writes, 'I hate a Waverer from the bottom of my soul. I like an *out* and *out man*, one who has a *fixed principle* & does not change at every moment... This at least no one can ever accuse me of ever having done.' Yet his new cabinet is hardly '*out* and *out*'.

The 'new morality' at Victoria's court amuses him, he tells Lady Georgina. 'To think that the Morals of the Duke of Beaufort, Lord Chesterfield & Wilton have been objected [to] when our little Queen has been living for the four past Years in habits of intimacy with Lords Melbourne & <*illegible* >, and *especially* this from the outset when she was emancipated in 1837 from the nursery. This is too absurd & ridiculous in my very humble opinion.' This last phrase, unexpected from Ernest, occurs often in these late letters, making him a sort of 'Disgusted of Hanover'.[17]

When Victoria had given Britain two more barriers against Ernest (the future Edward VII, and then Princess Alice in April 1843), she made the gesture of inviting him to be a baptismal sponsor. 'Many many melancholy remembrances of past happy Days will occur to my Mind,' he wrote to Princess Lieven, recalling 'so many pleasant Hours' spent at her country place at Richmond. 'All that is Alas gone by!!' Besides, the court had lost its tone under Victoria, 'for Jews, Turks and Infidels are not only admitted at Court, but come in private parties, balls and concerts at Buckingham House'.[18]

He arrived just too late for Alice's christening but was able to attend the wedding of a daughter of his brother Adolphus. Here he figured in a farcical way, trying to assert his precedence over Prince Albert, the 'paper' royal and non-king. After the service, when the queen was to lead the congregation out, he claimed his right, as a sovereign, to be the man to march out beside her — not Albert the non-sovereign. She refused. He persisted. Albert gave him a push. Ernest, aged 72 and stiff with rheumatism, nearly fell. 'Fuming with ire', he was escorted out by the Lord Chamberlain.

Next was the signing of the register, which lay on a table. Ernest placed his elbow on it and asked Victoria to sign so that he could sign next. Victoria nipped to the other side of the table and commanded the register to be passed across. She and then Albert signed before Ernest could get near. He left for Kew 'the moment the ceremony was over', he wrote to Princess Lieven (not mentioning his humiliations), 'to pass the melancholy *29th* [second anniversary of Frederica's death] *quite alone*', musing on former 'happy days'.[19]

He had looked forward to seeing Henry Brougham, for they could now speak of their hostilities as matters of history '& laugh at them, as I have often done with Lyndhurst'. And indeed he had a convivial dinner with these two former lord chancellors. He was still enjoying the memory months later. He told Princess Lieven, 'It would have made you laugh to have been present at the scenes and fun I had at Dinner with him & Lyndhurst, talking over my Battles with them ... especially the great annoyance I was to them all in the famous session of 1829 [over emancipation]... How all passes by in the world.' Brougham, once a great Whig activist, nicknamed Wickedshifts by Thomas Creevey, had veered towards the Tories. Ernest said he was in his heart a Conservative, even when 'we were daily at Daggers drawn and fighting like two Game Cocks'.[20]

During his three months in London, he complained, Victoria asked him to dinner only once. There were consolations. Ernest was 'feasted, invited and visited by all manner of men', Charles Greville was surprised to find. 'He is become the lion of the season with this foolish, inconsistent world.' This was not only in great houses. Ernest told Princess Lieven that in the streets of London 'the common people say to me, "God bless you, I am happy to see you."' And another time, 'they hail me with pleasure'. His gratitude is 'unbounded'.[21]

One must wonder if some of these greetings were sardonic cockney mock-praise. At any rate, Ernest was inspired to propose a public stroll with Prince Albert, who he knew still faced hostility as an upstart German import. Albert declined, saying he would be 'exposed to inconvenience from the crowd' (vulgar abuse, that is). Ernest replied, 'Oh, never mind that. I was still more unpopular than you are now, and used to walk about with perfect impunity.'[22] He counted on Albert's not knowing how much he had been reviled and pelted.

24

A royal commoner in Chelsea

The Tom Garth who left King's Bench Prison at the age of 35 was a sadder and no doubt a wiser man than the carefree Meltonian of the 1820s. Sir Herbert Taylor, having served the royal family so well in acquiring the dangerous documents, also saw that he got no money. (Only many years later, he was granted a little.) The funds that paid off his creditors, and that enabled him soon afterwards to set himself up in a fashionable part of Chelsea, came from his inheritance.

'Capt Garth' first appears in 1837 in the local ratebook as the owner of a house in Hans-place, west of Sloane-street in the Cadogan estate. This square, or rather long rectangle, was developed in the late 18th century by the architect Henry Holland when he was also engaged in grander projects, the prince of Wales's conversion of Carlton House into a palace and the first stages of his pavilion at Brighton. Garth bought No 30. He had sold the much grander Portland-place house left him by General Garth, which will have yielded money and to spare, for it was rated at £250 rental value and No 30 at £50. Among his Hans-place neighbours, the *Royal Blue Book* street directory says, were an army captain at 31, two superior naval captains at 33 and 45, and four reverend gentlemen. For his gentlemanly comfort he had his choice of the contents of the general's two mansions, and his bequest of a £1500 annuity. A supplement to his income was his half-pay as a captain in Ernest's old regiment, which continued all his life.

In this new home far from King's Bench Prison, he had servants to help him care for little Georgiana Rosamond Caroline. As a gentleman of some means, he could seek diversion. After so much shaming misfortune, was he willing to face old friends at Melton Mowbray? Two pictures of a foxhunting man on a horse have been claimed to be of him in middle age. One, by Henry Barraud, a prolific equestrian artist, was published by Lucille Iremonger in her book about Princess Sophia, *Love and the Princess*. Its owners, then living at Haines Hall, Berkshire, were descendants of General Garth's nephew and namesake, Captain Thomas Garth of the Royal Navy. They believed this horseman to be Tom Garth. He is likely however to be yet another Thomas Garth who was master of the Berkshire hounds in the 1840s — and who lived at Haines Hall.

The stronger contender is by John Ferneley, the artist who painted several of Garth's horses in the 1820s. It is signed and dated 'Melton Mowbray 1845'. In April 1989 it came up at Christie's, London, described as 'Captain Garth on his bay hunter with hounds in a landscape', and went for £44,000. The Melton provenance seems persuasive; and the rider does appear to be a *short* man, as Garth was.

Hans-place is about a mile and a half from Kensington Palace, where Garth's mother lived, more and more out of the world, until her death in 1848. There is evidence he visited her. William Childe-Pemberton, when working a century ago on his *Romance of Princess Amelia*, spoke to people whose memories went back to Sophia's time. He writes: 'An old female servant, known to the writer, lived when young in the service of Princess Sophia... She spoke gratefully of her royal mistress, never alluding to any scandals which she may have heard. One curious fact, however, she often mentioned. At certain times all the servants had strict orders not to enter the princess's apartments. Her Royal Highness was to be left for a day or two totally unattended. No questions were asked and no reasons vouchsafed. It was then that the unhappy mother received visits from her son.'

Childe-Pemberton, in a footnote about 'the shocking story of Princess Sophia', alludes sharply to Ernest: 'Her retribution was so terrible that it should silence the condemnation of all charitable persons. Of whatever indiscretions she may have been guilty, she was believed to have been brutally deceived by her own brother.' General Garth, he says, 'went through the form of marriage' with Sophia at Ilsington Manor. Sophia's son, he says, was guilty of 'unparalleled callousness and meanness', but he gives no instances. He says Garth boasted 'that he was the only commoner whose parents were both of royal birth' (a rare boast, but a true one).[1]

The census returns for Hans-place suggest a warning for researchers. Census-takers are told lies. In April 1851, Garth, aged 50 years and eight months, makes himself 45 and says his daughter, nearly 16, is 14. Perhaps they both wished to distance themselves a little from their aberrant origins. By April 1861, however, Garth is truthfully '60 – Capt H.P. [half-pay], 15th Hussars', born at Weymouth. He says he is married. Georgiana loses another year: she is 22. This census, giving more detail than formerly, lists a butler and two housemaids. Ten years later the butler has gone but there are two young servants. Georgiana, really 35, is a still more inventive 24. Garth says his wife is 30. She is to prove something of a puzzle.

The doubly royal gentleman died on 19 November 1875. His doctor certified 'Softening of brain, 1 year & 8 months'. The death was registered by 'George Willis Grey, nephew', a young clerk who lived nearby in Cadogan-street. If indeed a nephew, he must be the wife's. In a will signed in 1868 Garth left everything to 'my dear daughter'.

Two weeks after his death, his solicitor, Frederick Blake, with offices in South Sea House, Threadneedle-street, wrote a *Private and Confidential* letter that reveals that Garth did manage to win some money from his Aunt Victoria's court, but only long after Sir Herbert Taylor's death. Blake's letter is to a firm of solicitors in Great Marlborough-street who had been confidential advisers 'of the Queen and others of the Royal Family'. He encloses a copy of a letter written on Garth's behalf in 1863, in which 'the Parentage of our Client was referred to'. He presents evidence that a senior court official, Sir Charles Phipps, then instructed Coutts's Bank in May 1863 to pay Garth a pension of £300 a year from Queen Victoria's privy purse. This was paid until his death.

Blake's purpose now is to have Victoria continue the pension. He says Garth leaves a daughter, 'upwards of thirty' (in fact over forty) 'and a Widow, a Lady whom he married in 1852... As the Captain has virtually left nothing after payment of his debts &c, Miss Garth and her Stepmother are penniless... Under the circumstances I have ventured to open the story of Captn Garth again.'

Even in death, Garth troubles the palace. And Sir Herbert's name arises. Blake refers again to the reason for the pension grant of 1863, Garth's 'parentage', and says, 'Had General Garth known that his Son would not have received the benefits promised by Sir Herbert Taylor, he would in all probability not have altered the provisions of the Deed of 1820' (to leave Garth a £1200 annuity). Had Garth received the annuity he could have passed it on, making 'ample provision for his Daughter'. Presumably the general cancelled it when Sir Herbert had promised 'the benefits' in 1828, and died believing that Garth would receive them.[2]

Blake went too far in saying Georgiana Garth was penniless, but he was a lawyer making a case. The Inland Revenue's death-duty office valued Garth's estate at £11,689 and levied 10 per cent of that, leaving Georgiana the modern equivalent of £450,000. There was, besides, the annuity of £1500 that the general *did* leave Garth. According to the death-duty record, however, not Georgiana but Garth's wife, or alleged wife, had first claim on this. It says this annuity was 'secured' to the wife 'by a settlement of 9 June 1852'.

The date fits Blake's statement that Garth married in 1852 — but how then could the wife be only 30 in 1871? His census statement must have massaged her age as well as his daughter's. The Inland Revenue, at least, did not question that a wife existed: its record carries a final note, 'Widow died 21 December 1897.'[3]

Georgiana Garth's plea to retain the £300 pension seems to have failed. More than twenty-one years later she tried again: Blake's firm wrote to the Privy Purse, Sir Fleetwood Edwards, asking him to forward a petition from her to Victoria, her first-cousin-once-removed.[4]

One can assume that by then she was a sad relic. After Garth's death she had moved to an apartment building near St Margaret's, Westminster. For the 1881 census-taker she was still losing years. At 45, she alleged 32. She also changed her parish of birth from St George's, Southwark, to St George's, Hanover-square, where her mother had been fashionably married to Sir Jacob Astley fifty-two years earlier. She reported 'no profession or occupation'.

Little else is known about her. When Lucille Iremonger was writing *Love and the Princess* in the 1950s and visited descendants of Captain Thomas Garth of the Royal Navy, they said a tradition had been passed down that Georgiana Garth was 'a schoolmistress, who never married because, she said, she was so ashamed of her family history'. They gave Mrs Iremonger, 'under the seal of secrecy', the name of the man who they understood was Tom Garth's father. It was *not* General Garth.[5] A later descendant, when approached not long ago, would say only that the name 'will remain a mystery'.

Whatever else is a mystery, that name is not.

25

An old blind lady

Princess Sophia's bounteous devotion to Sir John Conroy continued after the dispersal of the Kensington Palace establishment — Victoria to Buckingham Palace, her mother to Clarence House and Conroy to one of his ill-gotten estates. Sophia helped him to acquire yet another property, a 16th-century Berkshire manor, Hurst House. In 1841 her income rose to £17,000 a year (each time one of the Sisterhood died, the rest shared in a richer pool). She was living more reclusively than ever. Out of her unneeded revenue she increased her annual payments to Conroy to £8000, according to his grandson John, the 3rd baronet.

Sophia's sight gradually failed. The *Court Journal* had reported in 1829 that she awoke one morning 'almost in darkness'. It credited an oculist with restoring sight to the right eye, 'but that of the left did not return'.[1] There was a further operation; but after 1840, quite blind, 'she was visited by such friends as valued her merits', Childe-Pemberton writes in his *Romance of Princess Amelia*. 'She had been a connoisseur and collector of curios, and when unable to see her treasures she could describe them from memory.' Her 'unmurmuring patient endurance' is described by the Hon Amelia Murray: 'Blind and suffering, no complaint ever issued from her lips... She had four readers who came to her every day — French, German, Italian and English; and as each was employed only for an hour, she observed, "The fatigue would not be too great for them." And she was thus kept *au courant du jour*, while she tore paper into small bits to fill pillows, which she found were acceptable to invalids.'[2] A visitor near the end was Conroy's grandson. Born in 1845, he was Sophia's godson. Years later he recalled being brought to see 'an old blind lady, sitting at a table' who 'gave me some tin soldiers, one of which took on and off his horse... I remember there were a great many clocks in the room, which all began to strike at once, at which I began to cry.'[3]

The passing hours of the blind princess ceased to be measured by readers and by clocks in her 71st year at 6.30 pm on 27 May 1848. The day happened to be devoted to a celebration of Queen Victoria's birthday (she was 29 three days earlier). The event was marked with special festivity and displays of military power — for a reason. 'These are anxious times,' Victoria wrote in her journal. Revolutions on the continent and hard times at home had inspired the Chartists to make their strongest campaign yet for rights that had not been granted in 1832, such as manhood suffrage, the secret ballot and paid MPs. Some of their leaders advocated 'physical force'. In April many thousands of these voteless men had converged on London with a plan to march to parliament to present a huge petition for the People's Charter. By the time they were assembled on Kennington Common, across the Thames from parliament, the 79-year-old Wellington had deployed artillery and thousands of soldiers to stop them from crossing the bridges. The Bank of England was guarded with troops and cannon, the staffs of government offices were armed, and 150,000 house-holders were enrolled as special constables. Victoria, Albert and their children were sent to the Isle of Wight.

On the day, the Chartist leader, Feargus O'Connor, was warned that he would be leading his men straight into gunfire. He called off the march, amid hot protests, and hired three cabs to deliver the peti-tion (with 5,700,000 signatures, he claimed; 1,975,496, ministers said).

For Wellington, there was irony in the event, if he cared to note it. In helping to defeat the radicals he was backing a Whig government under Lord John Russell, who in 1831–2 had been a strong advocate of the moderate reform which Wellington felt sure would bring revolution. In fact it resulted in Whig or Tory governments equally opposed to any extension of the franchise to the restive lower orders.

In Sophia's last weeks she had been visited by her sister Mary and by Victoria's mother. Not, however, by Victoria, who had been so pained by Aunt Sophia's intrigues with Conroy that for years she limited herself to a token annual visit. On the afternoon of 27 May she was told Sophia was very ill. Albert went to inquire; Victoria went for a drive in Hyde Park. Soon afterwards an officer announced 'to my utter astonishment', Victoria says in her journal, that Sophia had died. 'It was terribly sudden & melancholy in the midst of so much rejoicing & festivity. But it is a merciful release for her.' Sir John Conroy 'reported everything being in the greatest order but that there was no will'.[4] Soon came the surprising news that aside from personal possessions Sophia's wealth amounted to only £1607 at her bank and a few shares.

Sophia left a request to be buried in Kensal Green cemetery, thus ruling out a return to Windsor even in death. The funeral was to be 'as private as possible'. The cortège left Kensington Palace soon after dawn; but it was not a modest one: nine four-horse coaches of mourners (servants, doctors, court ladies, equerries and higher personages) with full military escort, and a six-horse hearse carrying a coffin covered with crimson velvet. Victoria, who until she was 18 had shared Kensington Palace with Sophia, was absent, represented by Albert. Ernest was represented by his London envoy.

On Sophia's imposing granite and marble monument can be read the inscription, COME UNTO ME ALL YE THAT LABOUR AND ARE HEAVY LADEN AND I WILL GIVE YOU REST.

The Chartists fought on. Victoria wrote in her journal, 30 May, 'We were surprised to see by the papers that there had been a procession of 1200 men... The mob had marched along in sullen silence in military array, & were composed of the lowest of the low.'[5] Many of them were hungry workless men. But one leader of these 'lowest of the low' was a man who, five years earlier, had been presented to Victoria by the Duke of Beaufort: the King of Hanover's godson Ernest Jones, now a lieutenant of Feargus O'Connor.

Truncheon-wielding police broke up Chartist meetings. Jones was charged with sedition and unlawful assembly. The attorney-general said at his trial that he excited people to arm themselves. He had been about to go in the mail-train to the disturbed manufacturing districts. A 'general rising of the working classes' was planned for 12 June. Had it succeeded, 'the country would have been placed under the fierce and uncontrolled democracy of the people ... the most grinding tyranny'. Jones and five others were sentenced to two years solitary confinement in Tothill-fields House of Correction, Westminster.[6]

Life in this place of 'correction' was brutal. Jones published a petition calling for an inquiry. In a cold, damp cell, allowed only summer clothing through the winter, and eating bad food, he became dangerously ill. Two fellow-Chartists died. For nineteen months he was not allowed pen and paper except to write a quarterly letter. A visitor was allowed four times a year, for twenty minutes. When he tried to appeal to MPs he was 'seized by the neck and ankles' and 'locked up in a refractory cell on bread and water'. He asked, 'For how long?' The reply, 'As long as I choose.' The prison used the 'silent system', an invention of Utilitarian thinkers to elevate criminals into good citizens. The discipline was 'so rigorous as to make an involuntary smile, turning the head to right or left or folding the arms a punishable offence', Jones says, and he was sharply reprimanded 'for even reading the Bible to himself, though in a scarcely audible voice'.[7]

He left jail more radicalized. He wrote an address to the authorities with passages such as this: 'Thanks! You have taught us what mercy to grant when the day of retribution shall be ours at last! ...Prosecutions and imprisonments make the weather that ripens revolutions... All England is a prison for the poor.'[8] Before his jailing he had been in contact with a German refugee, Karl Marx, whose Communist Manifesto was published in London in February 1848, and he corresponded with Marx for years. Contact with militant Chartists contributed to Marx's vision of a capitalist Britain ripe for proletarian revolution.

Had King Ernest come to the throne in 1837, the extirpation of Chartist ideas would have been the least of his desires. Eager to overturn the reforms achieved since 1829, and to 'stem the democratic spirit' and assert Monarchical Principles, he would have done everything in his power to promote ultra governments. Commentators of that time believed that he might well have brought about the republican upheaval that he was set on preventing.

Soon after Sophia's death, more was revealed of Conroy's roguery. The Duchess of Kent was forced to accept as comptroller the upright Colonel George Couper. He dismissed a clerk, William Rea, who had served Conroy for years. The duchess, after a long delay, gave Couper the keys to chests of accounts at Clarence House revealing that at least £60,000 was unaccounted for. The line she took was, 'I have no *head*... I blame myself severely... I *erred* in *believing blindly.'*

As for Sophia, Couper reported that over the years she must have had nearly £400,000 (say £16 million) to spare. He told the duchess, 'Where the money has gone no one can say.' Conroy 'declined to give any account' of Sophia's money. He had been 'for so many years gratifying his own vanity' — a kind phrase. His grandson Edward said Conroy was her *de facto* heir 'for she gave him nearly all her large income'.[9] She left no will because he did not need her to make one.

Just as Couper was making his last damning report in March 1854, Conroy died of a heart attack. Astonishingly, he proved insolvent. The old rogue's family were, equally astonishingly, given royal pensions.

26

King Ernest survives the canaille

Ernest's out-and-out principles were put to their sharpest test in 1848. Ever since Napoleon's defeat, a league of crowned heads, the Holy Alliance, had prevailed over most of Europe, with Metternich, the Austrian strongman and master censor, as overlord. He and other absolutists suppressed 'jacobinical' demands for effective constitutions and parliaments. Yet the democratic and idealist concepts that had led up to the revolution of 1789 lived on and took new forms. Agitators began using the disturbing words socialism and communism.

Before 1848 Ernest had had foretastes of trouble. Radicalism was 'making great strides', he said in 1845, so he banned all political meetings. He wrote to Princess Lieven, 'You never observed me in my long Career [he was now 74] ever swerve from those fixed principles of Politicks I had imbibed and learned from my late revered Father... Honesty is the best policy... The Ruin of the present day is that cursed word Expediency.' Soon 'things going on' were 'highly alarming': 'The spirit of innovation, reckless thirst for changes both in Church and State, demand the utmost vigilance. Thank God till now I have been able to prevent this evil gaining ground chez moi.' At the first appearance in Hanover of a reformist church movement, Lichtfreund (friend of enlightenment), he banned its meetings. 'Would to God the King of Prussia and other Sovereigns had done the same.'[1] By January 1848 unrest was so widespread that he feared 'a general blow-up'.

It came much sooner than he expected. That February (just when Karl Marx was publishing his Communist Manifesto) a revolution in Paris ousted King Louis-Philippe. This secondary Bourbon had been raised to the throne in 1830 on the back of a three-day street revolution that restored the liberty-equality-fraternity tricolor and granted a charter of citizens' rights. Many of the citizens soon found, however, that they had set up a king who enriched the few and who betrayed the charter. Years of disillusion culminated in his overthrow, another three-day event. France became a republic again.

Ernest was enraged ('my blood boils', he wrote) because the king fled instead of fighting. Had *he* been Louis-Philippe, he told Princess Lieven, he would have put himself at the head of his army 'and rather have been cut to pieces than run away'. Uprisings rapidly broke out elsewhere. It was 'too frightful'. Prussia and Austria were in 'complete anarchy', with students and ' proletaries' (a new word) dictating.[2] Metternich (one of Princess Lieven's ex-lovers) fled to England. The Prussian king lost control of Berlin. Italians rebelled against Austria, and Hungarians achieved a formidable year-long revolt.

In Hanover, Ernest had a running struggle. He reports fast-moving events in letters to Princess Lieven and to his friend Lord Strangford (a former ambassador and an odd one, of whom *The Times* said, 'The more than diplomatic freedom which His Lordship takes with matters of fact makes him the jest of all diplomatists'). Ernest writes, 'My mind is in a state of constant irritation, but I am determined to keep my temper and act coolly and manfully... I command the respect of even the rankest radicals... They know I play no dirty tricks.' But foreign rabble-rousers are a threat. They are too mobile. The railway had reached Hanover in 1847 and linked it to Paris and Berlin. 'These damned railways bring in daily hundreds of Poles, French and other *canaille* [rabble], which, had it not been for the watchfulness of the citizens, would have caused all sorts of rioting.'

He jailed 'a rascal attorney' at Hildesheim. The town rose in rebellion, so he sent 'three battalions of infantry, a squadron of cavalry, and artillery, and the town surrendered,' he reported. 'These are strange times.' He was certainly ready to open fire on his people. This is shown in his comments on events in Berlin. After street battles in which many people were killed, the Prussian king called off his army, so 'the *canaille* are ruling everything', Ernest wrote. The king should have 'surrounded and bombarded' the city, but many of his ministers are 'rank republicans and the vilest radicals'.[3]

Only Hanover, Ernest declared, was 'in a good state of law and order'. A fortnight later, violent protests so 'paralysed' his ministers that they resigned. Agitators were to blame: 'We were overrun — after the dreadful scenes at Berlin — by emissaries from that capital who were in communication with the communists in Paris.' To find new ministers, he renounced principles and turned to men 'who had been my most violent opposers'. More astonishing still, 'up to now I have no reason to complain'.[4]

Having opted for expediency in Hanover, he still advocated cannonading for Berlin. On 8 June he expected Berlin to declare a republic. 'Then the battle will begin... I flatter myself we shall be strong enough to put it down.' He seems ready to offer his army. 'By completely surrounding the town of Berlin (which must be sacrificed) we shall be enabled to restore peace and order... The idea of saving either property or lives not to be thought of.' Shedding blood 'is the only means of saving a greater deluge of blood in other places'.[5] This is very like the tsar's warning to Warsaw that Ernest had so admired.

Instead of cannonading, the Prussian king granted a constitution. In Austria the regime recovered by making concessions that split the reformers on class lines. Ernest and others similarly survived. Disparate liberals and radicals had failed to concert their fervour. Reaction, backed by armies, soon prevailed. In Paris, where the blow-up had begun, the confused republic chose a nephew of the great Napoleon as president — who soon suppressed republicans and made himself emperor. Yet the Holy Alliance was never quite the same again.

By this time Ernest was a grandfather. A wife had been found for his blind son, a princess of Saxe-Altenburg. According to the Duchesse de Dino, visiting Hanover in 1849, she was a gentle soul, ideal for the prince; being very unlike her sister, the 'animated, piquant' wife of Russia's Grand Duke Constantine. King Ernest, the duchesse noted, 'lives on oysters and ices, a singular régime that marvellously agrees with his eighty years' (really 78).[6]

He enjoyed playing with his grandchildren. Every evening the eldest grandson was brought to him, who 'seized the little tuft of hair that still adorned his grandfather's forehead' and 'uttering piercing cries ... fought to get hold of the king's monocle'. Then came a grotesque ritual, according to the wife of the Hanoverian Count Münster. 'The last amusement which the boy asked for and obtained every day was as follows: the king would open his mouth and put his tongue out and the child would rub his hands and cheeks against it, which gave great pleasure to the royal grandfather, but sickened the onlookers.'[7]

Ernest kept alert to every innovation in Britain. He deplored all 'meddling with old customs and habits'. It was shocking that bishops had been 'permitted to lay aside their wigs, purple coats, short cassocks and stockings' when in public. 'If ever the Lord Chancellor, judges, KCs, etc, lay aside their wigs and gowns it will mean adieu to respect for them,' he declared; but he had underestimated the barristers' devotion to wigs. Another proposed innovation, 'admitting Jews into Parliament', he thought 'revolting'. So indeed did many others: it was resisted for nearly forty more years.[8]

Popery was always a peril. He wrote to Georgina Bathurst, 'I hope you are cured of your Puseyism, which is neither more nor less than disguised Popery, & of the two, Popery, being open & avowed, is far preferable to infamous, hypocritical Puseyism.' It was an Oxford-based movement that promoted Roman practices in the Anglican church. In a postscript Ernest adds: 'Is it not disgusting reading the names of so many of our nobility becoming Romanists in order to kiss the Pope's slipper? Certainly to many it is a cheap way of getting rid of their sins, for I believe for half a crown you may purchase absolution & for a crown you have a week's or fortnight's permission to sin as much as you like.' Yet one day he found that some Roman Catholics were quite presentable: 'It is most extraordinary, but positively true, that I have lately had a cardinal & several Roman Catholic bishops to dinner' (in Hanover to introduce a new bishop). 'I never met with a more agreeable or distinguished man than His Eminence.'[9]

In Ernest's last year, a new target was Prince Albert's Great Exhibition of 1851. It was 'a folly and absurdity' to invite other countries to display their rival manufactures. Besides, the exhibition 'would bring all the ruffians and *canaille* from all parts of the world'. Queen Victoria would be wise to get out of town. Of course, she did not. In June she figured at a 'tomfool ball' and 'was loaded with my diamonds'.[10]

Ernest died at 80 in November 1851 and was buried in the uniform of a British field marshal — the rank he had been granted as a consolation for being ousted in 1814 as viceroy of Hanover. His loyal admirers erected a bronze statue of him on horseback. This image of Ernest the cavalryman survived RAF bombs when they destroyed much of central Hanover, and it can be seen outside the main railway station.

Few of Ernest's obituarists found much to praise. 'His evil disposition, his vicious propensities and his despotic tendencies', said the radical *Reynolds's News*, were formed in petty German courts, 'hotbeds of corruption'. He was hated for his politics and also as 'a detestable profligate ... so monstrous in his passions that he even seduced one of his own sisters into a criminal intercourse. From this revolting intercourse issue came. The amour ... has been productive of scandals to which we dare allude no farther' — perhaps because of

Garth's presence in London. As well as perjury, adultery and incest, *Reynolds's News* declared Ernest guilty of murder. It recalled the *Minute Detail*'s invention of a robbery motive for Sellis, and said this was ridiculous: if Sellis had wished to rob Ernest, 'he need not have commenced by an attempt at murder'. It closed with a flourish. 'The demon soul that for so many years tenanted a human shape has returned into those unfathomable worlds that lie beyond the grave.'[11]

The Times, though long free of any hint of radicalism, declared Ernest 'the most unpopular prince of modern times': 'As he passed along the streets of this metropolis, no hat was raised out of respect for him.' During the 1832 reform contest, 'bigots, obstructives and alarmists' saw him as 'a prince of their own hearts, tenacious of aristocratic privileges, reckless of popular opinion, and prepared ... to dare the worst that revolution might bring'.

On the Sellis case, *The Times* spoke of dark secrets that could not be uttered (though 'sodomy' *had* been uttered during Ernest's libel prosecution of 1833). It did say this: 'Rumour persisted in attaching to his excesses a certain criminal blackness below the standard dye of aristocratic debauchery.' In its comment on the libel convictions of White and Phillips in 1813 and 1833, *The Times* in effect found Ernest the guilty party: 'The probabilities against him fell short of legal proof. The impartial historian, however, will be likely to decide that there was little in the known character of Prince Ernest to exempt him from sore suspicions touching what remained concealed.'

The Times summed him up as 'a bad German prince of the last century', who in his translation to Hanover 'gained oblivion for his faults and opportunities for his talents'.[12]

From Ernest I to Ernest V

Ernest's successor, the blind George, was more devoted to music than to statecraft. A catalogue of his music library lists works from Bach onwards and also songs and dances composed by himself. Hanover allied itself with Austria against the growing power of Prussia, unluckily, for in 1866 Prussia defeated Austria and annexed Hanover. George went into exile in Austria, retaining some solid wealth, his Duke of Cumberland title and part of the royal jewellery that Britain had ceded at last in 1858. His son, Ernest Augustus II (1845–1923), built a lakeside palace near Salzburg, still used by the family.

A marital rapprochement between Prussia's Hohenzollerns and the

Hanoverians was achieved in 1913. Emperor Wilhelm (soon to be deplored and derided in Britain as 'Kaiser Bill') arranged a marriage between his daughter Victoria Louise and the next Ernest Augustus (1887–1953). This infusion of Hohenzollern blood produced some significant descendants. A daughter, Frederica, born 1917, spent a few years in the female Hitler Youth, married the future King Paul of Greece in 1947, and was later a dominant reactionary figure behind her son King Constantine. An army coup ousted them in 1967. Constantine, a cousin of both Queen Elizabeth and Prince Philip, has ever since been a London exile. Frederica's daughter Sophia, however, had the good fortune to marry the prince who became King Juan-Carlos of Spain after the death of the dictator Francisco Franco. So Ernest, the lifelong enemy of popery, has a great-great-great-granddaughter who reigns as a Roman Catholic, and whose son Felipe, born 1968, promises to be the next king of Spain.

In 1919 Ernest Augustus II had been stripped of the Cumberland peerage because during the 1914–18 war he was a vassal of Kaiser Bill (Queen Victoria's grandson) against George V of Britain (Queen Victoria's grandson). In the 1950s, however, Ernest Augustus IV (1914–87), to restore some lustre to the family, applied to be declared an English subject. He argued that a naturalization act of 1705, drafted solely to enable a duke of Hanover to be made King George I of England, was so worded that it also naturalized all George I's descendants, including of course descendants of George III's son Ernest. The Chancery Court said no; three appeal judges said yes. A Tory government challenged this, but five law lords upheld Ernest Augustus IV. As *The Times* pointed out, this ruling meant that many others in Europe might claim to be English. It also raised the question of 'Prince Ernest's technical position before the criminal law, seeing that he held a German commission in the war against George VI, who is now found to have been his lawful sovereign'.

His son, Ernest Augustus V, born 1954, is a godson of Queen Elizabeth and claims the title 'Prince of Great Britain and Ireland' as well as Prince of Hanover and Duke of Brunswick and Lüneburg. In 1999 he committed what his great-great-great-grandfather, our hero Ernest, would see as a popish offence. He married, as her third husband, Princess Caroline of Monaco. This marriage deprived him of a place somewhere far down in the line of succession.

He has a reputation for combativeness. He had to pay heavy

damages for an attack in 1998 on a television cameraman. In January 2000 a nightclub owner in Kenya accused him of violent assault, which he denied. In June 2000 he demonstrated his Ernest-like hostility to non-teutonic presences by pissing against the Turkish pavilion at a millennium exposition in Hanover — inspiring the city's mayor to say, 'I think His Royal Highness needs psychiatric help.' His vagaries do remind one of how often the blood boiled in his ancestor's veins.

A few family memories

The fate of other families in the story deserves a few words. The death of Garth's lover made Sir Jacob Astley free to remarry, but having two sons who could continue the baronetcy, he lived unmarried with a Frenchwoman. In 1841 he was granted the barony of Hastings, which dated from 1290, 'having proved that he was the junior coheir of the junior coheiress of that ancient barony', says the *Complete Baronetage*, 1903, 'but which for above 450 years ... had been unheard-of!' This advanced him from 6th baronet to 16th baron.

Of the two sons whom Lady Astley abandoned in their infancy, the elder, Jacob Henry Delaval Astley, had only illegitimate children, so after him the barony went to his brother, the Rev Delaval Loftus Astley, rector of Little Snoring, Norfolk. These details were kindly provided by Sir Jacob's great-great-grandson, the 22nd Lord Hastings, born 1912, who was for many years active in official and charitable work, and was at the time of writing still the happy possessor of Seaton Delaval Hall.

Joseph Sellis's family must not be forgotten. A few relics of him came down to a great-great-granddaughter, Miss Phyllis Sewell of Lever-hulme, Manchester. In 1981 she presented to the British Museum the key and nameplate of the Sellises' St James's apartment. These must have been passed in 1810 to poor Mrs Sellis by a sympathetic palace servant. The key, 4.5 inches long, with the royal G R on one side and SELLIS on the other, and the brass SELLIS nameplate, about 3.5 inches wide, are in the museum's department of medieval and later antiquities. Miss Sewell also made a gift of the *laissez-passer* issued to Sellis at Marseille (*see page 50*) on his fateful journey from Sardinia to London. It is in the British Library manuscript department.

'As I appear to be the only person left in my family to be interested,' Miss Sewell wrote to me, 'I wanted these items to be preserved for posterity.' She had family memories passed down from 1810: that Ernest 'was reputed to be the "bad boy" of the family', that Sellis's death was 'a bit of a mystery', that 'evidence showed that he had been murdered' and that he was buried as a suicide.

In his native city, Cagliari, memories may well survive of the young *parruchiére* who travelled north, prospered, and then was violently silenced. The latest Cagliari phonebook lists twenty-four people named Selis (the current spelling) and others elsewhere in Sardinia.

The Sellis children will have had various descendants, especially in the London region. The registers of St Martin-in-the-Fields, the church not far from where Sellis was shamefully buried, record the marriage of William Sellis to Mary Ann Pitt in June 1822, one witness being Mary Elizabeth Sellis; and of Mary Elizabeth herself to Joseph Seiffrett in September 1826 (she is probably the sad girl who was noticed in the crowd after Sellis's death). A third Sellis, James, and his wife brought twin babies to be baptized at the same church in March 1825. These three Sellises are surely Joseph's children. No listing appears of his youngest, Ernest's godson, baptized in 1810. Perhaps the baby did not survive the family's stressful sudden eviction from the palace.

Sons of William Sellis were baptized in 1825 and 1827 at St Pancras Old Church, so he is evidently the William Sellis listed in an 1828 directory as 'grocer and tea dealer' of Ossulston-street in that parish. This family soon moved to Chelsea: five further children were baptized at St Luke's, Sydney-street, during 1831–40.[13] This was Garth's church after he settled in Hans-place. It is thus probable that Ernest's son joined in communion with a son of the man Ernest murdered.

The uniquely royal person whose momentous birth on 8 August 1800 opened this biography has no known descendant. Garth's memory is not honoured like his father's by an equestrian statue, or like his mother's with a monument graced with a coronet. It is possible, however, to visit his grave — not near his mother's at Kensal Green, but three miles away in Brompton Cemetery. His modest headstone, now crumbling and bereft of its cross, is almost hidden in long grass. The inscription can just be made out. It perpetuates the false birthdate assigned to him: 'THOMAS GARTH / Born 5th August 1800 / Died 19th November 1875.' The biblical words chosen for him (John 11, 26) are, 'Whosoever liveth and believeth in me shall never die.'

APPENDIX
Exculpating Ernest

Some authors have presented Ernest outright as a much-maligned gentleman. Others have made a show of balance, yet have laboured inventively to acquit him over Garth and Sellis. A brief survey of the exculpators, in the light of what this book has established, should help to prevent their errors and biases from being eternally cited as truths.

The finest hagiography is that by Geoffrey Malden Willis (1954), who shared Ernest's ultra enthusiasms and deplored Catholic emancipation and the 1832 reform as grievous errors, ruinous for Britain. For him, Ernest is 'this great but infamously libelled man'.

Sellis, he says, was 'his master's favourite', and yet 'a cross between a scoundrel and a homicidal maniac'. Willis seizes on the slanders invented in the *Minute Detail* pamphlet (*see pages 65–6*). 'The madman,' he says, 'had conceived a bitter jealousy of his fellow-valet, Neale, to appease which he was prepared to sacrifice his master.' Ernest's wounds, Willis says, left him lying in agony 'for upwards of a month'. Curiously, he refrains from going so far as Ernest's own claim that he was in agony 'for six weeks to two months'. Perhaps Willis was aware that Ernest rose from his bed after three days.

The Sellis affair was followed, he says, by foul stories about 'rape, incest and unnatural obscenities'. Ernest was the victim of 'a violent campaign' over Garth, 'though nowhere did it appear in a tangible form that he could meet'. So much for the acute questions of *The Times* and others, and Ernest's self-wounding replies. Ernest is innocent too of any offence with Lady Lyndhurst. It is a scandal invented by 'a scurrilous paper, *The Age*' — in fact Ernest's scurrilous ally, here as elsewhere. As for Lady Graves, it is 'of course absurd' that he had an affair with her. He argues, charmingly, that she was 'in her fifties [in fact 46], the mother of thirteen children and wore spectacles'.

Other authors make the Garth story take odd turns. A pregnant princess discomposes them.

The late Sir Roger Fulford's *Royal Dukes*, which devotes a chapter each to George IV's brothers, dates from 1933 and has often been cited. Its most recent reissue was by Penguin in 2000. Over Ernest and Sophia, Fulford begins with fierce denial. He deplores 'the most atrocious scandal that has ever been spread about the reigning family of a civilised country': that Ernest fathered Sophia's son. 'It is still whispered over the port [at Fulford's club, Boodle's, one assumes] but it was not true.' The truth, he says, is in Lady Bath's story that Sophia was violently in love with General Garth and that he fathered the boy.

For a new edition in 1973, Fulford changes tack — but confusedly. In a revised version of the book's introduction he reconsiders Sophia. 'She was supposed to have had a child' by the general, he says, but if that were so 'we can hardly suppose that he would have kept his position at court' or continued 'on easy terms' with the princesses (a sound point). He now questions whether Sophia had a baby by anyone. It is 'completely unproven' and there is 'no evidence at Windsor'. However, *if* she did, possibly the general 'as a friend of the Royal Family assumed responsibility for it'. Having taken this line, Fulford forgets to amend his Ernest chapter. There, General Garth still impregnates the amorous Sophia. In this comical confusion the book has remained from 1973 until now.

Fulford creates a new muddle in a contribution to *Society Scandals* (1977). Now his Sophia definitely had no baby. We cannot, he says, 'hope to discover who first made up the tale' that her illness in 1800 'was not spasms' but 'a pregnancy'. Then who is Tom Garth? He is the general's son but by a non-royal mother. Why in that case the court should offer the fellow huge sums is a question Fulford wisely avoids. For an affirmation of Ernest's innocence he quotes *The Age*: 'The most injured man in His Majesty's dominions.'

Years earlier, two resourceful women had established that the boy was Sophia's. The first is Dorothy Margaret Stuart in *The Daughters of George III* (1939). She experiences difficulties, however, over the claim that General Garth was the father. 'It is practically beyond question' that he was, she says; but then 'not the least curious feature of the story is the cordial attitude of the family, including Queen Charlotte and the Prince of Wales', towards him. It is 'a matter for bewilderment' that he handed the son 'any documents susceptible of a sinister interpretation'. Yet when she comes to the contest over the documents she overcomes such doubts. She calls the talk of Ernest's guilt a 'hideous legend' and decries the challenging questions asked by *The*

Times, Globe and *Morning Chronicle* as 'loud baying'. It was impossible, she says, for Ernest 'to grapple openly with the slander' — ignoring, like Willis, his use of ultra papers for violent counterattacks.

Lucille Iremonger's *Love and the Princess* (1958) goes further into the Chancery suit and the conflict around it, but ends by endorsing Ernest's claim to be a victim of 'a malicious and ruthless campaign by the Whigs to rid themselves of an enemy'. She does hint at doubts over the assertion by Ernest's advocates of the 'physical impossibility' of his guilt. 'It might have been possible to establish a cast-iron and comprehensive alibi of this nature as late as 1829,' she says. She does not point out that they failed to do so, but suggests, oddly, that their having been 'bold enough' to make the claim 'is something'.

Even the fact that Sophia had a baby continued to be denied by some writers, out of devotion to the family. Olwen Hedley, who worked for years at Windsor Castle, dismissed the idea as 'slander' in her *Queen Charlotte* biography (1975).

Christopher Hibbert, a strikingly prolific writer on royalty and much else, says in his *George IV* (1972) that Sophia's child was 'more likely' to have been fathered by the general than by Ernest. A few sentences later he makes the general a certainty: he 'found himself alone with her'; he is 'Princess Sophia's lover'. In his *The Court at Windsor* (1977) Hibbert says Lady Caroline Thynne 'knew' Sophia 'was very much in love with the old general', but he returns to uncertainty in *George III: A Personal History* (1998): 'It was whispered that her dreadful brother the Duke of Cumberland, whose watchful affection for her was certainly felt to be unnatural, was the baby's father.' However, the baby 'was far more probably' the general's. What *is* one to believe?

On Sellis, Hibbert takes note in his *George IV* of Captain Jones's record of Ernest's confession, then newly revealed. He calls it 'a curious document' and adopts Arthur Aspinall's inventive subversion of it, saying, 'Whether Jones misunderstood the duke's meaning or intentionally wished to harm him it is, of course, impossible to say.' He contrives an additional escape-route for Ernest: 'The duke may for some strange reason, in keeping with his mysterious character, have wanted to mislead or shock his secretary or to impose some burdensome secret upon him.' One thing is 'clear enough' to Hibbert: 'Whatever he [Ernest] might or might not have said, he did not murder Sellis.' Five years on, however, it is not at all clear. In *The*

Court at Windsor he calls Ernest 'a strange and ugly man of the most reactionary opinions', who, 'so he claimed', was attacked by Sellis; and despite the inquest verdict, many people 'thought that Sellis had not cut his own throat'. Here is some slight progress.

These books (and there are others more unworthy) have a cumulative effect. Some historians dismiss every hint of wrongdoing by Ernest in a sentence. John Brooke says in his *King George III*, a biography warmly endorsed by the Prince of Wales, 'The most scandalous stories (entirely untrue) were told about his [Ernest's] private life.' Error flourishes by repetition. Biographies published in 2000 are recent examples. Claire Harman's *Fanny Burney* says Sophia was 'rumoured' to have had a child. Michael Bakewell in his *Augusta Leigh* (Byron's half-sister) discusses sibling incest and says of the Ernest/Sophia affair, 'The claim was proved to be false.'

Scholarly works of reference suffer. Dorothy George, in her generally admirable catalogue of caricatures in the British Museum, says of Garth, 'It was (falsely) alleged and believed that Cumberland was his father', and she cites Fulford in support. As for Sellis, she says Ernest 'was awakened by a murderous attack' and Sellis was 'found locked in his room and cutting [!] his throat'. That Ernest murdered Sellis was a 'popular and unfounded suspicion'.

The James Gillray exhibition at Tate Britain in 2001 provided a footnote to the Sellis drama. In June 1810 Gillray was sinking into dementia, but the news stirred him to attempt a print. The exhibition showed four outlines he sketched, with a caption about 'the Italian valet attempting the assassination of a prince of ye Blood Royal'. Gillray wanted 'all those who prefer Italian French & other Charlatans & cut throat adventurers' to consider the 'extreme Danger attendant upon employing Foreign Servants'. He was evidently roused by the xenophobic line taken by some papers; and of course he knew nothing of the questions raised about Ernest's story. But after 191 years the exhibition catalogue remained free of doubts about Sellis's guilt: there was 'a rumour' that Ernest murdered him, but 'this was a canard'.

The fallacious books have prevailed, but there can now be hope that the repetition of their baseless kindnesses to Ernest will cease at last.

References

The following abbreviations are used:

BL ms   British Library manuscript
BM   British Museum (department of prints and drawings)
PRO   Public Record Office, Kew
RA   Royal Archives manuscript, Windsor
WP   Wellington Papers, University of Southampton Library

Arbuthnot   *Journal of Mrs Arbuthnot*
Charlotte   *Letters of Princess Charlotte* (Aspinall)
G IV   *Letters of King George IV* (Aspinall)
Glenbervie   *Diaries of ... Lord Glenbervie*
Greville   *Greville Memoirs*
PoW   *Correspondence of George Prince of Wales* (Aspinall)

See the bibliography for details of these books, and of others cited below

NOTE: 'Harcourt mss' refers to manuscripts of the family at Stanton Harcourt. *The Harcourt Papers* is a multi-volume selection published by the family.

1 BIRTH OF A ROYAL BABY

1 PRO ms 30/29/4/9, Caroline Howe to Lady Stafford, May 14 1800
2 *Morning Post*, July 30 1800
3 PoW, vol IV, 150; court circular in *Morning Post*, *Morning Herald*, etc
4 George III, *The Later Correspondence*, vol III, 421, Oct 3 1800 (Portland's reply)
5 Greville, I, 271
6 Harcourt mss, Princess Elizabeth volume, July 25 1794
7 Glenbervie, I, 214, April 7 1801
8 Glenbervie, II, 87, Oct 1810
9 Harcourt mss, Elizabeth volume, Lady Harcourt's note
10 Harcourt mss, Elizabeth vol, July 23 1802; Nov 5, Dec 1 1808; Oct 28 [1811]
11 Papendiek, *Court*, I, 265; BL, Althorp mss, F39, Jan 8 1786; *Public Advertiser*, Jan 10 and Feb 7 1786
12 *Gazetteer*, Nov 6 1788
13 BM, 'The Gradual Abolition of the Slave Trade or Leaving off Sugar by Degrees', April 15 1792
14 Joseph Jackson Howard and Frederick Arthur Crisp, *Visitation of England and Wales*, V (1897), 4
15 Harcourt mss, Elizabeth vol [Aug 1794]
16 Burney, *Journals and Letters*, IV, 78, Feb 1798; Childe-Pemberton, *Princess Amelia*, 72
17 Edgeworth, *Letters*, 127; Harcourt mss, Elizabeth vol, Dec 22 1799
18 Childe-Pemberton, 124, 193; PoW, VII, 39; Edgeworth, ibid
19 Childe-Pemberton, 173–6
20 PoW, II, 285–7, Sept 24 1792
21 Pigott, *Female Jockey*, xxviii–xxx, 2, 7, 9
22 Greville, I, 272, March 17 1829
23 Bodleian Library, ms Dep Bland Burges 10, ff 133v–135v, Dec 2 1794
24 Hedley, *Queen Charlotte*, 223
25 Harris, *Diaries and Correspondence*, IV, 21, Oct 24 1788; Papendiek, II, 10
26 Hedley, 198; Stuart, *Daughters*, 269; PoW, II, 388, Sept 18 1793

27 PoW, II, 467, Oct 15 1794
28 PRO ms 30/29/4/10, f 1460v [1797]
29 William Rowley, *A Treatise on Female Nervous, Hysterical, Hypochondriacal, Bilious, Convulsive Diseases, Apoplexy and Palsy*, 1788, 52–63; Dr James Wilson, *On Spasm, Languor, Palsy and other Disorders, termed Nervous*, 1843, 31
30 Burney, *Journals and Letters*, IV, 10–11, Nov 3 1797
31 Harcourt mss (mixed vol, prince of Wales and others), Aug 24 1794

2 'TOO WILD FOR ENGLAND'

1 Morris Marples, *Princes in the Making*, 1965, 113–14
2 RA 46973, Jan 11 1787
3 RA Add 15/970, April 17 1788
4 RA 47029–30, July 14 1790
5 PRO ms 30/29/4/9, letter to Lady Stafford, Aug 17 1793
6 *Harcourt Papers*, V, 403–04, Nov 2 1793; 414, Nov 24; 422, March 25 1794
7 Willis, *Ernest Augustus*, 38, Feb 4 1794; PoW, II, 430, May 11 1794
8 RA 47123–4, July 24; RA 47126–7, Aug 28 1794
9 PoW, II, 444, July 11 1794
10 PoW, II, 497–8, 504, Nov 24 and 29 1794
11 PoW, III, 154, Feb 15 1796; 215, June 8 1796
12 RA 47182–3, April 1798
13 PRO, LC11/7, LC5/198, accounts
14 Farington, *Diary*, IV, 1326, Dec 15 1799
15 PRO, LS13/27, wine-cellar book
16 *Times*, Nov 4–9 and 11–13 1799

3 A CERTAIN LITTLE BOY

1 *Times*, July 1789, etc; and similar ads in *Morning Chronicle*
2 Dorset Record Office archives
3 Ham, *Elizabeth Ham by Herself*, 47–8
4 Harcourt mss (mixed vol), Dec 30 1800
5 Fraser, *Unruly Queen*, 97, quoting RA mss, early 1797
6 BL ms Add 61986, f 24v, about 1808
7 Glenbervie, I, 203–04, March 25 1801
8 Glenbervie, I, 363–4, Feb 12 1804
9 National Library of Scotland, ms Acc 10505/9, Glenbervie journal, ff 172v–175v, Oct 11 1810 (not in Bickley)

10 Glenbervie, II, 95–6, Nov 4 1810
11 Clarke, Mary Anne, *Recollections* (at PRO), 210–11 and 175–6
12 George III, *Later Correspondence*, III, 439–40, Evan Nepean, Secretary of the Admiralty, to the king, Nov 18 1800
13 Paul Baines, '"This Theatre of Monstrous Guilt": Horace Walpole and the Drama of Incest,' *Studies in Eighteenth-Century Culture*, vol 28, 287–309, Johns Hopkins, 1999; *Diary and Letters of Madame d'Arblay*, ed Charlotte Barrett, 1854, vol 3, 200; Glenda Hudson, *Sibling Love and Incest in Jane Austen's Fiction*, 1999
14 *Letters from George III to Lord Bute*, ed Romney Sedgwick, 1939, 37–9, winter 1759–60
15 *The Record of Old Westminsters*, ed Russell Barker and Alan Stenning, 1928, vol II, 678
16 PoW, V, 89–93, Aug 25 1804; and 112–18, memorandum ascribed to Sir Robert Wilson, Sept–Oct 1804; Clarke, *Recollections*, 115, 117
17 *Morning Chronicle*, March 18 and 24 1829
18 Charlotte, 151, 155, Sept 10 and 19 1814
19 Glenbervie, II, 153, Oct 1811
20 Charlotte, 151, 152, 154, Sept 1814

4 AT THE HEART OF THE COURT

1 Glenbervie, I, 147, Jan 28 1801; for Pitt's full exchange with George III see *Annual Register*, 1827
2 Glenbervie, I, 173, Feb 19 1801
3 BL ms Add 41692, Thomas Willis journal, f 8–11, Feb 21 1801
4 Add 41692, f 102, March 17
5 Add 41693, f 10–16, April 11 and 12
6 Add 41693, f 35, April 16
7 Add 41693, f 44; Glenbervie, I, 224
8 Add 41695, f 11–12, May 23; f 13–14v, May 25; f 91, undated
9 *Times*, June 3 and 5 1801; Add 41695, f 39v, June 6
10 Add 41695, ff 113–14, undated, probably June; f 59, June 27; f 82v, Oct 16 1801
11 Glenbervie, II, 54–5
12 *Parliamentary History*, XXXV, May 16 and 23 1800

13 Willis, *Ernest Augustus*, 26; PoW, II, 419

14 BM, 'The Illustrious Lover or the Duke of Cumberland Done Over', Aug 16 1801; 'The Coronation of the Empress of the Nairs', Sept 1 1812; 'A Cumberland Strut', undated

15 BL ms Add 51359, Lady Susan's journal, f 58v, July 26 1802; Clarke, Mary Anne, *Recollections*, 115

16 Stanhope, *Memoirs*, II, 52–3

17 PoW, V, 370–71 April 18 1806

18 PoW, V, 474–5, 484–6, Oct 13/16 1806

19 Wylly, *XVth*, 138

20 Leveson-Gower, *Private Correspondence*, II, 189, April 24 1806

21 *Times*, June 30 and July 4 1808

22 Francis Grose, *Military Antiquities*, II, 1812, 105; *Times*, May 11 1810

23 *The R[oya]l Brood; or An Illustrious Hen and Her Pretty Chickens*, 'Peter Pindar jun', 1813

5 DEATH IN ST JAMES'S PALACE

1 Sellis's laissez-passer, BL ms Add 61891, f 1; St James's chapel baptism register

2 *Star*, May 31 1810; *Star* and *Times*, June 1

3 BM, 'Progress of the Warrant', April 30 1810

4 PRO, ms HO 42/107; Glenbervie, II, 82;

5 BL mss Add 27851, f 6v; Add 27852, f 9v

6 Farington, *Diary*, X, 3643, April 27 1810

7 *Times* and *Star* reports; BL mss Add 27851, 27852 (Place)

8 PoW, VII, 34–5, 4.30 am, May 31 1810; 36–7, June 1

9 *Harcourt Papers*, VI, 254–5, May 31 1810

10 PoW, VII, 37–8, June 3

11 PRO ms HO42/107, June 3

12 *General Evening Post*, June 5; *Times*, June 6 1810

13 PoW, VII, running reports by Halford and Matthew Baillie

14 *Star*, June 4; *General Evening Post*, June 5

15 Spencer, *Correspondence*, 107, May 31

16 BL ms Add 48383, f 41–45v, Nov 18 1798; Add 48404A, f 68–9, June 7 1810

17 Calvert, *Irish Beauty*, 162, June 2 1810

18 *News*, June 3 1810; PoW, VII, 410, June 4; Charlotte, Jan 14 1812

19 Spencer, *Correspondence*, June 7 1810

20 *Times*, June 14, 16, 21

21 PRO, LS 13/163, Lord Steward's Cash Book, entry for June 22 1810

6 THE GHOST OF SELLIS RISES

1 Knight, *Autobiography*, vol I, 174–5

2 BL ms Add 61986, f 14–14v, Nov 4 1810, to Lady Glenbervie

3 Charlotte, 6, Sept 26 1811

4 Charlotte, 16, Dec 9 1811

5 *Diary and Correspondence of ... Lord Colchester*, 1861, II, 348 and 354

6 Charlotte, 18, Dec 14 1811

7 BL ms Egerton 3260, f 231–6, Dec 26

8 Charlotte, 16, 18, Dec 9 and 14 1811; 214, Nov 1815

9 *Independent Whig*, Aug 30 and Oct 11 1812; *A Minute Detail* (anon), especially pages 92 on; BL mss Add 27852, f 16v; *Independent Whig*, Oct 25 1812

10 Adams, *Complete Servant*, 361–4

11 *Independent Whig*, Nov 22 1812

12 BL ms Add 35143, f 100, f 119–22

13 *Independent Whig*, ibid; Clive Emsley, 'The Home Office and its sources of information ... 1791–1801', *English Historical Review*, July 1979; BL ms Add 35143, f 64–5; Thale, *Selections*, 428, 436–7; PRO, ms PC1/41/138, Powell to Wickham, April 27 and 28 1798

14 BL ms Add 35152, f 59v

15 PRO, HO48/14 and 48/15

16 PRO, TS11/40, *Political Review and Monthly Mirror of the Times*, Oct 1812, in Treasury Solicitor's file

17 *The Statesman*, Oct 6 1812

18 PRO, TS11/41, King's Bench indictment, March 5 1813; *Independent Whig*, March 7

19 PRO, TS11/41, March 14 1813

20 Charlotte, 9, Oct 14 1811

21 BL, Add 27851, f 125

22 *Times*, April 2 1813; G IV, I, 278, letter to prince regent, Aug 6 1813

23 BM, George Cruikshank for *Town Talk*, July 1 1813

24 *Midnight Dreams*, 'Peter Pindar', 1814

7 'MY BLOOD BOILS IN MY VEINS'

1 BM, 'The Princely Meeting at Stralsund', about June 1813

2 *The R[oya]l Brood*, 1813

3 BL ms Add 63610, Keppel Craven's journal, f 47

4 G IV, I, 260, June 18 1813; PRO, ms FO 34/5, July 13

5 Willis, *Ernest Augustus*, 104 and 111

6 G IV, I, 304–5, Oct 10 1813

7 Jackson, *Bath Archives*, II, 350–51, letter to Jackson, Nov 11 1813

8 G IV, I, 341–2, Dec 9 1813, Bloomfield and Ernest to prince regent

9 Hedley, *Queen Charlotte*, 200

10 G IV, I, 369, 373, 379, 375, Jan 8, 10, 18 and 11, 1814

11 Charlotte, 103, Jan 11 1814

12 G IV, I, 471, July 23 1814

13 Hedley, *Queen Charlotte*, 272

14 BL ms Add 38261, f 274, Oct 1 1814

15 *The General-Post Bag* by 'Humphrey Hedgehog', 1815

16 G IV, II, 47–8 and 54–5, March 25, April 8 1815

17 Charlotte, 173, Dec 21 1814

18 Jackson, *Bath Archives*, II, 487, June 1 1815

19 BL ms Add 38261, f 276v–277, June 13 1815

20 *Times*, July 1; Creevey, *Life and Times*, July 5

21 *Scourge*, Aug 1 1815

22 PRO, HO 48/15, April 4 and 24 1812; TS 25/5/208, 1813

23 *Salms for a R——l Duke! or Doleful Lamentations of a Hopeful Chick and his German Hen for the loss of £6,000 a Year!!*, 'Peter Pindar Esq', 1815

24 Farington, *Diary*, XIII, 4671, July 14 1815

25 Leicestershire Record Office, ms DG 24/850/2; G IV, II, 90, Aug 3 1815

26 BL ms Add 38261, f 328–328v, Aug 12 1815

27 BL ms Add 38261, f 377, Aug 28

28 *Mémoires de la Comtesse de Boigne*, ed Jean-Claude Berchet, Paris, 1971, I, 375

29 G IV, II, 95; BL ms Add 38573, f 29, both Sept 1 1815

30 G IV, II, 98, Sept 2; BL mss Loan 57 (Bathurst papers), Box 77, Sept 13 1815; *Times*, Nov 16 1815

31 Willis, *Ernest Augustus*, 144–5

32 G IV, II, 139–40, Dec 23 1815

8 SOPHIA OPENS HER HEART

1 BL, Bathurst mss, Loan 57, Box 77, Dec 26 1805

2 *The Gold-Headed Cane*, Dr William Munk, 1884, 169

3 Clarke, J F [surgeon], *Autobiographical Recollections*, 349, 351–2

4 Wellcome Trust Library, Halford mss, Jan 1837

5 Leicestershire RO, ms DG 24/835/59, four-page letter, Jan 26 [1811]

6 Charlotte, 11, 23, 32, 49–50, 51–2, 143–44, Nov 6 1811, Jan 10 and Oct 26 1812, Jan 27 and Feb 7 1813, Aug 18 1814; and page 9, Oct 14 1811

7 Stuart, *Daughters*, 286, Dec 12 1812

8 Charlotte, 87, Dec 1 1813; Leicestershire RO, ms DG 24/849/58; G IV, I, 409, March 12 1814

9 Edgeworth, *Letters*, 127, Oct 15 1818

10 Leicestershire RO, ms DG 24/842/13 and 18, Sept 13 and Nov 16 1818

11 Stuart, *Daughters*, 297

12 Granville, Harriet, *Letters*, I, 168–9

13 Burney, *Journals and Letters*, XI, 279–80, Sept 1821, and 289–90, Nov 1821; *Life of John Linnell*, Alfred Story, 1892, I, 124

14 Burney, XII, 878n

9 HUNTING FOR THE HEIR

1 G IV, II, 203–04, Oct 10 1817

2 G IV, II, 227, Dec 18 1817

3 Gillen, *Prince and His Lady*, 213–21

4 RA GEO/Add 15/1048 (June 11 1813), 996, 1004 (Feb 9 1810)

5 Buckingham and Chandos, *Memoirs*, II, 226, W H Fremantle to Marquess of Buckingham, April 4 1818

6 Derbyshire Record Office, St Helens papers, ms 239M/F11535, Feb 10 1818

7 Derbyshire R O, mss 239M/F11552, Nov 25 1821; F11554, Feb 5 1823; F11561, Aug 31 1830

8 *Hunting for the Hair!!! The R---l H-mb-gs*, 'Peter Pindar Esq'

9 *Times*, April 16 and May 9 1818

10 Creevey, *Papers*, I, 277

11 G IV, II, 141, Jan 3 1816; 251, July 22 1818

10 THE WILD MELTONIAN

1 *Morning Chronicle*, March 18 1829
2 Charlotte, 216
3 Gronow, *Reminiscences*, I, 123; II, 289
4 Stuart, *Daughters*, 294–5, General Garth to York, Oct 6 1818
5 One of six 'Scenes with the Smoking Hunt', published 1826
6 *Sporting Magazine*, July 1825, July 1828, May 1829
7 Paget, *Melton Mowbray*, 26 and 134
8 Wilson, *Memoirs*, 517–18
9 *Times* and *Morning Herald*, Feb 20 1827
10 Longford, *Wellington, Years of the Sword*, 166–7; *Confessions of Julia Johnstone* (1825), 213; Wilson, *Memoirs*, 617
11 *Stockdale's Budget*, March 7 1827; G IV, vol V, 501–03
12 *Blackmailing of the Chancellor*, ed Kenneth Bourne (1975), 34, 41–5
13 Metropolitan Archives, evidence at Consistorial Court, Doctors Commons; *Times*, June 9 1828
14 *Times*, June 16 and 23 1828
15 *Times*, Aug 6 1827, March 20 1828
16 *New London Rambler's Magazine*, 1828, 29

11 A JUST TITLE TO RANK AND FORTUNE

1 PRO, ms C.13/939/4, affidavit sworn Feb 28 1829
2 *Morning Chronicle*, March 14 1829
3 *Fraser's Magazine*, May 1834; or see William Bates's *Gallery of Illustrious Literary Characters*, 1873, or Maclise *Portrait-Gallery*, 1883
4 BL, Sadler's Wells collection, Crach I, Tab 4b.4/4, f 102, letter to Elliston, July 25 1819
5 *Times*, Feb 7 1823
6 *The Wasp*, 1826
7 *The Age*, July 3 and 24, 1825
8 *Spirit of the Public Journals for 1825*, 363
9 *Drury Lane Journal: Selections from James Winston's Diaries, 1819–1827*, ed Alfred Nelson and Gilbert Cross (Society for Theatre Research), 1974, 116
10 *Times*, Aug 15 1826; *Stockdale's Budget*, March 28 1827; *Times*, April 24 1827; *Age*, June 10 1827

11 *Times*, Nov 26 1827
12 PRO, Garth's affidavit

12 ERNEST'S TANGLED WEB

1 *The Age*, July 27 1828; *Spirit of the Age Newspaper for 1828*, xvi
2 Greville, I, 299; BL ms Add 58890, f 20, Thomas Grenville to Lord Grenville, Sept 2 1828
3 G IV, II, 432–3, 438, 446, Sept 19, Oct 11, Nov 17; *The Age*, Nov 23 and 30, 1828
4 BL ms Add 51600, f 178 and f 182, Jan 23 and 27, 1829
5 Northern Ireland PRO, Anglesey Papers, D.619/27A, Jan 27
6 BL ms Add 47361B, f 17, Feb 4 1829
7 Wellington, *Despatches*, V, 482–3, Feb 2; G IV, vol III, 453, Feb 4 1829
8 *Times*, Feb 10 and 14; Halford's notebook for February 1829, Royal College of Physicians ms 2786
9 Creevey mss (microfilm Reel 31, University College London), Feb 14 and March 2
10 Wellington, *Despatches*, V, 504–05, Feb 16
11 *Parliamentary Debates*, New Series, XX, Feb 19; Willis, *Ernest Augustus*, 188, Feb 25
12 Wellington, *Despatches*, V, 515–16; Greville, I, 261–62, March 2
13 Ellenborough, *Diary*, I, 370–77
14 Arbuthnot, II, 248
15 Ellenborough, *Diary*, I, 379–80; Wellington, *Despatches*, V, 518, March 5
16 *Correspondence of Daniel O'Connell*, ed Maurice O'Connell, Dublin, 1972–80, IV, 20
17 *Figaro in London*, April 4 1835
18 Ellenborough, *Diary*, I, 388, March 10 1829; Arbuthnot, II, 254–5, March 16
19 *Age*, March 1; *Times*, March 7
20 *Standard*, March 10
21 *Times*, March 14
22 Haydon, *Diaries*, III, 347–8
23 BL ms Add 60297, f 78v, March 21
24 Creevey mss, Reel 31, Feb 16; Greville, I, 270–72, March 14 and 17 1829
25 Niedersächsisches Hauptstaatsarchiv, Hannover, Dep 103 II, ms 1/26, May 15 1827

26 PRO, C.13/939/4
27 BL ms Add 56368, f 148, Feb 25 1829
28 *Morning Journal*, March 14 1829; PRO, ms 30/9/29, Ellenborough's journal, same day (not in printed version)
29 *Observer* and *Age*, March 15
30 *Times* and *Morning Chronicle*, March 16
31 PRO, Ellenborough's journal, March 18
32 *Globe*, March 18
33 Greville, I, 278, March 21
34 *Times*, April 11
35 Willis, *Ernest Augustus*, 193; Horace Twiss, *Public and Private Life of Lord Chancellor Eldon*, III, 86, Eldon's memorandum, April 9; Greville, I, 290
36 Arbuthnot, II, 264–5
37 Knighton's letterbook, RA 51347v, 51348, 51348v, April 3 1829

13 A STILL MORE TANGLED WEB

1 *Times*, Sept 14 1826; Sir William Holdsworth, *A History of English Law*, XI, 352–370
2 BL ms Add 56554, Hobhouse diary, May 30 1829
3 *Examiner*, June 14 1829
4 *Parliamentary Debates*, XIII, May 27 1825
5 Creevey (ed Maxwell), II, 198; Edgeworth, *Letters*, 486
6 *The Age*, Aug 2 1829
7 BL ms Add 47350, ff 102–104v, Aug 3 to 8; Greville, I, 306
8 Leveson-Gower, *Private Correspondence*, II, 349-50
9 Add 47350, f 104v, f 106v, Aug 9 and 18; Greville, I, 310, 322; Add 51547, f 177
10 BL ms Add 52095, ff 55–60, Dec 1–9 1829
11 Lieven, *Earl Grey*, I, 261
12 Add 47353, f 72–74, Aug 9, 17, 18, 1829
13 Dino, *Chronique*, I, 201; Lieven, *Earl Grey*, II, 466–9
14 PRO, TS11/1003/3795, marked copy of *Standard*, July 20 1829; WP, 1/1045/18, Sept 18
15 Wellington, *Despatches*, VI, 294, Nov 10 1829; Creevey (ed Gore), 313, Nov 14; Gronow, *Reminiscences*, II, 4
16 PRO, ms C.13/939/4, sworn June 17 1829
17 PRO, C.13/19/10, Sept 8 1829
18 *Times* and *Morning Chronicle*, both Nov 16 1829
19 *Standard*, Nov 16
20 *Times* , Nov 17
21 Taylor, *The Papers*, 279
22 *Age*, Nov 22 1829

14 ERNEST, A RAZOR AND THE THUNDERER

1 Anglesey, *One-Leg*, 100–01
2 Thomas Hague, *The Royal Urinead*, 1808
3 G IV, vol III, 470, Knighton's diary
4 BL ms Add 48233, f 187v
5 *Paget Brothers*, 144, July 15 1810; 249, June 1812
6 BL ms Add 48407A, f 191–3, Sept 21 1826
7 Greville, I, 362, Jan 22 1830
8 *The News*, Feb 14 1830
9 *Times*, Feb 9 and 10
10 *The Age*, Feb 14
11 Lieven, *Earl Grey*, I, 434, 454–5, Feb 9 and 24
12 G IV, vol III,, 505–08, Feb 14 to 23
13 Lieven, *Une Vie* (Daudet), 155
14 Granville, Harriet, *Letters*, II, 58–60
15 Arbuthnot, II, p 358, May 17 1830; *Next Door Neighbours*, ed Ethel Richardson, 1926, 144–5, letter of Aug 7 1830
16 *Figaro in London*, Feb 18 1832
17 *Satirist*, March 18 1832
18 *Satirist*, May 17 1835

15 THE MENACING CAPTAIN ASHE

1 PRO, ms TS11/469/1604, Ashe, late Sept 1829; Wellington to Maule, Oct 4 1829
2 PRO, ms HO48/15, report to Richard Ryder, home secretary, May 7 1812; RA GEO/Add 11/213–15
3 G IV, II, 364–6, Ashe to William Vizard, Sept 4 1820
4 WP, 1/1054/38; PRO, TS11/469/1604
5 PRO, TS11/469/1604, Oct 31, Nov 5 and 10, 1830
6 BL ms Add 40399, f 383
7 Ellenborough, *Diary*, II, 136
8 PRO, TS11/469/1604, May 27 1830
9 TS11/469/1604, July 13 and 15, 1830
10 TS11/469/1604, July 17; Const Quick's and superintendent's reports, July 18 and 19
11 BL ms Add 40315, f 324, about July 18

12 TS11/469/1604, to Birnie and Ernest, both July 22

13 TS11/469/1604, Maule ro Peel, July 26

14 ms HO48/28, Ashe to Maule, Aug 19

15 TS11/469/1604, Scarlett to Maule, Sept 10

16 *Times*, Sept 20 1830

16 GRAVE AND ALARMING CHARGES

1 PRO, ms C33/794, p 821v, March 8 1830

2 *Times*, April 2, 8 and 9 1830

3 PRO, ms C.33/841, p 496, July 12 1830

4 PRO, ms C.13/939/4, June 14 1830

5 Longford, *Wellington, Pillar of State*, 210–12

6 Wellington Papers at Stratfield Saye, July 17 1830

7 *Times*, 15 Feb and Dec 21 1832

8 PRO, ms C.33/826

9 BL ms Add 40315, f 324v

17 A MOST ROYAL PRISONER

1 Haydon, *Diaries*, June 20 1830

2 *A Description of the King's Bench Prison*, John McShee, 1823

3 *Times*, Nov 18 1829

4 *Times*, March 26 1830

5 *Times*, Dec 24 1831

6 PRO, ms PRIS 10/130; *Times*, July 18 and 19 and Aug 1 1832

7 PRO, PRIS 10/130

8 *Times*, August 24 1831

9 PRO, PRIS 10/131

10 *Sporting Magazine*, March 1826

11 *The Life of John Mytton*, 2nd edition, 1837, 21, 64-5, 120–22

12 Mytton's letters and his mother's are quoted in a Sotheby's sale catalogue, Dec 19–20 1938

13 PRO, PRIS 10/131

14 *Life of John Mytton*, 157–9

15 *Satirist*, Jan 18, March 29, May 3, Aug 2 1835

16 London Metropolitan Archives, Reel X92/035

17 *Satirist*, Oct 11 and 35 1835

18 THE REWARDS OF CHICANERY

1 BM, No 16036 in caricature catalogue; dated 'c 1830'

2 PoW, VIII, 425 (additional letters), note

quoting Knighton, Aug 18 1817

3 Greville, II, 193, quoting Wellington

4 *Archives*, vol xiii, 59, article by Sir Robin Mackworth-Young, royal librarian

5 *Times*, Feb 21 1834

6 Catherine Jamison, *The History of the Royal Hospital of St Katharine*, 1952

7 *The Devil's Visit*, 1830, anon

8 Grant, *Newspaper Press*, III, 16–18

9 *Fraser's Magazine*, Oct 1830; *Annual Register* 1830, quoting Westmacott; Clarke, *Autobiographical Recollections*, 109

10 *Portraits of Public Characters*, II, 16, 1841; *A Gallery of Illustrious Literary Characters*, ed William Bates, 1873, 130

11 *England and the English*, Edward Bulwer, 1833, 234–6

12 RA MP/39/97, Westmacott to Melbourne, Nov 29 1837; *Figaro*, July 2 1836

13 *The Bookseller*, Sept 1 1868

14 BL, Puttick & Simpson catalogue, sale of Dec 8–12 1868

19 'WE SHALL HAVE A REVOLUTION'

1 *A Trip to the Earth by the Man in the Moon!* Dedicated to Charles X, 1830

2 BL ms Add 60288, f 234v–235, Jan 11 1830

3 Arbuthnot, II, 324–6, Jan 9 1830; *Wellington and His Friends*, 70, 90, Sept 28 1826 and April 10 1830

4 Lieven, *Letters*, 234

5 Wellington, *Despatches*, VII, 383

6 WP, 1/1159: items 135, 162, 121, 95, 142, 109, dating from Nov 4 to Dec 15 1830

7 *Wellington and His Friends*, 95, May 1 1831

8 Greville, II, 197, Sept 1831

9 James Grant, *Random Recollections of the House of Lords ...1830 to 1836*, 79–82

10 *Times*, June 22 1831

11 *The Radical*, Oct 15 1831

12 WP, 1/1199/17, f 3–4, Oct 27

13 Strangford, *Letters*, 93–4

14 BL ms Add 56368, f 151–152v, Nov 6 1831; Leicestershire RO, ms DG 24/941, Halford diary, Nov 3 1831; *Diary of Frances Lady Shelley*, ed Richard Edgcumbe, II (1913), 214, to Lady Shelley, Jan 18 1832

15 BL ms Add 60289, f 18, Feb 20 1832
16 *Figaro in London*, Feb 11 1832; *Punch in London*, March 24 1832
17 Greville, II, 297 and 301; Anglesey, *One-Leg*, 258; *John Bull*, May 13 1832
18 *Times*, May 14 1832; *Wellington and His Friends*, Aug 27 1819
19 *John Bull's Picture Gallery*, May 1832
20 Greville, II, 301
21 Niedersächsisches Hauptstaatsarchiv, Dep 103 II, ms 3/40, May 17 1832
22 *Parliamentary Debates*, Third Series, XII, May 22 1832
23 BL ms Add 47354A, ff 37–41, June 4, 8
24 *Times*, June 6
25 WP, 1/1240/8, Dec 30 1832
26 Oman, *Gascoyne Heiress*, 86, 96, 127, 171

20 THE BLACK SECRET OF HIS GUILT

1 Greville, I, 272, March 17 1829
2 BL ms Add 35144, f 72–4
3 *Authentic Records*, 95, 97
4 *The Trial of Josiah Phillips for a Libel on the Duke of Cumberland*, 1833, 8, 13–16, 29, 32; BL ms Add 35144, ff 82–4
5 *True Sun*, April 18 1832; Hamilton, *Secret History*, 1832, I, 156, 165, 195
6 *Asmodeus, or The Devil in London*, April 28 1832
7 *Times*, June 26 1833; *Trial of Josiah Phillips*, 65, 74, 75; *Age*, June 30 1833
8 Wylly, *XVth*, 142, 181, 213, 235, 238–9; *Paget Brothers*, 103–4
9 PoW, vol VII, 373–7
10 PRO, TS11/120, Clarke, *Recollections*, 96–7
11 PoW, VII, 378
12 Niedersächsisches Hauptstaatsarchiv, Dep 103 II, ms 2/36, Sept 23 1842
13 Bishopsgate Institute, Jones collection, diary 1839–43
14 PoW, VII, 5–8

21 ERNEST AIMS AT THE CROWN

1 BL ms Add 37889, ff 37–47
2 BL ms Add 38253, f 292, to Lord Liverpool
3 BL ms Add 40373, f 286
4 *Times*, 24 Nov 1826, Feb 13, April 21 and May 22 1827
5 *The History of the Times*, G E Buckle,

Stanley Morison et al, 1935, I, 369
6 *Parliamentary Debates*, Third Series, XXXI, Feb 23 1836
7 *London and Westminster Review*, Jan 1836, 190; *The Orange Exposure*, H S Chapman, 1835
8 Lieven, *Une Vie* (Daudet), 179; Dino, *Chronique*, 68–70, May 12 1834
9 *Times*, Aug 10 1835; *News*, Aug 16; *Standard*, Aug 24
10 *A Letter to the Duke of Cumberland*, Pamphlets for the People series, ed J A Roebuck MP, 1835
11 *Annual Register*, 1835; *Correspondence of Lady Burghersh with the Duke of Wellington*, ed Lady Rose Weigall, 1903, 642
12 Greville, II, 110, Jan 25 1831
13 *Figaro in London*, Nov 7 1835; *Political Odds and Oddities*, no date; *Satirist*, Jan 31 and Feb 7 1836
14 *Parliamentary Debates*, Feb 23 1836
15 *Age*, Feb 28 and March 6 1836
16 *Parliamentary Debates*, March 7
17 Willis, *Ernest Augustus*, 262
18 Quoted in *London and Westminster Review*, Jan 1836, 223

22 SOPHIA AND THE AMAZING CONROY

1 Greville, IV, 199
2 Stuart, *Daughters*, 301–02
3 Wellington, *A Selection*, 85–94
4 Hudson, *Royal Conflict*, 147 (Queen Victoria's journal, March 14 1838); Greville, VI, 69
5 L G Mitchell, *Lord Melbourne*, 1997, 237 (Victoria's journal, Sept 4 1838)
6 Longford, *Victoria*, 119 (Victoria's journal, Jan 21 1839)
7 Childe-Pemberton, *Princess Amelia*, 87
8 BL ms Add 39873, ff 86–97, Oct 27 to Dec 24 1829
9 *Elizabeth Lady Holland to her Son*, ed Earl of Ilchester, 1946, 83; Arbuthnot, II, 182–3
10 BL ms Add 47354A, ff 54–60; Dino, *Chronique*, I, 201, July 31 1834
11 Longford, *Victoria*, 44–6
12 Woodham-Smith, *Victoria*, 434–5
13 Woodham-Smith, 142; Hudson, 189
14 *Times*, March 9 and April 5 1838

23 HIS MOST MOUSTACHIOED MAJESTY

1 Greville, II, 6–7, Jan 4 1838
2 *Figaro in London,* June 24 1837
3 Greville, III, 373
4 *Figaro,* July 1 1837
5 Taylor, *The Papers,* 400, July 1 1837
6 *Figaro,* July 22 and Aug 5
7 Greville, III, 385–6; *Figaro* , Sept 9 1837
8 BL ms Add 47351A, ff 5–9, Feb 9 1838; Leicestershire RO, ms DG 24/850/19, 1838
9 Leicestershire RO, ms DG 24/925/5, Aug 8 1840
10 Lieven, *Lieven–Palmerston,* 140, Nov 13 1837; Greville, IV, 258, March 29 1840
11 Woodham-Smith, *Victoria,* 183, quoting Victoria's journal
12 *Croker Papers,* II, 360, Mar 8 1840
13 Woodham-Smith, *Victoria,* 198–9; Greville, IV, 244–5, Feb 19 1840
14 BL ms Add 47351A, f 93, Feb 15 1840
15 Woodham-Smith, 217; Lieven, *Lieven–Palmerston,* 200
16 Dino, *Chronique,* III, 103; BL ms Add 47351A, ff 119–120, July 19 1841; Leicestershire RO, ms DG 24/ 925/1, July 25; Strangford, *Letters,* 3, July 20
17 Strangford, 4; BL ms Loan 57 (Bathurst Papers), Box 78, Ernest to Lady Georgina, Sept 13 1841
18 BL ms Add 47351B, f 40v, April 22 1843; f 44, May 12
19 Woodham-Smith, 233–4; BL ms Add 47351B, f 47
20 Add 47351B, f 41 and f 99v–100
21 Greville, V, 97, 123; Add 47351B, ff 46 and 48v
22 Greville, V, 123–4

24 A ROYAL COMMONER IN CHELSEA

1 Childe-Pemberton, *Princess Amelia,* 87–8
2 RA PP/VIC/1/80/21, Frederick John

Blake to Arnold White, Dec 3 1875
3 PRO, IR26/2894, folio 1682
4 RA PP/VIC/1/80/34
5 Iremonger, *Love and the Princess,* 269

25 AN OLD BLIND LADY

1 *Times,* Sept 14 1829, quoting *Court Journal*
2 Amelia Murray, *Recollections from 1803 to 1837* (1868), 70
3 Hudson, *Royal Conflict* , 179
4 RA VIC/QVJ/1848: May 27 and 29
5 RA VIC/QVJ/1848: May 30
6 *Times,* July 11 1848
7 *Times,* May 29 1851
8 *Life and Labour of Ernest Jones, Poet, Politician and Patriot,* 1869 (pamphlet by Marx's daughter Eleanor Aveling), 10
9 Woodham-Smith, *Victoria,* 257–60

26 KING ERNEST SURVIVES THE CANAILLE

1 Strangford, *Letters,* 75, Aug 24 1845; BL ms Add 47351B, ff 107–107v, 117–18, Oct 2 and Dec 1 1845
2 BL ms Add 47351B, ff 195–196v, May 22 1848
3 *Times,* Aug 7 1828; Strangford, *Letters,* 145–8, April 7, 19 and 29 1848
4 Strangford, 150–51, May 15
5 Strangford, 157, June 8 1848
6 Dino, *Chronique* , III, 381, Nov 5 1849
7 Ghislain de Diesbach, *Secrets of the Gotha,* 1964, 148
8 Strangford, 71–2, Jan 23 1845; 185–6, July 3 1849
9 BL mss Loan 57, Box 78, Jan 6 1851
10 Strangford, 222, 225, 227, Feb and June 1851
11 *Reynolds's News,* Nov 23 1851
12 *Times,* Nov 20 1851
13 Family Records Centre, London

Bibliography

Unpublished sources

Letters, diaries, legal documents, etc, in British Library, Bodleian Library, Public Record Office, Royal Archives and other collections, as cited in the References, pages 259–67

Newspapers and periodicals

Age, Alfred, Figaro in London, Gazetteer, General Evening Post, Independent Whig, John Bull, Morning Chronicle, Morning Herald, Morning Journal, Morning Post, News, Observer, Public Advertiser, Punch in London, Satirist, Scourge, Sporting Magazine, Standard, Star, Stockdale's Budget, Times

Letters, journals, memoirs, etc

Arbuthnot, Charles, *The Correspondence of...*, ed Arthur Aspinall, 1941

Arbuthnot, Harriet, *The Journal of Mrs Arbuthnot*, ed Francis Bamford and 7th Duke of Wellington, 2 vol, 1950

The Authentic Records of the Court of England for the Last Seventy Years, anon, 1832

Bessborough, *Lady Bessborough and Her Family Circle, Journals and Correspondence*, ed 9th Earl of Bessborough and Arthur Aspinall, 1940

Bessborough, *A Regency Chapter: Lady Bessborough and her Friendships*, ed Ethel Mayne, 1939

Boigne, Comtesse de, *Mémoires*, ed Jean-Claude Berchet, Paris, 1971

Buckingham and Chandos, Duke of, *Memoirs of the Court of England during the Regency*, 2 vol, 1856

Burney, Fanny, *Diary and Letters of Madame d'Arblay*, ed Charlotte Barrett, 1854; *The Journals and Letters of Fanny Burney (Madame d'Arblay)*, ed Joyce Hemlow et al, 12 vol, 1972—

Bury, Lady Charlotte, *Diary Illustrative of the Times of George the Fourth*, 4 vol, 1838–9; *The Diary of a Lady-in-Waiting*, ed A Francis Steuart, 2 vol, 1908

Calvert, Frances, *An Irish Beauty of the Regency ... Unpublished Journals of the Hon Mrs Calvert, 1789–1822*, ed Mrs Warrenne Blake, 1911: MP's wife, social/political

Charlotte, Princess, *The Letters of ...*, ed Arthur Aspinall, 1949

Clarke, J F, *Autobiographical Recollections of the Medical Profession*, 1874

Clarke, Mary Anne, *The Recollections of ... Exhibiting the Secret History of the Court of St James's and of the Cabinet of Great Britain ... Communicated to her by HRH the Duke of York*, 1813, 246 proof pages, set up to put pressure on Duke of York to pay up (PRO, TS11/120/X.1./7972)

Creevey, Thomas, *The Creevey Papers*, ed Sir Herbert Maxwell, 2 vol, 1903; *Creevey's Life and Times*, ed John Gore, 1934: life seen by witty Whig, 1802–38

Croker, John Wilson, *The Croker Papers 1808–57*, ed Bernard Pool, 1967: Tory

Dino, Duchesse de, *Chronique de 1831 à 1862*, ed Princesse Radziwill, 4 vol, Paris, 1909–10

Edgeworth, Maria, *Letters from England, 1813–44*, ed Christine Colvin, 1971

Elizabeth, Princess, *Letters of ...*, ed Philip Charles Yorke, 1898

Ellenborough, 2nd Lord, *A Political Diary 1828–1830*, 2 vol, 1881 (full ms in PRO)

Farington, *The Diary of Joseph Farington*, ed Kenneth Garlick and Angus Macintyre, 16 vol, Yale University Press, 1978–84: London art world, 1793–1821

George III, *The Later Correspondence of ...*, ed Arthur Aspinall, 5 vol, Cambridge, 1962–70

George Prince of Wales, *The Correspondence of ... 1770–1812*, ed Aspinall, 8 vol, 1963–71

George IV, *The Letters of ... 1812–1830*, ed Aspinall, 3 vol, Cambridge, 1938

Glenbervie, Lord, *The Diaries of Sylvester Douglas, Lord Glenbervie*, ed Francis Bickley, 2 vol, 1928 (for 1793–1804, 1807–11, 1815-19); *The Glenbervie Journals*, ed Walter Sichel, 1910 (for 1793,

1811–15): insider, court and politics

Granville, *Lord Granville Leveson Gower: Private Correspondence 1781 to 1821*, ed Castalia Countess Granville, 1916: for Lady Bessborough letters

Granville, *Letters of Harriet Countess Granville, 1810–1845*, ed F Leveson Gower, 2 vol, 1894

Greville, the Hon Charles, *The Greville Memoirs, 1814–60*, ed Lytton Strachey and Roger Fulford, 8 vol, 1938; politics and society, 1821–60

Gronow, Rees Howell, *The Reminiscences and Recollections of Captain Gronow ... 1810–1860*, 2 vol, 1889: especially for late-Georgian years

Ham, Elizabeth, *Elizabeth Ham by Herself, 1783–1820*, ed Eric Gillett, 1945: Weymouth memories

Hamilton, Lady Anne, *Secret History of the Court of England*, 1832, altered version of *Authentic Memoirs* (reissued 1903)

Harcourt, Edward, *The Harcourt Papers*, 14 vol, Oxford, 1880–1905

Harris, James, *Diaries and Correspondence of James Harris, First Earl of Malmesbury*, ed by 3rd earl, 4 vol, 1844

Haydon, Benjamin Robert, *Neglected Genius: The Diaries of Benjamin Robert Haydon*, ed John Joliffe, 1990

Jackson, Sir George, *The Bath Archives*, 2 vol, 1873: diplomat's diaries, letters, Napoleonic period

Knight, Cornelia, *The Autobiography of Miss Cornelia Knight, Lady Companion to the Princess Charlotte of Wales*, 2 vol, 1861; and ed Roger Fulford, 1960

Lieven, *Correspondence of Princess Lieven and Earl Grey*, ed Guy Le Strange, 3 vol, 1890

––––– *Letters of Dorothea Princess Lieven ... 1812–1834*, ed Lionel Robinson, 1902

––––– *Une Vie d'Ambassadrice*, ed Ernest Daudet, Paris, 1903: with many letters not in Robinson

––––– *The Lieven-Palmerston Correspondence, 1828–1856*, ed Lord Sudley, 1943

––––– *The Unpublished Diary and Political Sketches*, ed Harold Temperley, 1925

Next-Door Neighbours, ed Ethel Richardson, 1926: diaries, letters, 1820s–1830s

[Paget family] *The Paget Brothers, 1790–1840*, ed Lord Hylton, 1918

Papendiek, Mrs Charlotte, *Court and Private Life in the Time of Queen Charlotte: Being the Journals of Mrs Papendiek...*, 2 vol, 1887

Spencer, *Correspondence of Sarah Spencer, Lady Lyttelton*, 1912

Stanhope, Lady Hester, *Memoirs ... Related by Herself in Conversations with her Physician*, 3 vol, 1845

Strangford, *Letters of the King of Hanover to Viscount Strangford*, ed Charles Whibley, 1925

Taylor, Sir Herbert, *The Taylor Papers*, ed Ernest Taylor, 1913: the *unburnt* ones

Wellington, 1st Duke of, *Despatches, Correspondence and Memoranda*, 2nd series (1867–80), vols V–VII

––––– *A Selection from the Private Correspondence of the First Duke of Wellington*, ed the 7th duke, 1952

––––– *Wellington and his Friends*, ed the 7th duke, 1965

––––– *Political Correspondence*, ed John Brooke and Julia Gandy, 1976

Wilson, *Harriette Wilson's Memoirs*, preface by James Laver, 1929 (many other editions, 1825 on)

History, biography, etc

Adams, Samuel and Sarah, *The Complete Servant; Being a Practical Guide to the Peculiar Duties and Business of all Descriptions of Servants*, 1825

Andrews, Alexander, *The History of British Journalism*, 2 vol, 1859

Anglesey, *One-Leg: The Life and Letters of Henry William Paget, First Marquess of Anglesey*, by the 7th Marquess, 1961

Anon, *A Minute Detail of the Attempt to Assassinate H.R.H. the Duke of Cumberland*, 1810: defaming Sellis

Aspinall, Arthur, *Politics and the Press*, 1949 and 1973: news-management 1780–1850

Aspinall, Arthur (ed), *Three Early Nineteenth Century Diaries*, 1952: a Whig and two Tories, 1830–34

Bird, Anthony, *The Damnable Duke of Cumberland ... a Vindication*, 1966

Brooke, John, *King George III*, 1972: largely a eulogy

Buckle, G E, Stanley Morison et al, *The History of The Times*, 2 vol, 1935

Cannadine, David, *Aspects of Aristocracy: Grandeur and Decline in Modern Britain*, Yale University Press, 1994

Childe-Pemberton, William, *The Romance of Princess Amelia*, 1910

Diesbach, Ghislain de, *Secrets of the Gotha*, 1967: royal and noble realms, marriages, madness, etc

270

Fraser, Flora, *The Unruly Queen*, 1996: George IV's Caroline

Fulford, Roger, *The Royal Dukes*, 1933; revised edition 1973 (and 1977, 2000)

Gillen, Mollie, *The Prince and His Lady*, 1970: Victoria's father

Grant, James, *The Newspaper Press*, 3 vol, 1871

Hedley, Olwen, *Queen Charlotte*, 1975: the view from Windsor

Harvey's *Improved Weymouth Guide*, 1800

Hudson, Glenda, *Sibling Love and Incest in Jane Austen's Fiction*, 1999

Hudson, Katherine, *A Royal Conflict: Sir John Conroy and the Young Victoria*, 1994

Huish, Robert, *Memoirs of George IV*, 2 vol, 1830–31

Iremonger, Lucille, *Love and the Princess*, 1958: Princess Sophia

Laver, James, *The Age of Illusion: Manners and Morals, 1750–1840*, 1972

Longford, Elizabeth, *Victoria R I*, revised edition 1983

————— *Wellington, Years of the Sword*, 1969; *Wellington, Pillar of State*, 1972

Macalpine, Ida, and Richard Hunter, *George III and the Mad-Business*, 1969; controversial study of royal insanity

Midelfort, Erik, *Mad Princes of Renaissance Germany*, University Press of Virginia, 1994: including some early Brunswicks

Oman, Carola, *The Gascoyne Heiress*, *The Life and Diaries of Frances Mary Gascoyne-Cecil, 1802–39*, 1968: a lively Lady Salisbury

Paget, Major Guy, *The Melton Mowbray of John Ferneley*, Leicester, 1931

Pigott, Charles, *The Jockey Club, or a Sketch of the Manners of the Age*, 1792; *The Female Jockey Club…*, 1794: radical surveys of royal and other scandals

Rogers, Nicholas, 'Pigott's Private Eye', *Journal of the Canadian Historical Association*, n.s., vol 4, 1993

Rudé, George, *Hanoverian London, 1714–1800*, 1971

Stuart, Dorothy Margaret, *The Daughters of George III*, 1939: pioneering study

Thale, Mary, *Selections from the Papers of the London Corresponding Society 1792–1799*, Cambridge, 1983

Van Thal, Herbert, *Ernest Augustus, Duke of Cumberland and King of Hanover*, 1936: Ernest 'a terrible victim of rumour'

Warren, Martin, et al, *Purple Secret — Genes, 'Madness' and the Royal Houses of Europe*, 1998

Willis, Geoffrey Malden, *Ernest Augustus, Duke of Cumberland and King of Hanover*, 1954: hagiography, yet with useful detail

Woodham-Smith, Cecil, *Queen Victoria, Her Life and Times 1819–1861*, 1984

Wylly, Colonel H C, *XVth (The King's) Hussars, 1759 to 1913*, 1914

Index

274

278